Europe Recast

A History of European Union

2nd Edition

Desmond Dinan

Enniskillen Campus

palgrave
macmillan

First published in Europe 2014 by
PALGRAVE MACMILLAN

Palgrave Macmillan in the UK is an imprint of Macmillan Publishers Limited, registered in England, company number 785998, of Houndmills, Basingstoke, Hampshire RG21 6XS.

Palgrave Macmillan in the US is a division of St Martin's Press LLC, 175 Fifth Avenue, New York, NY 10010.

Palgrave Macmillan is the global academic imprint of the above companies and has companies and representatives throughout the world.

Palgrave® and Macmillan® are registered trademarks in the United States, the United Kingdom, Europe and other countries

ISBN: 978–1–137–43644–3 paperback

The paper used in this publication meets the requirements of the American National Standard for Permanence of Paper for Printed Library Materials Z39.48-1992.

A catalogue record for this book is available from the British Library.

A catalog record for this book is available from the Library of Congress.

Printed in the United States of America.

To Denis Smyth,
mentor and friend

Contents

Maps

Preface

IT IS A PRIVILEGE TO WRITE A SECOND EDITION OF *EUROPE RECAST.*
Since the first edition appeared, in 2004, there have been ten more years
of European Union (EU) history. Key events have included enlargement
from fifteen to twenty-eight member states, major treaty reform, and the
eurozone crisis. These events are examined in the new edition. Though it
will be several decades before they can be adequately evaluated in historical perspective, their impact is already clear. Enlargement has changed
not only the face but also the form of the EU. Treaty revision has proved
time-consuming and fraught, reflecting growing public unease with EU institutions and policies. The eurozone crisis has been wrenching—politically,
economically, and socially. All three events demonstrate the limits of European integration at this stage of the EU's development, and the importance
of studying the past in order to understand the present.

Apart from generating more raw material for historians eventually to
mull over, the past ten years have produced a wealth of historical work on
earlier periods of European integration. Despite the EU's current ills, the
history of European integration remains a flourishing subfield of modern
European history and of economic and diplomatic history. Recent scholarship on the history of European integration, together with my own reflections on the subject, have informed the writing of the second edition. Fur-
thermore, the introduction contains a section on the historiography of
European integration, which was absent from the first edition.

My fundamental view of the EU and of the nature of EU history has
not changed. As I noted in the preface to the first edition, although the EU
symbolizes European unity—the triumph of voluntarily shared sovereignty
over excessive nationalism, ideological division, and imperial ambition—

the reality is less clear-cut and more complicated. Member states (and prospective member states) are motivated not by nebulous visions of European unity, but by concrete calculations of national advantage. That was always the way historically for the EU. The difference now is that national interests are often undisguised and generally harder to reconcile. The EU today has a plethora of vital issues on the agenda, far higher political stakes, a cumbersome policymaking apparatus that has evolved over the years, and four times as many national governments as originally sat around the table. Inevitably, the EU is increasingly difficult to manage.

Ten years ago the EU had already entered a period of flux. Today, challenges of globalization, Europeanization (the growing intermingling of EU and national politics and policymaking), and Euroskepticism continue to buffet it from all sides. Nevertheless, the EU remains remarkably resilient. The impact of Central and Eastern European enlargement, the painful and protracted process of treaty reform, and the severity of the eurozone crisis have put the EU under enormous stress. Yet, what I wrote in the preface to the first edition still holds true: inasmuch as this book serves as a guide to the future, the lesson probably is that European integration will rumble along and the EU will muddle through whatever challenges lie ahead.

A note on style. It is difficult to write elegantly about the EU, a subject replete with abbreviations, acronyms, jargon, and excessive use of capital letters. I tried to improve the flow of the narrative by keeping these encumbrances to a minimum. For instance, I have not capitalized "member states," "common foreign and security policy," "justice and home affairs," "intergovernmental conference," and the like. I managed to keep the list of acronyms and abbreviations just over a page, surely a great achievement in a book on the EU. I use "national leaders" instead of "heads of state and government," and I use "EU leaders" to refer to members of the European Council, the EU's most powerful political body.

Finally, a note on nomenclature. First, the uninitiated invariably confuse the European Council and the Council of the European Union (the latter formerly and still known colloquially as the Council of Ministers). The European Council, consisting of national leaders plus its elected president and the European Commission president, meets regularly to direct EU affairs and resolve pressing problems. Given the seriousness of the eurozone crisis, the European Council and the Euro Summit—a variation of the European Council consisting of the leaders of countries in the eurozone, as well as the European Council president and the European Commission president—met increasingly frequently during the past five years. The Council of Ministers, by contrast, consists of ordinary government ministers. It meets regularly in a number of formations, such as the foreign ministers, finance ministers, and agriculture ministers, to make legislative and other policy decisions. When I refer to "the Council" alone, I am always referring to the Council of Ministers, never to the European Council. Second, the European Union officially came into existence only in November 1993; before that time it was known as the European Community (EC). In general, I refer to the EC until the early 1990s and the EU thereafter. Overall, I have tried to avoid pedantry without sacrificing accuracy, not an easy thing to do when speaking, teaching, or writing about the EU.

—*Desmond Dinan*

EUROPE
RECAST

Introduction

THE IDEA OF EUROPEAN UNION IS A RECURRING THEME IN THE long and often violent history of the continent. The Holy Roman Emperors, Napoleon, Hitler, and others sought, in sometimes horrifying ways, to achieve a continental unity based variously on princely alliances, ethnic cohesion, ideology, or raw power. Ever since the emergence of the modern state, in the mid–seventeenth century, philosophers and political thinkers have also imagined a united Europe triumphing over narrow national interests and allegiances. Today's European Union (EU) is singular among these competing visions. Tempering the nationalist ethos that had become the ruling principle of European political development, the countries that formed the European Communities, the basis of the EU, chose to limit (but not eliminate) their own sovereignty, the hallmark of a modern nation-state, in favor of collective peace, economic integration, and supranational governance.

Their reasons for doing so were rooted in the disastrous decades of the early twentieth century. The miserable legacy of heroic European nationalism —two world wars, countless millions dead, and economic ruin—was not lost on the peoples of Europe, who were receptive to the idea of treaty-based and highly institutionalized economic and political integration after World War II. European politicians wanted above all to end international strife, foster social harmony, and promote economic well-being. They sought to build a better world, free of the hatreds and rivalries that had destroyed their countries in recent years. For their generation, European integration became synonymous with peace and prosperity.

Yet there was nothing inevitable about the emergence of European integration in the form with which we are now familiar. European politicians were (and still are) instinctively averse to sharing national sovereignty, despite rhetorical flourishes to the contrary. National leaders decided to share sovereignty in supranational organizations primarily because they perceived

1

that it was in their countries' (and therefore their own) interests to do so. Ideas, intellectual fashion, opportunity, chance, conviction, calculation, personal predilection, and ambition all played a part. Ultimately, however, European integration emerged as it did because of a calculated response by politicians, businesspeople, and other actors to changing economic, political, and strategic circumstances, ranging from Germany's postwar recovery, to the fall of the Berlin Wall, to the acceleration of globalization. Despite growing public concern about the process and politics of European integration, Europeans generally acquiesced because the outcome seemed worthwhile and the alternatives less attractive.

The Interwar Experience

World War I, fought mostly in Europe, ended in November 1918 after more than four years of frightful slaughter. US intervention on the side of the Western allies tipped the balance against Germany, which had earlier forced the newly established Soviet Union to capitulate. The Versailles Treaty of 1919 imposed hefty war reparations on Germany and severely limited its sovereignty. John Maynard Keynes, the brilliant English economist, denounced the financial provisions of the treaty in a bestselling book, *The Economic Consequences of the Peace,* published in 1920.[1] As Keynes predicted, reparations became a huge drain on the German economy, a major irritant in Franco-German relations, and a rallying cry for ardent German nationalists who denounced the democratic Weimar regime for having signed the treaty.

Persistent, virulent nationalism in Western Europe between the wars was hardly conducive to voluntary European integration. To the east, new nation-states, jealous of their sovereignty, emerged from the wreckage of the Russian, Austro-Hungarian, and Ottoman empires. Because the Soviet Union, weakened by civil war, did not pose a serious threat to international security, other European countries were not inclined to unite "against" it. The absence of a Soviet threat accounted in part for the relative aloofness of the United States, which refused to become entangled in European affairs or even to join the League of Nations, the new international security organization. Nor were the Europeans, resentful though they were of the rise of the United States to global power, inclined to unite "against" the United States, a major market and potential ally.

The horrors of the Great War and uncertainty of the early postwar period nevertheless spawned a movement for European union: the Pan-Europa pressure group of Richard Coudenhove-Kalergi, a count of the old Holy Roman Empire. In his influential book *Pan-Europa,* published in 1923, Coudenhove-Kalergi called for a federal union of European states centered on France and Germany, but excluding the Soviet Union (because of its communism and foothold in Asia) and Britain (because of its imperial interests).[2] An aristocrat and elitist, Coudenhove-Kalergi initially sought the support of Italy's dictator, Benito Mussolini. Growing public interest in the idea of Pan-Europa, and Mussolini's rejection of it, led Coudenhove-Kalergi to appreciate the importance of democracy in building European union.

Although it generated chapters in most continental countries, Pan-Europa was an ephemeral political movement. Nevertheless, two of its members, Edouard Herriot and Aristide Briand, were leading French politicians who sought a rapprochement with Germany. Briand, foreign minister in the mid-1920s, worked with Gustav Stresemann, his German counterpart, to rescue Franco-German relations from the wreckage of the war and France's punitive policy toward Germany immediately afterward. Together with Britain's foreign minister, they were instrumental in concluding the Locarno Treaty of October 1925, which guaranteed the borders of Western Europe and paved the way for Germany's entry into the League of Nations. The "spirit of Locarno" hovered over the "years of hope" (1925–1929), when it seemed as if Western Europe was finally on the road to a better future.[3]

Briand and Stresemann had a celebrated summit meeting in the small village of Thoiry, across the French border from Geneva, in September 1926. There they addressed a number of contentious issues in hopes of paving the way for a Franco-German entente. France wanted Germany to make good on its promise to pay reparations; Germany wanted the allies to end their military occupation of the Rhineland, along the country's western border, on which France took a hard line. Despite good relations between Briand and Stresemann, Germany and France were too suspicious of each other to follow the Thoiry summit with detailed negotiations and a diplomatic breakthrough. The years of hope gradually gave way to despair as extreme nationalists in both countries entrenched their positions. Stresemann's death in October 1929 symbolized the death also of incipient Franco-German accord.[4]

In his last speech to the League of Nations, in September 1929, Stresemann advocated European integration and even raised the possibility of a common currency.[5] He followed in the footsteps of French prime minister Herriot, who, as early as 1925, spoke publicly about a United States of Europe. Briand was another leading proponent of Pan-Europa. Like Stresemann, he extolled the virtues of European integration in a speech to the League in September 1929. Spurred in part by Stresemann's untimely death, Briand followed up with a famous memorandum in May 1930 calling for an association of European states, subordinate to the League, to coordinate economic policies and promote political union. Although far-reaching by the standards of the time, Briand's initiative did not propose that governments share national sovereignty. Even so, it was too radical for most European countries, including Briand's own. The League established the Committee of

Enquiry on the European Union, which held a number of sessions in the early 1930s, after which nothing more was heard about the Briand memorandum.[6]

Germany and Austria used the language of European integration to float a proposal in March 1931 for a customs union open to other countries as well. The idea of an Austro-German customs union jogged historical memories of the Zollverein of 1834, the customs union among German states that presaged the rise of Prussia and unification of Germany in 1871. Many Europeans, who ascribed the continent's current ills to German unification, feared that an Austro-German customs union would lead inevitably to an Austro-German *anschluss* (political union). France blocked the proposal. Once Hitler came to power, any prospect of Franco-German reconciliation and voluntary European integration abruptly came to an end.

The 1930s was a dismal decade in Europe, bracketed by economic recession at the beginning and the outbreak of war at the end. Fascism seemed unstoppable in Germany, Spain, and the faltering democracies of Central and Eastern Europe, having already taken root in Italy. Emboldened by Anglo-French weakness and US detachment, Hitler scored one foreign policy triumph after another, until his invasion of Poland in September 1939 triggered an Anglo-French declaration of war. In August 1940, Coudenhove-Kalergi fled Europe for the United States, his Pan-Europa movement almost forgotten.[7]

The approach of war triggered a revival of interest in federalism as a way to bolster the democratic nations in the face of Fascist aggression. Federal ideas had flourished in Britain in the interwar years. Leading intellectuals such as Lionel Curtis, Philip Kerr (later Lord Lothian), and Harold Laski championed them. These and other federalists joined a new group, the Federal Union, established in November 1938, which attracted several thousand members. *Union Now,* a book by US academic Clarence Streit, calling for a transatlantic union of democratic states, had a big impact on British opinion.[8] As World War II ground on, British federalists produced a steady stream of books and pamphlets advocating the establishment of a federal system of European states in the postwar period. In September 1944, the Federal Union adopted as an "immediate aim the promotion of a democratic federation of Europe as part of the postwar settlement."[9]

Britain was home during the war to many exiled continental politicians, who both imbibed and shaped these federalist ideas. British federalism also influenced the non-Communist resistance movements throughout occupied Europe, especially in Italy. There Altiero Spinelli and other democratic socialists, detained on the island of Ventotene, smuggled out their Manifesto for a Free and United Europe, in July 1941 (it later appeared as an underground publication in Nazi-occupied Rome).[10] Drawing on a tradition of Italian federalism dating from the nineteenth century, the manifesto called for a postwar federation, including Germany, to ensure peace in Europe. Inspired by the

Ventotene Manifesto, Italian federalists conferred with the representatives of resistance movements from other countries during a clandestine conference in Geneva in the spring of 1944; the result was the International Federalist Declaration, which circulated secretly throughout Nazi Europe.

At the same time, driven by a malevolent racial nationalism, the Nazis integrated Europe by force. Yet Albert Speer, Hitler's young economic czar, speculated about a postwar European economic community based on voluntary cooperation rather than coercion. Referring to a meeting in September 1943 with Jean Bichelonne, the like-minded French minister of production, Speer told an interviewer decades later: "We agreed that in the future we would avoid the mistakes of the First World War generation, who were now at the helm. Irrespective of national frontiers, Europe had to be economically integrated."[11] According to his military liaison officer, Speer believed strongly in shared economic sovereignty: "He was certain that the only way towards a better and peaceful future, not only for Germany but for all of Europe, was if Germany could eventually be part of an economic European entity."[12]

Toward European Union

Speer never thought that the war would end in Germany's annihilation. That outcome, together with the emergence of the Soviet Union as the liberator and then the occupier of Central and Eastern Europe, completely changed the geopolitical configuration of the Continent. Eager to establish a new, open, international economic system and protect Western Europe from internal Communist subversion or external Soviet aggression, the United States became deeply embroiled in European affairs as the Cold War intensified. Susceptible to US pressure and mindful of the mistakes of the past, yet fearful as ever of eventual German resurgence, France sought a mutually agreeable strategy to deal with the new Federal Republic. The circumstances seemed propitious for France and its neighbors to share a degree of national sovereignty in a supranational organization. The Cold War facilitated such an initiative but also ensured that, instead of being pan-European in scope, it would be confined to Western Europe.

The movement for European integration reemerged in the aftermath of World War II and reached its apogee in 1948 at the Congress of Europe, a gathering of over 600 influential Europeans from sixteen countries, held in The Hague in May 1948. Yet the Schuman Declaration of 1950, which gave rise to the European Coal and Steel Community (ECSC), originated not in the ferment of the European movement but in the narrow confines of the French economic planning office, headed by Jean Monnet. It was an imaginative response to the challenge of rapid German economic recovery at a time of worsening East-West conflict, satisfying differing US, French, and German needs and objectives. For leading French and German politicians at the time, the coalescence of European and national interests made sharing sovereignty irresistible and set in train a lengthy, unpredictable, and intriguing process of economic and political integration.

In his famous article "The End of History?" Francis Fukuyama referred dismissively to "those flabby, prosperous, self-satisfied, inward-looking, weak-willed states whose grandest project was nothing more heroic than the creation of the Common Market."[13] The six countries that launched the European Community (EC) in the 1950s were far from flabby, prosperous, self-satisfied, or inward-looking. Nor were they weak-willed. Despite Fukuyama's scorn for a vision devoid of color and heroic derring-do, it took a leap of faith and rare political courage for most of those countries to turn their backs on traditional nation-state aspirations and agree to exercise some of their powers in common. For France, in particular, accepting the EC meant a drastic revision of the country's long-standing self-image as a leading great power. For Germany, largely destroyed at the end of the war, European integration offered salvation and international rehabilitation.

Plans for a European Defense Community (EDC), to be organized along lines similar to the ECSC, collapsed because of French fear of German rearmament, apparently poisoning prospects for further formal integration. Yet the European Economic Community (EEC) emerged soon afterward, not because of the kind of spillover predicted by Ernst Haas in *The Uniting of Europe,* his pathbreaking book on the ECSC, but because of the appeal of deeper economic integration at a time of intensifying intra-European trade.[14] Member states built the EC on a solid foundation of informal economic integration stretching back to the late nineteenth century, which they now shaped in particular geographical and functional directions.

Britain stayed outside the Communities because its national interests, or at least the government's perception of its national interests, pointed in a different direction. By the time Britain changed course and applied to join in the early 1960s, French president Charles de Gaulle saw British membership as a threat to France and promptly thwarted it. De Gaulle embraced the EC as an economic entity, not least because of its promise of a generous agricultural policy, but rejected its political pretensions. His espousal of an intergovernmental political union and dismissal of European Commission president Walter Hallstein's federal ambitions precipitated the greatest constitutional crisis in the history of European integration—the empty chair crisis of 1965–1966.

French opposition to British accession ended after de Gaulle's resignation in 1969 and in light of Germany's growing economic power. Unfortunately, British membership in the EC coincided with international financial instability and the oil crisis of the early 1970s. The enlarged EC struggled through a decade of brutal economic conditions: sluggish growth, rampant inflation, and rising unemployment. The recession reinforced British ambivalence toward the EC. Regular meetings of EC leaders, institutionalized in the European Council, helped hold the Community together. The chancellor of Germany and the president of France used the EC as a hook upon which to hang the European Monetary System (EMS), a mechanism for monetary policy cooperation in the late 1970s. Otherwise the EC seemed moribund, the butt of jokes about agricultural surpluses and excessive harmonization of industrial product standards.

The EC sprang back to life in the mid-1980s, rediscovered as the answer to the problems of Eurosclerosis and the lethargy of the previous decade and as a vehicle for Community members to confront together the challenges of incipient globalization. Commission president Jacques Delors deftly capitalized on the member states' determination to accelerate economic integration. He leveraged the single market program to win substantial spending from the EC budget to promote economic and social cohesion, aimed at closing the gap between richer and poorer member states, including recent entrants Portugal and Spain. The Single European Act (SEA), the first major treaty reform in the EC's history, committed member states to complete the single market by 1992; introduced far-reaching institutional reform with respect to single market measures; and enshrined cohesion as a key Community objective. Little wonder that the SEA came to be seen as a major turning point in the history of European union.

If legitimacy depends on success, then the EC enjoyed strong legitimacy in the late 1980s. The single market program proved popular with elites and ordinary Europeans alike. Delors reveled in the EC's newfound popularity. France and Germany returned to the driver's seat of European integration, their leaders calling for the ambitious, seemingly improbable goal of monetary union to consolidate the single market and strengthen the EC politically in the face of dissolution of the old order in Central and Eastern Europe. Increasingly alienated by moves toward monetary union and other forms of integration, British prime minister Margaret Thatcher warned that the EC risked becoming a "superstate." She and Delors had radically different visions of Europe: his ardently federalist, hers fervently antifederalist.

Popular support for European integration helped return Helmut Kohl of Germany, François Mitterrand of France, and Felipe González of Spain to power, and helped topple Thatcher from power, in the late 1980s. Driven by their respective national interests and a shared European interest, Kohl and Mitterrand pushed forward with plans for monetary union. Rapid change in Central and Eastern Europe, culminating in the imminent prospect of German unification, helped Kohl overcome domestic resistance to giving up the country's cherished currency, the deutschemark. The sudden end of the Cold War also emboldened member states to develop a common foreign and security policy (CFSP), which, together with economic and monetary union (EMU), became the centerpiece of intergovernmental negotiations in

1991 that resulted in the Maastricht Treaty. A new face of Europe was emerging: that of an aspiring global power, trying to achieve the unified political clout to match its rising economic weight.

But exaggerated claims of the single market's success and a severe economic downturn soured the public mood in the early 1990s. The Maastricht Treaty, which launched the EU, fanned popular unease about the pace of European integration. Responding to a near-fatal backlash against the treaty's scope and content, a chastened political establishment struggled to make the EU more open, accountable, and responsive to citizen concerns. Member states stressed the notion of subsidiarity—a principle of decentralization and quasi-federalism—to reassure a restive public. Despite these efforts, the EU failed to win widespread acceptance as it struggled to be effective in a harsh international environment.

The newly proclaimed EU faced formidable challenges. The road to monetary union, finally reached in 1999, was rocky, obliging member states to make hard economic choices in order to participate. Enlargement reemerged on the EU's agenda with the end of the Cold War. First the European neutrals (plus Norway), then the newly independent countries of Central and Eastern Europe (plus Cyprus, Malta, and Turkey), sought membership. The neutrals (Austria, Finland, and Sweden) joined without fuss in 1995; Norway chose to stay outside. Primarily because of their low level of economic development and poor administrative capacity, the Central and Eastern European countries faced major obstacles to membership. They eventually joined in two stages: the Czech Republic, Estonia, Hungary, Latvia, Lithuania, Poland, Slovakia, and Slovenia acceded in 2004 (along with Cyprus and Malta); Bulgaria and Romania acceded in 2007. Croatia, like Slovenia a former republic of Yugoslavia, which had collapsed in the 1990s, joined the EU in 2013. Turkey was a special case: geographically distant though strategically important; economically underdeveloped and politically unsteady; populous and predominantly Muslim. The Turkish occupation of the northern part of Cyprus complicated the Mediterranean island's otherwise straightforward membership application as well as Turkey's own membership prospects. Once Cyprus acceded, Turkey's chance of joining seemed even more remote.

Enlargement on such a large scale was bound to change the EU, especially at a time of growing public disillusionment with the EU itself. Having avoided far-reaching institutional change during previous episodes of enlargement, and aware of the need to address the yawning gap between "Brussels" and ordinary Europeans, national governments launched a new round of treaty reform in 2000 that would culminate a decade later in the Lisbon Treaty. First came the Nice Treaty of 2001, which proved patently inadequate either to prepare the EU for enlargement or to strengthen the EU's weak legitimacy. Next came the Convention on the Future of Europe, in 2002–2003, when representatives of EU and national institutions considered sweeping changes to the EU treaties, including the promulgation of a constitution.

The ensuing Constitutional Treaty was less innovative than its proponents had hoped, but alarmed many Europeans by drawing attention, as the adjective "constitutional" implied, to the EU's statelike characteristics. The rejection by Dutch and French voters of the Constitutional Treaty in 2005 was a severe political setback for the EU. National and EU leaders managed to salvage most of the contents of the discredited treaty in the unobjectionably named Lisbon Treaty, which itself had to be voted on twice before being ratified in Ireland (the only member state to hold a referendum on the issue). Though the Lisbon Treaty strengthened the EU institutionally and broadened its policy scope, the protracted and unsatisfactory experience of treaty reform over the previous decade deepened public unease with the EU and strengthened national resistance to further grand bargains to bolster European integration.

The outbreak of the eurozone crisis in the wake of the Constitutional Treaty debacle reinforced the impression that the EU was in serious trouble. The onset of the crisis, in 2009, exposed weaknesses in the design of EMU and a pattern of economic divergence among eurozone members. A "one size fits all" monetary policy had unintentionally encouraged excessive borrowing by some countries, notably Greece, and had fueled property bubbles in other countries, notably Ireland and Spain. Risky behavior by many European banks added to the eurozone's vulnerability when the financial crisis struck.

Regardless of the causes of the crisis, it was the seemingly sluggish EU response and the tough line that Germany took on conditionality for bailouts to the worst-affected countries that undermined confidence in EMU and in European integration more broadly. Germany's insistence on austerity seemed to exacerbate the economic downturn throughout Europe. Though Germany's chancellor, Angela Merkel, remained in power throughout, governments in more than half of the eurozone countries fell during the crisis. A huge rift opened between Germany and France when François Hollande, who strongly opposed austerity, became president of France in May 2012. Germany's preoccupation with austerity and apparent indifference to the plight of other eurozone countries, serious tension in Franco-German relations, and growing opposition in Britain to continued EU membership overshadowed the undoubted success of the European project during the previous decades.

Clearly, today's EU is very different from the European Communities of the 1950s. Yet certain features endure: the logic of economic integration; French fear of falling behind; concern about Germany's predominance; the significance of Franco-German leadership; British detachment; and the small-country syndrome (small member states' fear of hegemony). Like the EC before it, the EU is a political undertaking that is concerned primarily with economic integration. Although the common foreign and security policy, a nascent defense policy, and cooperation on justice and home affairs often grab the headlines, at its core the EU is mostly about managing the European marketplace. Economic integration is unglamorous but important. By eliminating barriers to trade and investment, and facilitating movement across borders, it benefits the peoples of Europe directly but largely imperceptibly.

The EU operates in a global context that has changed dramatically since the birth of the original European institutions. Some of the early proponents of European integration wanted Europe to assert itself internationally, seeing the EC as a possible "third force" alongside the United States and the Soviet Union. The Cold War put an end to their dream and to French efforts in the early 1960s to establish a European union independent of the United States. The end of the Cold War provided an opening for the EU to emerge not as a third force but, because of the disappearance of the Soviet Union, as a second force alongside the United States, in a world with several emerging economic powers such as China, Brazil, and India. By then the EU was a global economic power; becoming a global political and military power proved more difficult. The fallout from the terrorist attacks on the United States in 2001 and the war in Iraq in 2003, and from the great recession and the eurozone crisis, has greatly complicated the EU's efforts to match its economic power with diplomatic and military might.

Interpreting European Union History

Serious historical research on European integration started in the 1980s. Before then, the interpretation of European integration was not the work of historians, or to be more precise it was not historical work, given that the full range of raw material began to become available only in the late 1970s with the declassification of most government documents covering the early postwar years (under the standard "thirty-year rule"). Only as the ensuing archival-based research was disseminated at conferences and in publications did the historiography of European integration truly commence. By that time, the federalist interpretation of European integration, based on ideology rather than rigorous academic assessment, had firmly taken hold.[15]

The Federalist Interpretation

The federalist interpretation was spawned by a dedicated group of writers who viewed the demise of the nation-state and the emergence of European union as both inevitably and highly desirable. For them, the 1948 Congress of Europe was a high-water mark, after which the struggle for European union became more difficult though the outcome no less certain. In their opinion, the fault lay with intractable intergovernmentalism, epitomized by the United Kingdom and personified by former prime minister Winston

Churchill. Despite having made a famous speech in Zurich, in 1946, in which he called for a United States of Europe, Churchill was a nationalist with little sympathy for supranationalism.

Churchill's prominence at the Congress of Europe, where he ensured that the Council of Europe, which emerged from it, was organized along traditional intergovernmental lines, frustrated many federalists. Undaunted, federalists believed that European union would ultimately prevail, not least because history was on their side. Indeed, European federalism had been building steam for decades, even centuries. Its origins lay in "a continual hankering after some kind of European unity," notably since the glorious days of Charlemagne, who became Holy Roman Emperor in 800.[16] European federalists fondly cited subsequent calls for European unity made by a succession of Christian intellectuals and politicians, and pointed to a rich literature espousing the idea of a united Europe.

The spiritual dimension of European federalism gave many of its proponents a "holier than thou" attitude. In the long march of history, federalism seemed to them to have a better lineage and to be a worthier cause than modern nationalism, which had brought Europe such misery by 1945. Many federalist writers anticipated the sudden demise or gradual withering away of the nation-state and its replacement by a federation of states. In their view, supporters of traditional political arrangements and international relations were naive (at best) or malevolent (at worst).

Jean Monnet was an awkward character for many federalists to embrace. Although a proponent of European unity, Monnet took an unheroic, low-key approach, preferring to move piecemeal toward European union via the unglamorous path of functional economic integration. Nor was he religious, let alone a Christian Democrat. He was not a career politician either, but a prominent national and (before that) international civil servant.

By contrast, Robert Schuman, whose name became synonymous with the plan for the ECSC, was ideally cast for the federalist interpretation of European integration. Coming from the disputed province of Lorraine and having grown up in German-occupied territory, Schuman sought above all to promote reconciliation between France and Germany. He was not only a Christian Democrat but also a devout Catholic—celibate and saintly.[17]

Konrad Adenauer, postwar Germany's first chancellor, also fit the bill, being another Christian Democrat and advocate of European union. Federalists added to the mix Italian prime minister Alcide de Gasperi, yet another Christian Democrat and bona fide European idealist, who nonetheless played only a marginal role in the development of European integration and whose motives owed as much to concerns about the growing strength of the Italian Communist Party as to a burning desire for a federal Europe.

For all the excitement surrounding the Schuman Declaration, the ensuing ECSC was a far cry from the much-sought European federation.

Federalists' hopes soared again with the call (also engineered by Monnet) for a European Defense Community, and correspondingly plunged when the proposed community collapsed in 1954. According to the federalists, the failure of the defense community ranks alongside the stunted development of the Council of Europe as the greatest setback in the history of the European integration.

The new hero, in the federalists' view, was Belgian foreign minister Paul-Henri Spaak, who engineered the successful outcome of the Messina meeting of foreign ministers in June 1955, which resulted in the negotiations in 1956–1957 that brought about the European Economic Community. But Spaak was not as compelling a character in the federalist narrative as was Schuman. Without doubting his commitment and contribution to European integration, many federalists were discomfited by his socialism and anticlericalism.

Walter Hallstein, the first president of the European Commission, occupies a high position in the federalist pantheon. Hallstein was a zealous federalist who sought to assert the economic community's political character. That brought him into conflict with de Gaulle, the greatest scoundrel in the federalist interpretation (greater even than Churchill). What seemed to some federalists like a titanic struggle in the early 1960s between two great leaders, one (Hallstein) representing the future of Europe and the other (de Gaulle) clinging to the past, was in reality an unequal battle between a powerful national leader and the head of an emergent European institution.

The empty chair crisis contributed to a political malaise in the Community that stretched into the early 1980s. The economic recessions of the 1970s made matters worse. These were the dark ages for European federalists, a time when European integration seemed stagnant or even regressive. Salvation came in the form of Jacques Delors, who became Commission president in January 1985 and oversaw the single market program later in the decade. By that time, the federalist interpretation of European integration enjoyed wide currency. This was a story of chances seized and squandered; of setbacks and surges; of crises and opportunities; of a few far-sighted statesmen struggling for Europe's soul against atavistic nationalists; of supranational institutions embodying the ethos of European federalism and constituting an embryonic European government; of brave officials of Community institutions carrying the torch of European unity.

The European Commission had an obvious interest in encouraging research and writing on the history of European integration that would propagate the federalist interpretation. The Commission was instrumental in establishing the European University Institute (EUI), which opened in Florence in 1976. The Commission envisioned the EUI's Department of History and Civilization as a source of scholarship on European integration that would lay the academic foundations for what it hoped was an emerging European federation.[18]

Walter Lipgens, the first professor of history at the EUI, seemed ideally suited for the job and lent academic credibility to the federalist interpretation. A convinced federalist himself, Lipgens embarked on the monumental task of attempting to collect and publish every speech, statement, and scrap of documentary evidence, country by country, from the resistance movements and subsequent European movement in support of European integration. Lipgens's Herculean effort did not bear the abundant fruit that he had hoped for. Nor did he live to see the results, which appeared posthumously.[19] The three edited volumes may have had the contrary effect from that intended. For the contrast between the weight of documentary material contained in them and the actions of European politicians was striking. Why had so many speeches, policy papers, and other pronouncements on European integration produced such relatively paltry results?

Backlash

By that time, many historians of postwar Europe were highly critical of the federalist interpretation. With the opening of national archives covering the immediate postwar years, they were finally able to explore the dynamics of decisionmaking on issues ranging from the Marshall Plan to the ECSC. Alan Milward, a brilliant economic historian who succeeded Lipgens at the EUI, was the most prominent of them.

Initially, Milward was curious to know why reconstruction had been so successful after World War II compared to the aftermath of World War I. Presumably, Europe's success after 1945 was due largely to the role of the United States. Indeed, the prevailing view in the popular and academic literature was that the United States had saved Western Europe by implementing the Marshall Plan. Milward asserted that Europe's economic recovery had begun in 1945 and was well under way by 1947 when Europe faced a shortfall of dollars with which to continue to buy capital and consumer goods from the United States. Far from rescuing Western Europe, the Marshall Plan had merely helped Western Europe to overcome a balance-of-payments problem (although this was hardly an inconsiderable achievement).

If the Marshall Plan had not saved postwar Western Europe, Milward wondered what had. He concluded that the real saviors were the ECSC and the European Payments Union. The first facilitated a diplomatic settlement between France and Germany, without which a stable Western European order could not have come about; the second facilitated international trade, without which Western Europe could not have prospered. In Milward's view, Monnet devised the ECSC not because of altruism or high idealism but because of unrelenting US diplomatic pressure on France to come to terms with Germany's political and economic rehabilitation. By early 1948, French officials were groping for a strategy that would reconcile French economic modernization with German economic recovery. This was the genesis of the Schuman Plan, the substance of which emerged gradually over a two-year period and "did not, as all commentators on it have so far suggested, emerge as a *deus ex machina* from [Monnet's] Planning Commissariat in Spring 1950."[20]

Milward took particular pleasure in debunking the federalist interpretation of European integration and dismissed the political significance of the "extraordinary wave of enthusiasm for European federation" in the immediate postwar years, claiming that "it was no more than a faintly disquieting and soon stilled disturbance for the ship of state, their officer governments and their crews of civil servants."[21] The idea that European integration was the result of idealism or the weakness of the nation-state, Milward wrote, "is flatly contradicted by this book. Here the interpretation is that the very limited degree of integration that was achieved came about through the pursuit of the narrow self-interest of what were still powerful nation states."[22] Nor was there anything inexorable or inevitable about European integration.

The publication of Milward's *The Reconstruction of Western Europe* had a profound impact on the historiography of European integration. Milward's stellar academic credentials, together with the extent of the archival research on which the book rested, lent considerable credibility to his conclusions. Backed up by solid research, Milward's assertions about the state-centric nature of European integration seemed compelling, if somewhat overstated. Milward used the occasion of the publication of the paperback edition to take a swipe at those federalist who claimed that the book was "a denial of the role of idealism and an exaggeration of the role of national materialism in the making of post-war Europe," once again claiming that the historical evidence showed that the prevailing (federalist) understanding of European integration was "an inadequate foundation of belief and theory on which to build or explain the new European order."[23] Milward was so dismissive of the federalists as to argue that his own interpretation of the history of European integration was blindingly obvious: "it is no great thing to show to be wrong what few historians ever believed to be right."[24]

The study of postwar economic reconstruction had brought Milward to the study of European integration, which was squarely the subject of his next big book. Milward was struck by a paradox: at the same time that nation-states were becoming more powerful in the postwar period, having recovered (in most cases) from the devastation of the war itself, they were surrendering sovereignty to a supranational entity that, its proponents claimed, was the antithesis of the nation-state. How could nation-states be strengthening and weakening at the same time? Milward concluded that "there is no . . . antithesis between the nation state and supranationality" and that "the evolution of the Community since 1945 has been an integral part of the reassertion of the nation state as an organizational concept." Indeed, the two were inextricably linked: "to supercede the nation state would be to destroy the

Community. To put a finite limit to the process of integration would be to weaken the nation state, to limit its scope and to curb its power."[25]

Milward's thesis was that national governments went beyond traditional international interdependence and surrendered sovereignty in key policy areas in order to ensure their own survival and enhance their own authority. European integration, far from undermining the nation-state, as federalists believed that it would, was an essential means of strengthening the nation-state under the circumstances in which Europe found itself in the mid–twentieth century. "The development of the EC, the process of European integration, was . . . a part of [the] postwar rescue of the European nation-state, because the new political consensus on which this rescue was built required the process of integration, the surrender of limited areas of national sovereignty to the supranational."[26]

The publication of *The European Rescue of the Nation State* cemented Milward's reputation as the foremost historian of European integration and established his explanation of the origins and development of the EC as the new orthodoxy.[27] Rearguard actions to reassert federalism, or at least to provide a more balanced perspective, were largely unavailing.[28] *The Frontier of National Sovereignty,* a short book by Milward and colleagues, published in 1993, was essentially an addendum to *Rescue of the Nation State.*[29] It contained a number of case studies to demonstrate the primacy of national interests in the process of European integration and the mutual dependence of the nation-state and the supranation (the case studies were country-specific, focusing on the interests and preferences of Italy, France, Denmark, Britain, and the United States at various times in the postwar period).

Like *Rescue of the Nation State* only more so, *The Frontier of National Sovereignty* sought to develop a theory of European integration based on historical evidence. Milward's hypothesis, that nation-states chose to surrender sovereignty in a supranational entity when it suited them to go beyond traditional interdependence, had both descriptive and predictive value: it described the process of integration to date and provided a framework for envisaging when nation-states might agree to surrender sovereignty in new policy areas. Not surprisingly, Milward and his colleagues concluded that their approach to understanding the EC convincingly explained the acceleration of integration in the late 1980s, culminating in the Maastricht Treaty of 1992.

Another of the most important books on the history of European integration appeared at about this time, and could be described as an annex to Milward's edifice. That was John Gillingham's *Coal, Steel, and the Rebirth of Europe,* a compelling analysis of the background and negotiations that led to the ECSC.[30] Like Milward, Gillingham asserted the centrality of the ECSC to the stability and security, and therefore also the prosperity, of Western Europe after World War II. Like Milward as well, Gillingham emphasized the primacy of national interests. His chapter on the negotiation of the ECSC, aptly titled "From Summit to Swamp," followed the course of the intergovernmental conference from the rhetorical heights of the Schuman Declaration to the unseemly give-and-take of the bargaining that followed.

Another important feature of Gillingham's book was that it drew heavily on industry as well as government archives and placed the ECSC squarely in the history of nearly fifty years of interaction between French and German producers (almost half the book covered the period from the end of World War I to the end of World War II). The final chapter, titled "The Success of Failure," contrasted the economic inadequacy of the ECSC with its political success. Whereas the ECSC was unable to prevent reconcentration in the German steel industry and failed to bring about a fully functioning common market, it provided a practical peace settlement for postwar Europe, inculcated cooperative practices among participating groups and governments, and laid an institutional foundation for the European Economic Community.

Political Science and History

Political scientists—mostly American or US-based—had been among the most astute analysts and observers of the European Community in the 1950s and 1960s. Political scientists' interest in the EC waned in the 1970s and early 1980s, as the EC itself appeared to languish. With the renewal of European integration in the late 1980s, a new generation of political scientists, again mostly American or US-based, discovered the EC. Prominent among them were those who fused history and political science in an effort to explain European integration and predict future developments. Andrew Moravcsik was the most famous and influential of these scholars.

Like Milward, Moravcsik took an unabashedly state-centric view of European integration, beginning with a study of the negotiations that resulted in the Single European Act.[31] Moravcsik refined Milward's approach by focusing exclusively on the commercial interests of the big member states. In his view, commercial interests alone determined governments' preferences, and lowest-common-denominator intergovernmental bargaining accounted for the contents of the SEA. Again like Milward, Moravcsik wanted to develop a theory of European integration that was based on historical evidence. The case study of the SEA formed the basis for Moravcsik's trademark "liberal intergovernmentalism," an approach to understanding key constitutive moments (mostly treaty-making and reform) in the history of European integration.

The Choice for Europe, Moravcsik's monumental study of European integration "from Messina to Maastricht" (1955–1992), developed the theory of liberal intergovernmentalism on the basis of five case studies.[32] In addition to the SEA, these were: the negotiation of the Rome Treaty; the consolidation of the common market; the launch and management of the European Monetary System; and the negotiation of the Maastricht Treaty. Moravcsik not only insisted on the importance of historical research for understanding and theorizing about the EU, but also stressed his mastery of primary sources.

A number of critics claimed not only that Moravcsik's use of sources was incorrect but also that the sources themselves were "softer" than Moravcsik declared them to be. Accordingly, these critics went on to question the validity of Moravcsik's revisionist claims. Regardless of its possible impact on Moravcsik's scholarly reputation, such criticism accentuated the massive impact of Moravcsik's work. Moravcsik had managed to blend history and political science in the study of European integration, cast key developments in the history of the EU in a new light, and raise the visibility and status of EU studies.

Craig Parsons, another political scientist working on the history of European integration, focused on the key events of the 1950s, though he confined his analysis to France, the crucial member state at that time. In *A Certain Idea of Europe,* Parsons argued that a combination of ideological commitment and favorable domestic political circumstances, rather than economic or geopolitical forces, accounted for the success of the ECSC and the European Economic Community.[33] By contrast, the absence—for reasons not unconnected to the European question—of a ruling coalition that would support the defense community, sealed the fate of that initiative. Perhaps because the chronological scope and theoretical sweep of his research were narrower, and because his familiarity with French sources was so thorough, Parsons was not seriously criticized by historians, though his ideational explanation for the triumph of the community model in the 1950s has certainly been questioned.

Historical research is not the province exclusively of US political scientists working on the EU. Berthold Rittberger (of Ludwig Maximilians University of Munich) has long combined historical research and political science methodology to explore questions relating to democratic accountability and representation. His groundbreaking book *Building Europe's Parliament* was rooted in research on the origins of the Common Assembly of the ECSC, and the acquisition by the European Parliament of budgetary and legislative power in the 1970s and 1980s.[34]

Recent Work

Whereas Moravcsik developed a new theory grounded in historical research, John Gillingham embarked on an equally ambitious undertaking: a history of European integration (the book was titled simply *European Integration*) from the Schuman Plan in 1950 to the Nice Treaty in 2000. Gillingham's credentials as a leading historian of European integration were already well established. Aware of the importance of archival sources and their general unavailability for the period after the early 1970s, he nonetheless felt compelled and confident to continue his narrative into the early 2000s. The story that he told was not simply of national interests and supranational solutions, but of a struggle "between two principles of social, political, and economic organization: the state and the market"; Gillingham declared that "the tension between these two poles is responsible for the zigs and zags characteristic of the integration process."[35]

Gillingham starkly portrayed the process of European integration as a fight between good and bad, between market forces and statism. During the first stage of European integration, in the immediate postwar period, statism was on the ascendant. Monnet, the hero of Gillingham's book on the ECSC, became something of an antihero in *European Integration.* The difficulty with Monnet this time was his passion for planning and disinterest in democratic institutions, two problems that he bequeathed to the EC and later the EU. The epic battle between markets and statism took place, in Gillingham's opinion, in the 1980s; the main protagonists were Thatcher and Delors. Thatcher was Gillingham's hero in *European Integration,* Delors the villain, a characterization that turned the usual description of European integration in the 1980s on its head.

Arguably, Gillingham's ideological zeal undermined the credibility of *European Integration,* which appealed strongly to euroskeptics. Yet Gillingham remained profoundly appreciative of the benefits of European integration, regretting only its direction (or lack of direction) since the halcyon days of the single market program. The negative outcome of the French and Dutch referendums on the Constitutional Treaty in 2005 was fully consistent with Gillingham's conclusions in *European Integration* and was not necessarily a cause for alarm. Rather, it was a signal to EU leaders that the EU needed to return to first principles: the continuation of unspectacular but essential economic integration.

Other major contributions to the historiography of European integration in recent years have not been as ambitious as Gillingham's, and range from detailed studies of national involvement to in-depth analyses of particular events and developments. The creeping forward in time of the availability of national archives has meant that important turning points, such as the launch of the European Monetary System, are now subject to thorough scrutiny.[36] Meanwhile, the burgeoning of postgraduate studies in EU history and the increasing political salience of European integration have accounted for a growing number of young historians turning their attention to the EU. More recent scholarship has focused on the relationship between European integration and the Cold War, the institutional history of the EU, and particular policy developments.[37]

Britain and the EU

Given its highly emotional and politically charged nature, it is hardly surprising that the question of Britain's EU membership has attracted considerable academic attention. Concerned about the quality of the public and academic debate on Britain's involvement in the EC, Milward weighed in with a chapter on "Britain and Western Europe" in the first edition of *Rescue of the Nation State,* which he revised considerably in the second edition.[38] He also wrote the first volume of the official history of Britain's relationship with the EC, covering the period from the Schuman Plan to the failure of Britain's first application for membership, in which he argued that British policy throughout was consistent with a national strategy that sought to ease the country's transition from a great power to a middle-ranking European power but that proved difficult to implement for a variety of economic and political reasons.[39]

Stephen Wall, a former British diplomat, wrote the second volume of the official history, covering the period from the Britain's first membership application to the 1975 referendum.[40] Unlike Milward, Wall did not present a main thesis or argument, preferring to let the government documents, from which he quoted extensively, speak from themselves. Nevertheless, Wall emphasized the primacy of geopolitical rather than economic considerations for Britain's renewed membership efforts; and the adroit political maneuvering of Prime Minister Harold Wilson, who used the renegotiation of EC membership terms and the 1975 referendum to overcome strong opposition to the EC from within the Labour Party.

Purpose and Organization of the Book

Europe Recast examines the European Communities' and later the EU's political, institutional, and policy development in the context of fluctuating national fortunes and changing global circumstances. Drawing on original accounts of the establishment of the European Communities and a wealth of scholarship in a range of disciplines, the book seeks to explain and describe the development of European integration as comprehensively as possible within a manageable length, while hoping to avoid "Euro-fatigue" on the part of the reader. The history of the EU, because it lacks conventional heroics, often seems dull and dry. The empty chair crisis of the mid-1960s, when French representatives refused to take their seats in the Council of Ministers, is the most exciting political conflict in EU history—hardly on a par with the siege of Vienna or the Napoleonic campaigns. Yet as this book shows, the making of the EU combines idealism and ideological struggles, the initiative and political entrepreneurship of strong individuals, national interests and international relations, and institutional design and bureaucratic intrigue.

The story of European integration is worth telling not only because of its intrinsic interest but also because of its importance. Having begun as one of a number of competing European projects, the supranational EC quickly eclipsed all others and soon claimed center stage. As a result, today's EU is a regional integration organization unlike any other, with formidable economic power and political clout. Understanding the EU is fundamental to understanding Europe, and understanding EU history is fundamental to understanding the EU.

While arguing that national interests rather than Euro-idealism accounted for the emergence of the ECSC and that national preferences were paramount as well in later stages of European integration, this book acknowledges the sometimes pivotal importance of other influences and factors. Although pragmatism may explain the scope and shape of the EU, a felicitous combination of idealism and national self-interest characterized the early years of European integration. The architects of the new Europe grasped the political opportunities presented in the 1950s to pool national sovereignty and establish supranational organizations. European integration could not have flourished and Euro-idealism would have foundered if the undertaking had not worked to the advantage of the countries concerned.

Although the ideas that led to the founding of the European Communities reach back into the nineteenth century, the end of World War II is the critical point of departure for the story of contemporary European integration, and therefore for this book. Thus Chapter 1 explores the immediate postwar period. Chapter 2 examines the emergence of the three Communities in the 1950s, as well as the failure of the proposed defense community. Chapter 3 covers the construction of the EC, including the epic constitutional battle provoked by de Gaulle. Chapter 4 assesses the EC's fortunes during the economic upheavals of the mid-1970s. Chapter 5 explains the EC's gradual recovery in the late 1970s and early 1980s, due to changing domestic and international circumstances. Chapter 6 discusses the acceleration of integration in the late 1980s, focusing on the SEA and the single market program. Chapter 7 describes the achievement of European union in the early 1990s, focusing on the Maastricht Treaty. Chapter 8 examines the challenges that confronted the new EU, notably enlargement, further treaty reform, and implementation of EMU. Chapter 9 looks at the limits of European union, especially with respect to further enlargement, the Lisbon Treaty, and the eurozone crisis. Chapter 10, the conclusion, returns to key points of the narrative, highlighting the substance of the European idea that survived each new reinvention and expansion to keep the original vision alive.

Notes

1. John Maynard Keynes, *The Economic Consequences of the Peace* (New York: Harcourt, Brace, and Howe, 1920).

2. R. N. Coudenhove-Kalergi, *Pan-Europa* (Vienna: Pan-Europa-Verlag, 1923); translated as *Pan-Europa* (New York: A. A. Knopf, 1926).

3. See Raymond J. Sontag, *A Broken World: 1919–1939* (New York: Harper and Row, 1971), p. 127.

4. See Zara Steiner, *The Lights That Failed: European International History, 1919–1933* (Oxford: Oxford University Press, 2007), pp. 387–493.

5. On Stresemann's contribution to European integration, see Jonathan Wright, *Gustav Stresemann: Weimar's Greatest Statesman* (Oxford: Oxford University Press, 2002).

6. See Francis Deak, "Can Europe Unite?" *Political Science Quarterly* 46, no. 3 (September 1931), pp. 424–433.

7. On Coudenhove-Kalergi's exile in the United States and return to Europe after the war, see Arnold J. Zurcher, *The Struggle to Unite Europe* (Westport: Greenwood, 1958), pp. 10–27. Coudenhove-Kalergi received the first Charlemagne Prize, awarded annually by the city of Aachen for service to the cause of European union.

8. Clarence Streit, *Union Now: A Proposal for a Federal Union in the Democracies of the North Atlantic* (New York: Harper and Brothers, 1939).

9. Michael Burgess, *The British Tradition of Federalism* (London: Leicester University Press, 1995), p. 146.

10. See Charles F. Delzell, "The European Federalist Movement in Italy: First Phase, 1918–1947," *Journal of Modern History* 32, no. 3 (September 1960), pp. 244–245.

11. Quoted in Gita Sereny, *Albert Speer: His Battle with Truth* (New York: Knopf, 1995), pp. 386–387.

12. Ibid., p. 554.

13. Francis Fukuyama, "The End of History?" *The National Interest* no. 16 (Summer 1989), p. 8.

14. Ernst Haas, *The Uniting of Europe: Political, Social, and Economic Forces* (Stanford: Stanford University Press, 1958).

15. See Desmond Dinan, "The Historiography of European Integration," in Dinan, ed., *Origins and Evolution of the European Union*, 2nd ed. (Oxford: Oxford University Press, 2014), pp. 345–375.

16. Richard Mayne, *The Community of Europe: Past, Present, and Future* (New York: Norton, 1962), p. 35.

17. See A. P. Fimister, *Robert Schuman: Neo-Scholastic Humanist and the Reunification of Europe* (Brussels: Peter Lang, 2008).

18. O. Calligaro, "Negotiating Europe: EU Promotion of Europeanness and Non-Institutional Actors Since the 1950s," PhD thesis (Florence: European University Institute, 2011), pp. 49–52.

19. Walter Lipgens, ed., *Documents on the History of European Integration*, vol. 1 (Baden-Baden: Nomos Verlag, 1985); Walter Lipgens, ed., *Documents on the History of European Integration*, vol. 2 (Baden-Baden: Nomos Verlag, 1986); Walter Lipgens and W. Loth, eds., *Documents on the History of European Integration*, vol. 3 (Berlin: De Gruytes, 1988).

20. Alan Milward, *The Reconstruction of Western Europe, 1945–1951* (Berkeley: University of California Press, 1984), p. 164.

21. Ibid., p. 55.

22. Ibid., p. 492.

23. Ibid., p. xix.

24. Ibid., p. 493.

25. Alan Milward, *The European Rescue of the Nation State* (Berkeley: University of California Press, 1992), pp. 2–3.

26. Ibid., p. 4.

27. See F. Guirao, F. M. B. Lynch, and S. M. Ramírez Pérez, eds., *Alan S. Milward and a Century of European Change* (London: Routledge, 2012).

28. See, for instance, D. Sidjanski, *The Federal Future of Europe: From the European Community to the European Union* (Ann Arbor: University of Michigan Press, 2000).

29. A. Milward, F. M. B. Lynch, F. Romero, R. Ranieri, and V. Sørensen, *The Frontier of National Sovereignty: History and Theory, 1945–1992* (London: Routledge, 1993).

30. John Gillingham, *Coal, Steel, and the Rebirth of Europe, 1945–1955* (Cambridge: Cambridge University Press, 2005).

31. Andrew Moravcsik, "Negotiating the Single European Act: National Interests and Conventional Statecraft in the European Community," *International Organization* 45, no. 1, pp. 651–688.

32. Andrew Moravcsik, *The Choice for Europe: Social Purpose and State Power from Messina to Maastricht* (Ithaca: Cornell University Press, 1998).

33. Craig Parsons, *A Certain Idea of Europe* (Ithaca: Cornell University Press, 2003).

34. Berthold Rittberger, *Building Europe's Parliament: Democratic Representation Beyond the Nation State* (Oxford: Oxford University Press, 2005).

35. John Gillingham, *European Integration, 1950–2003: Superstate or New Market Economy?* (Cambridge: Cambridge University Press, 2003), p. xii.

36. Emmanuel Mourlon-Droul, *A Europe Made of Money: The Emergence of the European Monetary System* (Ithaca: Cornell University Press, 2012).

37. See N. Piers Ludlow, Frédéric Bozo, Marie-Pierre Rey, and Leopoldo Nuti, eds., *Europe and the End of the Cold War: A Reappraisal* (Abingdon: Routledge, 2008); Michel Mangenot and Sylvain Schirmann, eds., *Les institutions européennes font leur histoire* (Brussels: Peter Lang, 2012); Katja Seidel, *The Process of Politics in Europe: The Rise of European Elites and Supranational Institutions* (London: Tauris Academic, 2010); Maria Gäiner, *Aux origines de la diplomatie européenne* (Brussels: Peter Lang, 2012); Ann-Christina L. Knudsen, *Farmers on Welfare: The Making of Europe's Common Agricultural Policy* (Ithaca: Cornell University Press, 2009).

38. Alan Milward, *The European Rescue of the Nation State,* 2nd ed. (London: Routledge, 2000).

39. Alan Milward, *The UK and the European Community,* vol. 1, *The Rise and Fall of a National Strategy, 1945–1963* (London: Cass, 2002).

40. Stephen Wall, *The Official History of Britain and the European Community,* vol. 2, *From Rejection to Referendum, 1963–1975* (Abingdon: Routledge, 2012).

1

Finding a Way Forward

THE 1940S IN EUROPE SAW THE END OF ONE WAR AND THE BEGIN-
ning of another. World War II ended in 1945; the Cold War began almost
immediately afterward. The Cold War was not inevitable but occurred as a
result of deep-rooted antagonism, intense mistrust, and happenstance. It
gelled in the late 1940s, dividing Europe into two armed camps. Western
Europe gratefully accepted US protection from a menacing Soviet Union.
Eastern Europe lay under Soviet control, as the Red Army turned from a
liberating to an occupying force. The main fault line between East and West
ran through Germany, the geopolitical fulcrum of twentieth-century Europe.

World War II changed Europe completely. Germany was defeated, destroyed, and divided into four zones of occupation. Soviet-controlled Communist parties came to power throughout Eastern Europe, establishing dictatorial governments, seizing private property, and imposing command
economies. Coping with the consequences of the war and an emerging
threat from the East, Western European countries urgently sought economic
recovery, political stability, and military security. The United States made it
possible for them to achieve all three.

The United States promoted international interdependence through free
trade and unrestricted financial flows. Western Europe was an important element in the US-inspired global system. But Western Europe was too weak
economically and financially to participate fully in the emerging international order immediately after the war. The United States came to the rescue
with the Marshall Plan to expedite economic recovery and, with the European Payments Union, to facilitate currency convertibility. The North Atlantic Treaty, signed in Washington in April 1949, provided a security umbrella for Western Europe in the form of the US-led North Atlantic Treaty
Organization (NATO).

This chapter examines the early years of European integration in the context of the emerging Cold War. It shows how the United States supported European integration in order to enhance regional security and accelerate economic recovery, although Europeans were ambivalent about sharing national sovereignty. Very few advocated a United States of Europe; most subscribed to a vague notion of solidarity and transnational cooperation. Rhetorical support for integration reached its zenith in the Congress of Europe in 1948, leading to the establishment of the intergovernmental Council of Europe a year later. Economic integration along supranational lines emerged instead as a solution to a specific problem in postwar Europe: what to do with the new West Germany. The Schuman Declaration of June 1950 was a French initiative to resolve the German question by means of treaty-based economic integration.

From World War to Cold War

By the end of World War II, Germany was thoroughly defeated and utterly devastated. The former Reich was at the mercy of the four occupying powers (Britain, France, the Soviet Union, and the United States). For Germany, 1945 was "zero hour" (*Stunde Null*). The country changed shape as Poland and Czechoslovakia regained disputed territory in the east. Hundreds of thousands of ethnic Germans fled westward. Together with a huge number of displaced persons already in Germany (forced laborers and concentration camp survivors), these impoverished arrivals caused a refugee problem of unprecedented proportions. The official economy collapsed and a thriving black market emerged.

The situation varied elsewhere in Europe in the summer of 1945 but was generally grim.[1] Many countries in Central and Eastern Europe had suffered grievously under German occupation and were ravaged by the epic battles of 1944 and early 1945 between the retreating German and advancing Soviet armies. The German occupation regime in Western Europe had not been as harsh as in the east, nor had the scale and impact of fighting on the Western Front been as great as on the Eastern Front.

Conditions differed markedly within liberated Western Europe, although most countries endured considerable economic privation and social dislocation. Having been liberated before the end of 1944, Belgium was relatively well off in 1945. Parts of neighboring Holland, by contrast, were a battlefield almost until the end of the war. Some liberated countries, such as France and Italy, went through short but sharp civil wars at the time of the German army's retreat, as the resistance settled scores against local Fascists and against elements within its own ideologically diverse membership.

Under the leadership of Josef Stalin, the Soviet Union had withstood a series of ferocious German onslaughts since June 1941, suffering massive

Germany Under Occupation

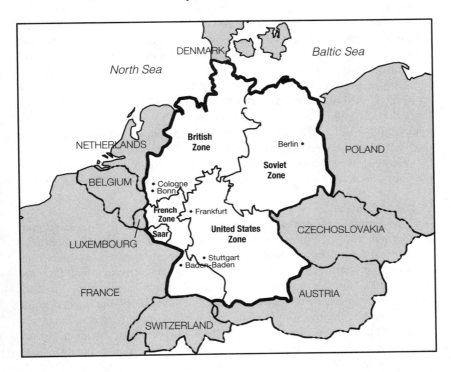

physical destruction and loss of life. Having pushed the progressively weaker German army all the way back to Berlin, the Soviet Union emerged from the war as a great power whose armies were encamped in much of Central and Eastern Europe. Thus Stalin was in a position to impose Communist regimes in a region that the United States and Britain, the two leading Western powers, recognized as a Soviet sphere of influence. Initially, Stalin seemed content to allow non-Communist parties to reorganize themselves in Central and Eastern Europe and participate in coalition governments with the Soviet-supported Communist parties. Nevertheless, historical enmity between Russia and most of its neighbors, as well as the generally loutish behavior of Red Army troops, fostered a climate of deep suspicion toward the Soviet Union.

The United States ended the war undamaged and more powerful than any of the other protagonists. It had global postwar ambitions and interests. The United States wanted above all to establish an international economic system conducive to free trade and investment. This required a tripartite institutional structure: the World Bank, the International Monetary Fund

(IMF), and the International Trade Organization, later the General Agreement on Tariffs and Trade (GATT). Only a country as self-confident and influential as the United States at the end of the war could have hatched such a grandiose scheme for global economic management. Ultimately, US plans for the postwar world foundered on domestic and foreign resistance and were only partly realized.[2]

Despite profound differences between their political and economic systems, the United States and the Soviet Union hoped to maintain a working relationship after the war. The United Nations (UN) was to have provided an overarching political framework for postwar diplomatic relations among the members of the wartime Grand Alliance (the countries that had fought against Germany). Instead, US-Soviet cooperation deteriorated rapidly after the end of hostilities. Mutual mistrust, widespread before the war, quickly resurfaced.

Postwar Politics

Independent national governments returned to power in Europe as soon as the German army withdrew. Apart from discredited collaborators who had no political future (in the short term at least), there were two main distinctions between politicians at the end of the war: the party to which they belonged and where they had spent the years of occupation. Some politicians had fled abroad and formed governments in exile; others remained at home and in many cases joined the resistance. Tension arose between those who stayed and those who left, even within the same party. But the main distinction among politicians after the war, as well as before and during it, was ideological orientation and party affiliation. Communists emerged stronger from the war because they had played a leading role in the resistance and had the support of the Soviet Union, a country widely credited with having defeated Hitler. Social Democrats were also popular because of their longstanding opposition to fascism and the appeal of the social market to voters wary of both communism and capitalism. Eager to distance themselves from disgraced right-wing political parties, conservatives recast themselves after the war as Christian Democrats, advocating compassionate capitalism and accepting the welfare state.

Most governments immediately after the war were coalitions of Communist, Socialist, and Christian Democratic parties. Often infused by the resistance ideals of partnership and shared sacrifice, and conscious-stricken by the failure of anti-Fascist popular fronts in the 1930s, they attempted to work harmoniously together to build better societies and fairer economic systems. Human frailty, lingering resentments, political ambition, and party rivalry soon drove them apart. Distrust between the Communists and non-Communists ran deep and erupted into the open at the onset of the Cold War. By the late 1940s, Communist parties were leaving or being thrown out of government in Western Europe (as in France and Italy) and were throwing non-Communist parties out of government in Central and Eastern Europe (for instance in Czechoslovakia and Poland). Socialist and Christian Democratic parties, sharing a common antipathy toward the Communists, generally continued to cooperate with each other in Western Europe.

Britain was an exception to the postwar European pattern. For one thing, Britain did not have a significant Communist party. Due to a series of political and economic reforms, the vast majority of the British working class had eschewed revolutionary socialism in the nineteenth century. Instead, most British workers supported the nonrevolutionary, social democratic Labour Party. For another thing, Britain had a two-party system in which one party alone traditionally formed the government. Following the collapse of the Liberal Party early in the twentieth century, Labour and the Conservatives were the two main parties. Although they had formed a national unity government under Winston Churchill during the war, the two parties competed against each other in the first postwar election, in July 1945. Despite their gratitude for Churchill's wartime leadership, most Britons did not trust the Conservatives to provide housing, jobs, and a generous welfare system. Promising comprehensive state care "from the cradle to the grave," Labour won by a landslide and remained in office until 1951.[3]

Continental Socialists looked to the Labour Party for leadership and inspiration. Denis Healey, later a leading British government minister, was Labour's international secretary in the late 1940s. He recalled that "among socialists on the Continent, the British Labour Party . . . had a prestige and influence it never enjoyed before or since. Britain was the only big country in Europe where a socialist party had won power on its own, without depending on any coalition partners. Britain had stood out alone against Hitler after the rest of Europe crumbled. And Britain had won."[4] Yet the Labour government pursued a foreign policy that placed relations with European countries third in line behind relations with the United States and with the Empire and Commonwealth (a collection of former colonies).

Germany was another exception to the postwar continental political norm, but for very different reasons. Life in postwar Germany initially remained under the strict control of the four powers, whose approach to local government varied considerably.[5] The occupying powers were supposed to have cooperated in governing Germany through the Allied Control Council, consisting of senior US, British, French, and Soviet officials, but never did so. Reparations became a major sticking point. The Soviets wanted to get hold of as much industrial plant and material as possible in the Western zones. Mindful of the economic mistakes made in Germany after World War I and realizing that it would ultimately have to foot the bill, the United States objected and eventually stopped delivering reparations to the Soviets in May 1946, triggering a series of events that drove the former allies further apart. One of the most dramatic of these was the Berlin Blockade of

1948–1949, when the Soviets blocked all rail, road, and water routes between Berlin and the West. The Western powers responded by supplying their beleaguered zones in Berlin with food and other essentials by air, before the Soviets lifted the blockade eleven months later. The Berlin Blockade symbolized the collapse of the Yalta and Potsdam agreements of 1945 among Britain, the United States, and the Soviet Union on Europe's future and the emergence of a bitter confrontation between East and West.[6]

Mindful of the Great Depression, European electorates wanted their governments to provide economic growth, full employment, and generous social welfare. That was a tall order at the best of times, let alone immediately after the war when disaster relief was the first priority. It was surprising, under the circumstances, that economic recovery proceeded as quickly as it did in postwar Europe. By 1946 a number of smaller countries—Belgium, Denmark, and Norway—attained a level of gross domestic product (GDP) equivalent to that of 1938, the last year before the outbreak of war. France and Italy followed suit in 1949. Britain, relatively unscathed in the war, continued to improve upon its 1938 level during the war itself, whereas Germany, greatly damaged at the end of the war, attained its 1938 level only in 1951.[7] This recovery took place despite the massive wartime destruction of industry and infrastructure, shortages of skilled labor in critical economic sectors, and millions of displaced persons. Nor did the weather help: the winter of 1946–1947 was exceptionally cold and wet, and the summers before and after exceptionally hot and dry.

The Marshall Plan

Following the abrupt termination in August 1945 of its wartime Lend Lease program, the United States continued to assist war-damaged Europe through the United Nations Relief and Rehabilitation Administration. That helped European countries meet pressing demands for food and fuel. As Europe's recovery gathered speed, Europeans looked to the United States for additional supplies of basic commodities as well as for machinery, raw materials, and consumer goods. The cost of imports depleted Europe's precious dollar reserves. Hence the emergence of a "dollar gap": the difference in dollars between what European countries needed and what they could afford to buy in the United States. The gap could have been narrowed by a combination of domestic austerity and more intra-European trade. But austerity was unpopular and therefore politically impracticable, especially so soon after the war; at the same time a plethora of restrictions on the movement of goods and capital, together with the hoarding of dollars for dealings with the United States, hobbled intra-European trade.

US officials were well aware of Europe's predicament. Reports of widespread hunger and poverty in Germany in early 1947 intensified State Department efforts to promote Europe's economic recovery. Although Germany's

The Cold War Divides Europe
Between East and West

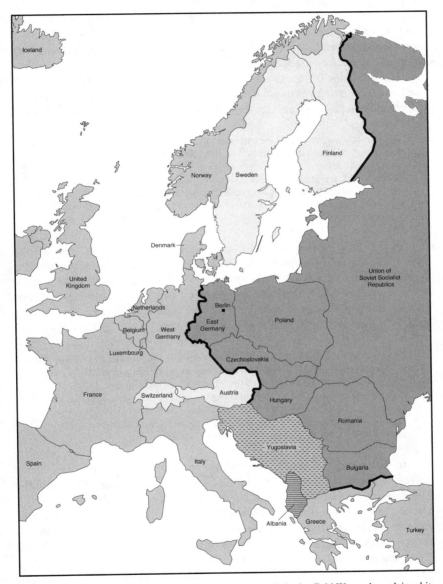

Notes: Yugoslavia broke away from the Soviet Bloc early in the Cold War and proclaimed itself "nonaligned." Albania proclaimed itself completely independent and self-reliant, and regulary and loudly denounced the United States, the Soviet Union, China, and just about everyone else in the world.

situation was not typical of the Continent's as a whole, the humanitarian motive proved useful when selling to Congress the idea of additional aid, as did the far more compelling case that an economically buoyant Western Europe would be less susceptible to communism. More than anything else, the consolidation of Soviet control in Central and Eastern Europe and the strength of Communist parties in Western Europe galvanized elite opinion in the United States in favor of a long-term assistance program.

The provision of massive assistance was also in the economic interest of the United States. As William Clayton, undersecretary for economic affairs, informed Secretary of State George Marshall in a memorandum in May 1947:

> Without further prompt and substantial aid from the United States, economic, social and political disintegration will overwhelm Europe. Aside from the awful implications which this would have for the future peace and security of the world, the immediate effects on our domestic economy would be disastrous: markets for our surplus production gone, unemployment, depression, a heavily unbalanced budget on the background of a mountainous war debt. *These things must not happen.*[8]

Based on reports of Germany's plight and more broadly on their assessment of Europe's economic and political situation—the dollar gap and the threat of communism—officials gave Marshall the outline of an idea to assist Europe's recovery through the provision of US assistance, in cash and in kind, for a period of several years. The United States would act in concert with Europe. As Marshall said in his famous speech in June 1947:

> It would be neither fitting nor efficacious for this Government to undertake to draw up unilaterally a program designed to place Europe on its feet economically. This is the business of the Europeans. The initiative, I think, must come from Europe. The role of this country should consist of friendly aid in the drafting of a European program and of later support of such a program so far as it may be practical for us to do so. The program should be a joint one, agreed to by a number, if not all, European nations.[9]

It took a year of intensive negotiations among the Europeans themselves, between the Americans and the Europeans, and especially within the US government before what became known as the Marshall Plan was fully fleshed out and functioning.[10] Its immediate objective was to close the dollar gap while simultaneously promoting intra-European trade. Its longer-term objectives were to inculcate US business practices and to fashion in Europe a marketplace similar to the one in the United States: large, integrated, and efficient. In US eyes a single market was an essential prerequisite for peace and prosperity in Europe and for Europe's full participation in the global economic system.

Earlier, in March 1947, President Truman had announced the doctrine that bore his name, promising military assistance to Greece (then fending off a Communist insurrection thought to be supported by the Soviet Union) and to any other European country that came under Communist attack. The Marshall Plan was the economic counterpart of the Truman Doctrine. The Americans were careful not to exclude the Soviet Union explicitly from the Marshall Plan, but Soviet participation was incompatible with the plan's anti-Communist intent. The Soviet foreign minister attended the conference of potential aid recipients in Paris in July 1947, but withdrew after failing to convince the others to reject the US insistence on a joint European request for assistance. Claiming that the Marshall Plan amounted to US interference in domestic affairs, the Soviets forbade the Central and Eastern European countries from participating as well.

Thus the Marshall Plan and the Soviet Union's negative response to it were pivotal events in the early history of the Cold War. For many Americans and Western Europeans, the Marshall Plan was synonymous with the selflessness and generosity of the United States toward allies and former enemies alike, in marked contrast to the rapaciousness of the Soviet Union in Central and Eastern Europe. The Communist seizure of power in Czechoslovakia in February 1948 and the Berlin Blockade three months later deepened the growing Cold War divide. Like the Marshall Plan, these events were immense propaganda coups for the United States.

The Marshall Plan was a resounding success. Politically, it signaled the intention of the United States to remain engaged in Europe after World War II, in contrast to the country's disastrous disengagement a generation earlier. Economically, the plan did not "save" Europe, because Europe was already on the road to recovery.[11] Nevertheless, Marshall aid helped close the dollar gap, even though a recession in the United States in 1948–1949 depressed US demand for European goods, causing the gap temporarily to widen again. Through the sale of goods supplied by the plan, recipient governments were able to generate revenue in local currency with which to pursue national economic objectives such as infrastructural development or debt reduction. According to Charles Maier, a leading historian of the period, "by easing balance-of-payments constraints and freeing key bottlenecks for specific goods, American aid allowed the European economies to generate their own capital more freely, certainly without returning to the deflationary competition of the 1930s. US aid served, in a sense, like the lubricant of an engine—not the fuel—allowing a machine to run that would otherwise buckle and bind."[12]

The European Movement

In May 1948, three years after the end of the war in Europe, several hundred people attended the Congress of Europe in The Hague, the political capital of the Netherlands. They included senior politicians from most European countries and political parties (excluding the Communists). All participated in a private capacity. Winston Churchill, the already legendary prime minister of wartime Britain, then the underemployed leader of the opposition Conservative Party, presided over the event.

The Hague Congress was the high point of the postwar European movement.[13] Inspired by appeals throughout the ages for European unity, and appalled by events in the interwar and wartime periods, the movement included several dozen organizations—some nationally based, others transnational—encompassing thousands of individuals in more than twenty countries.[14] Popular support for European unity in the immediate postwar years was widespread and deeply felt. The idea of European integration in the 1940s was not elitist but had reasonably broad public support.

Although members of the European movement subscribed to the general goal of European union, they disagreed among themselves on what form it should take. A few were ardent federalists, convinced by the lessons of the recent past that relations between European states needed radical recasting. Some of the more ideological of them, notably Altiero Spinelli, saw federalism as a panacea for Europe's ills, an antidote to the evils of nationalism and the corruption of modern capitalism.[15]

By contrast, most of those attending the congress had only a vague vision of Europe's future. Like the vast majority of Europeans, they were either indifferent to federalism or opposed to it. For them, a high degree of intra-European cooperation was desirable or even imperative, but the legitimacy and efficacy of the nation-state were not disputed. The idea of European union had political, economic, and cultural dimensions, without as yet having precise constitutional contours. For all its proponents, however, European union meant an unequivocal commitment to democracy, justice, and human rights. It also acknowledged the need to bring Germany back into the international fold. The rhetoric of European union was pan-European, but the reality of the emerging Cold War meant that concrete initiatives would be restricted to Western Europe and therefore also to West Germany.

The large and influential attendance at the congress reflected the appeal of European union. Yet ringing phrases in the final resolution could not disguise the difficulty within such a heterogeneous group of deciding on next steps. There was general agreement to transform the International Committee of the Movement for European Unity, the body that had organized the congress, into an umbrella organization called the European Movement. The new organization was launched in Brussels in October 1948 under the joint presidency of Churchill, Leon Blum (a French Socialist), Alcide de Gasperi (an Italian Christian Democrat), and Paul-Henri Spaak (a Belgian Socialist). There was general agreement also on establishing a postgraduate institution for the study of European integration. The College of Europe duly opened its doors in the picturesque city of Bruges, Belgium, in 1950.

On more substantive issues, however, a consensus could not be found. Efforts to establish a European Assembly, a tangible expression of the movement's commitment to democratic principles and responsiveness to public opinion, became the biggest bone of contention. Deep differences quickly surfaced over the assembly's purpose and organization. Federalists wanted a constituent assembly, organized on transnational lines, to draft a European constitution; antifederalists wanted nothing more than a consultative body, organized on national lines and responsible to a ministerial body. The congress agreed to disagree, leaving the precise nature of the proposed assembly for another day's work.

The French government, then groping toward a policy of rapprochement with Germany, took up the cause of a European Assembly in July 1948, under the aegis of the five-power Brussels group (made up of Britain, France, Belgium, the Netherlands, and Luxembourg). The French ran straight into strong British opposition. The governing Labour Party was uninterested in a European Assembly, however anodyne its responsibilities. Churchill himself, for that matter, liked to orate about European union without being either personally or politically committed to it. Churchill's most famous speech on European union, delivered in Zurich in September 1946, in which he called for "a kind of United States of Europe," is often cited as evidence of Euro-enthusiasm. In reality, Churchill was too nationalistic to champion a new European system based on shared sovereignty.

Regardless of what Churchill said or what people thought that he should say, official British policy toward European union was extremely negative. Britain saw itself as a global power whose foreign policy priorities were relations with the United States and relations with the Empire and Commonwealth. The idea of Eurofederalism was anathema to Britain, a country proud of its distinctive political institutions and culture and of its recent wartime record. The prevailing view in London was that shared sovereignty was for continental losers, not for British winners.

Eventually the British government agreed to the establishment of a Consultative Assembly, but one that was virtually powerless and that was answerable to an intergovernmental body, the Committee of Ministers. This was the institutional foundation of the Council of Europe, which ten countries— the Brussels powers plus Denmark, Ireland, Italy, Norway, and Sweden— formed in May 1949. British foreign secretary Ernest Bevin suggested that the Council be located in Strasbourg, a city long disputed between France and Germany and far enough away from national capitals to help ensure the Council's marginalization.

The assembly met for the first time in August 1949. Churchill led the delegation of British Conservatives at the inaugural session and gave a rousing speech in Strasbourg's war-damaged city center. It was vintage Churchill: emotional, entertaining, and enthralling. It also marked the zenith of Churchill's career as the champion of European union. Although the former prime minister presided over the newly launched European Movement and although popular interest in integration remained strong on the Continent, the Council of Europe's obvious weakness sapped political support for similar grandiose schemes.

Enthusiasts for European integration nevertheless continued to look to the assembly for inspiration and leadership, believing that it could act as a constituent body for a federal union. Spaak, Belgium's foreign minister and the assembly's first president, personified their hopes. His resignation from the assembly's presidency in December 1951, in protest against most governments' opposition to any federal initiative, signaled the end of the road for the Council of Europe as a possible instrument of political integration.

Prospects for Economic Integration

A number of international organizations existed immediately after the war with the aim of rebuilding national economies, but not necessarily integrating Europe economically. These included the United Nations Relief and Rehabilitation Administration, which closed down in 1949. The United Nations Economic Commission for Europe subsumed the remaining emergency organizations in May 1947. Walt Rostow, a US official who was special assistant to the Economic Commission's first executive secretary, wrote optimistically in 1949 that the commission "appeared a possible realistic first step along the long slow path towards a democratically negotiated, economic unity in Europe."[16]

The onset of the Cold War destroyed whatever potential the organization had to promote European integration. The Soviet Union was content to keep the commission in existence but had no intention of turning it into a forum for economic cooperation along capitalist lines. The United States and the countries of Western Europe focused instead on the Marshall Plan, which, unlike the Economic Commission for Europe, had the financial means to match its economic ambition and, the United States hoped, to stimulate European integration.

Undersecretary Clayton urged that the proposed package of US assistance "be based on a European plan which the principal European nations . . . should work out. Such a plan should be based on a European economic federation on the order of the Belgium-Netherlands-Luxembourg Customs Union. Europe cannot recover from this war and again become independent if her economy continues to be divided into many small watertight compartments as it is today."[17] Clayton's equation of "economic federation" and "customs union" shows that integration lacked a precise meaning at the time. Charles Kindleberger, then one of Clayton's officials and later an internationally renowned economist, noted in 1950 that "at no time was there in existence a single clear idea of what [integration] meant." Thus the Marshall Plan presented an opportunity for the United States "to usher in a new era of European collaboration, cooperation, unification, or integration—to run the polysyllabic gamut."[18]

Michael Hogan, one of the foremost historians of the Marshall Plan, has described the endeavor as "a grand design for remaking the Old World in the likeness of the New."[19] John Killick, another Marshall Plan historian, quotes a resentful British Treasury official complaining that "the Americans want an integrated Europe looking like the United States of America—God's own country."[20] What the Americans really wanted was what eventually happened in Europe not in 1952 but in 1992: a single market involving the free movement of goods, services, and capital. The free movement of people—the "fourth freedom" in the single market program—seemed neither desirable (except for Italy) nor obtainable in the early 1950s and was not fully implemented even in the early 1990s.

The Foreign Assistance Act of April 1948, which enacted the European Recovery Program (as the Marshall Plan was officially called), contained the following "Declaration of Policy":

> Mindful of the advantages which the US has enjoyed through the existence of a large domestic market with no internal trade barriers, and believing that similar advantages can accrue to the countries of Europe, it is declared to be the policy of the people of the US to encourage these countries [receiving Marshall aid] through a joint organization to exert common efforts . . . which will speedily achieve that economic cooperation in Europe which is essential for lasting peace and recovery.[21]

The countries of Western Europe had no objection to submitting to Washington a joint assistance request. Soon after Marshall's speech in June 1947, they formed the Committee on European Economic Cooperation, and upgraded it in April 1948 to the Organization for European Economic Cooperation (OEEC). But they balked at the suggestion that they should integrate their economies into a single European market. In effect, they paid lip service to the idea of economic union as a guiding principle for Europe's future. Western European governments were jealous of their prerogatives. In an uncertain economic environment, most of them sought maximum national advantage through a plethora of tariff and nontariff barriers. The lessons of the interwar years may have taught otherwise and the rhetoric of the postwar years may have claimed otherwise, but protectionism was deeply entrenched in Europe in the late 1940s.

A cursory examination of various calls at that time for the formation of customs unions bears out the point. Belgium and Luxembourg, which formed an economic union in 1921, agreed with the Netherlands in 1944 to form the Benelux customs union. It came into existence in 1948, but balance-of-payments problems and the persistence of nontariff barriers to trade impeded prospects for closer economic integration. Moreover, Benelux was conceived not as a first step toward wider European integration but as a defensive mechanism against possible postwar economic recession and protectionist measures by larger states.

French interest in forming a customs union was motivated not by a desire to open the European marketplace but by the goal of limiting Germany's economic recovery. The French idea of establishing a customs union without Germany had little appeal for Belgium and especially for the Netherlands, which, having had close ties to the prewar German economy, was eager to hasten Germany's postwar recovery. Nevertheless a series of negotiations followed in Brussels, under the auspices of the European Customs Union Study Group, from November 1947 to December 1948. Fourteen countries, including Britain, took part in the talks. It soon became clear that each country was jockeying for sectoral advantage rather than seeking to open markets, and that concern about sovereignty would preclude Britain from participating even in a customs union. The study group then transformed itself into the Customs Cooperation Council, a standing body that slaved away on tariff nomenclature. Finally, in April 1949, France called for a customs union with Benelux and Italy (to be known as Fritalux). Once again, Dutch insistence on including Germany thwarted the initiative.[22]

The fate of these efforts shows that economic integration was an idea whose time had not yet come. The OEEC was a prototypical organization for European integration. But the British were not about to concede economically to the OEEC what they refused to concede politically to the Council of Europe: a share of national sovereignty. The Americans wanted Spaak, a leading advocate of European union, to become director-general of the OEEC; the British successfully objected to the nature of the office and to Spaak holding it.[23] British obstructionism and continental indifference consigned the OEEC to the role of a clearinghouse for economic information, devoid of real decisionmaking power. In effect, the OEEC became a cover for European disregard of US insistence on closer integration in return for Marshall aid. The OEEC gave the impression that Europeans were integrating by providing a collectivist gloss to individual requests for national assistance. The Americans were not fooled. They realized the limits of their influence as well as the extent of European resistance to shared sovereignty in economic affairs.

Yet in the long term, as the success of the single European market program showed more than forty years later, the Marshall Plan and related US initiatives had a profound effect on European integration. As Killick observed, "US policy and the Marshall Plan pushed Europe towards an integrated and multilateral future, created mechanisms to transfer the best of US commercial organization, social patterns, and technology, and attempted to create an open and unified international market."[24] Marshall aid had an immediate impact on the growth of intra-European trade through the establishment in 1950 of the European Payments Union, which restored multilateral settlements and paved the way for the introduction of full currency convertibility by the end of the decade. Backed by the United States, the Payments Union allowed its members to run surpluses or deficits with each other without fear of either nonpayment or withdrawal of credits. The launch of the Payments Union coincided with the adoption by the OEEC of a code of trade liberalization, calling for the progressive removal of quantitative restrictions on a nondiscriminatory basis.[25]

The Marshall Plan, the OEEC, and the Payments Union triggered a virtuous cycle by encouraging countries to reduce tariff and nontariff barriers in order to promote cross-border trade. At the same time, participation in the US-sponsored GATT set European countries on the long road to global trade liberalization. The gradual abandonment of trade protection facilitated the emergence in the late 1950s of the European Economic Community. Yet the EEC could not have come about unless European countries had tackled a residual postwar problem of fundamental political and economic importance. That was the German question.

Tackling the German Question

The immediate question was how to realize Germany's enormous economic potential without risking a return to German hegemony and a new imbalance of power in Europe. A solution was as pressing for Germany as it was for the United States and for Germany's neighbors in Europe. The United States had long since abandoned plans that called for Germany to be politically and economically emasculated for a lengthy postwar period. By the late 1940s the United States wanted an economically strong Germany, particularly in view of the worsening Cold War. US thinking was clear and comprehensible: a weak Germany meant a weak Europe, and a weak Europe meant a weak Atlantic alliance.

Britain underwent a similar change in its approach to Germany after the war. So did France, but only up to a point, and certainly not to the point in 1949 of countenancing German remilitarization, as Britain and the United States were inclined to do. In the meantime, France was far more reluctant than either Britain or the United States to allow unfettered German industrial revival. The difference in allied thinking about Germany was due in part to geography: France was much closer to Germany than was either Britain or, more obviously, the United States. It was also due to history: since the industrial age, France had been economically weaker than Germany; Germany's greater economic strength had contributed to nearly a century of Franco-German conflict. Tackling the German question therefore amounted to allaying French security concerns about Germany's economic recovery. Properly speaking, the German question was the Franco-German question, or perhaps even the French question.

By contrast, there was no "Italian question"—no feeling of French insecurity toward Italy after the war. Although Italy, like Germany, had united late in the nineteenth century and fought against France in World War II, Italy's existence did not threaten France. Compared to Germany and even France, Italy had limited economic potential. Moreover, Italy was burdened by an impoverished and densely populated south. France and Italy made amends soon after the war, signing a peace treaty in February 1947. Italy's main postwar problem was political instability due to limited economic opportunity and the existence of a powerful Communist party. Alcide de Gasperi, Italy's postwar leader, used the threat of indigenous communism and the influence of Italian immigrants in the United States to maximize US economic assistance. This, in turn, helped the Christian Democrats to defeat the Communists in the decisive general election in 1948.[26]

France also faced political uncertainty immediately after the war. Charles de Gaulle, leader of the wartime Free French Movement, formed the first government of liberated France (it lasted from August 1944 until January 1946). Despite pressing domestic problems, de Gaulle was keenly interested in foreign affairs. The foreign policy that he pursued then, and later as president of the Fifth Republic between 1958 and 1968, is often described as one of *grandeur* (greatness). It took for granted that France was a great power with global interests. Not only that, but France was a *victorious* great power, having redeemed the defeat of 1940 with the participation of French forces in the allied victory of 1945. But France was not invited to attend the two conferences with the Big Three powers, held in Yalta in February 1945 and Potsdam in July–August 1945, where the fate of Germany and Eastern Europe was broadly decided. De Gaulle despised the Yalta and Potsdam settlements and abided by their terms only when it suited him. For instance, he rejected the acquiescence by Britain and the United States in a Soviet sphere of influence in Eastern Europe, but accepted the decision at Potsdam to give France a small zone of occupation in Germany. In de Gaulle's view, France had every right to occupy part of Germany and have an equal say with Britain, the Soviet Union, and the United States in deciding the country's future.

Yet de Gaulle was not so unrealistic as to think that other countries would take France at face value. France's economic weakness, stretching back a century or more, was as apparent to de Gaulle as it was to other allied leaders. Despite his supposed disdain for the dismal science, in 1945 de Gaulle devoted considerable attention not only to France's immediate economic needs but also to its eventual resurgence. In the short term, France could demand reparations and capitalize on Germany's economic demise.

De Gaulle shied away for political reasons from undertaking thoroughgoing monetary reform. French economic recovery, no matter how impressive, would therefore rest on a rickety financial foundation.

The Monnet Plan

Jean Monnet, a senior civil servant, advocated a modernization plan for France that held out the prospect of achieving economic recovery and long-term security. Monnet did not approach de Gaulle directly—Monnet rarely approached key decisionmakers directly—but hooked de Gaulle on his idea by first winning over one of the general's closest advisers. Monnet was wary of de Gaulle in any case because of their previous dealings with each other. Like de Gaulle, Monnet was in London in June 1940 at the time of the French military collapse. But Monnet did not join de Gaulle's Free French Movement, opting instead to work on allied economic policy in Washington, where he was attached to the British embassy. Monnet and de Gaulle met again in Algiers in 1943, where de Gaulle was fighting (politically) to wrest control of the provisional government-in-waiting from Henri Giraud, a senior French general who enjoyed US president Franklin Roosevelt's support. Roosevelt asked Monnet, whom he knew in Washington, to intercede in Algiers on Giraud's behalf. Once in Algiers, Monnet quietly switched sides and supported de Gaulle, who clearly was better qualified to lead the Free French than was the bumbling and autocratic Giraud.

De Gaulle should have been grateful to Monnet, but gratitude was not in the general's nature. Instead de Gaulle resented Monnet for a variety of reasons, including Monnet's refusal to serve under him in London in 1940, his subsequent service in the British embassy in Washington, his cultivation there of influential US policymakers, and his cosmopolitanism and internationalism. Nevertheless, de Gaulle appreciated Monnet's skill and experience as an economic planner. Monnet also had a major virtue in the general's eyes: he was not a member of any political party. De Gaulle hated political parties, especially those that had sprung back to life in France after the liberation. He craved strong presidential power. De Gaulle was hamstrung as president of the provisional government by what he saw as the machinations of small-minded political parties and their leaders. Those politicians prevailed over de Gaulle in the struggle for the constitution of the new Fourth Republic, which incorporated a parliamentary rather than a presidential system of government. Accordingly, in January 1946, de Gaulle resigned in a huff, but not before he had approved the appointment of Monnet to head the national planning commission (Commissariat Général du Plan), a government agency independent of the giant finance and economics departments.

Monnet spent the next few years absorbed in French economic affairs. He and his small staff oversaw the work of numerous sectoral committees that brought together representatives of all sides in industry, setting guidelines for resource allocation and production levels in order to meet domestic demand and fill foreign markets. For the moment, France depended far more on imports than exports for its economic survival. Clearly, international developments held the key to future French and European prosperity.[27] Monnet paid particular attention to the United States, the country at the center of the emerging international economic system and the source of badly needed dollars.

French planning was not at all like planning in the Soviet Union, which had a command economy. Monnet was not a Socialist, let alone a Communist. Having grown up in the brandy business and spent many years as an international financier before the war, he was a bona fide capitalist. Yet he personified the consensus in postwar France that capitalism could best be served by judicious government direction of key economic activities. This view was not anathema to Washington, where a number of New Dealers were still influential in government. The promulgation of the Marshall Plan, although very different from the Monnet Plan, showed that Washington also accepted the idea that market mechanisms alone would not suffice to get the European economy fully going again.

The Marshall Plan was a mixed blessing for France. It presented both an opportunity and a threat. The opportunity was the prospect of funding the Monnet Plan's strategy of investment in French industrial modernization. Funds from the sale of goods supplied to European governments were not supposed to have been used to implement national economic planning. But the Americans made an exception for Monnet, who had a host of influential friends in Washington. Historians often say that the Marshall Plan saved the Monnet Plan.

France Under Pressure

Yet the Marshall Plan also posed a threat to the Monnet Plan and to French security in general. Whereas the Marshall Plan sought German economic recovery as an integral part of European economic recovery, the Monnet Plan sought French economic recovery by exploiting German economic weakness. This was especially true of the coal and steel sectors, the basis of industrial power in mid-twentieth-century Europe. Historically, France's lack of coking coal, which Germany had in abundance, notably in the Ruhr region in the west of the country, hobbled French steel production. Monnet based his plan to modernize the French steel industry on the assumption that, with Germany on the ropes economically, France would have unlimited access to Ruhr coal and could exploit postwar markets previously filled by German producers. As François Duchêne, Monnet's biographer, put it, France would develop its steel industry "on a diet of Ruhr coke till it largely replaced German steel."[28] Because of the nature of Germany's prewar and wartime military-industrial complex, the Ruhr was synonymous in

France with militarism and the rise of Nazism. Controlling the Ruhr was therefore a vital French interest, economically and strategically.

The United States, by signaling through the Marshall Plan its intention to allow Germany to revive economically, challenged France's Ruhr policy and stoked French security concerns. Sensitive to France's situation, the United States sought somehow to reconcile French interests with its own determination, for economic and strategic reasons, to reconstitute Germany. As the terms of the Marshall Plan indicated, the Americans believed that European integration could provide the solution. Rather than impose a particular scheme, however, the United States wanted the Europeans themselves to come up with a proposal for economic and, ultimately, political integration. The United States looked primarily to France for a solution to the German question.

The ensuing swing from repression to rapprochement in French policy toward Germany, in response to pressure from the United States, is a key theme in the history of European integration in the late 1940s and early 1950s. As Robert Marjolin, a Monnet planner, reminisced:

The Ruhr

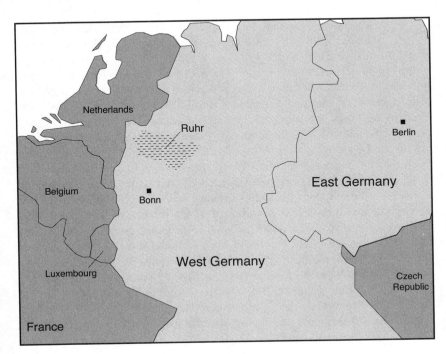

> Despite the violence of my feelings towards the Germans before and during the war, I had rapidly convinced myself after the hostilities ended that Europe could not recover unless Germany were rebuilt and became once again a great industrial country. . . . I did [not] believe in the dismemberment of western Germany, from which the Rhineland and the Ruhr, for example, would have been separated. That would have sown the seed for future wars. I was therefore quite ready to include the Germans in European cooperation.[29]

Marjolin was ahead of most of his compatriots in his attitude toward Germany so soon after the war. Thus France refused to merge its zone of occupation with those of Britain and the United States and acquiesce in the raising of Germany's allied-approved levels of industrial production. France found itself fighting a rearguard action as Britain and the United States merged their zones in 1947 and raised Germany's production levels regardless.

As long as the Communists were still in government, France was unable to work closely with its Western allies. The removal of the Communists from office in May 1947, a consequence of the deepening Cold War, increased the French government's freedom of maneuver vis-à-vis the United States, but closed the door on cooperation with the Soviet Union. The intensification of the Cold War in turn intensified US pressure on France to relax its policy toward Germany so that Germany's economic potential (and eventually its military potential as well) could be put at the disposal of the West.

France gradually yielded as western Germany rebounded politically sooner than any of the allies had expected. Germany's Social Democratic Party, proscribed since the Nazi seizure of power in 1933, was reconstituted relatively quickly after the war, and a new Christian Democratic Party came into being. Konrad Adenauer, a wily old conservative with impeccable anti-Nazi credentials, emerged as leader of the Christian Democrats. Kurt Schumacher, an implacable Socialist and ardent nationalist (but a bitter foe of National Socialism), was the undisputed leader of the Social Democrats.

In the London Accords of June 1948, France finally agreed to the formation of the Federal Republic of Germany through the merger of its zone of occupation with the previously merged US and British zones. France insisted on a federal, decentralized Germany, with the small city of Bonn as its capital, and on maintaining control of the Saar, a coal-rich region in southwest Germany. France also hoped to thwart German control of the Ruhr through the establishment of the International Ruhr Authority to oversee coal production and distribution. These conditions were enshrined in the Occupation Statute of April 1949, which regulated relations between Germany and the Western allies. The narrowness of the French National Assembly's approval of the London Accords indicated the depth of French distrust toward Germany despite the distance that France had traveled from its initial postwar position.[30]

Under the aegis of the London Accords and the Occupation Statute and of a Basic Law (constitution) drawn up by representatives of Germany's regional authorities, the Federal Republic came into existence in May 1949. Based on the results of national elections that had taken place some weeks earlier, the Bundestag (lower house of parliament) chose Adenauer to become chancellor by a single vote. The Christian Democrats and the small Liberal Party formed the first West German government. The Communists monopolized power in East Germany, which duly became the German Democratic Republic.

The sovereignty of the new West German state was limited, especially in the fields of foreign policy (including foreign economic policy) and defense. Understandably, Adenauer sought to restore to Germany as much sovereignty as possible.[31] Adenauer especially resented the International Ruhr Authority, which symbolized Germany's continued economic subjugation.

Accepting the Inevitable

The United States continued to press Paris to propose an alternative scheme that would allay French concerns about the Ruhr without engendering German resentment and therefore endangering Germany's economic and political rehabilitation. US pressure intensified under Dean Acheson, the new secretary of state. The solution, Acheson told his ambassadors in Europe, lay "in French hands."[32] On October 30, 1949, Acheson sent Robert Schuman, his French counterpart, a forceful message: "I believe that our policy in Germany . . . depends on the assumption by your country of leadership in Europe on these problems."[33] Acheson asked Schuman to come up with something new by May 1950, when allied foreign ministers were due to meet in London.

As the United States and France edged toward a resolution of the German question, Britain stood on the sidelines.[34] Britain's behavior in the OEEC and in the Council of Europe convinced many continental Europeans that Britain was uninterested in contributing much to European integration, through which a solution to the German question would have to be found. It seemed clear that Britain's continental neighbors would have to take further initiatives by themselves. Yet the idea of acting without Britain was unimaginable for most Europeans. After all, Britain was at the pinnacle of its postwar power and prestige. Britain's economic and military strength were formidable by European standards, although not by the standards of the United States and the Soviet Union.

If the experience of the OEEC and the Council of Europe implied that the continentals would have to go it alone, another development, in April 1949, suggested that they *could* proceed without Britain. This was the signing in Washington of the North Atlantic Treaty. As the contractual basis for the future North Atlantic Treaty Organization, the Washington treaty signaled the unequivocal commitment of the United States to Western Europe's defense, which had hitherto rested on the Brussels Pact of March 1947 between Britain, France, and the Benelux countries. Built around Britain, the Brussels Pact was originally intended to guard against a revanchist Germany.

With the onset of the Cold War, the Soviet Union replaced Germany as a more plausible security threat, and NATO replaced the Brussels Pact as a more effective military alliance. With the United States now committed to Western Europe's defense, continental Europeans were less dependent militarily on Britain. Although NATO's organizational structure was not fleshed out until the end of 1950, the North Atlantic Treaty gave France more security than did the Brussels Pact vis-à-vis Germany and Russia, and more confidence to take diplomatic initiatives in Europe without fear of offending or possibly alienating Britain.

Yet the political situation in France did not seem conducive to a bold foreign policy initiative. The country was in almost constant political flux. Governments followed each other in quick succession, often with the same cast of characters playing ministerial musical chairs. Prime ministers came and went, but two people, Georges Bidault and Robert Schuman, occupied the foreign ministry for most of the Fourth Republic's existence (1946–1958). Bidault, foreign minister for much of the earlier period, was witty, outgoing, and frequently inebriated. Schuman, his successor, was solemn, saintly, and always sober. Yet Bidault has a historical reputation for obduracy and Schuman for imagination. That is because Bidault is associated with a policy of hostility toward Germany, whereas Schuman is associated with a policy of reconciliation.

In fact, Bidault was moving toward a rapprochement with Germany when he left office in 1948, and Schuman supported a punitive policy toward Germany before replacing him as foreign minister. Bidault, as de Gaulle's foreign minister immediately after the war, was obliged to implement a harsh policy toward Germany. Even after de Gaulle's departure, public and official opinion in Paris did not countenance an improvement in relations with Germany for some time to come. When the thaw began in late 1948, it was Schuman's good fortune to be foreign minister. Undoubtedly, Schuman favored a new departure with Germany and genuinely supported European union. Unlike Bidault, he quickly grasped the significance of a supranational solution to the problem of the Ruhr and soon personified not only Franco-German rapprochement, but Franco-German reconciliation as well.

Coming from the disputed borderland of Lorraine, speaking French with a German accent and German without a French accent, and being a devout Catholic, Schuman became the living embodiment of Franco-German amity after generations of Franco-German enmity. He could easily have gone down in history the other way around, however. Had it been politically imperative to do so, Schuman might well have used his borderland background and experiences in Lorraine before 1919 to perpetuate distrust of Germany. Schuman's Catholicism and personality may have predisposed him to seek reconciliation with Germany, but political necessity ultimately determined his course of action. Fortunately for Schuman, a reappraisal of French policy toward Germany made it possible for him to combine personal predilections and political preferences and give his name to a declaration that symbolized a radical new departure by France. The declaration contained a proposal to pool sovereignty in the coal and steel sectors under a supranational High Authority, thereby reconciling US, German, and French interests without going too far down the road toward political union.

The Schuman Declaration

The announcement of the Schuman Declaration took place at a hastily convened press conference late in the afternoon of May 9, 1950, in the French foreign ministry. Schuman proposed both a specific solution to the problem of the Ruhr (a supranational coal and steel organization) and a general solution to the German question (implicit equality and nondiscrimination in the context of European union). It was an approach that combined economic, political, and social objectives. The immediate goal was to ensure "the modernization of production and the improvement of its quality; the supply of coal and steel on equal terms to the French and German markets . . . [and] to those of the [other] member countries; and the equalization as well as the improvement in the living standards and working conditions in those industries." Schuman linked this to the greater goal of European union, for which strong emotional support still existed despite the Council of Europe's disappointing development. Thus the coal and steel pool would "lay the first concrete foundation for a European Federation which is so indispensable to the preservation of peace."[35]

The immediate background to the declaration was equally dramatic. Monnet, by his own account, developed the idea while on one of his periodic hiking holidays in the Alps, in April 1950. After returning to Paris, Monnet instructed key people in his planning office to work out the details. Having gone through various drafts, Monnet sent the final version first to Prime Minister Bidault, who did not respond, then to Foreign Minister Schuman, who did. Monnet also contacted Adenauer through an intermediary. Aware of Adenauer's approval of it, Schuman slipped the proposal through a cabinet meeting on the morning on May 9, hours before the famous press conference.[36]

Monnet's account may be correct, but the manner of its telling, without adequate reference to the evolution of French foreign policy during the previous two years, gives the declaration a heroic quality to which early scholars of European integration eagerly subscribed. William Diebold, author of one of the first books on the Schuman Plan, wrote breathlessly about a foreign minister who took a major . . . initiative with little or no consultation with his own ministry; a rapid elaboration of the final version of the plan in great secrecy by a tiny group of people; only the briefest discussion before the Cabinet [of] . . . a measure that went well beyond foreign policy and would have a major effect on the defense and economy of France; almost immediate public announcement with only the shortest notice to allies and others on whose assent success would depend.[37]

Some historians of a later generation, notably Alan Milward, gleefully debunked the myth of May 9.[38] Monnet was certainly imaginative and far-sighted. But he did not conjure the proposed community out of nowhere. Ideas about a coal and steel association of some kind had been floating around France and Germany, in government and private circles, for several years; some could even be traced back to the interwar period.[39] Thinking along such lines had intensified as France came under mounting pressure in 1949 and early 1950 to adopt a radically new approach toward Germany. Monnet was more astute than most: the idea of a High Authority as the supranational instrument of sectoral integration was novel and timely. Yet even François Duchêne, Monnet's former collaborator and biographer, admits that the Schuman Declaration "may have been a lucky strike when other prospectors had given up."[40]

Nor was it surprising that Monnet devoted so much thought to the idea. After all, it was Monnet who bore the brunt of US pressure for a new French policy toward Germany. Monnet was the main conduit for US-French relations in the late 1940s and early 1950s. He was in almost daily contact with the highest representatives of the United States in France. Monnet knew how badly Washington wanted Paris to launch a new initiative and how keenly Schuman wanted to oblige. Moreover, the future of the Monnet Plan was at stake. Economic modernization in France could not be realized without a resolution of the Ruhr problem. Whereas maintaining French control through the International Ruhr Authority was no longer feasible, the creation of a supranational community might succeed.

Monnet was in his element when under pressure. He was an opportunist who thrived on crises (even his marriage involved elopement and intrigue). He was the right man (a fixer, a close friend of the Americans) in the right place (head of the national planning commission) at the right time (when France needed to come to terms with Germany's resurgence). With the Schuman Declaration, Monnet hit the jackpot. Not only did the Marshall Plan save the Monnet Plan but also, in Milward's memorable phrase, "the Schuman Plan was invented to safeguard the Monnet Plan."[41]

The Schuman initiative bore all the hallmarks of Monnet's approach to economic development. As outlined in the declaration, the High Authority would be an international version of the French planning office. Just as the planning office consisted of technocrats acting independently of government ministries, the High Authority would consist of technocrats acting independently of national governments, providing overall direction and arbitrating disputes between vested interests. As for achieving European union, the declaration reflected Monnet's preferred approach of sectoral economic integration, what Kindleberger described in a US State Department memorandum as a way of moving "crabwise through technical cooperation in economic matters."[42]

Monnet may have hatched the plan, but Schuman took the political risk. Most members of the French cabinet were still too hostile toward Germany and fearful of the future to take such a bold step. Hence Schuman's subterfuge, talking the initiative down in the cabinet and up at the press conference. Only after the press reported favorably on the declaration did the cabinet grudgingly accept a fait accompli. It is often said that Monnet, the architect, deserved to have had the declaration named after him. But the name of the declaration accurately indicates where the political credit belongs.

Diebold was half-right when he remarked that France's allies had received only "the shortest notice" of the declaration. Britain received no notice at all, because of Schuman's concern that London would again obstruct a major European initiative. The British were furious at not having been consulted, let alone notified in advance. Supposedly the United States was informed only on May 7, when Acheson visited Paris en route to the foreign ministers' meeting in London. In fact, US support was too crucial to have been left to chance. Monnet let his US interlocutors in Paris, as well as John J. McCloy, his friend the US high commissioner in Bonn, know that a major initiative was in the offing. Once assured that Schuman was not proposing an international cartel, Acheson was delighted with the declaration. Although the proposal was a lot smaller in scope than what the United States had called for in the Marshall Plan, Washington immediately recognized the declaration's political importance.[43]

Adenauer's response was equally positive. The chancellor wanted a resolution of the German question as much as the allies did. Chafing under the restrictions of the Occupation Statute and the International Ruhr Authority, inevitably Adenauer embraced an initiative based on the principles of equality and nondiscrimination. Fulfilling the promise of the Schuman Declaration became a key element of Adenauer's foreign policy, which sought to maximize German sovereignty, integrate Germany into the Atlantic system, and bring about a rapprochement with France. The Schuman Declaration was grist to Adenauer's mill (for Germany, shared sovereignty was better than limited sovereignty).[44]

Ironically, the Schuman Declaration came at a time when Adenauer's relations with France were under strain. France's virtual annexation of the Saar inflamed German opinion. A purported goodwill visit by Schuman to Bonn in February 1950 ended on a sour note when Adenauer vehemently protested French policy in the German region. Adenauer then floated an idea that may have been sincere but seemed jarring under the circumstances. In an interview with a US journalist on March 9, the chancellor proposed a Franco-German union, complete with a joint parliament.[45] Official reaction across the Rhine was far from favorable: victorious France, not defeated Germany, should make daring overtures. Two months later, with the Schuman Declaration, France took such a step on a less ambitious but more realistic basis. Eager to ease Franco-German tension, Adenauer enthusiastically endorsed the declaration at a press conference in Bonn several hours after Schuman's press conference in Paris.

Adenauer was often criticized at home for being subservient to the former occupying powers. Schumacher, leader of the opposition Social Democratic Party, famously called him the "Chancellor of the Allies."[46] Having stood up to the allies on a number of occasions during the previous few months, Adenauer was less vulnerable to charges of complicity with them on the question of the Schuman Declaration. Nevertheless, the declaration became a major political issue. The Social Democrats disliked the proposed coal and steel organization for ideological reasons (Schumacher dismissed it as "France, Germany, Inc.") and because they thought that it would perpetuate the division of Germany.[47] Adenauer conceded that a rapprochement with the West was incompatible at that time with an opening to the East, but countered that European integration would lead ultimately to German unification, with an economically weak East Germany eventually gravitating toward an economically strong West Germany.

The Schuman Declaration is now hailed as a major turning point in Franco-German relations and in contemporary European history. Those who heard or read Schuman's words at the time could not have foreseen the future and rendered such a verdict, but most grasped that something exciting was in the air. French and German leaders were now on the same wavelength, public opinion was generally on their side, and the United States stood squarely behind them. Only ardent nationalists, Communists, and doctrinaire Socialists in France and Germany strongly opposed the Schuman Declaration. Vested interests in the coal and steel industries were unenthusiastic about it, fearing a government sellout. France and Germany's prospective partners faced a similar set of domestic circumstances. Realization of the Schuman Plan, in the form of the European Coal and Steel Community, would therefore be tricky.

Notes

1. See Tony Judt, *Postwar: A History of Europe Since 1945* (New York: Penguin, 2005), pp. 13–40; Ian Buruma, *Year Zero: A History of 1945* (New York: Penguin, 2013).

2. Frederick S. Weaver, *The United States and the Global Economy: From Bretton Woods to the Current Crisis* (Lanham: Rowman and Littlefield, 2011), pp. 16–22.

3. Peter Clarke, *Hope and Glory: Britain, 1900–2000,* 2nd ed. (New York: Penguin, 2004), pp. 216–247.

4. Denis Healey, *The Time of My Life* (London: Penguin, 1990), p. 76.

5. See Giles MacDonogh, *After the Reich: The Brutal History of the Allied Occupation* (New York: Basic, 2007), pp. 201–277.

6. On the Cold War, see John Lewis Gaddis, *The Cold War* (London: Allan Lane, 2005); Melvyn Leffler, *For the Soul of Mankind: The United States, the Soviet Union, and the Cold War* (New York: Hill and Wang, 2007); Melvyn Leffler and Ode Arne Westad, *The Cambridge History of the Cold War,* 3 vols. (Cambridge: Cambridge University Press, 2012).

7. See Tim Geiger, "Reconstruction and the Beginnings of European Integration," in Max-Stephan Schulze, ed., *Western Europe: Economic and Social Change Since 1945* (London: Longman, 1999), pp. 23–41.

8. William L. Clayton, "GATT, the Marshall Plan, and OECD," *Political Science Quarterly* 78, no. 4 (December 1963), p. 497; emphasis in original.

9. The text of the Marshall speech is available at http://www.let.leidenuniv.nl/history/rtg/res1/marshall.htm.

10. On the Marshall Plan, see Greg Behrman, *The Most Noble Adventure: The Marshall Plan and the Reconstruction of Postwar Europe* (New York: Free Press, 2008); Michael Hogan, *The Marshall Plan: America, Britain, and the Reconstruction of Western Europe, 1947–1952* (Cambridge: Cambridge University Press, 1987); John Killick, *The United States and European Reconstruction, 1945–1960* (Edinburgh: Keele University Press, 1997); Alan Milward, *The Reconstruction of Western Europe, 1945–1951* (Berkeley: University of California Press, 1984), pp. 56–125.

11. Alan Milward made this point in *Reconstruction of Western Europe,* pp. 56–61.

12. Charles S. Maier, "The Two Postwar Eras and the Conditions for Stability in Twentieth Century Western Europe," *American Historical Review* 86, no. 2 (April 1981), p. 342.

13. See Hendrik Brugmans, *L'idée européenne, 1918–1965,* 2nd ed. (Bruges: De Temple, 1966); Frederick L. Schuman, "The Council of Europe," *American Political Science Review* 45, no. 3 (September 1951), pp. 724–740.

14. See Walter Lipgens, *A History of European Integration,* vol. 1, *1945–1947: The Formation of the European Unity Movement* (Oxford: Clarendon, 1982).

15. See Altiero Spinelli, "The Growth of the European Movement Since World War II," in C. Grove Haines, ed., *European Integration* (Baltimore: Johns Hopkins University Press, 1957), pp. 37–63.

16. Walt W. Rostow, "The Economic Commission for Europe," *International Organization* 3, no. 2 (May 1949), p. 255.

17. William L. Clayton, "GATT, the Marshall Plan, and OECD," *Political Science Quarterly* 78, no. 4 (December 1963), p. 498.

18. Charles P. Kindleberger, "Memo for the Files: Origins of the Marshall Plan, July 1948," quoted in Charles P. Kindleberger, *Marshall Plan Days* (Boston: Allen and Unwin, 1987), pp. 27, 48.

19. Michael Hogan, *The Marshall Plan: America, Britain, and the Reconstruction of Western Europe, 1947–1952* (Cambridge: Cambridge University Press, 1987), p. 53.

20. Killick, *United States and European Reconstruction,* p. 167.

21. The text of the act is available at http://www.let.leidenuniv.nl/history/rtg/res1/marshall.htm.

22. See Wendy Asbeek Brusse, *Tariffs, Trade, and European Integration, 1947–1957: From Study Group to Common Market* (New York: St. Martin's, 1997), pp. 52–63.

23. See Maier, "Two Postwar Eras," pp. 66–69.

24. Killick, *United States and European Reconstruction*, p. 185.

25. On the European Payments Union, see Barry Eichengreen, *The European Economy Since 1945: Coordinated Capitalism and Beyond* (Princeton: Princeton University Press, 2007), pp. 79–85; Jacob J. Kaplan and Günther Schleiminger, *The European Payments Union: Financial Diplomacy in the 1950s* (Oxford: Clarendon, 1989).

26. See John Lamberton Harper, *America and the Reconstruction of Italy, 1945–1948* (Cambridge: Cambridge University Press, 2002); James Edward Miller, *The United States and Italy, 1940–1950: The Politics and Diplomacy of Stabilization* (Chapel Hill: University of North Carolina Press, 1986).

27. On postwar French economic planning and recovery, see François Bloch-Laine and Jean Bouvier, *La France restaurée, 1944–1954: Dialogue sur les choix d'une modernisation* (Paris: Fayard, 1986); François Duchêne, *Jean Monnet: The First Statesman of Interdependence* (New York: Norton, 1994), pp. 147–180; Eichengreen, *European Economy*, pp. 97–117; Richard Kuisel, *Capitalism and the State in Modern France: Renovation and Economic Management in the Twentieth Century* (Cambridge: Cambridge University Press, 1981); Frances M. B. Lynch, *France and the International Economy: From Vichy to the Treaty of Rome* (London: Routledge, 1997).

28. Duchêne, *Jean Monnet*, p. 156.

29. Robert Marjolin, *Memoirs, 1911–1986: Architect of European Unity* (London: Weidenfeld and Nicolson, 1986), p. 186.

30. See William Hitchcock, *France Restored: Cold War Diplomacy and the Quest for Leadership in Europe, 1944–1954* (Chapel Hill: University of North Carolina Press, 1998), pp. 93–97.

31. See Hans-Peter Schwarz, *Konrad Adenauer: A German Politician and Statesman in a Period of War, Revolution, and Reconstruction*, vol. 1, *From the German Empire to the Federal Republic, 1876–1952* (Oxford: Berghahn, 1995), pp. 475–502.

32. US Department of State, *Foreign Relations of the United States [FRUS], 1949*, vol. 4 (Washington, DC: Department of State, 1986) p. 470.

33. *FRUS, 1949*, vol. 3, pp. 624–625.

34. See Alan Milward, *The UK and the European Community*, vol. 1, *The Rise and Fall of a National Strategy, 1945–1963* (London: Cass, 2002), pp. 10–47.

35. Robert Schuman, "Declaration of 9 May 1950," in Peter M. R. Stirk and David Weigall, eds., *The Origins and Development of European Integration: A Reader and Commentary* (London: Pinter, 1999), pp. 76–77.

36. On the origins of the Schuman Plan, see Duchêne, *Jean Monnet*, pp. 181–225; Raymond Poidevin, *Histoire des débuts de la construction européenne, mars 1948–mai 1950: Actes du Colloque de Strasbourg, 28–30 novembre 1984* (Brussels: Bruylant, 1986); Jean Monnet, *Memoirs* (Garden City: Doubleday, 1978); Raymond Poidevin, *Robert Schuman, homme d'état, 1886–1963* (Paris: Imprimerie Nationale, 1986), pp. 244–269.

37. William Diebold Jr., *The Schuman Plan: A Study in Economic Cooperation, 1950–1959* (New York: Praeger, 1959), p. 8.

38. Milward, *Reconstruction of Western Europe*, pp. 395–397; Alan Milward, *The European Rescue of the Nation State*, 2nd ed. (London: Routledge, 2000), pp. 318–344.

39. See John Gillingham, *Coal, Steel, and the Rebirth of Europe, 1945–1955* (Cambridge: Cambridge University Press, 2005).

40. Duchêne, *Jean Monnet*, p. 189.

41. Milward, *Reconstruction of Western Europe*, p. 395.

42. Kindleberger, "Memo for the Files," p. 27.

43. On US knowledge of the Schuman Declaration, see James Chace, *Acheson: The Secretary of State Who Created the American World* (Cambridge: Harvard University

Press, 1998), pp. 241–254; Thomas Alan Schwartz, *America's Germany: John J. McCloy and the Federal Republic of Germany* (Cambridge: Cambridge University Press, 1991).

44. See Schwarz, *Konrad Adenauer,* vol. 1, pp. 475–516.

45. See Ibid., pp. 493–494.

46. See Alfred Grosser, "France, Germany in the Atlantic Community," *International Organization* 17, no. 3 (Summer 1963), p. 556.

47. Quoted in F. Roy Willis, *France, Germany, and the New Europe, 1945–1963,* revised and expanded ed. (Stanford: Stanford University Press, 1968).

2

Europe of
the Communities

THE COLD WAR HUNG LIKE A DARK CLOUD OVER EUROPE IN THE
1950s. The decade began with the Korean War, a possible harbinger of hostilities in Europe, and ended with a Soviet-American standoff over Berlin. International tension eased after Stalin's death in March 1953, but rose again when the Soviets violently suppressed workers' demonstrations in East Berlin in June 1953 and broader reform movements in Poland and Hungary in 1956. West German remilitarization in the mid-1950s kept the Soviet Union on edge. In response, the Soviets launched a number of diplomatic initiatives. One of the most dramatic of them resulted in a treaty in 1955 for the establishment of a united, sovereign, neutral Austria, which had been divided between East and West since the end of World War II. The Soviets wanted the Austrian treaty to serve as a model for Germany, but German chancellor Konrad Adenauer feared that a united, neutral Germany would succumb to internal Communist subversion and external Soviet pressure. Soviet overtures to Adenauer and the Western allies ended in late 1955. Thereafter the division of Germany seemed set in stone.

The 1950s also saw the acceleration of decolonization as former dependencies of European countries, mostly Britain and France, gained independence. The process of decolonization was traumatic for France, which became embroiled in large-scale colonial conflicts, first in Indochina (Vietnam), where the French lost decisively in 1954, then in North Africa, where the increasingly brutal war in Algeria caused the collapse of the French Fourth Republic in 1958. Britain and France intervened militarily in Egypt in 1956 following Egypt's nationalization of the Suez Canal. The latter-day act of gunboat diplomacy ended when the Soviet Union threatened to come to Egypt's assistance and the United States refused to support Britain and France. Humiliated and distrusting each other, Britain and France withdrew with their tails between their legs.

Those colonial and postcolonial adventures drained French resources and compounded prevailing pessimism about the country's prospects. Foreign observers dismissed France as the "sick man of Europe," an epithet applied in the late nineteenth century to Turkey. Despite enjoying unprecedented growth, France seemed merely to be making up ground lost before the war, not entering into a new stage of dynamic development. A few farsighted French officials and politicians advocated liberalization and market integration in the mid-1950s. For them a common market, the cornerstone of what became the European Economic Community, was the key to France's future. They used every economic, political, and ideological argument to make their case, ultimately dragging France into the modern world.

The outlook in Germany was markedly different. By the mid-1950s, the country was prosperous, semi-sovereign, and, as a NATO member, relatively secure. Despite being unpopular early in his chancellorship, Adenauer won overwhelming election victories in 1953 and 1957. In his eighties at that time, he fit the German body politic like a comfortable old shoe. Yet Adenauer's support for the proposed common market divided his own party. Ludwig Erhard, Germany's economics minister, fretted that a common market would be protectionist, to the detriment of global trade liberalization through the General Agreement on Tariffs and Trade. The argument in Germany was settled not on economic but on political grounds. Apart from its economic merits, Adenauer saw the common market as an instrument of Franco-German reconciliation and European integration. Politics trumped economics, and the chancellor's view prevailed.

The EEC was the fifth initiative for a community of European countries in the 1950s. It accompanied a proposal to establish a European Atomic Energy Community (Euratom) and followed the failure of the European Defense Community and the related European Political Community. The quest for new communities demonstrated the increasing interdependence among Western European countries. The word "community," rather than simply "association" or "organization," connoted political ambitions that transcended economic goals. This chapter shows how officials and politicians sought to overcome the recent past, forge a better relationship between Germany and its neighbors, and improve Europe's economic prospects through deeper, highly institutionalized integration. The defense and political communities went too far, too soon after the end of the war. But the economic communities were an ideal means of pursuing national strategies in the broader European context.

The European Coal and Steel Community

According to the Schuman Declaration, the proposed coal and steel community, centered on France and Germany, would be "open to the participation of the other European countries." That was a bit disingenuous. Eastern Europe was excluded due to the Cold War; the Scandinavians had rejected supranationalism in the late 1940s; and Spain was isolated because of General Francisco Franco's support for Hitler during World War II. Effectively, the proposal was open to only a small group of countries—Belgium, Luxembourg, the Netherlands, and Italy—tied to France and Germany for economic and strategic reasons. Alcide de Gasperi, Italy's prime minister, embraced the proposal not only because he was a fervent Eurofederalist but also because it might help to strengthen his government's position vis-à-vis the strong Communist opposition. Although well aware of the proposal's strategic significance, most politicians in the Benelux countries were not much inclined toward Eurofederalism (Paul-Henri Spaak of Belgium and Joseph Bech of Luxembourg were notable exceptions). But they knew that their countries could not afford to stay out of an international economic organization centered on France and Germany.

Britain's Position

The proposal was open also to Britain. Although French foreign minister Robert Schuman made his declaration without consulting London, he hoped that Britain would overcome its reticence and play a leading role in European affairs. Other prospective members hoped so as well. Yet the British were uninterested in participating. Only a month after the Schuman Declaration, Britain's chancellor of the exchequer (finance minister) torpedoed in the Organization for European Economic Cooperation three relatively limited proposals for closer economic integration (the so-called Stikker, Pella, and Petsch plans).[1] As Alan Milward noted in his official history of Britain's involvement with European integration:

> The arguments that weighed in the balance against joining the Schuman Plan negotiations came from the Foreign Office: that by entering into the commitment to supranationality the United Kingdom would be accepting obligations to its European neighbors which would reduce its independence from, and thus its status and influence with, the USA, while at the same time weakening its links with the Commonwealth and thus even further reducing its influence over the USA. The foundations for Britain's post-war national strategy would have been shattered by accepting the concept of supranationality.[2]

Britain's concern about sovereignty seemed excessive. The contemporaneous case of the Netherlands is revealing. Although as skeptical of supranationalism as the British, the Dutch reluctantly paid Monnet's price of admission. Despite its small size, in the course of the negotiations the Netherlands managed to dilute Monnet's original supranational idea almost beyond recognition. As the outcome of the negotiations would prove, in practice supranationalism was not nearly as frightening as it looked in principle. As

Monnet himself conceded in July 1950, "the translation of this principle [of supranationality] into reality can be amended and undoubtedly improved."[3]

In a blistering indictment of Britain's reaction to the Schuman Plan, Edmund Dell, a prominent British academic, politician (in the 1960s), and member of the European Commission (in the 1970s), argued that Britain's political and economic circumstances did not preclude participation in the negotiations. Britain could have been "a global power . . . at the center of the Commonwealth and sterling area, and still [have subscribed to] the Schuman Plan."[4] Dell also asserted that Britain never assessed the plan adequately and that "the handling of the issue by the Attlee government and, in particular, by [Foreign Minister] Bevin and the Foreign Office, was governed too much by resentment at lack of consultation by France and too little by attention to the national interest."[5] This is similar to the conclusion of a leading British journalist that "at bottom there was [in Britain] a mysterious visceral hostility [toward European integration] great enough to transcend any amount of cool calculation."[6]

In view of Britain's position, France had no choice but to launch by itself "a diplomatic revolution in Europe."[7] In political terms, the Schuman Declaration was nothing less than "a dramatic reassertion of French leadership on the Continent."[8] Fearful of Germany's recovery, France finally responded with a creative and courageous initiative. Indifferent to France's plight and complacent about the future, Britain pursued an unimaginative foreign policy. Nor did Britain's position change after the election of October 1951, when the Conservatives replaced Labour in government and Churchill again became prime minister.

Although Britain was "absent at the creation," its presence was keenly felt around the table in Paris, where the others feared that Britain, for reasons of policy or pride, would attempt to derail the talks.[9] In the event, Britain did not do so, not least because the United States made its interest in the success of the negotiations abundantly clear. If anything, the British helped the negotiations by not floating alternative proposals and by pressuring Adenauer to reach agreement when it seemed in early 1951 that Germany's interest in the plan was waning.[10]

The Intergovernmental Conference

In June 1950, negotiations began among representatives of France, Germany, Italy, and the Benelux countries to flesh out the Schuman Plan and establish what became the European Coal and Steel Community.[11] The outbreak of war in Korea overshadowed the negotiations almost immediately. The question of German remilitarization, already in the background, suddenly leaped to the fore. Adenauer could now link remilitarization, an urgent US objective, to the restoration of full sovereignty, a pressing German goal. France feared that Germany would lose interest in the negotiations, but Ade-

The Six Original Member States

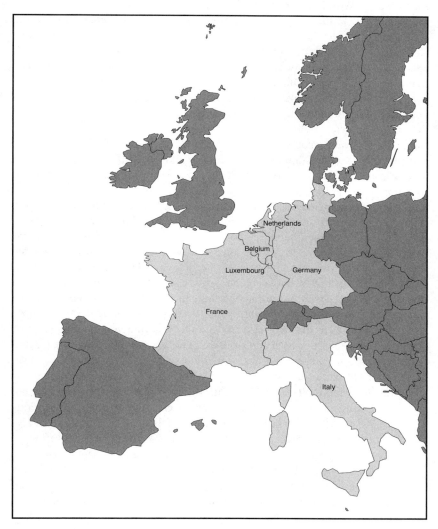

nauer was too sensitive to US and French opinion to shy away from them. The Schuman Plan remained an essential building block of Germany's policy of rapprochement with France and full integration into the West.

The negotiations were the first in a series of intergovernmental conferences—intense negotiations to conclude new treaties or revise existing ones—in the history of European integration. The Schuman talks set a procedural as well as a political precedent. A delegation of government officials represented each country. Working groups stood on the lowest rung of the conference ladder. Above them, the heads of delegation (most of whom went on to join the High Authority, the ECSC's executive body) met regularly in restricted session. At the top, the foreign ministers (including Adenauer, who was both chancellor and foreign minister of Germany) met occasionally to resolve particularly contentious problems.

Compared to later intergovernmental conferences, the Schuman Plan negotiations were atypical in one respect. Whereas foreign ministries dominated the other countries' delegations, the French delegation consisted mostly of Monnet's economic planners in Paris, with Monnet himself at its head. That gave the French delegation considerable flexibility and informality. Nevertheless, Monnet worked closely with Schuman, who provided overall political direction to the French delegation and to the talks themselves.

Monnet dominated the negotiations. He disliked large meetings, preferring to work directly with delegation heads, either bilaterally or multilaterally. Participants remembered the conference fondly, not so much as a set of negotiations but as a series of consultations with Monnet, in which all sides edged amicably toward an agreement. In fact, as in later intergovernmental conferences, there was intensive bargaining and occasional rancor. When things threatened to get out of hand, Schuman would reproach the delegates. Like a kindly uncle addressing unruly children, he would urge them to temper national interests for the sake of European union, while never losing sight of his own country's preference and priorities. Such was France's influence and Schuman's stature that the delegates invariably fell back into line.

Walter Hallstein, a former professor and a future European Commission president, led the German delegation. In the course of the conference, Hallstein became state secretary (director) of Germany's new foreign ministry and one of Adenauer's closest associates. His prestige, confidence, and assertiveness grew accordingly. So did his zeal for European integration.

Although a spirit of conciliation hovered over the conference, hard bargaining characterized the negotiations themselves. The prospect of better security through economic integration, rather than the ideal of European unity, drove the proceedings. As Milward observed of Belgium's approach to the negotiations, "there was no trace of idealism about the wider advantages to mankind of European integration. . . . It was taken for granted that peace between France and Germany was essential for Belgium's security, and that this was the strongest reason for accession to the treaty."[12]

An impatient Monnet thought that the negotiations could be completed in a few weeks. Typically, he wanted to focus on institutional issues to the exclusion of economic arrangements. Monnet's first draft treaty called for a High Authority, a parliamentary assembly, and a court. Monnet wanted to give the High Authority, the repository of shared sovereignty, virtually unfettered powers within its field of competence. As a sop to democratic control, he accepted a provision in the treaty allowing the assembly to dismiss the High Authority by a two-thirds majority. Otherwise the assembly would be relatively powerless.

The major institutional battle in the conference concerned the role of the High Authority. The main protagonist was the Dutch government, which distrusted supranationalism and sought to limit the power of the High Authority by means of national control.[13] Hans-Peter Schwarz, Adenauer's biographer, described the Dutch position generally as "an unfortunate mixture of trade calculations, aversion to French or German hegemony, openness to British influence, and deep concern about the prospect of being absorbed into larger units."[14]

The Dutch position irritated Adenauer and infuriated Monnet. But other national leaders, fearful of Franco-German dominance of the High Authority, shared Dutch concerns. Thus Monnet grudgingly acquiesced in the establishment of a Council of Ministers on the grounds that coal and steel questions could not be neatly separated from broader economic issues in which the High Authority lacked competence. The treaty supposedly established a balance between the Council and the High Authority, with the High Authority supreme in certain supranational areas. From the perspective of the original proposal, the institutional outcome represented a setback for supranationalism, as would the operational experience of the ECSC itself.

Just as one small country thwarted Monnet's hopes with regard to institutional design, another small country dug in its heels on economic issues. Belgian industry generally loathed the Schuman Plan, fearing the consequences of competition. The Belgian government saw the ECSC as an opportunity to replace national subsidization of the steel sector with European-level subsidization and to undertake painful industrial restructuring. The struggle inside Belgium, and in the negotiations between Belgium and its partners, was a harbinger of struggles within and among future ECSC member states on a wide range of issues. The outcome of the Belgian case was indeed prototypical: a complex regime of transfer payments, concessions, and transitional measures in the treaty to cushion the inevitable economic blow to cosseted national industries.[15]

The plan's overriding economic objective was to create a common market in coal and steel among participating countries. That meant removing a plethora of tariff and nontariff barriers, such as price fixing, turnover and sales taxes, subsidies, and differentiated freight rates, in order to facilitate the free movement of coal and steel across national frontiers. But the common market would not be an unregulated market. Using a variety of instruments and measures, the High Authority and Council of Ministers would try to improve productivity, rationalize distribution, safeguard employment, equalize working conditions, and minimize economic dislocation. The treaty's most innovative provisions were in the area of competition policy. Largely to allay US concern, the treaty included tough measures against restrictive practices and monopolies, including the possibility of fining companies up to 10 percent of their annual turnover. The treaty covered a period of fifty years (the ECSC duly came to an end in 2002).

Outstanding Issues

The treaty was all but wrapped up by December 1950, six months after the negotiations began. Yet it was another four months before the treaty was signed. The reason for the delay was German foot-dragging due to French insistence on the deconcentration of the coal and steel industries in the Ruhr. The big Ruhr conglomerates were to have been broken up under the terms of the Potsdam agreement, but the allies had not pressed the point. It was only in early 1951, with the ECSC hanging in the balance, that the French government launched an offensive. Afraid that the conglomerates would prove impervious to the treaty's antitrust provisions, and sensitive to growing domestic unrest about the relationship between the Ruhr and German rearmament, France linked deconcentration to a successful conclusion of the negotiations.

This aroused additional ill feeling in Germany, where many industrialists saw the Schuman Plan as a French plot to weaken German industry. French action and German reaction placed Adenauer in a dilemma: How could he reconcile economic interests at the national level and political interests at the European level? By backing France wholeheartedly and insisting on deconcentration, the United States resolved the dilemma for him. Even the most recalcitrant Germans acknowledged that Adenauer would have to bow to US pressure. Accordingly, Adenauer reached agreement with US high commissioner John McCloy on the terms of deconcentration at the end of March 1951, paving the way for the signing of the ECSC treaty in Paris in April.[16]

The International Ruhr Authority, which Adenauer abhorred, would cease to operate as soon as the ECSC came into being. The special status of the Ruhr, a bitter bone of contention in postwar Franco-German relations, would therefore come to an end. Yet the future of the Saar, a region of Germany controlled by France since the war, was still undecided. The French-imposed government of the Saar wanted the region to become the ECSC's seventh member state. That was too much even for the French government in Paris, which signed the treaty on behalf of France as well as the Saar. Adenauer insisted that, by signing the treaty, he was not abandoning Germany's determination eventually to reacquire the Saar. He and Schuman attached to the treaty an exchange of letters on the issue, affirming each side's position.

The foreign ministers had to resolve three other difficult issues, of a kind that would recur throughout the history of European integration, before the ECSC became operational. The first concerned the weighting of votes in the Council. Should Germany have more votes because its coal and steel sectors were the largest in the Community? Not surprisingly, France proposed equality of voting weight with Germany. Not surprisingly either, Germany agreed.

The second concerned the language regime in the Community. Speaking in German, the common language of the foreign ministers, Schuman proposed that French be either the sole or the preponderant language of the ECSC.[17] The ministers finally agreed that each country's language would have official status, but French would be the working language within the ECSC's institutions.

The third issue was the hardest to resolve. It concerned the location of the institutions. A protracted row erupted at a foreign ministers' meeting in Paris in July 1952, with each minister insisting on the location of one or more institution in his own country (Adenauer avoided chauvinism by championing the cause of Saarbrucken, the capital of the French-occupied Saar). The row seemed to make a mockery of the underlying purpose of the whole exercise. Dirk Stikker, the Dutch foreign minister, described what happened:

> The meeting [on the seat of the institutions] began at nine in the morning. . . . Questions of national prestige began to rise in importance. Proposals began to wander ever farther afield. No one was prepared to give way on any point before he had obtained another advantage. Europe was lost sight of. . . . As the confusion grew the discussion dragged on to midnight. At one point I rose in my place, ostensibly in wrath, told my colleagues in no uncertain terms what I thought of their high supranational principles, declared that I renounced any special position for the Netherlands, and walked out. . . . After some hours I returned, but it was still four o'clock [in the morning] before every national desire was satisfied.[18]

The foreign ministers finally agreed to hold meetings of the Council in Brussels, locate the court and High Authority in Luxembourg, and put the assembly in Strasbourg, where it could share facilities with the assembly of the Council of Europe.

Proceedings to ratify the treaty in national parliaments began in late 1951. Ratification was not a foregone conclusion. Various vested interests deployed a battery of political and economic arguments against the treaty. Anti-ECSC steel producers nearly unseated Schuman in the parliamentary elections of June 1951 (Schuman's constituency was in the steel-producing region of Lorraine). The biggest threat to ratification came not from business interests, which were often divided within and among the coal and steel sectors, but from nationalists on the right and Communists on the left. West Germany had only a small Communist party and an insignificant right-wing nationalist party. But the Socialists under Kurt Schumacher, who were both Marxist and nationalist, strongly opposed the treaty. In France the Communists and the recently constituted Gaullist Party, the largest party in parliament, failed to prevent ratification.

Launching the ECSC

The ECSC began operating in August 1952, at an inauspicious time politically. Adenauer's government was weak and unpopular. The French government was even weaker. The issue of German remilitarization, then at its height, cast European integration in a bad light. The political significance of the ECSC was lost in the bitterness of the controversy over the European Defense Community and the complexity of the new treaty's institutional and policy provisions. Perhaps it was just as well that the ECSC received only sporadic media attention (including in the United States) and that the new organization had a relatively low profile. Meetings of the High Authority and the Common Assembly went largely unreported. The ECSC had little impact on the everyday lives of Europeans.

Behind the scenes the organization got off to a good start, thanks to soaring demand for coal and steel. That was due partly to the continuing Korean War and consequent rearmament in Western Europe and the United States and largely to the postwar boom, epitomized by the so-called German miracle. Yet it is doubtful that the ECSC contributed much to Europe's rapid economic growth. The ECSC is barely mentioned in textbooks on national and European economic development in the 1950s.[19] Tariffs and quantitative restrictions were indeed removed in the coal and steel sectors, but nontariff barriers proved more difficult to identify and eradicate. The market remained fragmented, competitiveness did not increase greatly, productivity was not much improved, and cartels crept back into being.

A benign economic climate obviated the necessity for hard decisions by the High Authority, whose nine members and their staff, drawn mostly from national government ministries with a few international civil servants and academics thrown in, settled into Luxembourg. There was a great sense of excitement within the High Authority as the ECSC began its work. Despite the mundane reality of setting up a common market for coal and steel, most officials believed that they were serving the higher cause of European union.[20]

Monnet, at the head of the High Authority, missed Paris, but Paris did not miss him. His political shelf life was effectively over. Monnet's main use to the French government was close contacts with the Americans. But US assistance was now less important for France as US influence in Europe gradually diminished. Monnet was no longer needed to direct the modernization plan, and implementation of the Schuman Plan reduced his value as an entrepreneur of European integration. Moreover, because of his authorship of the unpopular defense community idea, Monnet had become a political liability. It was better for the French government to have Monnet far away in Luxembourg at a time when opposition to the EDC was boiling over in Paris.

As usual, Monnet was indefatigable. Now in his mid-sixties, he worked day and night to put the coal and steel community in place. But he was frustrated because the High Authority was too large and bureaucratic for his liking (in fact, it was a relatively small organization), and bored because the political action was in Paris, not Luxembourg. It was not surprising that, in August 1954, Monnet announced his intention to retire from the High Authority and return to Paris to try to reinvigorate European integration. His staff and fellow commissioners were relieved to see him go. While acknowledging his brilliance and creativity, they had been ground down by his poor management and chaotic work practices. Those with families looked forward to going home at a reasonable hour and staying there without risk of being summoned back to work late at night.

A steady stream of academic visitors had enlivened Monnet's life in Luxembourg. In addition to regulating the coal and steel industries, the ECSC spawned another industry: scholarship on European integration. The number of books and articles written on the ECSC in the 1950s and early 1960s is astounding. German academics were first on the scene, then French, then American. The three most important books of that epoch in English, by William Diebold, Hans Schmidt, and Ernst Haas, were based in part on lengthy observations of the High Authority in Luxembourg (before and after Monnet's departure).[21] Despite their best efforts, none of the authors was able to show that the ECSC was economically significant. Even Haas, the father of neofunctionalism, later admitted that the ECSC had not had a marked spillover effect.[22]

Significance of the ECSC

Nevertheless the ECSC was important politically and institutionally. The High Authority forged a good working relationship with the Council of Ministers and the member states' permanent representatives (ambassadors). According to Duchêne, Monnet's initial "narrow, technocratic view of relations between the High Authority and the industries and governments [developed into] a political system, which is substantially that of the Community today [1994]."[23] A blend of supranationalism and intergovernmentalism characterized the functioning of the Community from the beginning.

The ECSC achieved both its immediate goal of resolving the problem of the Ruhr and its long-term objective of overcoming entrenched Franco-German enmity. Robert Marjolin, who was far from starry-eyed about European integration, described the ECSC as "estimable on two counts. First, it represented a step forward, a new start on the road to a united Europe. Second, it represented a revolution in Franco-German relations. Nearly a century of wars, of attempts at domination, of an antagonism that had come absurdly to be called hereditary, had given way to a will to cooperate on completely equal terms."[24]

Milward, the arch-revisionist of European integration, saw the Community's significance as having "ended eighty years of bitter and deadly [Franco-German] dispute and made the reconstruction of Western Europe possible. It did so by avoiding all major questions of war and peace and creating instead a formalized network of institutional economic interdependence. International regulation of the economy was institutionalized as the alternative to the formal diplomatic resolution of major areas of political conflict."[25]

The ECSC set a profound historical precedent. John Gillingham, author of one of the best studies on the early years of European integration, characterized the outcome of the Schuman Declaration as a de facto peace treaty between France and Germany:

> This was no grand settlement in the manner of Westphalia or Versailles. The agreement to create a heavy industry pool changed no borders, created no new military alliances, and reduced only a few commercial and financial barriers. It did not even end the occupation of the Federal Republic. . . . By resolving the coal and steel conflicts that had stood between France and Germany since World War II, it did, however, remove the main obstacle to an economic partnership between the two nations.[26]

The European Defense Community and the European Political Community

Speaking in a debate in the French National Assembly in July 1949, Robert Schuman made a statement that came back to haunt him. The question of Germany's admission to NATO, he said, "cannot come up, either now or even in the future. Germany still has no peace treaty. It has no army, and it must not have one. It has no weapons, and it will have none."[27] Yet in little more than a year, the question of Germany's NATO membership *was* on the agenda, due to the outbreak of the Korean War. Schuman could not have foreseen that events would proceed as swiftly as they did in 1950.

Even before the Korean War, Adenauer wanted German remilitarization. His motive was less political (a quest for full sovereignty) than strategic (a quest for self-defense). Allied occupation forces in West Germany were small and weak. Adenauer feared that West Germany would be easily overrun in the event of an invasion by the Soviet army or an incursion by the East German paramilitary police. The answer, surely, was to build up allied forces and raise a West German army.

Adenauer knew only too well how controversial this idea was, having engendered a backlash against a statement about remilitarization that he had made in a newspaper interview in December 1949.[28] Circumstances changed suddenly with the outbreak of war in Korea. If the North Koreans had invaded South Korea, might not the East Germans invade West Germany? Improbable though it now seems, many Europeans feared that war with the

Soviet Union was imminent in the summer of 1950. The British and Americans spoke openly about the prospect of German remilitarization. At a meeting of the Council of Europe's Consultative Assembly in August 1950, Churchill called for German rearmament in the context of European integration. Matters came to a head at a NATO ministerial meeting in New York in September 1950 when US secretary of state Dean Acheson made it official: the United States wanted German military units to be raised and integrated into NATO forces in Europe.

Schuman cannot have been surprised by Acheson's announcement, but Acheson was surprised by the vehemence of Schuman's reaction to it. France was implacably opposed to German remilitarization in any shape or form. Bringing the issue into the open greatly strengthened Adenauer's hand. Inevitably, Germany's negotiating position in the coal and steel negotiations hardened. Inevitably also, Adenauer linked Acheson's call for German remilitarization to Germany's desire for abolition of the Occupation Statute and restoration of full sovereignty. French efforts to control Germany's postwar recovery were again endangered.

To protect the Schuman Plan and the overall strategy toward Germany of which it was a part, France needed a new initiative. Monnet provided it in the form of the Pleven Plan of October 1950: a scheme, named after French prime minister René Pleven, for a supranational European army, conditional on a successful conclusion of the ECSC negotiations. The difference between the Acheson and Pleven plans for German remilitarization was stark: Acheson wanted Germany to raise large armored units, if necessary as part of a reconstituted German army; Pleven wanted Germany to integrate small infantry units directly into a European army, without forming a German army. The original Pleven Plan was both politically inequitable and militarily infeasible. Acheson rejected it out of hand. Adenauer was more circumspect, protesting the plan's concrete proposals while welcoming its acceptance in principle of German remilitarization. Adenauer also assured Schuman that, despite the changing strategic circumstances, Germany remained committed to negotiating the ECSC treaty. Still sensitive to French security concerns, the United States pressured Germany to stick with the ECSC.

The Trauma of the European Defense Community
Thus began a four-year drama that traumatized France politically, tested Franco-German relations to the limit, and deeply alienated France and the United States from each other.[29] In February 1951, the six participants in the concurrent ECSC negotiations began a parallel intergovernmental conference to establish what came to be called the European Defense Community. Ever suspicious of supranationalism, Britain declined to participate.[30] For France and the Benelux countries, this was a serious setback. Britain was the leading military power in Western Europe and a traditional guarantor of the continen-

tal balance of power. Britain's membership in the EDC would have helped to allay French and Benelux concerns about Germany's military resurgence. In the hope that Britain might still join the negotiations, the Netherlands postponed its full participation in them until November 1951.

The prospect of German remilitarization reopened deep political wounds in France and energized the Communist and Gaullist opposition. The Gaullists made sweeping gains in the parliamentary elections of June 1951. Opinion in Germany was equally divided, with the Socialists tapping into a groundswell of pacifism. The EDC would not win Adenauer any votes, but the restoration of full sovereignty might. Hence, for domestic political consumption, he linked the negotiations to establish the EDC and to rescind the Occupation Statute, the former taking place in Paris, the latter just outside Bonn.

The EDC negotiations gathered speed in the fall of 1951. In the preceding months, Monnet had worked his magic on US high commissioner McCloy and General Dwight Eisenhower, the newly arrived NATO supreme commander. In return for French concessions on the size and equipment of German military units, McCloy and Eisenhower, whose influence in Europe was unrivaled, championed a revised version of the Pleven Plan, which they saw as a means of strengthening the European contribution to NATO. Acheson, in Washington, soon fell into line. Adenauer dropped his reservations about the plan's seemingly discriminatory proposals. He and the Americans still wanted the EDC to serve as a vehicle for German entry into NATO, but this was too much for the French. Nevertheless, with wholehearted US support, the negotiators in Paris gradually put the EDC's institutional and organizational elements into place.

A Soviet diplomatic note of March 1952, calling for Four Power talks to conclude a German peace treaty, "burst like a bombshell" into the EDC negotiations.[31] By raising the prospect of a neutral, unified Germany, the Soviets sought to prevent German remilitarization within the Western alliance. Adenauer would have none of it. Vulnerable to Communist subversion, a neutral Germany might slip into the Soviet sphere of influence. The Americans were aware of the danger. Accordingly, the Western powers decided to press ahead with the modified Pleven Plan. The six negotiating countries signed the EDC treaty in May 1952, in Paris. On the previous day in Bonn, Britain, France, Germany, and the United States had signed an accord replacing the Occupation Statute with a number of contractual agreements, thereby effectively restoring sovereignty to Germany.

A debate on the EDC in the French National Assembly in February 1952, three months before the treaty was signed, signaled that ratification would be difficult. Changes in the international situation, notably the ceasefire in Korea and the death of Soviet leader Josef Stalin in March 1953, emboldened opponents of the treaty. With a possible thaw in the Cold War, was German remilitarization necessary? Adenauer had no doubts on that score and pushed the treaty through a restive German parliament. The Benelux countries and Italy also ratified the treaty. That left France, the originator of the Pleven Plan, as the sole holdout. Eisenhower, now president of the United States, pressed France to ratify. So did Adenauer and Spaak, the zealous Eurofederalist foreign minister of Belgium.

A public debate raged in France on the merits of the treaty. It was likened at the time to the conflict-ridden Dreyfus affair of fifty years earlier, except that divisions over the EDC "were perhaps even more complicated and more irrational."[32] Charles de Gaulle, then in retirement, gave a celebrated press conference in November 1953 denouncing the treaty and Monnet, its unnamed "inspirer."[33] Indifferent to European integration and ambivalent about the EDC, Pierre Mendès-France, one of the most able politicians of the Fourth Republic, decided when he became prime minister in June 1954 to settle the issue. Having just ended France's disastrous involvement in Indochina and brokered an agreement with the nationalist rebels in Tunisia, Mendès-France was in a stronger position than most prime ministers of the hapless Fourth Republic.

The much-awaited parliamentary debate took place at the end of August 1954. Opponents of the treaty appeared less concerned about the fact of German remilitarization than about the implications of the treaty for France itself. Edouard Herriot, an influential old politician and former prime minister, claimed that membership in the EDC would mean "the end of France." Others emphasized the danger to France's two most cherished institutions, the army and the empire. Concern about France's future international stature also infused the debate. As one deputy put it, "we are still a nation . . . with rights equal to those of America and Great Britain. . . . The ratification of the EDC would put us on the level of two defeated and three tiny countries." By implication, Britain and the United States were eager to see France reduced in rank, so that they could deal "from now on with world strategy in an Anglo-Saxon tete-à-tete."[34]

It was almost impossible in the face of such emotion to make reasonable arguments in favor of ratification. Pro-EDC deputies were outnumbered and shouted down. In a final insult, the treaty was defeated not in a straight vote but on a procedural motion. By a majority of 319 to 264, the French parliament threw out the treaty "in an atmosphere of riot."[35]

Anthony Eden, the British foreign secretary, then suggested turning the old Brussels Treaty Organization (consisting of Britain, France, and the Benelux countries) into the Western European Union by the addition of Germany and Italy. Through the Western European Union, the former Axis powers could join NATO. The idea was fleshed out at a conference in London and reached fruition in the Paris agreement of October 1954. Consisting of a Council of Ministers and an assembly, and covering cultural and educational as well as military issues, the Western European Union was an intergovernmental organization. That fact, together with the reassurance of British membership in it, won over many French parliamentarians who had voted against the EDC. Nevertheless, it took a vote of confidence (meaning that the government would stand or fall on the result) to get a majority of deputies to back the Western European Union in December 1954. As a result, within a year of the collapse of the EDC, Germany was remilitarized and a member of NATO.

The European Political Community

The end of the EDC resulted also in the end of a related initiative for an overarching political community. This originated in a proposal by Italy's fervently federalist prime minister, Alcide de Gasperi, to attach to the EDC treaty a provision (Article 38) calling for the EDC's assembly, within six months of its inauguration, to consider establishing "a permanent organization . . . of a confederal or federal structure."[36] At the urging of the Council of Europe's Consultative Assembly, the foreign ministers of the EDC's prospective member states agreed in September 1952 to ask an ad hoc assembly to carry out the terms of Article 38 while awaiting ratification of the EDC treaty. Presided over by Spaak, the ad hoc assembly (in effect the assembly of the Coal and Steel Community) adopted in March 1953 a draft treaty to establish the European Political Community.[37]

The Political Community was to have provided an organizational umbrella for the Defense Community and the Coal and Steel Community. Thus the EDC's and ECSC's institutions would have been replaced or superseded by a bicameral parliament (consisting of a directly elected assembly and an indirectly elected senate), a European Executive Council whose president would be elected by the Senate, a Council of National Ministers, and a Court of Justice. Subject to swift ratification by the six prospective member states, the Political Community would have become operational at the same time as the EDC.

Spaak described the draft treaty as "neither the work of the maximalists nor the minimalists" in the ad hoc assembly. As for the polity he proposed to create, it was "neither federal nor confederal." By quoting George Washington on the draft constitution of the United States, however, Spaak revealed his federalist ambition. Nor can the first sentence of the first article have reassured intergovernmentalists: "The present Treaty sets up a European [Political] Community of a supranational character." Heinrich von Brentano, a leading German politician and chairman of the ad hoc assembly's constitutional committee, which drafted the treaty, enthusiastically described a community that would "be able to take on a more and more precise form . . . until it develops by a natural process into a real Federal State or Confederation. This appears particularly clearly from the fact that the supranational Community possesses one of the attributes of a State: . . . a directly elected Peoples' Chamber."[38]

In the increasingly heated climate of the EDC ratification debate, the proposed political community seemed far too ambitious. Yet the other foreign ministers must have known what to expect when they asked Spaak to preside over the ad hoc assembly. If so, with the exception of Italy's Eurofederalist foreign minister, they could not have intended to take the draft treaty seriously. It was hardly surprising, therefore, that the foreign ministers allowed it to languish procedurally in late 1953 and 1954, until the death of the Defense Community resulted also in the death of the Political Community. By that time even Italy had lost much of its federalist fervor, de Gasperi having died only twelve days before the French National Assembly rejected the EDC.

An Opportunity Lost?

For many proponents of European federalism, the demise of the Defense Community and the Political Community was the greatest lost opportunity in the history of European integration. Implementation of the EDC, they argue, would have brought defense policy under supranational control and resolved in the mid-1950s an issue with which the European Union began to grapple only in the late 1990s. Implementation of the Political Community, in turn, would have established an integrative framework for specific industrial sectors and for European defense, as well as for a growing array of socioeconomic policies. Yet the bitterness of the EDC debate in France suggests that, even if the treaty had been ratified, it could not have been implemented, which would have left the question of German remilitarization unresolved. As it was, German membership in NATO through the Western European Union settled the issue in a manner acceptable to France and removed from the agenda of European integration an otherwise intractable problem.

Far from being a historical accident, the defeat of the EDC was, according to one of Mendès-France's closest colleagues, "a historical necessity." In his view, ratification of the treaty would have opened "a permanent civil war in France. Imagine the Sunday ceremonies at the war memorial in every village, with the Gaullists and the Communists united behind every tricolor? The [Gaullist-Communist] alliance institutionalized from that point on would not only have made France ungovernable, it would have put it in a state of uncontrollable effervescence."[39] Alfred Grosser, an expert on France and Germany, concluded shortly after the event that defeat of the EDC benefited Franco-German relations and European integration. In addition to extremists on the right and left, most young people and many moderates in both countries generally opposed the EDC. Accordingly, ratification of the treaty could have alienated a constituency that was vital for the achievement of European integration and eventual Franco-German reconciliation.[40] Far from enriching the movement for European integration, the proposed EDC had muddied the waters. The entire episode fueled fears that integration meant militarization, to the detriment of economic cooperation among the six prospective member states.

Although defeat of the EDC seemed at the time to deal a near-fatal blow to prospects for further integration—"supranationalism" was a dirty word, Franco-German relations were soured, and federalist hopes were dashed—it cleared the air and allowed the countries concerned to focus on economic priorities. A key provision in the draft treaty for the Political Community identified one of those priorities: the establishment of a common market. The Dutch government, which in the early 1950s became the leading proponent of economic integration, insisted on a commitment to establishing a common market for industrial goods, in return for its lukewarm support of the EDC. This raised problems for France, which at that time was wedded to a protectionist trade policy. The inclusion of the common market clauses in the draft treaty suggests that, even if the EDC had been ratified, fundamental economic differences among the signatory states would have delayed or prevented implementation of the Political Community. As it was, it took another three years, including a new intergovernmental conference, before the Six negotiated, signed, and ratified the EEC treaty. The defeat of the EDC helped, not hindered, the road to the Rome Treaty.

The European Economic Community and the European Atomic Energy Community

The Coal and Steel Community, up-and-running by the mid-1950s, had little chance of leading automatically to deeper political and economic integration. Even the most ardent supporters of further integration were aware of the limits of the ECSC well before the defeat of the EDC. Monnet's disillusionment with the ECSC was long-standing. The collapse of the EDC merely confirmed in him the belief that he could best serve the cause of European integration by promoting a new initiative independently, at the head of an international lobby, rather than by staying in Luxembourg as head of the High Authority.[41]

Paradoxically, the EDC debacle contributed to a noticeable improvement in Franco-German relations in 1955 and 1956, as French officials sought to make amends for some of the fiercely anti-German rhetoric that had flowed during the debate on German remilitarization. It is hardly coincidental that a number of government-sanctioned "people-to-people" initiatives, in the cultural, educational, and linguistic fields, got off the ground at that time. The conclusion of a commercial treaty in August 1955 illustrated the extent of the thaw between France and Germany exactly one year after the collapse of the EDC. Similarly, the opening of a new bridge in September 1956, linking Strasbourg and Kehl across the Rhine, became a celebration of Franco-German rapprochement. Perhaps more than anything else on the political plane, the meeting of Adenauer and his French counterpart Guy Mollet in November 1956, at the height of the Suez crisis, demonstrated a newfound Franco-German willingness to work together.[42]

The improvement in Franco-German relations, and with it the beginning of genuine reconciliation, took place not only in the aftermath of the EDC debacle but also in the context of a new strategic situation. Germany's entry into NATO in May 1955 tied the country firmly into the Western camp. With Germany almost fully sovereign and remilitarized, the nature of the German question, and therefore of Franco-German relations, changed completely. France could no longer extract concessions from Britain and the United States by threatening to block Germany's recovery. Increasingly, France would base its policy toward Germany primarily on economic rather than geopolitical calculations.

Nevertheless, Franco-German relations retained a special quality. Given Germany's recent past (conduct in the war) and uncertain future (possible re-unification), dealings between Paris and Bonn could not be entirely normal. Adenauer was excessively deferential to French feelings. For sentimental and strategic reasons, he put a premium on maintaining harmonious relations with France. Adenauer's willingness to subordinate economic objectives to supposed strategic necessity irritated many of the chancellor's colleagues and gave France an advantage in bilateral and multilateral negotiations. This was especially the case in the intergovernmental conference of 1956–1957 that resulted in the Rome Treaty.

The resolution of the Saar problem was the most obvious manifestation of improved Franco-German relations in the mid-1950s. French control of the Saar since the end of World War II had caused deep resentment in Germany. France's proposal in 1954 to "Europeanize" the region under the auspices of the Western European Union failed to mollify German opinion. In an effort to ease tension with Germany and mute international criticism, France made the proposed change in the Saar's status contingent on the outcome of a referendum there in October 1955. To the embarrassment of the French, a large majority of the Saar's population rejected the proposal, clearly preferring to re-join Germany. Most of the region's residents seemed motivated not by nationalism but by economic self-interest (postwar Germany was already much more prosperous than France). Paris and Bonn then negotiated the return of the Saar to Germany in an atmosphere remarkably free of rancor. The Saar was eventually incorporated into the Federal Republic in January 1957, shortly before the end of the negotiations on the Rome Treaty.

Messina

The famous meeting of foreign ministers in the Sicilian town of Messina in June 1955 took place in a climate of growing Franco-German amity. The

Messina meeting looms large in the history of European integration. Casual accounts of the EU's origins credit Messina with deliberately relaunching the process of integration after the seemingly fatal setback of the EDC's defeat. In retrospect, Messina assumed the mantle of a Second Coming, after the initial incarnation of European integration in the Schuman Declaration of May 1950.

The ministers who gathered in Messina in 1955 would have been surprised to learn that the meeting would acquire such a retrospective gloss. The primary purpose of Messina was much less grandiose than relaunching European integration: it was to appoint a successor to Monnet as president of the High Authority. France still had a lock on the job. The other member states endorsed the French government's choice of René Meyer, a former prime minister (a distinction not uncommon in the French Fourth Republic).

The ministers then discussed proposals for further economic integration. Two stood out. One, championed by Monnet and strongly supported by Spaak as a means of reviving the European project, was for an atomic energy community analogous to the coal and steel community. The second was a reiteration of the Beyen Plan (named after Dutch foreign minister Johan Willem Beyen) for an industrial customs union, which had originally been incorporated into the draft treaty for the European Political Community.[43] Because he thought a customs union too ambitious, Spaak preferred Monnet's proposal for an atomic energy community. Under pressure from Beyen, however, Spaak incorporated the ideas for an atomic energy community and a customs union into a single package, the so-called Benelux memorandum of May 1955. Spaak and Beyen had different objectives in mind. Whereas Spaak saw economic integration as a steppingstone to political union, Beyen wanted to prioritize opportunities for economic growth.

The dependence of the Netherlands on international trade explains Beyen's interest in regional economic integration. Trade barriers were stifling the Dutch economy. The Dutch and other members of the so-called Low Tariff Club became fierce advocates of free trade. They were disappointed by the slow pace of tariff reduction in the GATT and especially of quota removal through the OEEC's Trade Liberalizing Program, launched in 1949. With decisionmaking in the OEEC subject to unanimity, it was easy for sovereignty-conscious and protectionist members to block progress. European free-traders soon lost patience with the GATT and faith in the OEEC. Hence their advocacy of a regional organization with real decisionmaking power to establish a common market, which would also increase their leverage to accelerate GATT negotiations for lower tariff barriers.[44]

The release of the Benelux memorandum in May 1955, two weeks before the Messina meeting, intensified political and business interest in the idea of a common market. Lively debates on regional economic integration took place in most ECSC members throughout 1955. The question in Germany was not whether, but how, to liberalize trade. Should Germany pursue liberalization globally through the GATT or regionally through a European organization? If regionally, was a free trade area or a customs union preferable? Ludwig Erhard, Germany's economics minister, favored a multilateral approach. As a doctrinaire economic liberal, he feared that regional arrangements would hinder rather than help the achievement of global free trade. Of the two regional options, he viewed a customs union as potentially protectionist and therefore undesirable.

Hallstein, in the foreign ministry, advocated a customs union for economic and political reasons. He thought it would afford Germany the economic benefits of market liberalization and the political benefits of deeper European integration. The rift between Erhard and Hallstein was personal (they cordially disliked each other), ideological (Erhard disdained Hallstein's Eurofederalism), and bureaucratic (their respective foreign and economics ministries vied for leadership in the field of trade policy).

Adenauer arbitrated between his two strong-willed ministers. The chancellor's preferences suggested that he would favor Hallstein over Erhard, as indeed he did. But Adenauer proceeded carefully, not least because Monnet pressured him to opt for the idea for an atomic energy community instead of the proposal for a common market. Also, Erhard was immensely popular in the country (he was known as the father of the economic miracle) and had the backing of influential interest groups. Adenauer wanted to assuage Erhard rather than confront him outright.

Advocates of free trade were rare in France in the mid-1950s. Robert Marjolin, who resigned as head of the OEEC in April 1955 because of the organization's impotence, was one of the few prominent French people to champion market liberalization. Marjolin was not an ideologue. He was less interested in the form than the substance of European integration. Marjolin believed that France could realize its full potential only through membership in a common market. High trade barriers and an overvalued currency were holding France back. Pessimistic about its economic performance, France was in danger of falling further behind unless it embraced regional economic integration.

French political and business elites were deeply protectionist. The only European initiative that caught their imagination was the proposed atomic energy community, known as Euratom.[45] Monnet and the French establishment supported Euratom for different reasons. Whereas Monnet saw it as an opportunity to advance supranationalism and relaunch European integration, French leaders championed it on narrow nationalistic grounds. Their main goal was to put European resources at the disposal of the French atomic energy industry for both civil and military purposes. French objectives were so transparent that other countries instinctively recoiled from the idea. Only Monnet's dogged advocacy of it, and French insistence on linking the proposals for an atomic energy community and a common market, kept the prospect of Euratom alive.

Contrary to the impression now widely held, governments did not commit themselves at Messina unreservedly to reignite European integration. Although most of the ministers present were ardent Europeanists, and although prospects for integration were increasingly propitious, most governments preferred to proceed slowly. Franco-German relations had improved greatly since the collapse of the EDC, but French distrust of German calls for trade liberalization and German distrust of French calls for atomic energy cooperation ran deep. The Benelux countries wondered how protectionism in France and internal divisions in Germany could ever be overcome.

Not wanting the Messina meeting to end inconclusively, the foreign ministers agreed at the last minute to establish an intergovernmental committee to continue work on the proposals for an atomic energy community and a common market. Antoine Pinay, the French foreign minister, was the last holdout. Under pressure from his colleagues, Pinay went along with the idea of an intergovernmental committee in order to end the conference on a positive note and prevent France from being isolated. The decision to keep existing options open, reached reluctantly and at the last minute, marks the real significance of Messina. Understandably, however, the foreign ministers couched the meeting's outcome in verbose language. "The time has come to enter a new phase in the construction of Europe," they declared, "through the development of common institutions, the gradual merger of national economies, the creation of a common market, and increasing harmonization of social policies."[46]

Toward the Intergovernmental Conference

The committee that emerged from Messina met in the summer and fall of 1955, under Spaak's energetic chairmanship. The governments and peoples of France and Germany had more immediate concerns. The question of the Saar and Adenauer's historic visit to Moscow in December 1955 preoccupied Germany, while the escalating conflict in Algeria preoccupied France. Whereas the Schuman Declaration and the EDC had been front-page stories, the activities of the Spaak committee were lucky to get an occasional mention in the media.

Relevant government ministries and interest groups nevertheless focused on the committee's work. The stakes were high, especially for France, which faced the greatest barrier to establishing a common market. Political instability increased French uncertainty until the election in January 1956 of the pro-European government of Guy Mollet. Even so, France insisted in the Spaak committee on numerous safeguards and special concessions. By working closely at home with various industrial and agricultural interests and in committee meetings in Brussels with sympathetic national delegations, the French government helped fashion a final report that could serve as a basis for an intergovernmental conference to negotiate a treaty establishing a common market.

In October 1955, at the height of the committee's deliberations, Monnet launched the Action Committee for the United States of Europe to lobby for further integration.[47] Monnet invited leading politicians and trade unionists (excluding Communists) to join. Most accepted out of respect for Monnet and because the obligations of membership were not onerous. Initially, Monnet used the committee to push exclusively for Euratom, his pet project. Most members of the Action Committee were uninterested in Euratom, preferring the idea of a common market, which Monnet eventually endorsed.

Given that France would not proceed with negotiations on a common market without negotiations also on Euratom, and that Germany would not proceed with negotiations on Euratom without negotiations also on a common market, inevitably the Spaak report, drawn up in April 1956, endorsed both options. Nevertheless, the report focused mostly on the proposed common market, with a customs union at its core and possibly including agricultural policy, the "harmonization of social and fiscal charges" (due to higher taxation and social benefits in France), the free movement of labor, cooperation on monetary policy, a "readaptation fund" to help compensate for job losses, and an investment fund for poorer regions.[48]

Meeting in Venice in late May 1956, almost a year after Messina, the foreign ministers considered the Spaak report. At the same time, interest groups were mobilizing for and against the proposed common market and Euratom. In most countries they strongly favored the common market, but not Euratom. France was the exception. Complicating the issue further, the French insisted in Venice that a final agreement on the common market include free access for products from French colonies. Reluctantly, Germany agreed to put the latest French demand on the agenda of the negotiations. The foreign ministers then gave a green light to launch the intergovernmental conference to conclude treaties for the two communities.

Membership in the proposed communities was not formally restricted to the Six. Britain had declined to attend the Messina conference and sent only a mid-level official to observe the work of the intergovernmental committee. The government recalled him to London in October 1955, fully six months before the committee presented its report. The British poured scorn on the efforts to integrate further. The disdain with which British politicians and officials dismissed the move toward a common market is now legendary. It could never happen, they said, because France would not allow it to happen. The idea of a common market was pie in the sky, further evidence of federalist fantasizing. As planning for the common market progressed, the British became even more dismissive.[49]

For those who believed that Britain's absence from the ECSC was a fundamental mistake, Britain's nonparticipation in the negotiations that resulted in the EEC seemed like an unmitigated disaster. In their view, Britain's approach to European integration in the mid-1950s suggested irrationality, rigidity, and shortsightedness. From the British point of view, however, the balance of economic and political interests did not yet weigh in favor of participation in a common market. Britain did not want to lock itself into a small customs union, preferring to pursue a larger European free trade area. In Germany, Adenauer supported the putative common market because of his overriding commitment to partnership with France. In Britain, by contrast, there was no desire to privilege relations with France over broader economic and political interests. Nor was there much sympathy for supranationalism. Alan Milward argued persuasively that, far from being motivated by delusions of grandeur or anti-European prejudice, which undoubtedly existed, Britain's decision not to become a founding member of the EEC was consistent with a national strategy aimed at strengthening security and promoting prosperity that was based on a careful calculation of the country's strengths and weaknesses and of regional and global opportunities and threats.[50]

A European free trade area limited to industrial goods would have suited the British. It would have suited Erhard and other economic liberals in Germany too, but was unacceptable to most political leaders in the Six. France wanted an agreement that included agriculture, social protection, and other safeguards. The Six generally wanted a more cohesive and dynamic economic organization than a loose free trade agreement would provide. As it was, by the mid-1950s the Six constituted an informal trading bloc. A customs union, with a common external tariff and a common commercial policy, made sense for them, but not for the United Kingdom.

Concern about the future of the Anglo-American "special relationship" is often cited as a reason for British aloofness from European integration. Yet the United States consistently supported European integration and British participation in it. To the extent that the special relationship existed, it did so despite, not because of, Britain's refusal to join the European communities. Phrases in the Messina resolution, such as "the construction of Europe" and "the establishment of a united Europe," appealed to the United States. Economically, the United States wanted to ensure that the common market would benefit US investors and exporters. Regardless of Britain's position, the United States strongly supported deeper European integration.

Negotiating the New Communities

The intergovernmental conference took place in Brussels, in recognition of Spaak's successful chairmanship of the committee that had prepared it.[51] Egypt's nationalization of the Suez Canal, which culminated in October

1956 in a failed Anglo-French military expedition to restore international control of the strategic waterway, dominated the headlines. The coincidence of the two events suggested a link between the success of the negotiations and the end of the Suez debacle. France supposedly reacted to the Suez situation by grasping the strategic importance of European integration and enthusiastically embracing the common market. According to this analysis, Gamal Abdul Nasser, the Egyptian leader, unintentionally became the "federator" of Europe.[52]

If a link existed between Suez and the intergovernmental conference, however, it lay in Mollet's use of the crisis as a strategic argument to bolster a policy in Europe to which he was already committed for economic reasons.[53] It also lay in the fact that, with the all-consuming Suez affair out of the way, the French government could devote more attention to the ongoing Brussels negotiations. Nevertheless, by cementing official Franco-German ties (Adenauer wholeheartedly supported the French intervention and went ahead with a previously planned visit to Paris at the height of the crisis), Suez contributed in a roundabout way to cementing European integration.

Similarly, developments in the Soviet bloc in October and November 1956 provided a strategic backdrop to the conference without impinging on the negotiations themselves. The failed uprisings in Poland and Hungary heightened Cold War tension but did not directly affect European integration, especially as NATO was already well established. Indirectly, however, the Soviet invasion of Hungary helped European integration because it triggered a popular reaction in Western Europe against local Communist parties that supported the Soviet intervention. As Communist parties were implacable and influential opponents of European integration, the decline of their fortunes in Western Europe benefited the European movement.

A contemporary observer described the 1956–1957 negotiations as "an intricate mixture of academic exercises in abstruse economic theory and poker games of political skill."[54] The theorizing took place mostly in the two expert groups, one on Euratom and the other on the common market; the poker playing took place in regular meetings of the heads of delegations and occasional meetings of foreign ministers. The heads of government met once toward the end of the conference, along with their foreign ministers, to resolve the most contentious issues. Adenauer and Mollet, who met alone in Paris in November 1956 and at the joint meeting of prime ministers and foreign ministers, also in Paris, in February 1957, were the dealmakers and powerbrokers. Reflecting the reality of Franco-German hegemony within the Six, the others generally went along with what Adenauer and Mollet decided.

As host of the conference, Spaak was particularly influential. Taking care not to alarm protectionists in France and economic liberals in Germany, Spaak moderated his usual Euro-enthusiasm and assumed the role of honest broker. His closest assistant was Pierre Uri, a French official of the

ECSC dispatched to Brussels for the duration of the negotiations. That was the extent of supranational involvement in the conference.

An array of government officials, parliamentarians, and interest-group leaders labored intermittently on the intergovernmental conference in Brussels and the national capitals. Mindful of the EDC debacle, governments sought to form coalitions with opposition parties and interest groups to ensure support for their positions. The German Social Democratic Party, then in the course of abandoning doctrinaire anticapitalism, accepted the idea of the common market. Two key parliamentary victories in France, one on Euratom in July 1956 and the other on the common market in January 1957, strengthened the government's negotiating position in Brussels.

Fear of the future, of the brave new world of market integration, nevertheless remained pervasive in France. Mollet's strategy was not to confront opponents of further integration head-on, but to win as many concessions as possible in the negotiations while cultivating key vested interests at home. French foreign minister Christian Pineau and Robert Marjolin, Pineau's special adviser, ably assisted Mollet. Together they conducted a campaign on two fronts: one in Brussels at the conference, the other at home in the cabinet, parliament, boardrooms, and offices of interest groups (what Marjolin called the "Battle of Paris").[55] Knowing the fragility of French domestic support, the Five cut France as much slack as possible in order to ensure ratification in the French parliament. Naturally the French delegation turned that to advantage, occasionally exaggerating the extent of domestic opposition in order to win even more favorable terms from the other delegations.

The French got away with this because France was central to the project for deeper integration in a way that Britain, for instance, was not. A large country with great economic potential, France already constituted part of a dense, though informal, continental trading bloc. It would hardly have been worth it for the Five to form a common market without France. Moreover, for political reasons, Germany placed a premium on cooperation with France. Thus France was in a privileged position at the conference, a position that its negotiators exploited to the full.

Nevertheless, there were limits to what France could demand. The Euratom treaty, in particular, contained far less than France wanted. France was able to retreat on Euratom because, as the conference progressed, domestic political support for the common market grew. In particular, many rural, right-wing parliamentarians swung behind the proposed EEC for the sake of the promised agricultural provisions.

The other member states, having experienced severe food shortages during or after the war, and having subsidized their agricultural production to some extent, disputed not the principle of a common agricultural policy but the practical application of it. France, because it had the largest farming sector, had the most at stake in the negotiations politically and economically. Indeed, Marjolin and other advocates of an industrial common market stirred up French enthusiasm for a common agricultural policy partly to generate a powerful domestic lobby in favor of what became the Rome Treaty. The Five eventually agreed to go along with a provision in the treaty endorsing a common agricultural policy, with the details to be negotiated soon after implementation of the treaty.

With Belgian support, France insisted during the conference on associating the member states' overseas territories with the common market. The idea had great emotional appeal in France, where it helped allay concerns that deeper European integration would drive a wedge between France and its colonies (and former colonies). Germany wanted nothing to do with the other member states' overseas territories, fearing especially that trade with Latin America would suffer as a result. The issue became one of the most difficult to settle in the conference. Adenauer and Mollet finally agreed to give preferential trade terms to the overseas territories and to establish a special fund for development assistance outside the Community budget, to which Germany, as the largest member state, would contribute the largest share. For the sake of Franco-German friendship, Adenauer rammed this concession through an indignant cabinet.

France accepted the Spaak report's recommendation that the customs union be established over a twelve-year period, in three stages of equal length. Fearful of the impact of international competition, France wanted to make the launch of the second stage subject to a unanimous decision of the member states. That would have given France a veto over implementation of the customs union, which the Five refused to countenance. As a compromise, the treaty would allow a member state to delay transition to the second stage for two years, after which the question would go to arbitration. Thus a country could delay but not prevent implementation of the customs union. Negotiators presumed in any case that implementation of the customs union would assume an almost unstoppable momentum.

France complained that the cost of providing generous employment benefits—lengthy paid holidays, high rates of overtime pay, and the like—as well as equal pay for men and women, would put the country at a competitive disadvantage in the common market. The solution, according to France, was for the other member states to subscribe to the much-vaunted French social model. The demand for social "equalization" or "harmonization" became a mantra of French employers and workers and a rallying cry for opponents of the common market. As the Five were not about to burden themselves financially for France's sake, the issue became a major stumbling block in the conference.

Adenauer and Mollet resolved it in November 1956. Germany agreed to a provision in the treaty promising equal pay for men and women to be included in a section on social policy that paid lip service to "the harmonization of social systems" in the common market. Germany also agreed that a special protocol attached to the treaty would allow France to take "protective measures" in industries affected by "disparities [among member states] in the method of payment for overtime," should such disparities continue to exist after implementation of the first stage of the common market.[56]

It is often said that the common market was a trade-off between France and Germany: an agricultural common market for France in return for an industrial common market for Germany. That was not the case. The French government—more specifically, the prime minister and foreign minister—wanted both and used one (the promise of an agricultural common market) to get the other (an industrial common market). Germany wanted an industrial common market above all but accepted an agricultural common market not only as a means of ensuring French participation but also for the sake of its own agricultural sector.

Some of the treaty's signatories, notably Spaak, Hallstein, and Bech, were ideologically committed to European integration. The others saw the EC primarily as a means to meet the challenges and exploit the opportunities of international economic interdependence. Yet this was no ordinary common market. Everyone involved in the negotiations remembered the war vividly. Few of them would have predicted that such an agreement would have been reached among the Six so soon after 1945. The central role of the foreign ministers, and occasionally the heads of government, in the negotiation and subsequent operation of the EC demonstrated that the Community's importance was more than merely commercial.

The Rome Treaties

Foreign ministers signed the EEC and Euratom treaties in Rome on March 25, 1957. Italy, which had not played a big part in the negotiations themselves, organized the elaborate signing ceremony. The symbolism of the occasion pleased Adenauer (Germany's foreign minister as well as chancellor) and some of the other signatories, especially as it came so soon after the failure of the EDC.

The preamble of the Euratom treaty included two key words in the lexicon of European integration: "peace" and "prosperity." The preamble of the EEC treaty, by contrast, not only mentioned peace and, indirectly, prosperity, but also suggested that the EEC was a means to a greater end: "an ever closer union among the peoples of Europe."[57] As is often the case with international agreements, the preambles stood in marked contrast to the utilitarian nature of the treaties themselves.

Though there were two treaties, the term "Rome Treaty" soon came to refer exclusively to the treaty establishing the EEC. Even before Euratom came into existence, most member states regarded it as irrelevant. Far from forging deeper integration, Euratom became a clearinghouse for information exchange among the Six. With imported oil becoming abundant and cheap, and consumer resistance to nuclear energy on the rise, Euratom languished. Instead, France successfully pursued a national route to atomic energy for both civil and military purposes.

The EEC treaty's provisions ranged from the general to the specific, the mundane to the arcane. Mind-boggling lists of existing tariffs constituted a lengthy annex. Other attachments—lists of overseas territories, the implementing convention on the association of overseas territories, protocols, and a final act consisting of various declarations on specific national interests—ran to many more pages than the treaty itself. Some of the protocols and declarations were for domestic political purposes. Without affecting implementation of the treaty itself, they acknowledged national sensitivities in areas likely to be affected by the common market.

The treaty proper included provisions for a customs union, a common commercial policy, a common transport policy, competition policy, limited cooperation on monetary policy, and coordination of macroeconomic policy. A provision on social policy called for the establishment of a European Social Fund to contribute to retraining and other assistance to workers. The treaty also established a European Investment Bank to provide cheap loans for regional development and other modernization projects. The treaty's provisions for the free movement of persons, services, and capital were tentative, reflecting the tension between what was theoretically desirable and what was politically practicable in the establishment of the common market.

The treaty established an assembly, council, commission, and court. The European Commission was the most distinctive new institution. Eager to play down supranationalism, the Six agreed to use the less controversial name "Commission" rather than the value-laden name "High Authority." Nevertheless the Commission, supposedly independent of national governments, was potentially powerful, notably with respect to upholding Community law and initiating and implementing Community legislation. But the Council of Ministers would be the EC's chief decisionmaking body. Depending on the issue under discussion (in accordance with the relevant treaty article), decisions would be taken by unanimity, simple majority vote, or qualified majority vote. Votes in the Council were allocated according to the size of the member states, with Germany and France having equal representation.

Ratification

National parliaments ratified the treaties before the end of 1957. Some opponents raised the specter of a European superstate, but the reality of the intergovernmental conference and its outcome was too pedestrian to sustain fantasies of that kind. The old charge of German domination recurred in the French debate, although many Germans, especially economic liberals, saw the Rome Treaty as a sellout to France. Gaullists were divided on the EEC:

some went along with it for economic reasons; others opposed it for political reasons (because it would erode national sovereignty). De Gaulle himself mostly kept quiet on the issue.

Other objections to the Rome Treaty, in France and elsewhere, focused on fears of mass migration and of large-scale job losses. In France, at least, the parliamentary votes of July 1956 (in favor of negotiating Euratom) and January 1957 (in favor of negotiating the common market) had essentially decided the issue. Ratification of the treaty in July 1957, by a margin of almost a hundred votes, was a foregone conclusion. In yet another turn of the French political carousel, Mollet's government collapsed in May 1957, two months after the treaty was signed and two months before it was ratified. But the government's fall had nothing to do with the EEC.

Adenauer faced more difficulty over ratification of the Rome Treaty than did his French counterpart. Not that ratification was ever in doubt in Germany, as the treaty clearly benefited the Federal Republic economically and politically. The problem lay in Erhard's resentment of Adenauer and dissatisfaction with the direction of Germany's foreign economic policy. Erhard accepted the treaty only grudgingly. He would have preferred to explore Britain's alternative proposal for a free trade area limited to industrial products. Erhard never forgave Adenauer for deferring to France. This opened a chasm within the ruling Christian Democratic Party that eventually cost Adenauer the chancellorship of Germany.

Much is made of Monnet's contribution to ratification of the Rome Treaty, especially in Germany. According to this line of thought, the membership of prominent German Social Democrats in Monnet's Action Committee for the United States of Europe helped reconcile the Social Democratic Party to the EC and undermine potential opposition to the treaty in the German parliament.[58] Undoubtedly, membership in the Action Committee brought German Social Democrats into contact with supporters of European integration in neighboring countries. But German Social Democrats had tempered their ideological opposition to European integration before Monnet launched his committee in October 1955, and developments in East-West relations in the mid-1950s meant that further European integration would have little immediate bearing on the division of Germany, an issue close to the hearts of many Social Democrats.

Ratification of the Rome Treaty in France and Germany presaged swift ratification in the other prospective member states. There was a flurry of activity in late 1957 to prepare for the Community's launch in January 1958. One of the most important decisions still to be taken was where to locate the EEC's institutions. Luxembourg, home of the High Authority, the assembly's secretariat, and the Court of Justice, was bursting at the seams. Having conducted the negotiations in Brussels, the Six decided to locate the Commission there. In addition to hosting the World's Fair in 1958, Brussels became the headquarters of the new Communities. Memories of the World's Fair soon faded, but playing host to the EEC saved Brussels, the declining capital of a declining country, from relative obscurity.

A more crucial political decision was the selection of the Commission's first president. As France, a big country, had the presidency of the High Authority, by common consent it was the turn of a small member state to nominate the Commission president. Belgium, the unofficial leader of the Benelux countries, chose instead to host the Commission in Brussels. That put the ball back in Germany's court. Hallstein seemed a natural choice. A confidant of Adenauer's, he was steeped in the workings of the ECSC and in the negotiations that led to the EEC.

Yet the choice of Hallstein may have been unfortunate. Despite having held high government positions, he had never held elective office. As Commission president, Hallstein personified the new institution's weak political legitimacy. Hallstein saw himself and the Commission primarily in political terms. A zealous federalist, he was determined to put the EEC politically on the map. That ran counter to most member states' view of the organization and set him on a collision course with de Gaulle, who became leader of France soon after the Community came into existence. The unequal struggle between de Gaulle and Hallstein personified the unequal struggle between intergovernmentalism and supranationalism in the development of the European Community in the decades ahead.

Notes

1. As Dutch foreign minister Dirk Stikker observed, these were irreverently called "The St. Pee-Pee Plans." Dirk Stikker, *Men of Responsibility* (New York: Harper and Row, 1965), p. 188.

2. Alan S. Milward, *The UK and the European Community,* vol. 1, *The Rise and Fall of a National Strategy, 1945–1963* (London: Cass, 2002), p. 75.

3. Quoted in Dirk Spierenburg and Raymond Poidevin, *The History of the High Authority of the European Coal and Steel Community: Supranationality in Operation* (London: Weidenfeld and Nicolson, 1994), p. 17.

4. Edmund Dell, *The Schuman Plan and the British Abdication of Leadership in Europe* (Oxford: Oxford University Press, 1995), p. 4.

5. Ibid., p. viii.

6. Hugo Young, *This Blessed Plot: Britain and Europe from Churchill to Blair* (Woodstock: Overlook, 1999), p. 69.

7. William Hitchcock, *France Restored: Cold War Diplomacy and the Quest for Leadership in Europe, 1944–1954* (Chapel Hill: University of North Carolina Press, 1998), p. 129.

8. Michael Hogan, *The Marshall Plan: America, Britain, and the Reconstruction of Western Europe, 1947–1952* (Cambridge: Cambridge University Press, 1987), p. 367.

9. Christopher Lord, *Absent at the Creation: Britain and the Formation of the European Community, 1950–1952* (Aldershot: Dartmouth, 1996).

10. See Alan Milward, *The Reconstruction of Western Europe, 1945–1951* (Berkeley: University of California Press, 1984), pp. 405–406.

11. On the negotiations that resulted in the European Coal and Steel Community, see John Gillingham, *Coal, Steel, and the Rebirth of Europe, 1945–1955* (Cambridge: Cambridge University Press, 2005); Klaus Schwabe, ed., *Die Anfänge des Schuman-Plans, 1950–1951* (Baden-Baden: Nomos, 1988); Raymond Poidevin, *Robert Schuman, homme d'état, 1886–1963* (Paris: Imprimerie Nationale, 1986), pp. 240–274; François Duchêne, *Jean Monnet: The First Statesman of Interdependence* (New York: Norton, 1994), pp. 207–220; Milward, *Reconstruction of Western Europe*, pp. 397–420; Spierenburg and Poidevin, *History of the High Authority*, pp. 9–43.

12. Alan Milward, *The European Rescue of the Nation State*, 2nd ed. (London: Routledge, 2000), pp. 82–83.

13. On the Dutch position, see Albert Kersten, "A Welcome Surprise? The Netherlands and the Schuman Plan Negotiations," in Schwabe, *Die Anfänge*, pp. 285–303.

14. Hans-Peter Schwarz, *Konrad Adenauer: A German Politician and Statesman in a Period of War, Revolution, and Reconstruction*, vol. 1, *From the German Empire to the Federal Republic, 1876–1952* (Oxford: Berghahn, 1995), p. 613.

15. On the Belgian case specifically, see Milward, *European Rescue of the Nation State*, pp. 64–83; M. Dumoulin, "La Belgique et les débuts du Plan Schuman (mai 1950–février 1952)," in Schwabe, *Die Anfänge*, pp. 271–284.

16. On the deconcentration issue, see Gillingham, *Coal, Steel, and the Rebirth of Europe*, pp. 255–262, 266–281; Thomas Alan Schwartz, *America's Germany: John J. McCloy and the Federal Republic of Germany* (Cambridge: Cambridge University Press, 1991).

17. De Gasperi was also a fluent speaker of German. Stikker tells the story of de Gasperi's first meeting with Schuman, in Paris: "As the Italian, who had been, just before the First World War, a member of the Austrian Parliament, struggled along in his heavily accented French, [Schuman], educated in Imperial Germany, spoke to him in German. 'Shall we try it in the mother tongue?' asked Schuman." Stikker, *Men of Responsibility*, p. 306.

18. Stikker, *Men of Responsibility*, pp. 304–305.

19. See, for instance, Alan Kramer, *The West German Economy, 1945–1955* (New York: Berg, 1991).

20. See Katja Seidel, *The Process of Politics in Europe: The Rise of European Elites and Supranational Institutions* (London: Tauris Academic, 2010).

21. William Diebold Jr., *The Schuman Plan: A Study in Economic Cooperation, 1950–1959* (New York: Praeger, 1959); Hans A. Schmidt, *The Path to European Union: From the Marshall Plan to the Common Market* (Baton Rouge: Louisiana State University Press, 1962); Ernst Haas, *The Uniting of Europe: Political, Social, and Economic Forces, 1950–1957* (Stanford: Stanford University Press, 1958).

22. See Gillingham, *Coal, Steel, and the Rebirth of Europe*, p. ix.

23. Duchêne, *Jean Monnet*, p. 214.

24. Robert Marjolin, *Memoirs, 1911–1986: Architect of European Unity* (London: Weidenfeld and Nicolson, 1986), p. 273.

25. Milward, *Reconstruction of Western Europe*, p. 418.

26. Gillingham, *Coal, Steel, and the Rebirth of Europe*, pp. 297–298.

27. Quoted in F. Roy Willis, *France, Germany, and the New Europe, 1945–*, revised and expanded ed. (Stanford: Stanford University Press, 1968), p. 130.

28. See Schwarz, *Konrad Adenauer*, vol. 1, p. 522.

29. On the EDC initiative and negotiations, see Edward Fursdon, *The European Defense Community: A History* (New York: St. Martin's, 1980); Hitchcock, *France Restored*, pp. 133–202; Daniel Lerner and Raymond Aron, eds., *France Defeats the EDC* (New York: Praeger, 1957); Kevin Ruane, *The Rise and Fall of the European Defense*

Community: Anglo-American Relations and the Crisis of European Defense, 1950–1955 (Basingstoke: Macmillan, 2000); David Clay Large, *Germans to the Front: West German Rearmament in the Adenauer Era* (Chapel Hill: University of North Carolina Press, 1996), pp. 111–204.

30. On Britain and the EDC, see Milward, *UK and the European Community*, vol. 1, pp. 78–125.

31. Schwarz, *Konrad Adenauer*, vol. 1, p. 652.

32. Jean Lacouture, *Pierre Mendès-France* (New York: Holmes and Meier, 1984), p. 268.

33. Charles de Gaulle, *Mémoires d'espoir, suivi d'un choix d'allocutions et messages sur la IVe et la Ve républiques* (Paris: Plon, 1994), p. 564.

34. The quotations are from Nathan Leites and Christian de la Malene, "Paris from EDC to WEU," *World Politics* 9, no. 2 (January 1957), pp. 193–219.

35. Lacouture, *Pierre Mendès-France*, p. 278.

36. See Fursdon, *European Defense Community*, p. 86.

37. On the Political Community, see Richard T. Griffiths, "Europe's First Constitution: The European Political Community, 1952–1954," in Stephen Martin, ed., *The Construction of Europe: Essays in Honor of Emile Noël* (Dordrecht: Kluwer, 1994), pp. 19–39.

38. These quotations are from Herbert W. Briggs, "The Proposed European Political Community," *American Journal of International Law* 48, no. 1 (January 1955), pp. 110–122.

39. Quoted in Lacouture, *Pierre Mendès-France*, p. 279.

40. Alfred Grosser, "France and Germany: A Confrontation," in Lerner and Aron, *France Defeats the EDC*, pp. 54–70.

41. Spierenburg and Poidevin, *History of the High Authority*, pp. 228–229.

42. See Schwarz, *Konrad Adenauer*, vol. 2, pp. 243–245.

43. See Richard T. Griffiths, "The Beyen Plan," in Griffiths, *The Netherlands and the Integration of Europe, 1945–1957* (Amsterdam: NEHA, 1990), pp. 165–182.

44. See Wendy Asbeek Brusse, *Tariffs, Trade, and European Integration, 1947–1957: From Study Group to Common Market* (New York: St. Martin's, 1997), pp. 143–184.

45. John Gunther, author of a popular book on Western Europe, pointed out that Euratom is pronounced "You're at 'em." Gunther, *Inside Europe Today* (New York: Harper and Brothers, 1961), p. 263.

46. Messina Declaration, available at http://www.let.leidenuniv.nl/history/rtg/res1/messina.htm.

47. See Walter Yondorf, "Monnet and the Action Committee: The Formative Years of the European Communities," *International Organization* 19 (1965), pp. 885–912; Duchêne, *Jean Monnet*, pp. 285–308; Pascal Fontaine, *Le Comité d'Action pour les États Unis d'Europe de Jean Monnet* (Lausanne: Centre de Recherches Européennes, 1974).

48. See Andrew Moravcsik, *The Choice for Europe: Social Purpose and State Power from Messina to Maastricht* (Ithaca: Cornell University Press, 1998), pp. 142–144.

49. See John W. Young, *Britain and European Unity, 1945–1999* (Basingstoke: Macmillan, 2000), pp. 26–52.

50. Milward, *UK and the European Community*, vol. 1, pp. 177–264.

51. On the Spaak committee and the subsequent intergovernmental conference, see Moravcsik, *Choice for Europe*, pp. 86–158; Jeffrey Glen Giauque, *Grand Designs and Visions of Unity: The Atlantic Powers and the Reorganization of Western Europe, 1955–1963* (Chapel Hill: University of North Carolina Press, 2002), pp. 23–33; Enrico Serra,

ed., *Il Rilancio dell'Europa e i Trattati di Roma* (Brussels: Bruylant, 1989); Anne Deighton, ed., *Building Postwar Europe: National Decision-Makers and European Institutions, 1948–1963* (New York: St. Martin's, 1995); "Laurent Warlouzet, France, and the Negotiations for the Treaty of Rome (1955–1957)," December 18, 2013, http://www.cvce.eu/content/publication/2008/3/18/b5e074bc-e1fa-486f-9c85-be1ebeffa806/publishable_en.pdf; Frances M. B. Lynch, *France and the International Economy: From Vichy to the Treaty of Rome* (London: Routledge, 1997); H. J. Küsters, *Die Gründung der europäischen Wirtschaftsgemeinschaft* (Baden-Baden: Nomos, 1982).

52. See, for instance, Hans Jurgen Küsters, "The Treaties of Rome," in Roy Pryce, ed., *The Dynamics of European Union* (London: Croom Helm, 1987), pp. 90–91.

53. On Mollet's pivotal role, see Craig Parsons, "Showing Ideas As Causes: The Origins of the European Union," *International Organization* 56, no. 1 (2002), pp. 47–84.

54. Uwe Kitzinger, "Europe: The Six and the Seven," *International Organization* 14, no. 1 (Winter 1960), p. 28.

55. Marjolin, *Memoirs*, pp. 284–297.

56. Rome Treaty, available at http://www.europa.eu.int/abc/obj/treaties/en/entoc05.htm.

57. Ibid.

58. See, for instance, Yondorf, "Monnet and the Action Committee," pp. 900–905.

3

Constructing the European Community

THE YEAR 1958 WAS NEWSWORTHY IN EUROPE NOT FOR THE BIRTH
of the European Economic Community (henceforth referred to as the European Community or the EC) but for two major political crises. One centered
on Berlin, the other on Paris. Soviet president Nikita Khrushchev provoked
the Berlin crisis by issuing an ultimatum to the three Western occupying powers, demanding a change in the city's status. Khrushchev's efforts to oust the
Western allies from Berlin, an enclave of Four Power control deep inside East
Germany, culminated in the Cuban missile crisis in 1962, which resulted almost in nuclear war. The Berlin and Cuban crises, as well as crises in the
Middle East and the Straits of Taiwan, caused a sharp drop in the temperature
of the Cold War and dominated international affairs in the EC's early years.

The French crisis was less far-reaching in its international implications
but had more impact on the EC. Only five months after the launch of the
Community, the French army mutinied in Algiers and threatened to over-
throw the government in Paris. That brought the unloved Fourth Republic to
an ignominious end. Reluctantly the French parliament granted Charles de
Gaulle, who had resigned as leader of the first postwar government in 1946
and had lived in self-imposed political exile ever since, extraordinary power
to rule unopposed for six months while drafting a new constitution. A large
majority of the French electorate endorsed the constitution, with its presidential system of government, in September 1958. De Gaulle duly became president. He resigned in 1969 following widespread student and worker protests
the previous year against the conservatism that he personified.

De Gaulle could have wrecked the EC at the outset. Instead he saved it
not only by rescuing France in the late 1950s but also by fending off a British
proposal for a rival free trade area and by sticking to the schedule for implementation of the customs union in the 1960s. The EC offered a means to
achieve key French economic objectives: industrial modernization and agri-

87

cultural subsidization. De Gaulle also saw the EC as a possible foundation for a Europe independent of the United States, stretching, in his famous phrase, from the Atlantic to the Urals (in western Russia). Britain's attachment to the United States and opposition to the emerging agricultural regime disqualified the country, in de Gaulle's mind, from joining the EC. Hence his celebrated vetoes of Britain's membership applications in 1963 and 1967.

De Gaulle had a more profound political impact on the emergent EC than on the wider international system. An avowed intergovernmentalist, in 1965 de Gaulle challenged the EC's supranationalist ethos by withdrawing French representation in the Council of Ministers, hoping to force other member states to curb the use of qualified majority voting. The ensuing constitutional crisis ended with an agreement not to call a vote in the Council when a member state claimed that important national interests were at stake, thereby enshrining the right to veto. The outcome of the crisis weakened the Commission's political authority and tilted decisionmaking in the Community in an intergovernmental direction for the foreseeable future.

Notwithstanding these developments, the 1960s was a good time to establish the EC. Gorging on cheap oil imports and engaging in greater international trade, Western Europe enjoyed high employment, low inflation, and unprecedented economic growth. In such a benign economic climate, member states completed the customs union in 1968, eighteen months ahead of schedule. Détente broke out in East-West relations and survived the shock of the Soviet intervention in Czechoslovakia in 1968.

This chapter examines the EC's early development, in the shadow of de Gaulle. The record was mixed. By the end of the 1960s the customs union and the common agricultural policy (CAP) were in place, although member states had not yet negotiated a permanent funding mechanism to cover agricultural expenditure. Despite de Gaulle's successful assault against qualified majority voting, supranationalism survived in other areas. In one of the most striking developments of the decade, the European Court issued a number of key rulings that buttressed the supranational character of the Community.

Setting Up Shop

The European Commission set up shop in Brussels in January 1958, in nondescript offices in the appropriately named Avenue de la Joyeuse Entrée. Walter Hallstein presided over a college of nine commissioners, two each from France, Germany, and Italy and one each from the Benelux countries. The number of commissioners matched the Community's range of responsibilities, so that each member had a weighty portfolio to manage. Most of the commissioners were either "political officials" (like Hallstein) or senior politicians. All had participated in various European initiatives and knew each other reasonably well.

The Hallstein Commission is generally seen in a glowing light. Its stature, compatibility, and competence are rarely questioned. Even before the Commission imploded during the constitutional crisis of 1965–1966, however, stresses and strains were evident in the college. Hallstein, a workaholic, was austere and aloof. Nobody doubted his commitment to the Community, knowledge of the Rome Treaty, or experience of European integration. Nobody doubted either that he was cold and lacked charisma. He was a good chairman but a poor chief. Hoping to cultivate a presidential style of leadership, he kept a greater distance from his colleagues and staff than would otherwise have been the case. Unmarried, he lived alone and rarely entertained. A minority of fellow commissioners shared Hallstein's fervent Eurofederalism. The rest knew that economic integration was a political endeavor but were not ideologically motivated.

As with any group of ambitious individuals, there were resentments and bureaucratic rivalries among the commissioners. Member states allocated portfolios on the basis of perceived national interests rather than the commissioners' abilities and experience. Some commissioners were unhappy with their lot; others were well suited to their portfolios. All fought for resources, which Hallstein allocated on the basis not of immediate needs but of the Community's anticipated activities. As a result, some busy departments were short of staff while others, not yet fully operational, were overstaffed.

Commissioners formed *cabinets* (private offices) and adopted other French administrative practices. Sensitive about being German, Hallstein tried hard to be French. The Commission's location in Brussels reinforced the use of the French language (it would have been politically incorrect to use German so soon after the war), and the appointment as secretary-general of Emile Noël, a senior French official, reinforced the use of French administrative norms. Commissioners met as a college once a week for an all-day session, prepared by their *chefs de cabinet*. The Commission established directorates-general (departments) corresponding to its main tasks and activities.[1]

Hallstein took responsibility for administrative affairs in the first Commission. Remembering the mess that Monnet had made of setting up the High Authority, Hallstein put his managerial experience in the German foreign office to good use. Unlike the High Authority, which had its own funds and immediate objectives to achieve, initially the Commission depended on the Council for money and had a more relaxed timetable for implementing the EC's main objectives.

Hallstein had a hand in the appointment of most of the Commission's early recruits, at least at the professional (administrative) level. He wanted a meritocracy but appreciated the political constraints on recruitment and promotion in an international organization such as the EC. With commissioners appointed on the basis of national affiliation, it would have been impossible to keep the Commission staff entirely free of national quotas, however informal.

Hallstein failed to prevent the establishment of national fiefdoms within the Commission, an almost inevitable by-product of informal quotas and often encouraged by governments. The most striking example was the lock that France established on the agriculture directorate-general.

Many of the Commission's staff came from national civil services; others came from the High Authority or straight from university (or from the College of Europe in Bruges). Idealism, adventure, and high remuneration attracted them. Initially there was little job security. The EC was a risky career choice. It looked in 1958 as if the Community might not last long, first because of the political crisis in France and then because of de Gaulle's hostility to supranationalism. Those who joined the Commission from national bureaucracies kept a right of return to their old jobs.

Despite initial uncertainty about the Commission's future, most of the pioneering officials looked back nostalgically on their first years of service. They lived a privileged life in Brussels, with high salaries, generous allowances, and distinctive license plates. They enjoyed working and socializing in an international milieu. As an early observer later recalled, "The Commission staff didn't just speak several languages; they joked in them, fought in them, made love in them. Speaking of making love, there were lots of European marriages in the early years. Germans married Italians and their children's first language was French. In the backyards of the suburbs surrounding Brussels lived a polyglot of people who were literally married to the European idea."[2]

The Commission introduced legislative proposals, took various policy initiatives, and became a lobbyist for further integration. The Commission came under attack in its early years from Wilhelm Röpke and other leading members of the conservative Mont Pèlerin Society (organized by Friedrich Hayek, the famous Austrian liberal economist). Röpke characterized the Commission as evil incarnate: namely, the institutionalization of state intervention at the European level. The EC, he claimed, was inherently protectionist. It would reverse the trend toward global liberalization and impose a planned economy on Europe.[3] By its nature the Commission was indeed more interventionist than liberal, but interventionist in the cause of the social-market economy. As the Commission remarked in its first action plan, "an economic order based on freedom can only exist in the world of today at the price of constant state intervention in economic life."[4] The liberal economists' fears of the common market were unfounded, except in the case of the CAP, although their onslaught may have helped to counteract a tendency in the Commission toward undue involvement in other policy areas.[5]

The Council of Ministers and the Committee of Permanent Representatives

The Council of Ministers came into existence in the form of the Interim Committee even before the official launch of the Community. The Interim

Committee met in late 1957 to consider the Community's approach to the General Agreement on Tariffs and Trade and to negotiations then in progress for a wider European free trade area. The Council proper held its first meeting in early January 1958, in Brussels, under the presidency of Belgium (the presidency rotated every six months in alphabetical order of the member states' official names, in their own language). The presidency's role was ill defined; at first it consisted mostly of chairing meetings. A small Council secretariat, recruited from national civil services but independent of national governments, served the presidency. Initially there were few Council formations (such as the foreign ministers or agriculture ministers), reflecting the Community's relatively limited competence. Foreign ministers (forming the General Affairs Council) met most frequently (only once a month). Originally the Council met in the new Palais de Congres before moving in the late 1960s to the Charlemagne building at Schuman Circle, a traffic roundabout at the heart of the new Community district.

Because of the need for continuity in relations between the Council and the Commission, national governments availed themselves of a provision in the treaty to establish a Committee of Permanent Representatives, made up of their most senior officials (at ambassador level). The committee, known by its French acronym, Coreper, met weekly to exchange national positions on Commission proposals and prepare Council meetings. The permanent representatives became key intermediaries between the Council and the Commission as well as between national governments and the Community. They spent the working week in Brussels promoting national positions, and weekends in their national capitals explaining Community developments. Each permanent representative headed an office, the Permanent Representation, staffed by officials from relevant national ministries. By the early 1960s, the big member states had staffs of forty or fifty officials in their Permanent Representations.

At first the Commission resented Coreper's existence. Commissioners wanted to deal with national ministers, not ambassadors. They feared, correctly, that Coreper would usurp some of the Council's decisionmaking authority. Because Coreper quickly became so important, the Commission had little choice but to come to terms with it. Commissioners soon swallowed their pride and attended Coreper meetings in order to explain and defend the Commission's positions.[6]

The history of the EC is really a history of meetings: meetings of the Commission, the Council, and Coreper; meetings of Council working groups, composed of national and Commission officials; meetings within the Commission of heads of divisions, directors, directors-general, *cabinet* members, and *chefs de cabinet;* meetings of national experts and Commission officials to discuss Commission ideas in the pre-proposal stage; meetings of officials and ministers in national capitals to consider Community developments; meetings among lobbyists and national and Community officials; and bilateral or multilateral meetings of ministers and national officials, often on the margins of other international meetings, to discuss Community affairs. As the Community consolidated its position in the early 1960s, the number and importance of these meetings grew proportionately.

The European Parliament

The history of the EC also included meetings of the European Parliament (EP), ranging from plenary sessions, to committee meetings, to the participation of members of the EP (MEPs) and their officials in meetings with representatives of other Community institutions, national governments, and interest groups. Initially the EP was relatively unimportant. It had little legislative authority, and its ability to dismiss the Commission, by a two-thirds majority, was as unusable as a nuclear weapon. Officially called the European Parliamentary Assembly, it was a combined institution of the Coal and Steel Community, Euratom, and the EC and had 142 members appointed by national governments from national parliaments (holders of the so-called dual mandate). The Rome Treaty obliged the EP to meet only once a year to hear a report on the Commission's activities. Like the ECSC's Common Assembly before it, the EP met in Strasbourg but held committee meetings in Brussels.

The EP attempted from the outset to assert itself and enhance its authority. It could, and did, meet more often than once a year. The EP held its first plenary session in March 1958, when members elected Robert Schuman president. In doing so, they honored one of the EC's founding fathers and asserted their independence from the Council, which wanted to have an Italian elected EP president because France, Germany, and the Benelux countries held the presidencies of the executive bodies of the three Communities.

Besides their willingness to confront national governments, parliamentarians sent a number of important signals during their first plenary session. One was a determination to press for direct elections, which the Rome Treaty provided for subject to a unanimous decision of the Council. Another was an interest in the Community's everyday affairs. Despite its limited legislative role, the EP established committees along functional lines to report on Commission proposals and Council decisions. The Commission indicated early on that it viewed the EP as an institutional ally and a potential source of legitimacy.[7]

Implementing the Customs Union and Fending Off the Free Trade Area

Taking the first step toward implementing the customs union—reducing intra-Community tariffs by 10 percent and increasing quotas by 20 percent in January 1959—assumed greater political than technical importance as the deadline approached. Would the new French government stick to the treaty timetable or, by letting the deadline slip, signal its lack of interest in the Community? Other national leaders, as well as the Commission, presumed that because de Gaulle disdained supranationalism, he also disdained the EC. Yet de Gaulle's economic and financial reforms since coming to office in June 1958 put France in a position materially to meet the January 1959 deadline. Indeed, domestic reform and external liberalization were inextricably linked in de Gaulle's approach with economic modernization. Much to the relief of its EC partners, France announced in late October 1958 that it would honor the treaty timetable.[8]

That approach was fully in accord with de Gaulle's longtime goal of revitalizing the French economy. Just as he had promoted Monnet, a supranationalist, to head the office for economic modernization in 1945, de Gaulle embraced the EC, a supranational organization, as the best means of pulling the French economy into the late twentieth century. Despite its supranationalist trappings, the EC offered something that France needed at the time and could not get elsewhere.

The other member states remained leery of France. The legalistic nature of France's announcement that it would honor the treaty suggested that de Gaulle was merely meeting an obligation, not fully embracing trade liberalization. The true test of de Gaulle's attitude would be his approach to the negotiations then taking place between the EC and the other members of the Organization for European Economic Cooperation to establish a free trade area. By pursuing a larger free trade area, de Gaulle could kill the EC without breaking any treaty obligations; by killing the free trade proposal, de Gaulle could demonstrate his commitment to the EC on more than legal grounds.

Britain had launched the idea of a free trade area in the mid-1950s, hoping that it would lure Germany and the Netherlands, with their lower tariffs and higher volumes of trade, away from the prospective EC.[9] With the imminent conclusion of the Rome Treaty, Britain proposed that the free trade area include the EC as a bloc. Britain and the other non-EC members of the OEEC therefore pressed for a free trade agreement by December 1958, the eve of the EC's first tariff cuts and quota increases. Otherwise, they argued, the EC's action would discriminate against them.

The proposal got a warm welcome in Germany from its economics minister, Ludwig Erhard, a longtime proponent of a free trade area, and in The Hague from a government instinctively sympathetic toward Britain. France, however, was opposed. Why should the government there accept a wider free trade area at the risk of jeopardizing the EC? An agreement acceptable to France would require broad coordination in a range of policy areas, strong institutions, and common rules. It would also need to include a special regime for agriculture, which Britain opposed.

Discussions came to a halt in April 1958 as the French Fourth Republic effectively ceased to function. The ministerial committee of the OEEC that was charged with exploring the idea did not meet again until July, after de Gaulle's return to power. The British then put their hopes in de Gaulle's well-known aversion to European integration. Instead, de Gaulle chose to implement the common market and end the negotiations on the free trade area. His decision made domestic political sense. As Miriam Camps observed at the time, "The opposition of French industry to a free trade area was fierce and articulate. . . . Virtually no one in France saw any appreciable economic advantage in the arrangement."[10]

Adenauer resisted pressure from Erhard to keep negotiating with Britain and sided with de Gaulle at their crucial first meeting, in September 1958. Two months later the French government announced its intention of formally ending the discussions. The Council of Ministers soon endorsed what became a Franco-German position. Here was an early example in EC history of the Franco-German axis at work. Paradoxically it was Erhard, the advocate of a free trade agreement, who informed the British officially of the EC's decision (Germany was then in the Council presidency).

British prime minister Harold Macmillan told the US administration that "the UK would organize a counter movement of their own and would have to reevaluate her position in NATO."[11] Britain followed through by inviting six other non-EC Western European countries (Austria, Denmark, Norway, Portugal, Sweden, and Switzerland) to open negotiations to establish a rival trade bloc, the European Free Trade Association (EFTA). This would not benefit Britain greatly, as Britain's economy dwarfed those of the other prospective EFTA members, and Scandinavian tariffs were already low. The main purpose of the proposal was to increase pressure on the EC to reopen negotiations for a free trade area. Britain hoped that the United States, concerned about a Europe "at Sixes and Sevens" (six EC members and seven prospective EFTA members) would twist the EC's arm.

Yet the United States disliked the idea of EFTA, which was much less advantageous economically than the EC. A common market had the potential for greater trade not only among EC member states but also between them and the United States. EU trade creation, the Americans thought, would far outweigh trade diversion. The United States also strongly supported the EC for political reasons, hoping that it would anchor West Germany firmly in Western Europe, strengthen Western Europe's ability to withstand Communist subversion and Soviet pressure, and stand shoulder to shoulder with the United States in a strong transatlantic community.[12]

Yet the United States was reluctant to oppose EFTA publicly. Only when negotiations to establish the new organization intensified did Washington lose patience with London. The United States held that a liberal Community trade policy and a successful round of GATT negotiations were the best solutions for all concerned. France, Germany, and the United States were in complete agreement. Even Erhard, surprised by the EC's liberal ori-

The EEC Six and the EFTA Seven

Notes: The EEC Six included the Netherlands, Belgium, Luxembourg, Germany, France, and Italy. The EFTA Seven included Norway, Sweden, Denmark, the United Kingdom, Switzerland, Austria, and Portugal.

entation in trade policy and impressed by strong US support for the EC, abandoned his initial support for a free trade area.

The United States finally took a stand at the end of 1959. Domestic pressure from business interests concerned about EFTA's emergence and about a possible proliferation of regional free trade areas around the world forced the US administration to act. The State Department hatched a plan to transform the OEEC into a broader economic organization that would include the United States, Canada, and possibly Japan. As the US secretary of state informed President Dwight Eisenhower in November 1959, this "would constitute an act of creative United States leadership in a recently deteriorating situation. It would greatly increase the opportunity of the United States to influence the makers of European economic policy in two directions—greater European development efforts and actions to compose European trade quarrels on a basis consistent with sound trade relations."[13] That was the genesis of the Organization for Economic Cooperation and Development (OECD), in which the proposal for a Western European–wide free trade area was finally buried.[14]

France and Germany readily accepted the US proposal; Britain did so grudgingly, holding fast to the idea that the EC was a protectionist bloc that would liberalize only under pressure from EFTA. Macmillan continued to warn about the possible consequences of an EFTA-EC split for Western European security and even threatened to withdraw British troops from Germany. A telegram to the US State Department from its embassy in London lamented the increasing number of "exaggerated and emotional statements" by the British prime minister on the EC, EFTA, and NATO.[15] Under the circumstances, Macmillan's about-face the following year, when Britain applied for EC membership, was truly remarkable.

The launch of the EC brought France, Germany, and the United States closer together on a range of economic issues and further alienated Britain. Fears about the impact of de Gaulle's return to power on the EC were so far unfounded. Despite France's reputation for economic protectionism and de Gaulle's hostility to supranationalism, the government of the new Fifth Republic had endorsed the EC's first tariff cuts and quota increases in 1959, opposed the free trade area, and supported a reasonably liberal commercial policy.

The development of the EC along lines congenial to the traditionally protectionist French was due to a number of factors. Political stability allowed France to undertake economic and financial reforms, but as the US embassy noted in January 1959, "some lever was required to gear internal corrective measures to world conditions and competition. That lever was supplied by the Common Market and its convenient deadline of January 1, 1959 for action on quotas and tariffs." Implementing the common market, suppressing the proposed free trade area, and supporting a liberal EC commercial policy, the US embassy observed, were clearly in the French national interest and were *"Gaulliste* in [the] fullest sense of the word."[16] Under the circumstances, the EC's prospects looked far brighter in 1960 than they had at the end of 1958.

The Common Agricultural Policy

At French insistence, the Six committed themselves in the Rome Treaty to establishing a common agricultural policy. Like most countries, France subsidized its farmers. By the late 1950s, France produced more food than the country could consume, but French agricultural products were not competitive internationally. France therefore wanted guaranteed high prices in an EC-wide market, subsidized through the Community budget, as well as export subsidies to close the gap between higher internal EC prices and lower prices in world markets.[17]

That set France on a collision course with two countries: Germany and the United States. Germany had fewer farmers than France (about 15 percent as opposed to 23 percent of the total population). Germany subsidized its farmers too, but German farmers could never produce enough to feed the entire German population. France longed to make up the difference, but French exports could not compete with cheaper exports from other countries, including the United States. US farmers did not want to be excluded from Germany and other EC markets by a French-inspired CAP.

France also clashed with the Commission over agricultural policy. Despite its commitment to a *common* agricultural policy, implying shared sovereignty and Commission supremacy, France and other member states were reluctant to relinquish responsibility for agriculture entirely to the Commission. At the instigation of France, governments set up a standing committee of national representatives in Brussels, the Special Committee on Agriculture, to deal with the Commission on the CAP. Unlike the permanent representatives, who reported to the foreign ministers and therefore had an ecumenical outlook on EC affairs, members of the agriculture committee reported to the agriculture ministers, a notoriously parochial group who were firmly under the thumb of national agricultural lobbies.

De Gaulle had to work with the Commission in order to realize the CAP (under the terms of the Rome Treaty, the Commission proposed and implemented policy). But de Gaulle rejected supranationalism and distrusted Sicco Mansholt, the commissioner for agriculture and an ardent Eurofederalist. That set the scene for a power struggle between France and the Commission over the CAP, with each side needing but distrusting the other.

The struggle did not begin until 1960, when the Commission submitted a CAP proposal followed by various draft regulations on specific products. The challenge for the Commission was to devise Community-wide organizations of agricultural markets that would guarantee farmers a decent living but not generate excessive surpluses, cost too much, and alienate the Community's trading partners. It proved an impossible task. On the one hand, the Commission wanted to base the CAP as much as possible on free-market principles; on the other, the Commission endorsed market intervention, including fixed prices and guaranteed sales for basic products and a system of levies on agricultural imports based on the difference between lower world prices and higher Community prices. The cost of the CAP would depend to a great extent on who set the price levels. Being susceptible to pressure from farmers, the Council would likely set high prices; the Commission, less susceptible to such pressure, would likely set lower prices. As a compromise, the Commission proposed that the Council set general price guidelines within which the Commission would determine precise prices per product.[18]

France pushed for an interventionist CAP with a greater role for the Council than the Commission wanted. Germany was divided on the issue. Erhard and other economic liberals protested that the proposed CAP was too protectionist; the agriculture ministry and farm lobby protested that it was not protectionist enough and would lower German farm incomes. Prevailing prices in Germany were higher than in France, but were too high to be adopted on a Community-wide basis. De Gaulle raised the stakes by announcing in June 1961 that France would block transition to the second stage of the customs union at the end of the year unless the Council reached agreement on the CAP by that time.[19] De Gaulle also impressed upon Adenauer the importance of the CAP for harmonious Franco-German relations, one of the chancellor's key foreign policy objectives.

A series of legendary Council meetings ensued between mid-December 1961 and mid-January 1962. Technically they ended successfully at midnight on December 31, thereby allowing progress on the common market. The agricultural negotiations were really between France and Germany, whose representatives often met separately on the margins of the Council before presenting their colleagues with a fait accompli. Germany went along with France for the sake of the industrial customs union (a greater economic prize for Germany than an agricultural common market) and good Franco-German relations (an overriding strategic objective).

The United States also acquiesced in the CAP for the sake of further European integration, over the objections of US farmers and their political supporters, who feared being shut out of the lucrative European market. The issue became increasingly acrimonious as the CAP was put in place. Karl Brandt, of the US Council of Economic Advisers, warned in September 1960 that the EC "must refrain from agricultural autarky. . . . [T]he situation is extremely dangerous because it is politically most difficult to unlodge the agricultural interests from their new protectionist position in the [EC] once they have entrenched themselves in it. . . . The European farm organizations, particularly in France and Germany, are past masters in the riot techniques and all sorts of revolutionary pressure tactics."[20] Brandt wanted the United States to end its "kid-glove tactfulness" and apply all possible pressure on the Europeans to abandon the CAP. On his return from a trip to Europe in November 1962, US agriculture secretary Orville Freeman complained bitterly about the CAP to President John Kennedy, lamenting that "the French are intractable."[21]

The situation was especially embarrassing for the US administration as it promoted the Trade Expansion Act in 1962. Although the administration touted the act as a means of dealing with the economic challenge of the EC by enhancing the president's authority to negotiate trade agreements, it accepted the implementation in Europe of a trade-distorting CAP. The United States had little choice but to sacrifice economic goals for political ends. William Diebold, a trade specialist who observed the construction of the CAP, reminisced years later that there was "much sweet reason in what American officials said to their European colleagues" about the discriminatory aspects of the CAP, "but the situation was thought to be delicate and there were [limits] to what the Americans were willing to do as they accepted the argument that a common agricultural policy was essential to the integration of the Community."[22]

The "Chicken War" of 1962–1963 set a pattern for transatlantic trade relations in the context of the CAP. The dispute erupted in July 1962 when the EC's import regime for poultry came into effect. Whereas US exporters had previously faced a German tariff of around 4.5 cents per pound, they now faced an EC import levy of about 13.5 cents per pound. The increase caused an immediate drop in US sales, sending farmers and politicians on the warpath. Although poultry exports to Germany represented a fraction of overall US-EC trade, the dispute generated considerable publicity. Hostilities ended when both sides accepted the opinion of a special GATT panel, delivered in November 1963, that upheld US complaints but recommended less compensation than the United States demanded. The EC tacitly acknowledged that the poultry regime, and the CAP in general, was discriminatory; the United States lost market share but won some compensation; and agricultural disputes became a fact of life in a US-EC relationship driven by broader political and economic interests.[23]

The CAP, British Accession, and Grand Designs

Agriculture, Britain's application for EC membership, and contending designs for Europe's future combined to produce the first major setback in the EC's history when de Gaulle vetoed Britain's application in January 1963. In a remarkable change of policy toward the Community, Britain applied to join in August 1961. Britain needed easy access to Western European markets and could get it only by entering the EC. Neither the Commonwealth nor EFTA was an adequate alternative. Sensitive to domestic concerns about possible loss of sovereignty, Macmillan played down the political implications of accession, treating it as an exclusively economic affair.[24]

Britain's application coincided with the launch by the new Kennedy administration of a Grand Design for transatlantic relations. The United States sought to organize transatlantic relations along more equitable lines in order to mollify Europeans' resentment of its preponderant power and strengthen the alliance's political cohesion. Thus the United States wanted a strong EC to emerge as part of a stronger Western Europe, which in turn would strengthen the Atlantic alliance.[25] In Kennedy's famous words, the transatlantic partnership would bind the United States and Europe "on a basis of full equality in all the great and burdensome tasks of building and defending a community of free nations."[26]

Commission president Hallstein's design for Europe and for transatlantic relations complemented that of the United States. Speaking in New York, Hallstein compared the histories of US federalism and European integration. "By its very nature," Hallstein observed, "the Community must be an ever-growing, ever-developing organism. . . . Essentially, [it] may be described as a federation in the making. . . . History is on our side." He subscribed fully to the idea of transatlantic partnership at the core of the Grand Design, an idea that sought to harness "one giant with a number of comparative dwarfs [in] a new system which joins in partnership . . . twin units [that] today are already comparable and which one day will be equal."[27]

De Gaulle had a radically different understanding of history and a competing vision of European union and transatlantic partnership. He envisioned a Europe based on intergovernmentalism rather than supranationalism; a "Europe of the states" rather than a federal Europe; and a Europe genuinely equal with the United States in NATO rather than militarily subservient to Washington.[28] Britain shared de Gaulle's antipathy toward supranationalism but shared Washington's vision of the transatlantic relationship, a vision that sought to hide US hegemony behind a facade of Euro-American equality.[29]

Britain was an important element in the Grand Design of the United States. But the United States viewed Britain's nonmembership in the EC, the nucleus of a uniting Europe, as politically awkward. The Americans were therefore pleased when Britain signaled in early 1961 its intention to apply for EC membership. The decision would have to be Britain's alone. As US undersecretary of state George Ball emphasized in May 1961, France would portray US support for British membership in the EC as an "Anglo-Saxon conspiracy."[30]

Behind the scenes, the United States wanted Britain to join the EC without reservation: Britain should embrace supranationalism, accept the CAP, and not try to negotiate concessions for the Commonwealth and EFTA.[31] The United States presumed that EC enlargement would benefit

US industrial exporters, by expanding the already sizable EC market. British membership would also help orient the EC's trade policy in a liberal direction. Nevertheless, agricultural exporters would lose out because of the emerging CAP. Despite US and British concerns about agricultural policy, there is no indication that Washington pushed London to join the EC in order to wreck the CAP from the inside.

The Americans assumed (as did the British) that de Gaulle would not look favorably on Britain's application. American doubts about French intentions were not dispelled when de Gaulle told Kennedy in June 1961 that "his position towards British membership is either/or; either full, or none."[32] Belgian foreign minister Paul-Henri Spaak, who carried considerable weight in Washington, told Ball in February 1962 that "on balance de Gaulle did not want the British in, as it might threaten France's leading role in the Community."[33]

The Fouchet Plan

The EC was germane to de Gaulle's as well as to Kennedy's geopolitical designs. Between 1959 and 1962, de Gaulle made two proposals to promote European political union. The first was for foreign policy cooperation among the Six, supported by a secretariat in Paris. The second was a more ambitious initiative, launched in September 1960, for regular meetings of national leaders to direct intergovernmental cooperation on political, economic, cultural, and defense matters. De Gaulle linked his proposal with separate calls for NATO reform.[34]

Representatives of the Six, meeting under the chairmanship of French ambassador Christian Fouchet, worked on the proposal in 1961 and early 1962. A number of delegations were suspicious of de Gaulle's intentions. The Dutch and the Belgians, in particular, were wary of possible French or Franco-German hegemony in the EC and of the possible impact of de Gaulle's plans on NATO. The negotiations veered between near-agreement and near-collapse for more than a year, depending on the issue in question. Finally, the Dutch refused to carry on until Britain was invited to take part, a demand that de Gaulle refused to concede. When the talks collapsed, de Gaulle turned his strategic attention to bilateral relations with Germany and unilateral action in NATO.

The United States had been surprisingly sanguine about the proposed Fouchet Plan. Monnet, who remained influential in Washington, reassured US officials. He was generally optimistic about the EC's prospects and was confident that Britain would soon join. (We now know that Monnet and de Gaulle drew up a secret memorandum in October 1960 in which Monnet agreed to support the Fouchet Plan and de Gaulle promised to maintain the integrity of the Rome Treaty.)[35] If Monnet, an arch-supranationalist, was not concerned about de Gaulle's motives, then surely Washington need not be either. But Spaak warned Ball in November 1961 that the United States should not be complacent; that the French proposals were "not a step toward political unification, but [were] actually retrogressive."[36] Ultimately, the United States relied on the ability of the other EC member states to keep de Gaulle in check.

Yet Adenauer's susceptibility to de Gaulle's influence caused some disquiet in the United States. Adenauer was trying to strike a balance between Paris and Washington. Although Germany depended on the United States for its security, Adenauer had doubts about America's military commitment during the Berlin crises of 1958–1962. By contrast, de Gaulle had supported Germany unreservedly. But Adenauer surely knew that France could not substitute militarily for the United States.

Regardless of military security, de Gaulle hoped that Adenauer would go along with his efforts to organize Europe along intergovernmental rather than supranational lines. Adenauer's difficulty lay in reconciling de Gaulle's vision of Europe with the Grand Design of the United States, and in allaying domestic concern that he was alienating Washington by embracing de Gaulle. The collapse of the Fouchet Plan got Adenauer off the hook, in Washington and in Bonn, at least until de Gaulle turned his attention to developing the Franco-German axis as the basis for what he called his "European Europe."[37]

The question of Britain's EC application was also bothersome for Adenauer, who disliked Macmillan (the feeling was mutual) and distrusted the British, especially because of their vacillation during the Berlin crises. Nevertheless, Adenauer saw the advantage of British membership in the EC. He knew that the United States wanted Britain to join, but that de Gaulle was equivocal, to say the least. Erhard strongly supported British membership for both economic reasons (market access) and political reasons (pro-American and anti–de Gaulle), and feared that Adenauer was veering too much in de Gaulle's direction.

De Gaulle Says No

In December 1962, Kennedy and Macmillan struck a deal in Nassau to provide US missiles for Britain's nominally independent nuclear force. De Gaulle saw this as further evidence of British subservience to the United States. Given Washington's oft-stated objective of building an Atlantic partnership on the foundation of the EC, and de Gaulle's opposition to the kind of partnership envisioned by the United States, the Nassau agreement demonstrated to de Gaulle the potential political difficulties that Britain's EC membership could pose for France.

The Nassau agreement could not have come at a worse time for Britain's EC prospects. The enlargement negotiations in Brussels were at a critical stage.[38] The British would not, or could not, drop their long-standing misgivings and accept the Rome Treaty wholeheartedly. They remained skeptical of supranationalism (a skepticism that de Gaulle shared), committed to the

Commonwealth, and attached to an agricultural system that was incompatible with the emerging CAP.

The CAP may well have precipitated de Gaulle's rejection of Britain's membership application, planned in late 1962 and announced in dramatic fashion at a press conference in Paris in January 1963. Whereas de Gaulle was able to pressure or cajole current member states to accept his agricultural proposals, he would have faced formidable—perhaps insurmountable—opposition if Britain, with its radically different agricultural interests and considerable political clout, acceded to the EC before the CAP was fully in place. That was the gist of de Gaulle's well-rehearsed answer to a prearranged question at the press conference, which amounted to a veto of Britain's application.[39]

France followed up by formally opposing British membership at a Council meeting at the end of January 1963, prompting the Six to end the accession negotiations. The other member states protested de Gaulle's abruptness and unilateralism. Given de Gaulle's personality and previous behavior, they cannot have been too surprised. In an indirect dig at de Gaulle, Hallstein wrote that the Community should not allow itself "to be subject to . . . those older methods [in international relations] of hegemony . . . reprisal, and blackmail."[40] Yet even Hallstein appreciated that British membership might not have been in the EC's immediate interest. Arguably, the EC survived the shock of de Gaulle's veto better than it would have survived the shock of British accession, which would have brought into the emerging EC a large member state that was strongly opposed to core Community principles and policies.

Britain took de Gaulle's rebuff as a national affront. The political consequences of the veto were indeed profound. Macmillan, personally slighted by de Gaulle, soon resigned, ostensibly on grounds of ill health. He was the first of many political casualties of Britain's involvement with the EC.

The Elysée Treaty

De Gaulle and Adenauer signed a treaty on Franco-German cooperation in the Elysée Palace at the end of January 1963, a week after the notorious press conference in which de Gaulle rejected Britain's candidacy.[41] Following the failure of the Fouchet negotiations, de Gaulle envisioned the treaty as an alternative approach to political union. The Commission, the small member states, and Italy worried more about the implications of the new treaty than about de Gaulle's veto of British membership. Already suspicious of the emerging Franco-German axis, they feared that the treaty would institutionalize Franco-German hegemony in the EC. Hallstein thought that Adenauer was entirely under de Gaulle's influence. Having once been close, Hallstein and Adenauer now differed fundamentally on the EC's political prospects.

The United States saw a link between de Gaulle's press conference and the Elysée Treaty. In his press conference, de Gaulle rejected British membership in the EC, an intrinsic element of Washington's Grand Design. In the Elysée Treaty, he tried to tie Germany to a rival French design for Europe. Adenauer attempted to assuage the Americans, arguing that the Elysée Treaty would not undermine German support for European integration and Atlantic partnership. After all, a treaty of Franco-German friendship was fully in accord with the postwar European policies of both Germany and the United States.

Those reassurances were not enough for the Americans or for Adenauer's domestic critics. The United States took comfort in the resolution passed by the German parliament and attached to the treaty, affirming Germany's commitments to the EC, NATO, and the GATT. The resolution humiliated Adenauer and infuriated de Gaulle. Adenauer's resignation later in 1963 and Erhard's appointment as chancellor ended the ascendancy of the German Gaullists in Bonn and brought German-US relations back to an even keel.

The events of January 1963 left a lasting impression in Washington, where mention of de Gaulle's name was enough to incite invective in the White House and State Department (not to mention the Pentagon). Ball, an avid Eurofederalist, could barely contain himself. "Never at any time since the war," he wrote to President Kennedy in June 1963, "has Europe been in graver danger of back-sliding into the old destructive habits—the old fragmentation and national rivalries that have twice brought the world to disaster in the past." What was to blame? "[T]he halting, and at least momentary reversal, of the drive toward unity in Europe. This has come about, as the whole world knows, from [de Gaulle's] abrupt reassertion of old-style competitive nationalism . . . [and] assault on the structure of European unity."[42]

Ball's fears were unfounded. The Fifth Republic was more stable than any regime in modern French history and remained so after de Gaulle's departure. The process of European integration was not thrown irrevocably off-course in 1963. Even without de Gaulle it is doubtful that the EC would have moved at the time in a more federal direction. De Gaulle's quest for *grandeur* continued to pit Paris and Washington against each other, notably on NATO and nuclear issues.[43] But the EC was no longer a battleground for competing French and US visions of Europe. Nor, despite these political problems, did the EC falter economically. The customs union remained on track, and other policies were gradually put in place.

The Empty Chair Crisis and the Luxembourg Compromise

No sooner did the dust settle in 1963 than another, more serious, dispute appear on the horizon. It began over Commission proposals for a new financial arrangement for the CAP for the period after July 1965, when the current system of national contributions would expire. In 1970, following completion of the final stage of the transition to the customs union, the EC was supposed to acquire its "own resources," consisting of duties from agricultural and industrial imports, from which the CAP would be permanently funded. With the advent of own resources, the Dutch wanted a transfer of budgetary power from national parliaments to the EP in order to counterbalance the transfer of moneys from national budgets to the EC's budget. In the process, the Commission might also acquire additional authority. Eager for those institutional changes, Hallstein wanted to bring the advent of own resources forward to 1965, in place of another interim financing measure. Hallstein knew that de Gaulle opposed giving more power to the EP and the Commission, but he also knew that de Gaulle wanted the introduction of own resources, which would greatly reduce the financial burden on France.

Presuming that de Gaulle would trade a desirable financial outcome for an undesirable political one, Hallstein introduced his budgetary proposals in April 1965. At first the issue took on the character of a personal battle between Hallstein and de Gaulle. In a celebrated passage in his memoirs, de Gaulle dismissed Hallstein as "first of all a German who is ambitious for his Fatherland."[44] Yet de Gaulle was an unapologetic nationalist, whereas Hallstein considered himself the personification of European postnationalism. Hallstein relished the trappings of power (the title "president," the diplomatic niceties, the red carpet) not for personal aggrandizement (or so he said), but because he wanted to establish the Commission's political preeminence. De Gaulle scorned Hallstein's posturing. The president of the French Republic dismissed the president of the European Commission as an upstart and the Commission itself as a collection of stateless technocrats. Hallstein's greatest weakness, de Gaulle knew, was that the Commission president was appointed, not elected.

Politically isolated, Hallstein had few friends in the national capitals, least of all in Bonn, where Erhard was now the chancellor. Erhard could not come out publicly against Hallstein, but made his position crystal clear. Hallstein backed down even before the fateful Council meeting of June 1965. Other member states, equally unhappy with the Commission's original proposal, wanted instead to negotiate another temporary financial arrangement for the CAP. Such a negotiation would be difficult and time-consuming and might not finish by the stipulated deadline of midnight on June 30, 1965. But there was ample precedent for continuing to negotiate after the deadline while technically reaching agreement on-time by "stopping the clock." The Five presumed that this is what would happen during the Council meeting that began on June 28.

France Walks Out

De Gaulle had other ideas. Claiming that his partners had violated their commitment to conclude a new financial arrangement by the agreed deadline, Maurice Couve de Murville, de Gaulle's foreign minister and president-in-office of the Council, abruptly ended the meeting in the early hours of July 1, 1965. France then withdrew its representation from the Council but pointedly continued to participate in routine Community business.[45]

De Gaulle did not spell out the seriousness of the situation until September 1965, when he held a typically imperious press conference. Following a diatribe against the Commission, de Gaulle declared his unwillingness to accept provisions permitting the use of qualified majority voting in a range of new policy areas that were due to come into force in January 1966. De Gaulle had two objections: on principle he refused to countenance qualified majority voting, which smacked of supranationalism; in practice he feared the impact of qualified majority voting on French agricultural and trade interests, lest a coalition of liberal member states alter the CAP and thwart French efforts to protect agriculture in the GATT. De Gaulle threatened to continue the boycott until member states agreed upon a new financial regulation for the CAP, the Commission curbed its political ambition, and provisions for more use of qualified majority voting were dropped from the Rome Treaty.

It is difficult to disentangle principle and pragmatism in de Gaulle's conduct of the ensuing crisis. As in other case studies of de Gaulle's policy toward the Community, Andrew Moravcsik argued that pragmatism triumphed over principle; that de Gaulle was much more concerned with protecting the CAP than scuttling supranationalism.[46] Undoubtedly de Gaulle was preoccupied with the CAP, but the extension of qualified majority voting in 1966 would not necessarily have been detrimental to French interests. Provisions existed before 1966 to use qualified majority voting in certain policy areas. Even so, governments were reluctant to outvote each other on issues that were politically sensitive. An unwritten rule had already emerged whereby decisions in the Council were generally taken by consensus. Presumably this would have continued after 1966, regardless of a government's right to call for a vote in a greater number of policy areas. Yet the fact that de Gaulle objected to the extension of qualified majority voting in 1965, when it would cover agricultural and trade policy, rather than in 1961, when it was first introduced, shows the extent of his concern about the CAP.

The other member states had no intention of renegotiating the Rome Treaty. While also aware of the possibly negative consequences of qualified majority voting, they would not succumb to de Gaulle's political blackmail. As with his veto of Britain's membership application, the Five strongly resented de Gaulle's intemperate oratory and unilateral action. They resolved to stand together, but not with the Commission. Spaak, a supranationalist and no friend of de Gaulle's, called for an extraordinary meeting of the Council to resolve the standoff. The meeting was extraordinary in that it was out of sequence and the Commission was not invited to participate.

Both Erhard and de Gaulle faced elections in late 1965. The crisis hardly affected the German contest but dominated the French one—the first European election in which the EC was a central issue. German business and agricultural interests strongly supported Erhard's handling of the crisis. Erhard's relatively easy victory allowed the new chancellor finally to move out of Adenauer's shadow and stand up to de Gaulle. French business and agricultural interests, by contrast, criticized de Gaulle's handling of the crisis. Farmers especially feared that de Gaulle's antics would destroy the CAP, although de Gaulle was arguably trying to protect the CAP against the possible vagaries of qualified majority voting. De Gaulle suffered a sharp rebuff in the election, failing to win the first round outright and winning the second round by a smaller margin than expected.

Ending the Crisis

De Gaulle liked to think that he was above populist politics; that he was a leader, not a follower; that he was not beholden to the electorate. Yet the result of the December 1965 presidential election shocked de Gaulle, as did the continuing hostility of farming and business interests to his handling of the crisis. The result also emboldened the Five, who remained united in opposition to de Gaulle's assault on the Community system.

The Five made little headway at the Council meeting in Luxembourg in mid-January 1966 (de Gaulle objected to holding the meeting in Brussels, the Commission's home town). Couve reiterated French objections to qualified majority voting and requested a written agreement among member states to use unanimity in the Council when key national interests were at risk. He also presented a ten-point document on the Commission's behavior and future relations with the Council. A series of bilateral discussions followed, leading to a second extraordinary Council meeting at the end of January. It was there that the Six hammered out the Luxembourg Compromise, according to which, when "very important interests are at stake," the Council would refrain from taking a decision by qualified majority vote.[47] In effect, the Luxembourg Compromise acknowledged a government's right to veto legislative proposals. With that, France agreed to take its seat again in the Council.

Member states also approved a code of conduct for the Commission that went some way toward meeting French demands. The Five successfully defended the Commission's exclusive right of legislative initiative but agreed with France on reducing the Commission's political profile. Hallstein faced an uncertain future. De Gaulle detested him, and the German government offered only lukewarm support. Wisely, Hallstein announced in May 1967 that he would soon step down.

Resolution of the crisis cleared the way for negotiation of a new financial arrangement for the CAP. Member states reached agreement at two marathon (but otherwise orthodox) meetings of the Council, in May and

July 1966. As part of the deal, France agreed to a German request that all remaining intra-EC tariffs on industrial goods be abolished by July 1968, when the common external tariff would take effect. Thus the customs union would come into being eighteen months ahead of schedule. The agreement on the CAP and the customs union allowed the EC to relaunch the Kennedy Round of the GATT, which had run aground during the crisis.

The outcome of the crisis looked like a victory for the Community: the Rome Treaty was intact, the Five stood as one, France took its seat again in the Council, and the Six soon reached agreement on completing the CAP and the customs union. The adverse effects of the crisis soon became apparent, however, with the Commission becoming less assertive and ambitious, and the Council increasingly resembling a forum for traditional intergovernmental negotiation. Taking a lead from France, other governments grew less reticent about asserting their national interests.

Qualified majority voting was used in the Council after 1966, perhaps even more so than before, but not on politically sensitive issues. Governments rarely invoked the Luxembourg Compromise: it was enough for them to hint that an important national interest was at stake in order to prevent a vote from being taken. Because there was no objective measure of what constituted an important national interest, governments used the term loosely, often under domestic pressure. The Luxembourg Compromise therefore cast a long shadow over legislative decisionmaking and elevated the national veto to a sacrosanct principle.

A Decade of European Community Integration

The tenth anniversary of the Rome Treaty, in March 1967, was a somber affair. Governments marked the occasion two months later with a meeting of national leaders in the Eternal City. As the only head of state present (the other leaders were prime ministers), de Gaulle was ceremonially supreme. More than six feet tall, he dominated the affair, both literally and figuratively. By then the world's most senior and best-known statesman, he was the center of political and media attention.

De Gaulle came to Rome not to bury the treaty but not to praise it either. There were perfunctory discussions about political union and enlargement, but it was clear that the other member states were treading water until de Gaulle left office. Hallstein stayed in the background. In a classic display of personal pique, de Gaulle insisted on relegating the Commission president to second-class citizenship at the anniversary event.[48]

Despite the heavy atmosphere in the aftermath of the empty chair crisis, the EC continued to conduct a remarkable amount of business. Indeed, in its first ten years of existence the EC weathered a number of political storms and accomplished impressive institutional and policy goals. These ranged from consolidating the EC's institutional architecture, to putting various internal policies in place, to concluding bilateral and multilateral agreements with diverse international interlocutors.

Institutional Accomplishments

In the wake of the empty chair crisis, the Commission was eclipsed. Morale sagged not only in the college but also in the Commission's services. Nevertheless the wide scope of Community activity kept Commission officials busy. The Commission established new directorates-general throughout the 1960s to reflect real or anticipated increases in Community responsibility. Although many Commission officials fervently believed in Eurofederalism, by the late 1960s enthusiasm for "building Europe" was giving way to a degree of apathy and careerism. By the late 1960s the Commission was a singular international bureaucracy, but not a truly supranational one.[49]

The Commission faced a particular administrative challenge in the late 1960s: implementation of the Merger Treaty (fusing the executive bodies of the three Communities). Some advocates of European integration hoped that this event, envisioned in the Rome Treaty, would boost the Commission's fortunes. France thought otherwise, and few of its partners advocated strengthening the Commission's powers against de Gaulle's wishes. Instead of discussing the Commission's role, the short intergovernmental conference that presaged the Merger Treaty dealt almost exclusively with administrative details. It took the newly merged Commission some time to overcome the organizational and cultural challenges of fusing three distinct bureaucracies. For an interim period between 1967, when the treaty came into effect, and 1970, when its provisions were fully implemented, the college of the Commission had fourteen instead of the usual nine members.[50]

The EP, which also suffered a setback at de Gaulle's hands, displayed a resilience and ingenuity characteristic of its development throughout the EC's history.[51] Most MEPs were strongly pro-integration (few Euroskeptical members of national parliaments put themselves forward for appointment to the Strasbourg assembly). MEPs resented their limited legislative role (their institution could give only nonbinding opinions on draft legislation) and pushed for greater power. Thus, MEPs passed numerous resolutions in the 1960s on a wide range of policy and procedural issues, and managed to insinuate themselves into areas from which the EP was originally excluded.

The European Court of Justice, the EC's third "supranational" institution, developed slowly but strikingly in the 1960s. The evolution of EC law was one of the least obvious but most important advances in European integration at the time. In two landmark cases, in 1963 and 1964, the Court promulgated the key principles on which Community law rests: direct effect and supremacy. In *Van Gend en Loos* (1963), a Dutch trucking firm brought a case against Dutch customs for raising the duty on a product imported from Germany, in breach of the Rome Treaty's common market provisions. Declaring that the EC "constitutes a new legal order of international law for the benefit of which the states have limited their sovereign rights," the Court ruled that the Dutch firm was indeed protected by the direct effect of Community law. The following year, in *Costa v. ENEL,* a case involving Italy's national electricity supplier, the Court upheld the supremacy of EC law over national law. As member states had definitively transferred sovereign rights to the Community, EC law could not be overruled by national law without the legal basis of the Community itself being called into question.[52]

These were audacious rulings by a new international court, especially in the prevailing climate of Gaullist intergovernmentalism. Governments knew what the rulings portended. Even the most Community-minded of them submitted statements to the Court arguing against direct effect and supremacy, rightly fearing that the Court's rulings would undermine national control of the integration process.[53] Governments may have thought that the two principles were unenforceable without the support of national courts, which would surely be more responsive to public opinion and more attached to national legal prerogatives. If so, member states misjudged the situation. Far from trying to fend off the encroachment of Community law, national courts worked closely with the Court of Justice in subsequent decades to implement the principles of direct effect and supremacy.[54]

Internal Policy Developments

The EC made considerable progress in the 1960s in policy areas subject to precise provisions in the Rome Treaty, such as the customs union, or to intense pressure from a powerful member state, such as the CAP, but made little progress in areas covered only generally by the treaty or of interest primarily to less influential member states. Nontariff barriers (such as different national rules on product standards) remained a major obstacle to the free movement of goods, a cornerstone of the customs union. The Commission began the laborious process of harmonizing national regulations, but soon ran into resistance, with many proposals languishing in working groups and never reaching the Council for a decision. Workers had the right to employment anywhere in the Community, on paper at least. Similarly, citizens of one member state could set up businesses and provide services in another member state, although governments dragged their feet on the harmonization of relevant national laws.

Big business generally welcomed the emergence of the common market, despite its imperfections. According to Hans von der Groeben, "Entrepreneurs were convinced of the project's potential: they procured the necessary equipment and labor ready for the enlarged market, invested appropriately and established trade connections with the other Member

States."[55] US multinationals eagerly exploited new opportunities in the European marketplace. Indeed, European businesses complained that US multinationals were better-placed and better-prepared than European companies to operate in a larger economic space.

The Union of Industrial Federations, one of the earliest and most powerful interest groups in Brussels, also complained that the Commission's ethos and activities were not friendly to European business.[56] Private enterprises were wary of competition policy rules that prevented restrictive agreements or abuse of dominant position. Governments complained about another branch of competition policy, one that sought to control "state aids" (public subsidies) and liberalize "regulated industries" (companies either owned by or having a special relationship with governments). Backed by the European Court of Justice, the Commission took a number of tough competition policy decisions, although increasing intergovernmentalism in the late 1960s inevitably curbed the Commission's willingness to confront flagrant violations by governments and national champions (big businesses closely associated with governments). Nevertheless, the Commission and the Court succeeded in the 1960s in establishing the principle, if not yet the practice, of a full-fledged Community-wide competition policy.[57]

Transport was an area where the EC made little progress. The Rome Treaty called for a common transport policy, without specifying a schedule. Only the Netherlands, home to Europe's largest seaport and having the most competitive truckers in the EC, as well as lower fuel prices and vehicle taxes than those of other member states, pushed for implementation of the policy. Germany, a target of intense Dutch competition, resisted. France was indifferent. Far from cooperating more closely, by 1968 the Dutch and the Germans were on the verge of a trade war over draft German legislation to reduce further the number of permits for Dutch trucks on German roads.

Alongside the customs union and common commercial policy, the CAP was the most striking policy innovation in the EC's first decade. It was also the best-known, due to media coverage of farmers' protests. By the late 1960s the CAP had a number of unintended consequences: it led to overproduction and environmental degradation, rewarded large-scale producers unduly, and failed to keep many small farmers on the land. The first sizable food surpluses—butter mountains and milk lakes—appeared in 1968. As with other policy areas, people directed their criticism of the CAP not at member states, where it belonged, but at the Commission, which epitomized the Community system.

The EC made little progress in the 1960s on regional policy. The preamble of the Rome Treaty mentioned the need to reduce regional disparities, but the treaty itself included few redistributive measures. On the contrary, the prevailing ethos, as stated in the treaty, was that the common market should, of its own accord, "promote throughout the Community a harmonious development of economic activities" and thereby achieve cohesion. As an exception to that general rule, the treaty permitted government subsidization of industry in those parts of the EC where "the standard of living is abnormally low or where there is serious unemployment."[58]

The Commission did not believe that market integration alone would boost regional development. Nor did Italy, the only member state in the 1960s with major regional disparities (the south of Italy was impoverished). Italy and the Commission therefore wanted the EC to develop a strong regional policy, including a greater portion of the CAP budget devoted to infrastructural improvements. But most governments resisted extending Community competence into an area not explicitly covered by the Rome Treaty.

Member states were even more protective of their tax policies, although the Commission scored a big success in the 1960s in the area of harmonization of indirect taxes. The large number of different tax systems and rates in the Community militated against the successful operation of the common market. The Commission's response focused initially on turnover taxes. Specifically, the Commission proposed that governments introduce a common value-added tax (VAT) system. Although France already had such a system and Germany was moving toward it, years of hard bargaining ensued before governments reached agreement, in 1967. The Commission got nowhere with a related initiative to harmonize direct taxes, an area not covered in the Rome Treaty.

The treaty called for some economic policy coordination, but not for monetary union. The Commission made a strong case for a common economic policy, including cooperation on monetary policy, in its action program for the second stage of the common market, published in 1962. The Council agreed to establish committees to discuss current economic trends and assist the Commission should the Council, acting unanimously, decide to "take special measures to cope with undesirable economic developments."[59] In May 1964, the Council established a committee on budgetary policy to examine the impact of national budgets on the EC's overall economic development.

Von der Groeben criticized Marjolin, his colleague in the Commission with responsibility for economic policy, for being too timid.[60] Marjolin was more realistic than reticent: he understood the political situation in France and did not want to risk further conflict with de Gaulle. Nevertheless, Marjolin supported "Community programming": regular economic forecasts and blueprints for policy coordination. Some of the more liberal member states, as well as business interests, resisted this approach, fearing excessive government interference in economic affairs. Nevertheless, the Council adopted the Community's first medium-term economic policy program in March 1966, covering employment policy, budgetary policy, regional policy, and research policy. Far from presaging close economic coordination, however, the program amounted mostly to an exchange of information.[61]

Monetary union seemed unnecessary in any case during the heyday of the Bretton Woods system of quasi-fixed exchange rates. Nor could the EC reach a joint position as the system began to unravel in the late 1960s. De Gaulle saw the balance-of-payments deficit of the United States, and the swing from what had been a postwar dollar gap toward a potential dollar glut, as an opportunity to attack the United States on the financial front. Instead of holding on to its excess dollars, France began to convert them into gold in 1967 to protest US expansionary macroeconomic policies and dominance of the international monetary system.[62] Although critical of US economic and monetary policies, the other national leaders were more forgiving of an ally who had bailed out their countries immediately after the war and on whom they depended for military security. De Gaulle's position precluded the adoption of a common EC position on international monetary issues, although frequent contacts among national central bankers, government officials, and Commission officials presaged the emergence in the early 1970s, when the Bretton Woods system finally collapsed, of a plan for monetary union.[63]

External Relations

The new EC quickly acquired an international persona and presence. The conclusion of the Kennedy Round of GATT negotiations, in 1967, was a concrete manifestation of the EC's international impact and of the advantages of European integration.[64] The fifty-three members of the GATT agreed to reduce tariffs over a five-year period by an average of nearly 40 percent. Acting as a bloc, the Six played a decisive part. The satisfactory outcome of the round demonstrated the value of a common EC negotiating position.

Yet the conduct of the Kennedy Round generated considerable friction. Within the EC, France and the Five, unofficially led by Germany, clashed over the possible inclusion of agriculture and the extent of the industrial tariff cuts. France did not want the CAP, negotiated and defended at considerable cost, undercut by a global agreement to liberalize trade in agricultural products. Nor did France want to expose its industrial producers, already coping with intra-EC liberalization, to greater global competition. As global industrial liberalization was a lesser evil for France than global agricultural liberalization, de Gaulle struck a deal with Germany to defend the CAP in return for French support for industrial tariff cuts in the GATT.

The Kennedy Round was also a source of friction between the EC and the United States. The United States hoped that the round would yield greater economic and political benefits than turned out to be the case. The United States had drafted its landmark Trade Expansion Act, the legislative basis for participation in the round, partly in anticipation of early British accession to the EC. Among other provisions, the act authorized the US president to eliminate duty on articles in categories of goods in which the United States and the EC together accounted for 80 percent or more of world trade. Once Britain had joined the EC, the United States and the EC together would account for at least that amount of world trade in a large number of categories. De Gaulle's veto of Britain's membership negated the provision of the Trade Expansion Act that anticipated EC enlargement and reduced the possible benefit of the Kennedy Round for the United States.[65]

While advocating the Trade Expansion Act, members of the US administration harped on the political as well as the economic importance of the proposed legislation for US-EC relations. In their view, the act and the ensuing Kennedy Round would help cement US relations with Brussels and build the Atlantic partnership. Instead, de Gaulle's assault against the Grand Design of the United States eroded US optimism about EC-US relations. More than anything else, de Gaulle's veto of British membership "struck a heavy blow at the idea of partnership which seemed . . . [to have] had such a bright future only several months before."[66]

Association Agreements

Apart from the Kennedy Round, the most significant development in the field of external relations during the EC's first decade was the conclusion of association agreements with Greece, Turkey, and a group of African countries, all former colonies of EC member states. The association agreements with Greece and Turkey were different, as both countries aspired to EC membership, albeit in the long term. The agreement with Greece, signed in July 1961, called for a customs union within twelve years; the agreement with Turkey, signed in September 1963, aimed for a customs union after a transition period of unspecified duration. The difference reflected Turkey's lower level of economic development. The EC acknowledged Greece's aspiration for membership but was more circumspect in its dealings with Turkey. While lauding Greece's contribution to European culture and civilization, the EC doubted Turkey's European credentials.

The EC suspended the association agreement with Greece in response to the right-wing coup in Athens in 1967, which ushered in a military dictatorship. At the same time, political instability and economic turmoil in Turkey caused Ankara's association agreement to languish. By the end of the 1960s, the EC had little to show for its association with two strategically important countries whose hostility toward each other would complicate the Community's involvement in the eastern Mediterranean for many years to come.

The association agreement with seventeen African states and Madagascar, signed in Yaoundé, in the Cameroon Republic, in July 1963, superseded the association between the EC and its member states' overseas territories (most of them French colonies), negotiated as part of the Rome Treaty and implemented in January 1958, when the treaty came into operation. In effect, the original association created a free trade area for the EC and the overseas territories. It also channeled aid to the associated territories through a development fund. The nature of the association and the size of the fund, which was separate from the EU budget, divided France and Germany. As with the CAP, France saw Community support for overseas territories as an opportunity to spread the cost of development assistance while continuing to reap the economic rewards. By contrast, Germany resented both the size of its financial contribution and the Community's close association with a part of the world in which it had little interest.

Although the treaty stipulated that the Council could extend the original association agreement, the granting of independence in the late 1950s and early 1960s to most of the overseas territories meant that a new agreement was necessary. Once again, Germany was in an anomalous position, on the one hand wanting to support global development while on the other hand not wanting to perpetuate postcolonial dependency. Negotiation of what became the Yaoundé Convention therefore took place on two fronts: externally between the EC and the African states, and internally among the EC's member states.

In the negotiations with the African states, the EC was in the driver's seat politically, economically, and administratively. The African states had little choice but to take what the EC offered them. Within the EC, France prevailed over Germany because of an implicit link between the GATT and the Yaoundé negotiations: in return for French support in the Kennedy Round, Germany acquiesced in the new convention. The United States doubted the Yaoundé agreement's compatibility with the GATT and fretted about its possible discriminatory impact on Latin American exports to the EC. Like Germany, however, the United States overcame its misgivings for the sake of a GATT agreement and for the cause of European integration.[67]

Britain's Second Application

In contrast to various internal and external developments, the most notable setback at the end of the EC's first decade was de Gaulle's veto of Britain's second membership application. This time it was a Labour government, led by Harold Wilson, that spearheaded Britain's accession effort.[68] Wilson was no more committed to European integration than Macmillan had been, but he knew that Britain needed to join for economic reasons. Britain's situation had worsened since de Gaulle's first veto. By 1967, the "battle for sterling" was at its height. Determined to defend the exchange rate and maintain sterling's reserve-currency status, Wilson refused to devalue or take harsh fiscal measures. Instead, the government tightened capital controls and asked the International Monetary Fund for help. As a means of redressing Britain's balance-of-payments deficit and restoring the country to economic health, membership in the EC seemed more essential than ever.

The issue continued to divide domestic opinion. The Labour Party included a number of die-hard Euroskeptics, most of whom opposed the EC for doctrinaire reasons, seeing it as a capitalist endeavor that was hostile to workers' rights and as an economic arm of NATO. Some Conservatives opposed the EC for economic reasons—in their view it was socialistic and hostile to business interests—but most disliked the EC because it threatened national sovereignty. Aware of deep divisions in the party and the country, Wilson argued the case for membership on solid economic grounds. He built parliamentary support through a series of lengthy debates, culminating in a successful vote in May 1967 in favor of a second application, which the government duly lodged in Brussels.

Wilson carried none of Macmillan's emotional baggage from having dealt with de Gaulle during the war. Wilson's advocacy of intra-European technological collaboration and criticism of US policy in Vietnam resonated with de Gaulle. But Wilson could not convince de Gaulle that British accession to the EC was compatible with French economic and strategic interests. De Gaulle outlined his misgivings at a press conference only four days after Wilson submitted Britain's second application. Rather than risk "destructive upheavals" by admitting Britain into the EC, especially because of sterling's vulnerability, might it not be better "to preserve what has been built until such time as it would appear conceivable to welcome an England which . . . [will] have undergone a profound transformation?"[69]

The British media immediately dubbed this "the velvet veto," although Wilson was still optimistic about Britain's chances because he seemed to have the support of France's EC partners. Wilson put great store in the advent in Bonn of the Grand Coalition of Christian Democrats and Social Democrats, under Chancellor Kurt Kiesinger and Foreign Minister Willy Brandt. Wilson hoped that Bonn's growing irritation with Paris, and Kiesinger's apparent willingness to stand up to de Gaulle, would strengthen Britain's prospects. Wilson also had a good relationship with Brandt, a fellow Social Democrat. Wilson used Brandt's support for Britain's EC membership to undermine opposition to the EC in his own Labour Party.

The Commission issued a favorable opinion on Britain's application in September 1967.[70] The Council discussed Britain's application and the Commission's opinion on a number of occasions, but another statement by de Gaulle, in a press conference at the end of November 1967, brought the matter to a close. Referring to the Commission's opinion, de Gaulle declared that Britain's economic and political situation precluded EC membership. Earlier in the month, Britain had devalued sterling by 17 percent, partly in response to publicly expressed French doubts about sterling's stability. De Gaulle now twisted the knife, saying that the sterling crisis, as well as Britain's commercial and agricultural policies, made it impossible to open accession negotiations. "To enter at present into any negotiations with Britain and its associate countries," de Gaulle declared, "would lead to the destruction of the European Community."[71]

The irony of this statement was not lost on the British and the Five, considering that de Gaulle had risked destroying the EC during the empty chair crisis in order to safeguard French interests. De Gaulle continued to worry about the possible impact of British accession on the CAP. Although the big battles on agricultural policy were over, a permanent financial arrangement (the final piece of the CAP puzzle) would not be put in place until 1970. Clearly, de Gaulle did not want Britain to join before then.

Strategic considerations also played a part in de Gaulle's decision. In 1966 de Gaulle launched various efforts to undermine US hegemony in NATO and loosen Soviet control in Eastern Europe. The most dramatic of these were his withdrawal from NATO's integrated military command, expulsion of NATO's headquarters from France, and much-publicized visit to Moscow. De Gaulle still saw the EC as a potential platform for a pan-European economic and security organization independent of the superpowers; letting Britain in might have given the appearance that the EC was moving closer strategically to the United States.

For Wilson, the most disappointing aspect of de Gaulle's veto was that Germany went along with it. Whatever Kiesinger and Brandt said privately to Wilson, publicly they were unwilling to confront de Gaulle. Undoubtedly de Gaulle's behavior exasperated Kiesinger and Brandt, but neither would risk alienating France for the sake of an eventuality that looked increasingly inevitable once de Gaulle was out of office. Germany saw economic and strategic advantages in British accession, but not enough to risk a crisis in Franco-German relations and Community affairs by antagonizing de Gaulle. Faced with French intransigence and Germany's diffidence, Britain put its application on hold in December 1967.

Impact on Everyday Life
For all its accomplishment and setbacks in the 1960s, the EC generally remained remote and largely unknown outside relatively small business, legal, and political circles. Avid readers of the quality press could have followed the story of the empty chair crisis or of Britain's membership applications. Otherwise, ordinary people knew little and cared less about what happened in Brussels.

The EC's existence directly affected the lives of relatively few people. Farmers depended on the CAP for their livelihoods, and some businesspeople enjoyed the benefits of market integration, however limited. Transnational interest groups representing farmers, workers, and employers sprang up in Brussels. Many national politicians and bureaucrats developed a European dimension to their work, perhaps coordinating positions on Community issues at home or participating in working groups and

Council meetings in Brussels. A vibrant Brussels apparatus, involving interaction among the EC's institutions, policy coordination at the national and European levels, and lobbying in Brussels and the national capitals, came into being. Although still largely out of the limelight, EC politics and policymaking were beginning to envelop Europe's political, bureaucratic, and business elites.

Notes

1. On the Commission's early years, see Michel Dumoulin, ed., *The European Commission, 1958–72: History and Memories* (Luxembourg: Office of Official Publications of the European Communities, 2007); Michel Mangenot and Sylvain Schirmann, eds., *Les institutions européennes font leur histoire* (Brussels: Peter Lang, 2012); Katja Seidel, *The Process of Politics in Europe: The Rise of European Elites and Supranational Institutions* (London: Tauris Academic, 2010).

2. George M. Taber, "Remembrance of Things Past: A Former Eurocrat Recalls the Dreams and Ideals of the Early Commission," *Time International,* March 29, 1999, p. 23.

3. See Hans von der Groeben, *The European Community: The Formative Years* (Luxembourg: Office for Official Publications of the European Communities, 1987), p. 48.

4. Commission, "Introduction to the Action Program for the Period 1964–1968," Bulletin EC 12-1962, p. 1.

5. On the struggle between the state and the market in the EC's early years, see John Gillingham, *European Integration, 1950–2002: Superstate or New Market Economy?* (Cambridge: Cambridge University Press, 2003), pp. 6–16.

6. See N. Piers Ludlow, "The European Commission and the Rise of Coreper: A Controlled Experiment," in Wolfram Kaiser, Brigitte Leucht, and Morton Rasmussen, eds., *History of the European Union: Origins of a Trans- and Supranational Polity, 1950–72* (Abingdon: Routledge, 2009), pp. 189–205.

7. For an account of the EP's early years and eventual impact on the EC system of governance, see Berthold Rittberger, *Building Europe's Parliament: Democratic Representation Beyond the Nation State* (Oxford: Oxford University Press, 2005).

8. See Andrew Moravcsik, *The Choice for Europe: Social Purpose and State Power from Messina to Maastricht* (Ithaca: Cornell University Press, 1998), pp. 179–182.

9. On the origin and outcome of the free trade area proposal, see Alan Milward, *The UK and the European Community,* vol. 1, *The Rise and Fall of a National Strategy, 1945–1963* (London: Cass, 2002), pp. 231–309; James Ellison, *Threatening Europe: Britain and the Creation of the European Community, 1955–1958* (London: Macmillan, 2000); Jeffrey Glen Giauque, *Grand Designs and Visions of Unity: The Atlantic Powers and the Reorganization of Western Europe, 1955–1963* (Chapel Hill: University of North Carolina Press, 2002), pp. 47–76.

10. Miriam Camps, "The Free Trade Area Negotiations," Policy Memorandum no. 18, Center for International Studies, Woodrow Wilson School of Public and International Affairs, Princeton University, February 10, 1959, p. 36.

11. US Department of State, *Foreign Relations of the United States [FRUS], 1958–1960,* vol. 7, pt. 1, *Western European Integration and Security; Canada* (Washington, DC: US Government Printing Office, 1993), pp. 67–68.

12. See ibid., p. 121.

13. Ibid., p. 173.

14. See Richard T. Griffiths, "The End of the OEEC and the Birth of the OECD," in Griffiths, ed., *Explorations in OEEC History* (Paris: OECD, 1997).

15. *FRUS, 1958–1960*, vol. 7, pt. 1, p. 281.

16. Ibid., p. 98.

17. On France and the CAP, see Andrew Moravcsik, "De Gaulle Between Grain and Grandeur: The Political Economy of French EC Policy, 1958–1970," pt. 1, *Journal of Cold War Studies* 2, no. 2 (Spring 2000), pp. 3–43. On the history of the CAP, see Ann-Christina L. Knudsen, *Farmers on Welfare: The Making of Europe's Common Agricultural Policy* (Ithaca: Cornell University Press, 2009).

18. On the Commission's role in the development of the CAP, see von der Groeben, *European Community*, pp. 70–78, 101–108.

19. Ibid., p. 102.

20. *FRUS, 1961–1963*, vol. 13, *West Europe and Canada* (Washington, DC: US Government Printing Office, 1994), pp. 275–277.

21. Ibid., p. 279.

22. William Diebold Jr., "A Watershed with Some Dry Sides: The Trade Expansion Act of 1962," in Douglas Brinkley and Richard T. Griffiths, eds., *John F. Kennedy and Europe* (Baton Rouge: Louisiana State University Press, 1999), p. 252.

23. See Herman Walker, "Dispute Settlement: The Chicken War," *American Journal of International Law* 58, no. 3 (July 1964), pp. 671–685; Ynze Alkema, "European-American Trade Policies, 1961–1963," in Brinkley and Griffiths, *John F. Kennedy and Europe*, pp. 226–234.

24. On Britain's early relationship with the EC and its application for membership, see Milward, *UK and the European Community*, vol. 1, pp. 310–441; Wolfram Kaiser, *Using Europe, Abusing the Europeans: Britain and European Integration, 1945–1963* (London: Macmillan, 1996); George Wilkes, ed., *Britain's Failure to Enter the European Community, 1961–1963: The Enlargement Negotiations and Crises in European, Atlantic, and Commonwealth Relations* (London: Cass, 1997); N. Piers Ludlow, *Dealing with Britain: The Six and the First UK Membership Application* (Cambridge: Cambridge University Press, 1997).

25. On the Grand Design, see Pascaline Winand, *Eisenhower, Kennedy, and the United States of Europe* (New York: St. Martin's, 1993), pp. 245–264; Giauque, *Grand Designs*, pp. 98–125.

26. John F. Kennedy, "Address at Independence Hall, Philadelphia," July 4, 1962, in *Public Papers of the Presidents of the United States: John F. Kennedy, January 1 to December 31, 1962* (Washington, DC: US Government Printing Office, 1963), p. 538.

27. Walter Hallstein, "The European Economic Community," *Political Science Quarterly* 78, no. 2 (June 1963), pp. 167–168, 174, 176. The article was based on a speech that Hallstein gave at Columbia University. See also Walter Hallstein, *United Europe: Challenge and Opportunity* (Cambridge: Harvard University Press, 1962).

28. On de Gaulle's strategic vision and European policies, see Frédéric Bozo, *Two Strategies for Europe: De Gaulle, the United States, and the Atlantic Alliance* (Lanham: Rowman and Littlefield, 2001); Alain Peyrefitte, *C'était de Gaulle*, vol. 1, *La France redevient la France* (Paris: De Fallois/Fayard, 1994), and vol. 2, *La France reprend sa place dans le monde* (Paris: De Fallois/Fayard, 1997); Eric Roussel, *Charles de Gaulle* (Paris: Broché, 2002); Maurice Vaïsse, *La grandeur: Politique étrangère du général de Gaulle, 1958–1969* (Paris: Fayard, 1997).

29. On Anglo-American relations and the Grand Design, see Stuart Ward, "Kennedy, Britain, and the European Community," in Brinkley and Griffiths, *John F. Kennedy and Europe*, pp. 317–332.

30. *FRUS, 1961–1963,* vol. 13, p. 11.

31. Ibid., p. 6.

32. Ibid.

33. Ibid., p. 66.

34. On this proposal, which came to be known as the Fouchet Plan, see Robert Bloes, *Le "Plan Fouchet" et le problème de l'Europe politique* (Bruges: College of Europe, 1970); Susanne J. Bodenheimer, "The 'Political Union' Debate in Europe: A Case Study of Intergovernmental Diplomacy," *International Organization* 21, no. 1 (Winter 1967), pp. 24–54; Pierre Gerbet, "In Search of Political Union: The Fouchet Plan Negotiations (1960–1962)," in Roy Pryce, ed., *The Dynamics of European Union* (London: Croom Helm, 1987), pp. 105–129; Giauque, *Grand Designs,* pp. 126–157.

35. See Moravcsik, "De Gaulle Between Grain and Grandeur," pt. 1, p. 39; Oliver Bange, *The EEC Crisis of 1963: Kennedy, Macmillan, de Gaulle, and Adenauer in Conflict* (London: Macmillan, 2000), pp. 27–28.

36. *FRUS, 1961–1963,* vol. 13, p. 52.

37. On Adenauer's relations with the Western allies, see Hans-Peter Schwarz, *Konrad Adenauer: German Politician and Statesman in a Period of War, Revolution, and Reconstruction,* vol. 2, *The Statesman, 1952–1967* (Oxford: Berghahn, 1997), pp. 513–627. On his relations specifically with de Gaulle, see Hermann Kusterer, *Der Kanzler und der General* (Stuttgart: Neske, 1995). On de Gaulle's policy toward Germany and relations with Adenauer, see Pierre Maillard, *De Gaulle et l'Allemagne: Le rêve inachevé* (Paris: Plon, 1990).

38. Ludlow, *Dealing with Britain,* pp. 169–199.

39. Andrew Moravcsik argued that de Gaulle vetoed Britain's application because "British membership would kill the CAP." Moravcsik, "De Gaulle Between Grain and Grandeur: The Political Economy of French EC Policy, 1958–1970," pt. 2, *Journal of Cold War Studies* 2, no. 3 (Fall 2000), pp. 4–68. See also Bange, *EEC Crisis,* pp. 108–116. The text of the press conference is in Charles de Gaulle, *Mémoires d'espoir, suivi d'un choix d'allocutions et messages sur la IVe et la Ve républiques* (Paris: Plon, 1994), pp. 832–848.

40. Hallstein, "European Economic Community," p. 175.

41. On the Elysée Treaty, see Giauque, *Grand Designs,* pp. 96–113.

42. *FRUS, 1961–1963,* vol. 13, pp. 204–209. George Ball's reverence for Monnet and loathing for de Gaulle are evident in his memoirs. See Ball, *The Past Has Another Pattern* (New York: Norton, 1982), pp. 96–98.

43. See Thomas Alan Schwartz, *Lyndon Johnson and Europe: In the Shadow of Vietnam* (Cambridge: Harvard University Press, 2003).

44. De Gaulle, *Mémoires d'espoir,* pp. 195–196.

45. On the empty chair crisis, see Miriam Camps, *European Unification in the 1960s: From the Veto to the Crisis* (New York: McGraw-Hill, 1966); John Newhouse, *Collision in Brussels: The Common Market Crisis of 30 June 1965* (New York: Norton, 1967); Françoise de la Serre, "The European Economic Community and the 1965 Crisis," in F. Roy Willis, ed., *European Integration* (New York: New Viewpoints, 1975), pp. 130–153; Moravcsik, *Choice for Europe,* pp. 159–237; Jean-Marie Palayret, Helen Wallace, and Pascaline Winand, eds., *Visions, Votes, and Vetoes: The Empty Chair Crisis and the Luxembourg Compromise Forty Years On* (Brussels: Peter Lang, 2006).

46. See Moravcsik, "De Gaulle Between Grain and Grandeur," pt. 2; Moravcsik, *Choice for Europe,* pp. 159–237.

47. For the text of the Luxembourg Compromise, see http://europa.eu.int/scadplus /leg/en/cig/g4000l.htm.

48. See F. Roy Willis, *France, Germany, and the New Europe, 1945–1967,* revised and expanded ed. (Stanford: Stanford University Press, 1968), p. 362.

49. See David Coombes, *Towards a European Civil Service* (London: Chatham, 1968).

50. See Finn Laursen, "The 1965 Merger Treaty: The First Reform of the Founding European Community Treaties," in Finn Laursen, ed., *Designing the European Union: From Paris to Lisbon* (Basingstoke: Palgrave Macmillan, 2012), pp. 77–97.

51. See Rittberger, *Building Europe's Parliament.*

52. Case 26/62, *Van Gend en Loos v. Nederlandse Administratie der Belastingen,* 1963, ECR 1; Case 6/64, *Costa v. ENEL,* 1964, ECR 585.

53. See Youri Devuyst, "The European Union's Constitutional Order? Between Community Method and Ad Hoc Compromise," *Berkeley Journal of International Law* 18, no. 1 (1999), pp. 1–52; Francesca Bignami, "Rethinking the Legal Foundations of the European Constitutional Order: The Lessons of the New Historical Research," *American University International Law Review* 28, no. 5 (2013), pp. 1311–1335.

54. See Karen Alter, "The European Court's Political Power," *West European Politics* 91, no. 3 (July 1996), pp. 458–486.

55. Von der Groeben, *European Community,* p. 87.

56. Ellen Frey-Wouters, "The Progress of European Integration," *World Politics* 17, no. 3 (April 1965), pp. 460–477.

57. See Kiran Klaus Patel and Heike Schweitzer, eds., *The Historical Foundations of EU Competition Law* (Oxford: Oxford University Press, 2013).

58. Rome Treaty, available at http://www.europa.eu.int/abc/obj/treaties/en/entoc05 .htm.

59. Ibid.

60. Von der Groeben, *European Community,* p. 209, n. 53.

61. On economic policy cooperation generally, see ibid., pp. 64–66, 141–144, 206–213.

62. See Jacques Rueff, *The Monetary Sin of the West* (London: Macmillan, 1972).

63. See Barry Eichengreen, *The European Economy Since 1945: Coordinated Capitalism and Beyond* (Princeton: Princeton University Press, 2007), pp. 242–251.

64. See Lucia Coppolaro, *The Making of a World Trading Power: The European Economic Community in the Kennedy Round Negotiations (1963–67)* (Farnham: Ashgate, 2013).

65. On the Trade Expansion Act, see Alkema, "European-American Trade Policies," pp. 226–231; Diebold, "Watershed," pp. 235–260.

66. John B. Rehm, "Developments in the Law and Institutions of International Economic Relations: The Kennedy Round of Trade Negotiations," *American Journal of International Law* 62, no. 2 (April 1968), pp. 406–407.

67. See von der Groeben, *European Community,* pp. 83–84, 205; Werner Feld, "The Association Agreements of the European Community: A Comparative Analysis," *International Organization* 19, no. 2 (Spring 1965), pp. 223–249; Isebill V. Gruhn, "The Lomé Convention: Inching Towards Interdependence," *International Organization* 30, no. 2 (Spring 1976), pp. 241–262.

68. On Britain's second application, see Oliver J. Daddow, ed., *Harold Wilson and European Integration: Britain's Second Application to Join the EEC* (London: Cass, 2002); Stephen Wall, *The Official History of Britain and the European Community,* vol. 2, *From Rejection to Referendum, 1963–1975* (Abingdon: Routledge, 2012).

69. The text of the press conference is in de Gaulle, *Mémoires d'espoir,* pp. 1033–1050.

70. Commission, *First Report on the General Activities of the European Communities* (Luxembourg: European Communities, 1968), pp. 346–347.

71. The text of the press conference is in de Gaulle, *Mémoires d'espoir,* pp. 1057–1075.

4

Setbacks and Struggles

THE END OF THE 1960S SEEMED TO HERALD A NEW BEGINNING IN
international relations and a new departure for the European Community.
The United States and the Soviet Union settled into a period of détente or
reduced tension in their adversarial relationship. This culminated in the
Helsinki Accords in 1975, which instituted the Conference on Security and
Cooperation in Europe, a vehicle for East-West dialogue and human rights
monitoring that helped gradually to undermine Soviet control in Central
and Eastern Europe. Ostpolitik, West Germany's new policy of rapprochement toward the Soviet bloc, was a regional manifestation of global détente. Enthusiastically espoused by Willy Brandt, who became chancellor of
Germany in 1969 as head of the first Social Democratic government since
the war, Ostpolitik stirred domestic as well as international controversy and
dominated German politics in the early 1970s.

Charles de Gaulle unexpectedly resigned as president of France at
about the same time that Brandt came to office. The sighs of relief in Washington and Western European capitals were audible. De Gaulle's resignation
facilitated an improvement in US-European relations and a revival of interest in European integration. Georges Pompidou, de Gaulle's successor, was
open-minded on the hitherto vexed question of British accession and on
new policy initiatives in the Community. At Pompidou's request, national
leaders convened in The Hague, in December 1969, for what promised to
be an epochal event in the history of the EC.

Developments nevertheless proved disappointing. International economics and finance were on the verge of a major upheaval. The Bretton Woods
system of quasi-fixed exchange rates, synonymous with economic stability
since World War II, teetered on the brink of collapse in the late 1960s. A bal-
looning US trade deficit and inflationary pressure generated by the Vietnam
War prompted the United States to float the dollar in August 1971. EC mem-

ber states responded by launching a plan for economic and monetary union with a target date of 1980 for irrevocably fixing intra-EC exchange rates.

Plans for EMU collapsed under the weight of the oil crisis that followed the October 1973 Arab-Israeli war. The ensuing recession in Western Europe saw rising unemployment, spiraling inflation, and plummeting rates of growth. Far from converging on the path to EMU, member states' economic policies and performances diverged drastically. The EC failed to meet the challenge of widespread economic and financial uncertainty. Despite protestations to the contrary, member states went their own ways. Although the customs union remained intact, efforts to remove nontariff barriers ground to a halt and new obstacles to intra-EC trade came into being. Narrowly defined national interests predominated. The circumstances were hardly favorable for Britain's entry into the EC in 1973.

The greatest political change in Europe at the time took place outside the Community and outside the Soviet orbit as well. In 1974 the Greek military junta collapsed following Turkey's invasion of northern Cyprus, an event regarded in Greece as a national disaster. Two other authoritarian regimes, in Portugal and Spain, ended as well in the mid-1970s. Greece, Portugal, and Spain promptly applied to join the EC. While celebrating the EC as a source of stability for emerging democracies, member states fretted about the financial, institutional, and policy implications of enlargement.

This chapter examines the vicissitudes of European integration during a distinctly unpropitious period. Preoccupied by domestic problems—the resurgence of communism in Italy; violent left-wing protests and terrorism in Germany; strikes and financial collapse in Britain—member states mostly looked inward. For those who bothered to think about it, European integration in the mid-1970s meant regulatory zeal, agricultural overproduction, and a sullen bureaucracy in Brussels. Nevertheless, developments in the EC were not unremittingly gloomy. There was notable progress on regional policy, social policy, and environmental policy. The European Court continued to produce a body of law that helped to tie the member states together at a time of threatened disintegration. On the institutional front, national leaders launched the European Council in 1975, to facilitate regular summit meetings. The European Parliament acquired limited budgetary authority in 1970 and prepared to hold its first direct elections before the end of the decade. The conclusion of a new aid and trade accord between the EC and a group of African, Caribbean, and Pacific countries in Lomé in 1975 enhanced the Community's international profile, as did the launch of European Political Cooperation, a mechanism to coordinate member states' foreign policies.

The Spirit of The Hague

The EC's fortunes looked distinctly unpromising at the beginning of 1969. The Luxembourg Compromise continued to cast a shadow over legislative decisionmaking. De Gaulle's second veto of Britain's application still rankled with the other member states. Following the domestic upheaval of May 1968, de Gaulle regained control in France and looked set to stay in power until at least the next presidential election, scheduled for December 1972. The Franco-German engine of European integration stalled. Despite widespread growth in the 1960s, economic trends diverged rather than converged within the Community as a whole. The Commission spoke openly "of crisis, paralysis and even the possible disintegration of the Communities," with advocates of deeper integration "discouraged and pessimistic."[1]

The fallout from the demonstrations and strikes in Paris, in May 1968, glaringly demonstrated French economic weakness and German economic strength. Germany was also beginning to make diplomatic overtures toward Eastern Europe and the Soviet Union, thereby stoking French fears that the Federal Republic might loosen its moorings in the West. Under the circumstances, France may have seen British accession as a way to counterbalance Germany's economic weight in the EC and tie Germany more firmly into Western Europe. Nevertheless, the EC had not yet agreed on a permanent financial arrangement for the common agricultural policy. Until it did so, de Gaulle's opposition to British accession would likely remain entrenched.

De Gaulle's resignation in April 1969, after losing a referendum on minor constitutional matters that became a vote of confidence, brought the question of British accession suddenly to the fore. So closely was de Gaulle associated with the Community's malaise that his resignation raised hopes of a rapid revival of European integration. Deep-rooted frustration with de Gaulle and relief at his departure accounted in large part for the wave of optimism about the EC's future that swept Western Europe at the end of 1969.

Brandt and Pompidou

Georges Pompidou, "solid, dependable, avuncular," won the French presidential election in April 1969.[2] As de Gaulle's prime minister for much of the 1960s, Pompidou was a well-known quantity. In some respects his approach to the EC was typically Gaullist: he defended the Luxembourg Compromise, advocated intergovernmentalism, and strongly supported the CAP. Pompidou embraced the EC primarily for economic reasons. Although keenly interested in the CAP, Pompidou's main goal was to modernize French industry.

Pompidou's election heralded a major breakthrough on enlargement. It coincided with Brandt's appointment as chancellor of Germany. The advent of a new chancellor with an impeccable anti-Fascist past and a desire to reinvigorate Franco-German relations augured well for the EC's revival. Nevertheless, Brandt and Pompidou were not on the same wavelength. Brandt was a Socialist, Pompidou a conservative. Brandt was a moderate supranationalist, Pompidou an avid intergovernmentalist. Pompidou was primarily a technocrat (he had served as prime minister for five years before being elected to parliament for the first time in 1967), Brandt a natural politician. Pompidou, despite his humble origins, was highly educated and detached; Brandt, because of his humble origins, was streetwise and down-to-earth.

Those differences need not have divided the two men. What really set them apart was Pompidou's unease about Germany's growing economic and political power. Pompidou fretted incessantly about Ostpolitik, Brandt's foreign policy priority, and resented Germany's behavior during the exchange rate crises in late 1969 when Germany, far from deferring to France, acted unilaterally by revaluing the mark. Loud German criticism of the CAP, with its runaway budget and rising food surpluses, also irritated the French.

The Hague Summit

The idea of a post–de Gaulle summit of the Six hovered over Community capitals in mid-1969 before France proposed it formally in July. Concerned about unilateral German monetary measures and the impact of exchange rate fluctuations on the all-important CAP, and keen to project a European "monetary personality" in transatlantic relations, Pompidou championed closer monetary policy cooperation. Having linked enlargement and CAP funding, Pompidou added EMU to the summit agenda. "Completion, deepening, enlargement"—meaning the budget (completion), EMU (deepening), and British accession (enlargement)—became a mantra in the run-up to the summit, scheduled for December in The Hague (the Dutch were then in the Council presidency).

The Hague summit generated considerable interest. Support for European integration reemerged with a revival of the European Movement, a host of pro-European demonstrations, and a profusion of newspaper articles and letters to the editor. Eager to seize the moment, the Commission and the EP called for a new commitment by national leaders to greater European integration. Hoping that the summit would give "a new political impetus to the creation of Europe," the Commission stressed the need for enlargement, a financial regulation for the CAP, EMU, greater use of qualified majority voting, and direct elections to the EP.[3]

Brandt stole the show at the summit, from which the Commission president was mostly excluded. The summit communiqué did not personalize the proceedings but inevitably played up the importance of the event, claiming that Europe was at "a turning point in its history." National leaders stressed in the communiqué their determination to make a definitive financial arrangement for the CAP, based on an agreement to fund the EC by its "own resources" rather than contributions from national budgets. They agreed in principle to open accession negotiations but did not stipulate a date, and approved a range of initiatives related to deepening, including "a plan in stages" to be worked out in 1970 to achieve EMU; Community support for industrial research and development; and reform of the European Social Fund "within the framework of a closely concerted social policy." National leaders also asked their foreign ministers to explore options for foreign policy cooperation.[4]

The summit gave rise to "the spirit of The Hague" or, as the Commission put it, "a rediscovered political will [among] the Six" to get the Community going again.[5] Most participants and observers hailed the summit as a landmark in the history of European integration, comparing it to the Messina meeting of foreign ministers in 1955 that led to the Rome Treaty. Their exuberance was understandable, given widespread support for enlargement and closer integration immediately after de Gaulle's departure. Subsequent setbacks in the 1970s served only to strengthen the summit's claim to fame.[6]

Completion

Completion meant bringing the transitional period of the common market formally to an end and switching to a system of "own resources" to fund the EC. There were two such resources: tariffs on industrial imports, and levies on agricultural imports, whose rates were determined by common EC policies (the common commercial policy and the CAP, respectively). As those would not be sufficient to cover all the EC's expenditures, member states would have to supplement them with a portion of their value-added taxes.

Commission proposals for a switch to own resources in 1965 had triggered the empty chair crisis. Now the Commission was more circumspect and France less defensive. At the end of a marathon session in mid-December 1969, the Council agreed to the phased introduction of own resources, including a national contribution of up to 1 percent of value-added tax, between January 1971 and January 1975, when the system would become fully operational. The Commission hailed the "friendly and constructive atmosphere" in the Council as evidence of "the spirit of The Hague."[7]

Related negotiations in the Council on the role of the EP amounted to a mini intergovernmental conference. Member states signed the Luxembourg Treaty in April 1970, amending a number of budgetary and institutional provisions in the Rome Treaty. Thus the EP and the Council became the EC's two budgetary authorities, although the distribution of power tilted toward the Council. The agreement also called for the Commission to introduce new proposals within a couple of years for further budgetary reform, thereby implying that member states would grant the EP additional responsibility. Indeed, national leaders agreed in principle in October 1973 to strengthen further the EP's budgetary authority and at the same time set up an independent Community audit board. Further negotiations culminated in the Brussels Treaty of 1975, which included provisions to establish the Court of Auditors.[8]

Deepening

Of the three goals declared at the Hague summit, deepening was the least precise. It referred primarily to EMU, but included also foreign policy cooperation and regional policy. Foreign policy cooperation added a new dimension to the EC, albeit of an intergovernmental kind. The development of regional policy, an area with considerable integrative potential, became bound up with EMU and, later, with enlargement.

Deepening was supposed to complement enlargement, lest the accession of new member states weaken the cohesiveness of the EC. Yet enlargement had little bearing on French and German motives for EMU. The French saw EMU primarily as a vehicle for constraining German monetary independence and projecting a European identity at a time of global financial turbulence. After May 1968, as the franc came under growing pressure, the French also saw EMU as a means of garnering support for their beleaguered currency.

Germany's interest in EMU was more strategic than economic. Brandt weighed every foreign policy option against Ostpolitik. Accordingly, he saw EMU as a way to assuage French concerns about Germany's new foreign policy direction. At the same time, Brandt played down the latent anti-Americanism inherent in Pompidou's conception of EMU, and played up the evidence that EMU provided of Germany's continuing commitment to the West, a commitment that reassured the United States as much as it did France.

The Commission's interest in EMU stretched back to Britain's first application for EC membership. In its 1962 action program, the Commission claimed that EMU would help to deepen integration in an enlarging EC. As it happened, an enlarged EC would have been unable to manage EMU in the 1960s because of Britain's chronic monetary problems. The deteriorating international monetary situation in the late 1960s offered the Commission another opportunity to advocate EMU even before de Gaulle resigned and Britain reactivated its membership application.

The Commission therefore submitted a memorandum on EMU in February 1969, named after Raymond Barre, Commission vice president with responsibility for economic policy.[9] The Barre memorandum was less a bold initiative for further integration than a cautious call for what the French government now wanted: coordination on monetary policy and short-term support for balance-of-payments difficulties. Barre was a pillar of the French establishment; he would not have taken such an important step without the French government's knowledge.

The development of the CAP in the late 1960s gave France an additional incentive to coordinate monetary policy, lest exchange rate fluctuations distort common prices and lower farmers' incomes. That is exactly what happened in 1969 when the French devalued their currency in August and the Germans revalued theirs in October. Pending the possible achievement of EMU, member states agreed to establish a complicated system of additional subsidies and border taxes—so-called monetary compensatory amounts—to compensate farmers for exchange rate fluctuations.

France and Germany changed their exchange rates in 1969 without consulting the other member states, despite an earlier undertaking to do so.

Apart from their impact on the CAP, the French and German realignments shook prevailing confidence in the stability of exchange rates, something taken for granted in the 1960s. Because quasi-fixed rates were presumed to have contributed decisively to the decade's unprecedented economic growth and prosperity, policymakers were generally averse to exchange rate flexibility and floating regimes.

At the Hague summit, national leaders instructed the Council to draw up a plan in 1970 for the establishment in stages of EMU. The Council entrusted the task to Pierre Werner, prime minister and finance minister of Luxembourg and a longtime advocate of deeper integration.[10] The Werner committee comprised the chairmen of the EC's monetary and economic policy committees as well as a representative of the Commission. In effect, an official of each government sat on the committee.

The goal of EMU seemed simple enough—fixed exchange rates, a common monetary policy, and a single monetary authority—but member states differed about how to achieve it. Governments disagreed among themselves about the necessity for economic convergence, the design and role of common institutions, and the desirability of a common currency. A major split emerged among finance ministers and within the Werner committee between the "economists," reflecting German and Dutch preferences, and the "monetarists," reflecting French and Belgian preferences. The economists insisted that a high degree of economic policy convergence had to precede monetary union; the monetarists held that monetary union would bring economic convergence in its wake. The issue was far from academic. Countries with balance-of-payments surpluses, such as Germany and the Netherlands, did not want constantly to bail out countries with chronic balance-of-payments deficits, such as France and Belgium. By contrast, the French and Belgians wanted to enjoy the benefits of monetary stability at the expense of the more stringent member states, without having to pay the domestic political price of undertaking macroeconomic policy reforms.

Although the Werner committee's initial report veered toward the monetarist position, its final report of October 1970 endorsed what Brandt later called the "iron rule" of parallel progress on economic convergence and monetary policy coordination.[11] Thus, in the first stage of the road to EMU, member states would narrow their exchange rate margins and launch medium-term monetary support measures. In the final stage, they would revise the Rome Treaty in order to establish new institutions at the European level and transfer power to the EP to counteract the loss of national authority over economic and monetary affairs. The Werner Plan was hazy about what would happen in the second stage. According to one of the earliest academic assessments of EMU, the gap between the first and the third stages "was simply enormous."[12]

The Werner Plan's endorsement of parallelism and call for institutional change discomfited Pompidou. So did the plan's call for treaty reform. Although un-Gaullist in his willingness to contemplate EMU, Pompidou was neo-Gaullist in his opposition to supranationalism, especially when it involved the power of the EP. Thus, on institutional as well as substantive grounds, France and Germany stood on opposite sides of the EMU divide.

The differences between the two countries became fully apparent at a rancorous meeting of the Council in December 1970, before Brandt and Pompidou patched things up at a bilateral summit in January 1971. Brandt faced conflicting domestic pressures. On the one hand, the Christian Democratic opposition castigated him for unnerving France by his pursuit of Ostpolitik. Brandt could assuage France and undermine domestic criticism by making concessions to Pompidou on EMU. On the other hand, the Bundesbank (German central bank), a hallowed institution, preferred flexible exchange rates over fixed, as a means of promoting price stability. Brandt attempted to square the circle by endorsing EMU in principle while playing down its institutional implications.[13] The outcome of the bilateral summit allowed the Council soon afterward to endorse the general goal of EMU, adopt various measures originally proposed in the Barre memorandum, and approve the Commission's third medium-term economic program. Ever inclined to grasp at straws, the Commission hailed the "far-reaching political implications" of these "historic" developments.[14]

The Council's decisiveness on relatively minor aspects of EMU disguised major differences between France and Germany, which would have become more apparent had EMU gone according to the Werner Plan. In the event, the international monetary crises of 1971 blew it off course. The first crisis struck in May, when a massive flow of funds from the United States into Germany put pressure on Bonn to revalue the mark. Germany pressed for a joint EC float, threatening otherwise to float the mark unilaterally. France opposed floating, fearing that a rise in the value of the franc would render French exports uncompetitive (German exporters had similar concerns about the mark). France instead advocated a de facto devaluation of the dollar through a rise in the price of gold. This was something that Germany, more sensitive than France to US interests, was unwilling to countenance. Having failed to reach agreement on a joint EC strategy, Germany and the Netherlands floated their currencies while other member states imposed capital controls. Thus member states found it impossible to narrow the range of intra-EC fluctuations in June 1971, as called for in the Werner Plan.

The second monetary crisis struck in August 1971, when the United States officially ended the convertibility of the dollar to gold, introduced a hefty import surcharge, and launched various measures to promote the sale of US goods at home and abroad. Once again, EC member states failed to act together. The United States and other countries agreed in December

1971 to realign exchange rates and finally devalue the dollar. The so-called Smithsonian agreement established a margin of fluctuation of 2.25 percent on either side of the new dollar parity. That meant a possible fluctuation of 4.5 percent between any two EC currencies.

Concerned about the consequences for the CAP of such a wide spread, Pompidou pressed Brandt to limit intra-EC margins to 2.25 percent within the permissible 4.5 percent range. The Council agreed to do so, in February 1972, through a system of intra-EC intervention and debt settlement. That was the origin of the wonderfully evocative "snake in the tunnel," an arrangement that allowed the currencies of member states to wiggle up and down within a narrower band than the one prescribed in the Smithsonian agreement.

The exchange rate crises of 1971 undermined the EC's confidence and sowed additional discord between Brandt and Pompidou. Although the snake in the tunnel seemed to put EMU back on track, monetary developments in 1972 were almost as rocky as before. The snake gyrated widely, shedding participating currencies like old skins.[15] As a concession to Pompidou, national leaders agreed in October 1972 to establish within the next few months a European Monetary Cooperation Fund for the second stage of EMU. In what many of them knew to be a leap of faith, they also reaffirmed their commitment "irreversibly to achieve [EMU] . . . with a view to its completion not later than December 31, 1980."[16]

Enlargement

Britain's hopes of joining the EC revived in 1969 after de Gaulle's resignation, when the Council asked the Commission to submit a new opinion on Britain's application. The Commission advocated the reopening of negotiations as soon as possible. Britain interpreted the Hague communiqué at the end of the year as an endorsement of the Commission's position and as a sign that rapid progress was possible.[17]

Although a Labour government revived Britain's application in 1969, it was a Conservative government, led by Edward Heath, that conducted the ensuing negotiations. Unlike Harold Wilson, the Labour Party leader, who was equivocal about EC membership, Heath was enthusiastic. Yet like Wilson, Heath faced deep divisions in his party.

Heath's conservatism, paternalism, and moderate intergovernmentalism appealed more to Pompidou than Wilson's socialism, egalitarianism, and indifference to the EC. Heath's personal interest in European integration heightened the government's determination finally to join. As Sir Con O'Neill, Britain's chief negotiator, put it, "What mattered was to get into the Community and thereby restore our position at the center of European affairs which, since 1958, we had lost. The negotiations were concerned only with the means of achieving this objective at an acceptable price."[18]

From Six to Nine

Accession involved two sets of negotiations: one between Britain and the Six, represented by the Council presidency; the other among the members states themselves. Formal negotiations took place in Brussels at ministerial and deputies levels. Ministerial meetings were ceremonial and stilted; deputies meetings were more productive. As in any set of negotiations, most of the important work took place in bilateral and multilateral meetings in the margins of official sessions. As the talks progressed, the feeling grew that the decisive negotiations were not between Britain and the Six or even among the Six themselves, but between Britain and France. Thus, diplomatic contacts between the two governments were crucial to the success of the negotiations.[19]

Despite the air of inevitability about eventual enlargement, there was no guarantee that the negotiations would succeed. Pompidou could hardly veto Britain's membership application outright, even if he wanted to. The Five would not defer to Pompidou as they had deferred to de Gaulle. Brandt made it clear that another French veto was unacceptable. But Pompidou could drag out the negotiations or insist on terms unacceptable to Britain.

The negotiations began in earnest only when member states ratified the Luxembourg Treaty (on Community funding) at the end of 1970. Thereafter, progress was slow. As O'Neill recalled, "The first four months of 1971 were months of stagnation, exasperation, virtual deadlock and increasing apprehension about the outcome."[20] Despite general agreement on the desirability of British accession, deep differences separated both sides on specific issues. The most contentious of these were fish, food, and finance.

Much to the annoyance of Britain and the other three applicants—Denmark, Ireland, and Norway—the Council adopted a common fisheries policy, which had long been on the EC's agenda, on the same day that the negotiations on Britain's accession began. This looked like a blatant effort to reach an agreement among the Six on an issue of great interest to the applicant states. Under pressure from the applicants, the Six relented and agreed to reopen the discussions on the fisheries policy.[21]

This was the only Community policy that the Six agreed to revise as a result of enlargement. By contrast, the CAP was sacrosanct, though Britain and the Six fought over specific commodities that enjoyed privileged access to the British market: Commonwealth sugar and New Zealand butter. Britain wanted to extend the terms of the Commonwealth sugar agreement that permitted large-scale importation into Britain of sugar from developing Commonwealth countries. The sugar lobby, led by wealthy British importers rather than poor Commonwealth producers, "was perhaps the best organized and most active of all the British interest groups seeking to influence the negotiations."[22] On the other side, France defended the interests of domestic sugar beet producers as well as the interests of producers in countries associated with the EC under the Yaoundé Convention.

New Zealand butter was a stickier point. Implausible though it seems, it was an issue dear to the hearts of many British voters. Britons were less enamored of the product than of the people of New Zealand, due to close family connections between the peoples of the two countries and to New Zealand's steadfastness during World War II. (New Zealand lamb, another British favorite, did not pose a problem, because the Community did not yet have a market organization for sheep meat.) New Zealand supplied about 40 percent of Britain's butter needs, a market share that French and Dutch producers wanted to acquire.

The question of New Zealand butter was so sensitive politically that, as Sir David Hannay, a senior British official, observed, "without the acquies-cence of the New Zealand government [in a butter deal] it was rather doubt-ful that the terms of Britain's accession would have been approved by the House of Commons."[23] France drew the obvious conclusion and leveraged New Zealand butter to win concessions from Britain on another issue in the accession negotiations: the EC budget. Britain's initial offer in the budget negotiations—a contribution of 3 percent in 1973, increasing to 15 percent in 1977—was ludicrously low. In the end, Britain agreed to pay 8.64 per-cent in 1973, with an increase to 18.92 percent in 1977. That was a great deal for New Zealand farmers, at British taxpayers' expense.[24]

The success of the negotiations ultimately hinged on agreement at the highest political level, presumably at either a Franco-German or an EC summit. Instead, the breakthrough came at a summit between Britain and France in May 1971. The contrast with previous summits between de Gaulle and supplicant British prime ministers could not have been greater. With the CAP financially secure and Germany increasingly assertive, Pom-pidou was willing to allow enlargement to proceed. He and Heath got on well and were determined to send a positive signal about enlargement and about the EC's future. They held a glowing postsummit press conference in the same room in which de Gaulle had launched his famous diatribes against British accession.

The foreign ministers and their officials still had a lot of work to do, notably on the linked problems of New Zealand butter and Britain's bud-getary contribution. But the political agreement reached by Heath and Pom-pidou ensured that the talks would ultimately succeed. Nevertheless, the ne-gotiations would not formally come to an end until January 1972.

There was intense media speculation in the aftermath of the Heath-Pompidou summit about the demise of the Franco-German axis and the rise of an Anglo-French axis within the enlarging EC. Undoubtedly, Pompidou was increasingly impatient with Brandt's approach to monetary policy and Ostpolitik and embraced Heath partly to snub the German chancellor. But Brandt was unperturbed. He knew that Franco-German ties were stronger than either Anglo-French or Anglo-German ties. British and French antipathy toward supranationalism bothered Brandt more. Heath and Pompidou were equally obdurate when it came to the defense of national interests in Community decisionmaking. Back in London after the Paris summit, Heath gave a ringing defense of the Luxembourg Compromise. Member states, he told the House of Commons, "should not attempt to override a single country in something which it considers to be of vital national interest."[25]

Heath's defense of national interests did little to assuage British public opinion, which, never at ease with European integration, turned more and more against accession. The British government, by playing down the political costs and exaggerating the economic advantages of membership, gave ample ammunition to British Euroskeptics.[26] In a harbinger of things to come, Wilson, the Labour Party leader, complained openly about the terms of accession.

Most British newspapers applauded the outcome of the negotiations. The *Times* and the *Telegraph,* though rabidly Euroskeptical twenty years later, swam against the tide of opinion in the early 1970s by championing British entry into the Community. In an October 1971 editorial, the *Telegraph* made "no apology for the fact that the balance is in favor of entry. We have supported entry in principle from the start, and consider the present terms acceptable." The tabloids were almost evenly split on the issue, with the mass-circulation *Express* then, as later, venting its spleen against Brussels bureaucrats, lost sovereignty, and the inevitable end of British greatness. The *Mirror* illustrated its support for British accession by featuring scantily clad "Euro-Dollies" (photos of women from the six member states).[27]

The key debate in the House of Commons took place in October 1971, shortly before the negotiations ended but when the contours of the accession treaty were already known. The government won by a comfortable majority, with most members of the two main parties voting in favor. Nevertheless, a sizable minority of Conservatives and almost half the Labour parliamentary membership voted against British accession. Positions hardened in 1972, when Britain ratified the accession treaty through parliamentary enactment of the European Communities Bill. Wilson denounced Heath's accession terms in uncompromising language, Labour antimarketeers were in full cry, and Heath had difficulty reining in his own anti-EC dissidents. The depth of division on the European question, and Wilson's determination to exploit it politically, caused concern across the Channel.

The Other Applicants

Ireland, Norway, and Denmark—the other applicant states—had close economic ties to Britain (although Denmark's and Ireland's were much closer than Norway's). The four applicants negotiated separately but contemporaneously with the Six. Like Britain, each of the three smaller countries had strong Euroskeptical elements.

There was some concern in Ireland about the impact of EC membership on neutrality, a legacy of the independence movement earlier in the century. The Irish government had declined Washington's invitation to join NATO in 1949 because of Britain's "occupation" of Northern Ireland. Although the EC was not a military organization, the Rome Treaty's commitment to "ever closer union" suggested that the EC would develop a defense policy some time down the road. Regardless, most Irish people accepted that, for economic reasons, Ireland could not stay out of the EC if Britain went in. For political reasons too, Ireland was better off inside a larger association of states than living permanently in Britain's shadow. A majority of Irish people saw EC membership as an opportunity to modernize their society and transform their economy. Simply put, the Irish wanted to be more worldly and wealthy. The prospect of "Brussels money" flowing into the pockets of Irish farmers made the EC even more attractive. Ireland's negotiations were relatively easy, although the Irish government complained about the common fisheries policy and successfully pressed for derogations in certain policy areas.[28]

Euroskepticism was more entrenched in Norway. As Norwegians liked to point out, having become independent of Sweden in relatively recent times, Norway was leery of joining another union of states, albeit voluntarily. Yet Ireland, which had also emerged from an unhappy union with a larger neighbor, avidly pursued EC entry in order to enhance its de facto independence. Moreover, joining a Community of which Sweden was not a part would surely have enhanced Norway's position vis-à-vis the old imperial power. But Norway's antipathy toward the EC ran deeper than national identity. Farmers were concerned that subsidies would fall if they participated in the CAP, conservatives fretted about the social impact of accession, and fishermen resented the common fisheries policy.[29]

Opinion in Denmark was equally divided over EC membership, although the economic arguments weighed heavily in favor of joining. Denmark could not afford to reduce its market access to Britain and looked forward to gaining unrestricted access to German markets. Yet Nordic solidarity, a cultural rather than an economic concept, pulled many Danes away from the EC. Remembering the war years, some Danes opposed the idea of closer association with Germany. A change of government in October 1971 brought the Euroskeptical Social Democrats to power. The new government took a harder line on a number of issues, including fisheries, important in Denmark because of the country's control over Greenland and the Faeroes.[30]

The 1972 Referendums

Four countries held referendums on enlargement in 1972: three of the applicant states and one member state. The applicants were Ireland, Denmark, and Norway; the member state was France. Legally, France could ratify the accession agreements only by a vote in parliament. Therefore the referendum was purely advisory. Pompidou, who was seriously ill (he died two years later), wanted to be remembered as a European as well as a French statesman. Already he envisioned the Paris summit later in the year as making a major contribution to the construction of Europe, albeit along intergovernmental lines. A successful referendum would emphasize France's commitment to the Community and burnish Pompidou's European credentials.

Domestically, Pompidou wanted to split the opposition and strengthen his position within the Gaullist camp. The Communists opposed the existence of the Community, whereas the Socialists supported British accession. A referendum on enlargement was a sure way to accentuate the division between Pompidou's left-wing rivals. As for the Gaullists, what better way to cut the feet from under critics of enlargement within his own party than by using a classic Gaullist device—a referendum—to buttress his own position? Yet Pompidou was careful not to follow de Gaulle's precedent by threatening to resign if the result was negative. As it happened, the result was favorable, but not overwhelmingly so. In a disappointing turnout, only 61 percent of the French population voted in favor of enlargement, a result that reflected domestic rather than European concerns.[31]

The referendum was soon forgotten in France, but its legacy was more enduring in Britain because of the ammunition that it gave to Euroskeptics in the Labour Party. Referendums were contrary to Britain's cherished principle of parliamentary sovereignty (a nationwide referendum had never been held in Britain). Labour opponents of EC membership seized on the French example as one to be emulated in Britain. In response, Wilson promised that, if returned to power, he would renegotiate the terms of membership and hold a referendum on the outcome. Wilson might have adopted that position anyway, but the impact of the French referendum was obvious.

The outcome of the Irish referendum, held in May 1972, was never in doubt. The two biggest political parties vigorously advocated membership; the small Labour Party campaigned against. The Irish people knew on which side their bread was buttered. A whopping 83 percent voted in favor of membership (the turnout was 77 percent). Next came the Norwegian referendum at the end of September. Those opposed to membership, drawn from all walks of life but representing especially agricultural and fishing interests, polled 54 percent (the turnout was 78 percent). The prime minister, who had turned the referendum into a vote of confidence, duly resigned (he was the first politician to lose office as a direct result of his country's involvement in the EC). The final referendum took place in Denmark, one week later. The result was a respectable 63 percent in favor of membership (the turnout was an impressive 90 percent).

These were the first in a number of referendums on European union held mostly in these same countries in the years ahead. From the perspective of 1972, they seemed like onetime events. The referendums showed that opinion in Norway and Denmark, Scandinavian countries that eschewed participation in earlier stages of integration, was finely poised between supporters and opponents of EC membership; that Irish support for EC membership was solid; and that the situation in France was less certain than the government thought.

The European Community on the Eve of Enlargement

EC leaders convened in Paris in October 1972 for their first meeting since the Hague summit in 1969. Recalling the spirit of The Hague, Pompidou wanted another summit to symbolize the EC's continued revival. Indeed, it seemed as if the Community was on the move again. The Luxembourg Treaty of 1970, which established the system of "own resources" and granted budgetary authority to the EP, was in effect. The first stage of EMU was under way, with member states frequently reaffirming their determination to launch the second stage on-time, in January 1974. Most impressive of all, the accession negotiations had ended successfully. Despite the disappointing results of the French and Norwegian referendums, the Community was about to encompass Britain, Denmark, and Ireland. Member states billed the summit as a celebration of enlargement and invited the leaders of the three candidate countries to attend. In the aftermath of the French referendum and in the run-up to the German general election, both Pompidou and Brandt had reason to accentuate positive aspects of European integration.

Superficially, the summit was a success. Pompidou made a strong speech in favor of deeper integration. He claimed that EMU was necessary in order to fight inflation, create "a distinctive European monetary zone," and contribute to reform of the international monetary system. Brandt kept a low profile, thereby allowing Pompidou and Heath to share the limelight. The summit communiqué contained an impressive list of immediate objectives, ranging from the establishment of the European Monetary Cooperation Fund and the launch of the second stage of EMU, to the creation of a European Regional Development Fund, to the strengthening of social, industrial, and science and technology policies. The communiqué contained a short final paragraph proclaiming that EC leaders had "set themselves the major objective of transforming, before the end of the present decade . . . the whole complex of the relations of [the] member states into a European union." It called on the EC's institutions to draw up a report on the subject before the end of 1975.[32]

Taken out of context, the communiqué's endorsement of European union became a caricature of the wildly optimistic state of integration in the early 1970s. In fact, national leaders tacked the statement onto the communiqué almost as an afterthought. It was Pompidou's idea. Far from connoting a commitment to supranationalism, the communiqué's final paragraph merely indicated Pompidou's general support for integration and concern about his legacy. None of the summiteers took literally the idea that there would be a European Union by 1980.

Despite the conviviality and apparent success of the Paris summit, the EC was in some disarray in the early 1970s. Like most spectral beings, the spirit of The Hague proved more apparent than real. There were major institutional and policy differences among member states, a growing chasm in Franco-German relations, and a marked decline in the Commission's fortunes. Smaller member states resented the drift toward intergovernmentalism that was evident not only in the Commission's decline but also in the persistence of the Luxembourg Compromise, the rise of summitry, and the big member states' dominance of European Political Cooperation (foreign policy cooperation).

Launched in 1970 in response to Germany's preoccupation with Ostpolitik, European Political Cooperation sought to improve the flow of information among governments on major foreign policy issues and help them to formulate joint positions. At French insistence, foreign policy cooperation was rigidly intergovernmental, with no role for the Commission and the EP. In order to emphasize the difference between governments meeting "in European Political Cooperation" and in the Council, on one infamous occasion foreign ministers met in the morning in Copenhagen to discuss foreign policy (Denmark was then in the Council presidency) before flying to Brussels in the afternoon to discuss Community business.

The Dutch government pressed in the early 1970s for an end to the rigid distinction between foreign policy cooperation and Community business, for greater use of qualified majority voting in the Council, and for reform of the Rome Treaty to counter growing intergovernmentalism in the EC. They were rebuffed not only by the French but also by the Germans, who, despite supporting supranationalism, were unwilling to confront France on the matter. The Dutch campaign petered out in 1972, when Britain's impending accession put the final nail in the coffin of treaty reform along supranational lines.

The Germans had more pressing issues to raise with the French, especially the runaway costs of the CAP. Helmut Schmidt, Germany's finance minister, made no secret of his opposition to excessive agricultural subsidies.[33] That put Schmidt at loggerheads with France and with the agriculture minister in his own government, who wanted the highest prices possible for Germany's farmers. France's agriculture minister at the time was none other than future French president Jacques Chirac. Chirac's combative style exacerbated Franco-German tension over agricultural prices. Schmidt especially resented the widespread perception that Germany, on account of its recent past, should be the paymaster of Europe. As one observer remarked, there was a tendency to view Germany's large contribution to the EC budget as "a form of delayed war reparations."[34]

French concern about the conduct and direction of Ostpolitik overshadowed Franco-German relations at the time. Pompidou was pathologically suspicious of Brandt's motives. Ostpolitik's growing momentum and Brandt's increasing international stature alarmed Pompidou and his influential foreign minister, Michel Jobert. Although Brandt was at pains to inform the French, bilaterally and in European Political Cooperation, about developments in the East, he could never put their minds at rest.

On one thing, at least, Brandt and Pompidou saw eye-to-eye. Both disliked the Commission: Pompidou for ideological reasons, Brandt because he never warmed to it. The Commission still drafted reports, communications, and legislation on a wide range of issues, but its political influence languished without support from Paris or Bonn. By common consent it was Italy's turn to nominate a candidate for president in 1970 when Jean Rey stepped down. No prominent Italian wanted to go to Brussels. Eventually the government nominated Franco Malfatti, the minister for post and telegraphs. A skilled speaker, Malfatti liked to orate about the lamentable state of European integration. Beyond that he had little impact on the EC. He resigned as Commission president in 1972 to return to Italian politics, leaving Sicco Mansholt, the father of the CAP, to finish his term of office. François-Xavier Ortoli, a senior French official with close connections to the French government, became the next Commission president.

Member states' determination to keep control over the two main items on the EC's agenda in the early 1970s, EMU and enlargement, further undermined the Commission. The process of enlargement strengthened the role of the Council presidency and the member states' permanent representatives in Brussels at the expense of the Commission. Con O'Neill, the British negotiator, noted how the governments "made it very clear that the Commission must operate as the servant of the Six."[35] Indeed, national leaders did not allow the Commission to sign the accession treaties. This triggered a typical outburst from Malfatti: "There are times," he told the EP in February 1972, "when prejudice replaces judgement, when an academic, legalistic approach replaces considerations of what is politically desirable."[36]

Surviving the Storm

The year 1973 should have been a banner one for the EC. Instead, enlargement seemed anticlimactic, despite lofty statements by politicians from the acceding and existing member states. Their words had a hollow ring, not only because of prevailing political and economic circumstances but also because Britain and Denmark were reluctant new entrants. At a time when the European ideal appeared to be faltering, it was highly unlikely that British accession would spark a renaissance in the EC.

A change of government in Britain in early 1974 brought Wilson back to power, partly on the strength of a promise to renegotiate Britain's entry terms and put the result to a referendum. The ensuing renegotiation and referendum overshadowed Britain's membership in 1974 and early 1975, to the intense irritation of the other member states. By that time the EC was battling gale-force winds. In late 1973, following the war in the Middle East, Arab producers quadrupled the price of oil and embargoed the port of Rotterdam to protest the Dutch government's support for Israel. The sudden, astronomical rise in oil prices threw Europe's economies into a tailspin, while the embargo tested the member states' solidarity and the nascent procedure for foreign policy cooperation.

The response of the Community and its member states was far from flattering. Efforts to negotiate an energy policy failed dismally. Governments initially went their own ways on policy toward the Middle East. Recession and spiraling inflation hastened economic divergence among member states, put an end to EMU, and threatened to roll back existing levels of market integration, notably through the proliferation of nontariff barriers to trade. The Commission remained weak, and governments haggled over the size and composition of an EP whose membership was soon to be directly elected.

Under the circumstances, the EC showed remarkable resilience. Although EMU stalled and an energy policy never emerged, there were noteworthy developments in other areas, such as regional policy, social policy, environmental policy, and overseas assistance. The EC also acquired a higher political profile, due largely to the coordination of the member states' positions at the Conference on Security and Cooperation in Europe through the mechanism of European Political Cooperation. Governments appreciated the benefits of the customs union and the CAP, despite obvious faults. After twenty years of European integration, habits of transnational cooperation were deeply ingrained.

Harmonization

The Rome Treaty empowered the Community to harmonize member states' laws in order to promote and maintain the common market. This required the Council to take legislative decisions, in many cases by qualified majority voting. The Commission, with a monopoly on legislative initiative, took an aggressive approach in the early 1960s until the onset of the empty chair crisis and adoption of the Luxembourg Compromise. Apart from a spurt of harmonization of customs legislation in the late 1960s, following completion of the customs union and, in other areas, in the warm afterglow of the Hague summit, the rate of harmonization slowed in the early 1970s.[37]

Faced with growing intergovernmentalism and the disruptive impact of enlargement, the Commission adopted a more pragmatic, politically sensitive approach, proposing fewer and better measures. In 1973 the Council

The Nine Member States

approved a program on harmonization and an action program on industrial policy. These contained a legislative agenda for undertaking harmonizing measures, with a deadline of December 1977 for the enactment of many of them. But progress was slow. By the mid-1970s, numerous draft directives were stuck in the EC's decisionmaking pipeline.

Faced with a serious economic downturn, Community governments were more susceptible than ever to pressure from businesses resisting harmonization in order to protect domestic market share. Lack of consensus gave governments an excuse to prevent the Council from enacting harmonization measures, despite provision in the Rome Treaty for proposals to be put to a vote. Enlargement made matters worse, given that "political attitudes to harmonization in Denmark and the United Kingdom . . . [varied] from the politely skeptical to the stridently hostile."[38] National politicians pilloried the Commission for its alleged obsession with uniformity. In its defense, the Commission admitted that "technical obstacles and quantitative restrictions . . . are both utterly depressing terms," but argued that the persistence and proliferation of nontariff barriers to trade gravely impaired the common market's potential and eroded public confidence in the Community.[39]

Economic and Monetary Union

By the mid-1970s, soaring inflation, rising unemployment, widening trade deficits, and oil price shocks made a mockery of the Community's commitment to EMU. Taking a pragmatic approach, Commission vice president Carlo Scarascia Mugnozza told the EP in January 1974 that "until our economic structures have been truly harmonized, and until we really begin removing disparities between the Member States, EMU will remain at the stage of abstract ideas and pious wishes. This is one of the main lessons, perhaps even the most important lesson, to be learnt from the events of 1973."[40]

Efforts to achieve EMU became increasingly unreal. As if to emphasize the point, the franc floated free of the snake in January 1974, just as the second stage of EMU was due to begin. Far from becoming an instrument of exchange rate stability, the snake shrank to accommodate only a handful of currencies centered on the mark.[41] EC leaders had little choice but to note, in December 1974, that "internal and international difficulties have prevented . . . the accomplishment of expected progress on the road to EMU," while affirming for the record that "in this field their will has not weakened."[42]

By the mid-1970s, EMU was a "non-issue" relegated to "the second division of Community interests."[43] Instead of deepening integration, EMU had driven France and Germany further apart while becoming a symbol of the Community's impotence in the face of international monetary turmoil and economic recession. Commission president Ortoli lamented in February 1976 "the absence of any decisive progress towards EMU." Although circumstances were largely to blame, Ortoli identified "a lack of conviction too."[44]

This was the gist also of a report on progress toward EMU by a group headed by Robert Marjolin, the influential former commissioner. Convened by the Commission, the Marjolin report concluded that EMU owed its demise to a lack of understanding of what was involved, as well as to a lack of political will: "It was as if the governments had undertaken the enterprise in the naive belief that it was sufficient to decree the formation of an EMU for this to come about at the end of a few years, without great effort or difficult and painful economic and political transformations."[45] The hard-hitting report, a fitting sequel to the optimistic Werner Plan, closed a troubled chapter in EMU history.

Regional Policy

Like a rising tide lifting all boats, the impact of market integration was supposed to close the gap between the Community's rich and poor regions. The Six were relatively homogeneous economically, apart from a big gulf between the rich north and poor south of Italy. The Italian government had little faith in the ability of market integration to help the impoverished south unless accompanied by generous financial instruments for regional development. Lacking political leverage, the Italians failed in the 1960s to convince other member states to establish and endow a munificent regional policy. Only the Commission strongly supported Italy, but the Commission's influence was weak in the aftermath of the empty chair crisis.

The political situation changed in the early 1970s, first with the onset of EMU, then with the prospect of enlargement. The Commission and Italy argued that EMU would widen regional disparities within and among member states. French and German interest in EMU gave the Commission and Italy some leverage to press for a regional policy with teeth.[46]

The impending accession of Britain and Ireland, two countries with pressing regional problems—there were large disparities among Britain's regions, and between Ireland as a whole and the other member states—drew more attention to regional policy. Even before enlargement formally took place, Britain, Italy, and Ireland formed an unofficial bloc of countries agitating for a European Regional Development Fund. Apart from the presumed merits of financial assistance for poorer regions, the British government had a strong political incentive to establish the fund. Because it had a small farm sector, Britain would receive relatively little in agricultural subsidies from the CAP. That was a sensitive point domestically and a political gift for the increasingly anti-EC Labour opposition. The government badly needed to establish the fund, not only to help Britain's disadvantaged regions but also to strengthen the case at home for EC membership.

Every Community government thought regional development a good thing, worthy at least of rhetorical support. While sympathizing with the goal of equitable regional development, however, the rich member states did not want to pay for a financial instrument to achieve it. Already opposed to greater EC expenditure on agriculture, Germany, the perceived paymaster of Europe, strongly resisted the establishment of the fund. Yet Brandt understood Heath's domestic political predicament (although Brandt was a Socialist and Heath a Conservative, they shared the goal of keeping Britain in the Community).

National leaders struck a deal at the Paris summit in October 1972, giving "a high priority . . . to the aim of correcting, in the Community, the structural and regional imbalances which might affect the realization of economic and monetary union." They undertook to coordinate their regional policies and instructed the EC's institutions to establish the Regional Development Fund before the end of 1973, to be financed from the beginning of the second stage of EMU from the Community's own resources.[47] That was a considerable coup for Heath, because it guaranteed a new source of Community expenditure in Britain.

Agreeing to establish the fund was one thing; coming up with the money was another. The summit communiqué did not mention a sum, leaving the Commission and the Council to work out the details. Preoccupied with the oil crisis, national leaders floundered about for a common energy policy, rather than trying to reach agreement on the fund, at the Copenhagen summit in October 1973. With no prospect of an energy policy agreement, little of substance emerged from the summit.

The outcome of the summit did nothing to help Heath in the ensuing election campaign. He was defeated largely on domestic economic grounds (Britain was riven by strikes), although growing popular discontent with developments in the Community undoubtedly helped his opponents. Wilson came back to office in February 1974, demanding a renegotiation of Britain's accession terms and an agreement on the fund. A change of leadership in Germany three months later, when Schmidt replaced Brandt, hardly boosted the fund's prospects. Like Wilson, Schmidt was a Socialist. But Schmidt had a reputation for holding the line on Community spending. Schmidt's position was popular at home, except among farmers when it came to the CAP.

In the run-up to the Paris summit in December 1974, the Commission proposed a compromise on the fund's size and disbursement (each country should get something). By that time a change of leadership in France proved fortuitous. Valéry Giscard d'Estaing, the country's new president, saw himself as the EC's savior and wanted the Paris summit to succeed (Ireland and Italy threatened to stay away unless there was a good prospect of a deal on the fund). Giscard successfully lobbied Schmidt, who was unwilling in the end to jeopardize the success of the Paris summit for the sake of a larger German contribution to the EC's coffers and, more importantly, for the sake of a revived Franco-German axis.

The deal struck in Paris in December 1974 established a fund for the years 1975–1977, with Italy (40 percent), Britain (28 percent), and France (15 percent) getting the lion's share. According to the summit communiqué, the fund was to become operational in January 1975, but negotiators wrapped up the details only in March of that year.[48] Thus a fund smaller than originally envisioned, spread out among more countries than originally contemplated, eventually came into being.

Repeated delays in establishing the fund, protracted disputes among governments about its size and operation, and open association of the issue with Britain's budgetary contribution diminished the fund's immediate importance for the EC. The size of the fund was a pittance compared to the amount of money necessary to improve the poorer regions' prospects, particularly at a time of economic recession. Nevertheless, the launch of the fund was a noteworthy development. Governments learned to collaborate with each other and with the Commission to develop regional policy at the European level. The story of the European Regional Development Fund could be interpreted as an egregious example of horse-trading among national governments, but it also showed that further integration was possible even at the worst of times.

Social Policy

Developments in social policy also belie the impression that the mid-1970s was a time of unremitting setbacks for the EC. The 1969 Hague communiqué acknowledged the importance of social policy and the desirability of reforming the European Social Fund, an item of EC expenditure provided for in the Rome Treaty. Brandt, a Social Democrat, had a particular interest in this. Pompidou, not wanting to be seen as a callous conservative, and aware of France's original insistence on including social policy provisions in the Rome Treaty, also advocated an active social policy for the EC. Accordingly, the 1972 Paris communiqué called on the EC's institutions, in consultation with labor and employers, to draw up an action program by January 1974, including reform of the social fund.[49]

The Commission drafted the social action program, which the Council adopted in January 1974. The program included measures to promote employment, better living and working conditions, worker participation in industrial decisionmaking, and equal treatment of men and women in the workplace. With the onset of the oil crisis and ensuing recession, however, the program seemed a luxury rather than a necessity, despite its supposed employment-enhancing measures. At the 1974 Paris summit, EC leaders merely reaffirmed the importance of the social program and, in a sure sign of inaction, emphasized the role of the Economic and Social Committee, a purely consultative body. As for the European Social Fund, the communiqué declared that the Council would decide, "when the time is ripe . . . whether and to what extent it will be necessary to increase the resources of the social fund."[50]

The Council enacted some social policy legislation in the early and middle 1970s, including directives on workers' information and consultation rights and on equal pay and equal treatment for men and women. A number of landmark rulings of the European Court of Justice further strengthened equal rights for women in the workplace. In addition, the EC established two agencies—the European Foundation for the Improvement of Living and

Working Conditions and the European Center for the Development of Vocational Training—to conduct research on social policy issues. By contrast, at the level of company law, measures that included provisions for worker participation became bogged down in disputes among governments and between trade unions and employers' organizations over which model of industrial democracy to use. Although disappointing by the rhetorical standards of summit communiqués, the EC's record on social policy was nevertheless significant at a time of serious political and economic uncertainty.

Environmental Policy

Environmental policy was not specifically mentioned in the Rome Treaty. Environmental legislation in the 1960s was therefore narrow and technical, justified either as an internal market measure or on the basis of a vague commitment in the preamble of the treaty to improve "the living and working conditions" of the people of Europe. As the environmental movement gathered momentum throughout Western Europe, governments and the Commission developed a keen interest in broader aspects of environmental policy. Hence the short statement in the 1972 Paris communiqué inviting the EC's institutions "to establish, before July 31, 1973, a program of action [on the environment] accompanied by a precise timetable."[51] That was the genesis of the EC's first environmental action program, which, like the second one in 1977, listed various measures that were essentially corrective in nature. The action plans and attendant legislation were a humble beginning for a policy area that would assume great importance for the European Union.

Energy Policy

Unlike most other policy areas, energy policy was an unmitigated disaster for the EC in the mid-1970s, a time of obvious need for common action in the aftermath of the oil crisis.[52] The Rome Treaty did not mention a common energy policy, largely because the other founding treaties dealt explicitly with coal and atomic power. It was only in 1968 that the Commission submitted to the Council the first guidelines for a common energy policy, which languished for years. The Council's inaction can be explained by member state inertia as well as by wide variations within the Community in national energy use and industry ownership. As the energy situation worsened in the early 1970s, Heath pressed successfully for a paragraph in the 1972 Paris communiqué calling for "the Community institutions to formulate as soon as possible an energy policy guaranteeing certain and lasting supplies under satisfactory economic conditions."[53]

When the oil crisis broke a year later, Britain drew back from a common energy policy, preferring to make sweetheart deals with the oil-producing countries and develop its own North Sea reserves. More ominously, the oil crisis split France and Germany, with France choosing to strike out alone and

Germany advocating a common approach. Franco-German relations, already under strain over Ostpolitik and EMU, now faced an "extraordinary mood of suspicion and recrimination generated by the energy issue."[54] Inevitably, the oil crisis dominated the Copenhagen summit of October 1973. Equally inevitably, national leaders failed to reach a common position on energy. A separate, nonbinding declaration attached to the communiqué merely reiterated the need for the "orderly functioning of a common market for energy" and "concerted and equitable measures to limit energy consumption."[55]

Relations with the United States complicated matters. Henry Kissinger, Nixon's hard-charging national security adviser, declared 1973 the "Year of Europe." Although intended to mend fences with Europe following recent transatlantic financial turmoil, its effect was to antagonize the Europeans further. Sensitive to Kissinger's overbearing manner and especially to US concerns about the EC's emerging mechanism for foreign policy cooperation, Europeans reacted skeptically to the US initiative. When the oil crisis broke, some Europeans, notably the French, saw Kissinger's call for a concerted Western response as additional evidence of US determination to dominate transatlantic relations.[56]

France eventually relented, consenting to Community as well as member state representation there. But France criticized Germany, then in the Council presidency, for its handling of the EC's position at the international energy conference convened by the United States in Washington in February 1974, and declined to join the International Energy Agency, a US-sponsored group of oil consumers. Community disarray over energy policy continued in the mid-1970s. At the Paris summit in December 1974, national leaders called on the Community's institutions "to work out and implement a common energy policy in the shortest possible time." That was wishful thinking, as was a plea by Ortoli that 1975 become "the year of the common energy policy."[57]

The Lomé Convention

The year 1975 was notable for the conclusion of the Lomé Convention between the EC and forty-six developing countries. Lomé was more than a successor agreement to the second Yaoundé Convention, which expired in January 1975. As well as including Britain's former colonies in Africa, the Caribbean, and the Pacific (as a result of Britain's recent accession to the Community), Lomé sought to put relations between the EC and the developing countries on a new footing, in keeping with prevailing global concerns about the yawning North-South divide. Instead of renegotiating a traditional donor-recipient relationship, the EC sought to establish a new partnership with its member states' former colonies. Negotiations with the African, Caribbean, and Pacific countries began in July 1973 and ended in February 1975 when both sides signed the new convention in Lomé, the capital of Togo.[58]

Unlike the prelude to the earlier conventions, the Lomé negotiations involved a genuine give-and-take between both sides. The disparate grouping of African, Caribbean, and Pacific countries was surprisingly united. Growing sympathy in the developed world for the plight of poor countries, especially in the aftermath of the global oil crisis, buoyed the negotiators of the African, Caribbean, and Pacific countries. The conclusion of the complex negotiations during Ireland's first time in the rotating Council presidency gave the Irish government an opportunity to bask in the international limelight. Garret FitzGerald, Ireland's foreign minister, claimed that "Ireland had a clear advantage in presiding over this negotiation. The [African, Caribbean, and Pacific countries] knew that we were sympathetic to them and that . . . we had no national interests to defend"[59]

The resolution of last-minute disputes over sugar and EC financial assistance paved the way for the final agreement, which included a development assistance package; a system of generalized preferences in trade; an export stabilization mechanism to guarantee commodity export prices regardless of global market fluctuations; a host of innovative aid and technical assistance programs; a special agreement on sugar that was favorable to exporters from the African, Caribbean, and Pacific countries; and a revised institutional framework. Both sides hailed the agreement as marking a new departure in North-South relations.

Although the Lomé Convention drew welcome attention to the EC's international role at a time of internal economic difficulties, its impact on European integration was mixed. Institutionally, the Commission played an important supporting role in the negotiations. But in keeping with the prevailing intergovernmental direction of the EC, the Council presidency predominated.

Britain's Renegotiation and Referendum

Developments in the EC in the mid-1970s played out against the backdrop of Britain's renegotiation and referendum.[60] Under pressure from a strong Euroskeptical faction within the governing Labour Party, Wilson called for a renegotiation of Britain's entry terms after narrowly winning the February 1974 general election. Wilson increased Labour's lead in the general election that he unexpectedly called in October 1974, but not enough to lessen his dependence on the anti-EC faction.

James Callaghan, Britain's foreign secretary, kicked off the renegotiation at a Council meeting in April 1974. Britain's demands were mostly financial: Britain wanted to contribute less to the budget and get more from it, mainly through the proposed European Regional Development Fund. The other foreign ministers acknowledged the justice of Britain's demands but disliked the way that Callaghan made his case. It looked to them as if Callaghan was presenting a diktat rather than a reasonable set of requests.

As with the original accession negotiations, France was pivotal to the success of the renegotiations. Because the stakes were so high, a final settlement could be reached only at an EC summit. Giscard's evident disdain for Wilson did not help matters. Schmidt, a fellow Social Democrat who sympathized with Wilson's difficult domestic situation, acted as honest broker. Schmidt made a highly influential speech in favor of Britain's continued EC membership at the Labour Party conference in November 1974. Wilson, in turn, publicly signaled a commitment to continued EC membership, conditioned on a successful end to the renegotiation. Schmidt then organized a dinner for Giscard and Wilson on the eve of the Paris summit in December 1974, giving the French and British leaders an opportunity to explain their positions to each other.

The breakthrough in Paris on the size and distribution of the Regional Development Fund satisfied one of Wilson's main demands. As for Britain's budgetary contribution, EC leaders asked the Commission and the Council "to set up as soon as possible a correcting mechanism . . . in the framework of the system of 'own resources' . . . [to] prevent . . . the possible development of situations unacceptable for a member state and incompatible with the smooth working of the Community."[61] The phrase "correcting mechanism" became code for a British rebate. The Commission published a set of proposals in January 1975, which the Council of Ministers used as a basis for negotiations on the size of Britain's rebate. Given the importance of the issue, national leaders became involved in last-minute bargaining, before reaching a deal at the Dublin summit—the first meeting of the European Council—in March 1975.[62]

Based on the Dublin agreement, Wilson advocated support for Britain's continued EC membership in the June 1975 referendum.[63] Yet the Labour Party remained deeply divided on the question of EC membership. The opposition Conservative Party was also divided, but less so. Margaret Thatcher, the new Conservative leader, personified the approach of many in her party: she liked the EC economically but not politically. That is, she supported economic integration and intergovernmentalism but opposed political integration and supranationalism. For constitutional reasons, Thatcher wanted the British people to decide the issue through their elected representatives in parliament, not directly in a referendum. Once parliament approved the referendum, however, she campaigned wholeheartedly for continued EC membership.

With leaders of the two main parties, as well as the business establishment, advocating continued membership, the outcome of the referendum was hardly in doubt. Roy Jenkins, a leading Labour Party moderate, and Edward Heath, the former Conservative prime minister, led the bipartisan "Britain in Europe" campaign. The result of the referendum was a solid 67 percent in favor of continued EC membership and 33 percent against, with a turnout of 64 percent. That should have put the matter to rest, but Britain's EC membership remained a bitterly divisive issue in the Labour Party.

The process of EC enlargement was inherently disruptive, bringing with it a need to absorb new languages, administrative cultures, officials, and national perspectives. The process of British accession was especially disruptive because it brought into the EC a large country with a strong strain of Euroskepticism. The impact of British accession was immediately apparent in the Council, where leading Euroskeptics such as Tony Benn, a prominent Labour minister, represented Britain until Labour lost the 1979 general election. It was also evident in the EP, where Labour members initially refused to take their seats. By contrast, British officials in Brussels generally favored European integration and contributed to the smooth operation of the EC's institutions.

Shortly after the referendum, Wilson announced that "the debate is now over . . . the historic decision has been made . . . we look forward to continuing to work with [our partners] in promoting the Community's wider interests and in fostering a greater sense of purpose among the member states."[64] Those were hollow words, with Britain growing increasingly Euroskeptical over the years. According to one academic assessment, "all that British diplomacy appeared to have accomplished was to persuade the [other member states] that the French, though still in many respects unregenerate nationalists, were tolerable compared with the British. Community politics was still too often a case of one against the rest."[65] Now the "one" was Britain, not France.

Franco-German Friendship
Close Franco-German relations in the mid-1970s contrasted not only with the sorry state of Anglo-French and Anglo-German relations but also with strained Franco-German relations earlier in the decade. The coming to power of Giscard and Schmidt brought a breath of fresh air to relations at the highest level between Paris and Bonn. Giscard and Schmidt had worked together as finance ministers in the early 1970s. They understood economics and, as Michel Jobert, France's former foreign minister, noted acerbically, "ils se tutoient en anglais" (they chatted familiarly to each other in English).[66] Giscard, notoriously haughty, regarded Schmidt as an intellectual equal. Yet Giscard was a head of state and not merely a head of government. On ceremonial occasions, Giscard always took precedence over Schmidt and other EC leaders.

Giscard was a moderate conservative, not a Gaullist. In his view the EC was intellectually interesting, economically important, and politically advantageous. Giscard was neither a rigid intergovernmentalist nor an ardent supranationalist. He was willing to allow majority voting in the Council and direct elections to the EP, though the narrowness of his election victory and the vigilance of the Gaullists in the French National Assembly kept his propensity toward more integration firmly in check.

Schmidt faced no such domestic political constraints. By the mid-1970s, Ostpolitik had run its course, and the Christian Democrats could no longer make political capital out of the risk it supposedly posed to European stability and German security. Brooding by nature, Schmidt became preoccupied later in the decade with a deadly terrorist campaign by far-left extremists and what he saw as the irresponsible global leadership of the United States. Schmidt viewed European integration as inherently beneficial for Germany but was far from enthusiastic about the process. He liked dealing with Giscard and generally shared his partner's perspective on the EC.

Close personal relations between Giscard and Schmidt complemented a convergence of French and German interests in the EC. Germany had the strongest economy in the Community; the Federal Republic weathered better than the other member states the international economic turmoil of the mid-1970s. Giscard wanted to emulate German economic policy in order to replicate Germany's economic performance. As a result, France's preferences moved closer to Germany's on a range of hitherto divisive issues. Thus Giscard accepted the primacy of fighting inflation, agreed to cooperate on international energy issues, and echoed Schmidt's criticism of the US global economic role (in that regard Schmidt moved more in the direction of traditional French thinking).

Institutional Adaptation

One of the most striking institutional developments in the 1970s, closely associated with Giscard and Schmidt, was the emergence of a new body, the European Council, to provide general strategic direction for the EC.[67] A trend toward summitry already existed before Giscard and Schmidt came to power. As the range of issues covered by the Community increased and the domestic stakes rose, national leaders, rather than ordinary government ministers, needed to reach political agreement on a host of important issues. As governments sought to coordinate their foreign policies more closely, notably through the mechanism of European Political Cooperation, regular meetings of national leaders seemed essential rather than discretionary. Accordingly, national leaders decided in Copenhagen in October 1973 to meet more frequently "whenever justified by the circumstances and when it appears necessary to provide a stimulus or to lay down further guidelines for the construction of a united Europe . . . [or] whenever the international situation so requires."[68]

According to the Copenhagen communiqué, "it will be for the country providing the President [of the Council] to convene these meetings and to make detailed proposals concerning their preparation and organization."

France, in the Council presidency, convened a summit in Paris in December 1974. It was there that the national leaders agreed "to meet, accompanied by the ministers of foreign affairs, three times a year," in a format called the European Council. They also instructed their foreign ministers to end the rigid distinction between the conduct of Community business and European Political Cooperation. Henceforth, foreign ministers meeting in the General Affairs Council could hold foreign policy discussions. In a related measure, the leaders declared that "greater latitude will be given to the permanent representatives so that only the most important political problems need be discussed in the Council."[69]

Giscard's advocacy of European summitry initially raised the hackles of the small member states. Garret FitzGerald, Ireland's foreign minister, saw in the proposed European Council "an initiative preconcerted between the 'Big Three,' a move towards the 'Directoire' or Directorate that some of us [in the Council of Ministers] had begun to fear."[70] It reminded the Dutch of de Gaulle's proposals for closer intergovernmental cooperation, which they had blocked after a bitter political battle in 1962. The small member states were mollified only when Giscard agreed that the European Council would not be a formal decisionmaking body and would respect the Commission's role in the Community system.

The decisions taken in Paris to launch the European Council, legitimize European Political Cooperation as a Community activity, and boost the position of the Council presidency suggested a strong tilt toward intergovernmentalism. Eager to provide at least the appearance of a counterbalance toward supranationalism, national leaders agreed in Paris on a number of other procedural and institutional changes, notably an accord that direct elections to the EP "should be achieved as soon as possible," which meant in practice "at any time in or after 1978." They also agreed, despite Danish and British reservations, to strengthen the EP's role, "in particular by granting it certain powers in the Communities' legislative process." Together with a call for the EP to "be more closely associated with the work of the Presidency" in the conduct of European Political Cooperation, the outcome of the 1974 Paris summit was a success for supranationalism as well as for intergovernmentalism.[71]

Yet measures to strengthen intergovernmentalism went into operation immediately, whereas those intended to strengthen supranationalism languished for some time. Governments squabbled for years over the composition of the directly elected EP and over the date of the first direct elections. Small member states were overrepresented in the existing EP. Giscard wanted to increase the size of the directly elected EP and redress the balance in favor of the large member states. The small member states resisted, seeing the issue as further evidence of French insensitivity to their interests.

Another row erupted over when exactly to hold the elections. Most governments wanted to hold the elections on the same day, in May or June

1978. But there was no consensus on what that day should be. Some favored a Sunday, others a Thursday. All agreed eventually to spread the elections over Thursday through Sunday and to start the count only after the last ballots were cast throughout the Community. Agreement on the number and allocation of seats proved more difficult, with the British pressing for more seats so that Scotland would not be underrepresented in relation to Ireland and Denmark (Scottish nationalism was then on the rise). The dispute over apportionment began at the April 1976 summit, where the small member states stood their ground and Giscard left in a huff. Governments finally hammered out an agreement at the next summit, in July 1976. By that time it was too late to schedule the first elections in 1978, hence the decision to hold them in June 1979. In the meantime the idea of increasing the EP's legislative powers fell by the wayside.

Governments failed to deliver another reform implicitly promised in the 1974 Paris communiqué: making greater use of qualified majority voting in the Council and reining in the national veto. As the Luxembourg Compromise (the right to veto) was originally a French device, Giscard's openness to qualified majority voting seemed revolutionary. It was equally surprising that the British, the new guardians of intergovernmental orthodoxy, appeared willing to abandon unanimity.

In fact, the Luxembourg Compromise remained firmly in place. FitzGerald, in the Council presidency in early 1975, tried valiantly to wean member states away from unanimity. Despite scoring a minor coup for qualified majority voting at the end of Ireland's presidency—in the form of a decision to exempt Botswana beef from the EC's import levy—FitzGerald lamented that "the Council soon reverted to the practice of deciding all issues, however trivial, on the basis of unanimity."[72] And so it remained until the early 1980s.

Apart from British and French recalcitrance, economic and political circumstances in the mid-1970s were not conducive to moving away from unanimity. Reeling from the impact of recession and rising unemployment, governments were unwilling to be outvoted in Brussels on legislation that could, in the short term at least, exacerbate the situation at home. Under intense pressure from businesses clamoring for protection, ministers were on the defensive in the Council. In what appeared to be a zero-sum game, governments would not abandon the right, as they saw it, to block legislation in Brussels by invoking or threatening to invoke the Luxembourg Compromise.

Giscard's and Schmidt's attitudes toward the Commission also undermined supranationalism. Schmidt's "disapproval of the Brussels bureaucracy was notorious."[73] He never nominated top-flight Germans to join the Commission. Giscard was even more dismissive of the Commission, although the French fought hard to mold the institution in their own image and to insinuate their officials into its upper echelons. Obsessed with status, Giscard tried to deny the Commission president membership in the European Council.

Commission president Ortoli, perhaps because he was French and therefore appreciated Giscard's preoccupation with protocol, meekly acquiesced in Giscard's treatment of him. Yet Ortoli was aware of the threat posed by the European Council to the Commission's already weak position. The European Council, Ortoli told the EP in February 1975, "represents a major change in spirit and may, if we are not careful, shake the institutional structure set up by the Treaties to their foundations."[74] A year later, Ortoli seemed assuaged. "The risk is still there," he told the EP, "but I am in no doubt that something has been gained: the European Council has provided us with a new organ capable of taking major decisions under the Treaties which set the future course of the Community and its member states. . . . On the whole, the European Council can be said to be an asset."[75] Undoubtedly the European Council was an asset, but as long as the Commission president was merely tolerated at its meetings, neither the Commission nor the Community could reach their full potential.

The Commission was hamstrung in the mid-1970s not only by poor leadership but also by the disruptive impact of enlargement. The addition of four new commissioners (two British, one Irish, and one Danish) increased the college to thirteen members, not an unreasonable number given the scope of the Commission's responsibilities. The influx of new officials into the Commission's services (departments) was more difficult to digest. There was a major reshuffle in the senior ranks in order to accommodate officials from the acceding member states and maintain the informal system of national quotas. The arrival of British, Irish, and Danish officials in the Commission gradually undermined the ascendancy of the French language and administrative culture, just as Pompidou had feared that it would. Cultural, organizational, and personnel changes preoccupied the Commission for some time after enlargement. Nevertheless, the new officials were generally communitarian in their outlook.

Prospects for European Union

At the Paris summit in December 1972, national leaders requested the EC's institutions to draw up in 1975 a report on how best to transform, by the end of the decade, "the whole complex of the relations of member states into a European union."[76] Referring to discussions among foreign ministers on the subject, FitzGerald confessed that "no one knew what European union meant."[77] Meeting in Paris in December 1974, EU leaders stressed the importance of institutional input in order to help them understand the "overall concept of European union." They asked Leo Tindemans, Belgium's prime minister and a Eurofederalist, to submit a comprehensive report by the end of 1975, based on reports from the EC institutions, consultations with national governments, and input from "a wide range of public opinion in the Community."[78]

The Commission, Parliament, and Court of Justice duly presented reports in mid-1975. Both the Commission and the Parliament called for more supranationalism in the Community, but refrained from promoting an ambitious agenda or timetable for European union. The Court, a highly supranational but apolitical body, restricted itself to calling for judicial reform. During visits to national capitals, Tindemans heard a variety of opinions, ranging from the Europhoric Italians to the Europhobic Danes. The British government received Tindemans warmly after the successful outcome of the referendum in June 1975, but impressed upon him London's lack of enthusiasm for further integration.

Tindemans presented his report to the European Council in December 1975.[79] It described European union as a stage of integration located between the existing EC and a full-fledged federation. In keeping with its author's predilection, the report urged member states to move in a federal direction, however slowly, and contained a set of policy and institutional prescriptions. Tindemans stressed the importance of EMU and a common foreign and security policy. In deference to Atlanticist sentiment in Denmark and neutralist sentiment in Ireland, he ruled out the development of a common defense policy. Tindemans recommended deeper integration in other areas as well, notably social and regional policy, and urged the EC to become more citizen-friendly by launching new policies and programs intended to counter growing public apathy about integration.

Institutionally, Tindemans recommended a stronger Commission and Parliament, while endorsing the emergence of the European Council. He suggested that the Commission president be appointed by the European Council and approved by the EP, and have the freedom in turn to appoint his own commissioners (it would have been revolutionary at the time to suggest that the Commission president might be a woman). Tindemans recommended increasing the legislative and oversight authority of the EP, whose membership was soon to be directly elected. More controversially, he proposed giving the EP a shared right of legislative initiative. Tindemans suggested reforming the Council by curtailing the use of unanimity in favor of qualified majority voting, extending the presidency's time in office to one year, and coordinating the work of the various sectoral councils. One of his most contentious recommendations was that the more integration-minded countries be allowed to cooperate more closely in a number of policy areas. This was an obvious reaction to British and Danish recalcitrance and to Ireland's reticence about defense policy cooperation.

The Tindemans report went too far for most member states and ran afoul of the Commission, which did not like the idea of a two-tier EC or of losing its exclusive right of initiative. Each member state rejected one or more of Tindemans's key proposals. France and Britain were the most reactionary. France disliked almost everything in the report; Britain resented particularly the proposals for differentiated integration and more qualified majority voting (Britain seemed open to the idea of a stronger Commission president, perhaps because by common consent it was Britain's turn to nominate the next incumbent). Germany reacted positively to the report but insisted that member states undertake major economic reforms before revisiting the issue of EMU.

Not surprisingly, the report had a short shelf life. The European Council discussed it fleetingly before asking the foreign ministers to report on it. The foreign ministers duly sent it to the permanent representatives, who eventually drafted a report on the report for the foreign ministers, who then reported to the European Council. By that time Tindemans knew the score. His fellow EC leaders thanked him effusively for his efforts on their behalf and asked the Commission to draft an annual report on progress toward European union.[80]

It seems surprising that the European Council even bothered to ask Tindemans, an avowed Eurofederalist, to write the report on European union. Yet the request fit a pattern in the post–de Gaulle period of ratcheting up the rhetoric of European integration without providing much follow-through. Clearly, most politicians were attached to the idea of European union but were unwilling to do much about it during difficult political and economic times.

Despite its lamentable fate, the Tindemans report proved prescient for a later stage of European integration. The European Union that emerged in the 1990s contained many elements mentioned in the report: economic and monetary union, cooperation on foreign and security policy, an emerging defense policy, stronger regional and social policies, greater parliamentary power, generalized use of majority voting, and differentiated integration. Although far from being a blueprint for the EC's development, the report provided a reference point for the European Community's revival and transformation into the European Union. For that reason alone it was a worthwhile political exercise, and a reminder that the 1970s was not such a disastrous decade for the EC after all.

Notes

1. Commission, *Third Report on the General Activities of the European Communities* (Luxembourg: European Communities, 1970), p. 12.
2. Philip Malcolm Waller Thody, *The Fifth French Republic: Presidents, Politics, and Personalities* (London: Routledge, 1998), p. 56.
3. Commission, *Third Report,* pp. 484–486.
4. Ibid., pp. 486–489.
5. Commission, *Fourth Report on the General Activities of the European Communities* (Luxembourg: European Communities, 1971), p. x.
6. On the Hague summit, see *Journal of European Integration History* 9, no. 2 (2003) (special issue on this topic); Haig Simonian, *Privileged Partnership: Franco-German Relations in the European Community, 1969–1984* (Oxford: Clarendon, 1985), pp. 83–84.

7. Commission, *Third Report,* p. 18.

8. See Ann-Christina L. Knudsen, "The 1970 and 1975 Budget Treaties: Enhancing the Democratic Architecture of the Communities," in Finn Laursen, ed., *Designing the European Union: From Paris to Lisbon* (Basingstoke: Palgrave Macmillan, 2012), pp. 98–123; Berthold Rittberger, *Building Europe's Parliament: Democratic Representation Beyond the Nation State* (Oxford: Oxford University Press, 2005), pp. 114–142.

9. For an account of monetary integration before 1972, see Harold James, *Making the European Monetary Union* (Cambridge: Harvard University Press, 2012), pp. 62–88; Barry Eichengreen, *The European Economy Since 1945: Coordinated Capitalism and Beyond* (Princeton: Princeton University Press, 2007), pp. 238–246; Emmanuel Mourlon-Droul, *A Europe Made of Money: The Emergence of the European Monetary System* (Ithaca: Cornell University Press, 2012), 15–29.

10. On the Werner committee and its report, see Loukas Tsoukalis, *The Politics and Economics of European Monetary Integration* (London: Allen and Unwin, 1977); James, *Making the European Monetary Union,* pp. 89–145; Eichengreen, *European Economy Since 1945,* pp. 246–251.

11. Willy Brandt, *My Life in Politics* (New York: Viking, 1992), pp. 245–246, 266–267.

12. Tsoukalis, *Politics and Economics of Monetary Integration,* p. 102.

13. See Simonian, *Privileged Partnership,* pp. 91, 127.

14. Commission, *Fifth Report on the General Activities of the European Communities* (Luxembourg: European Communities, 1972), p. ix.

15. On the "snake," see James, *Making the European Monetary Union,* pp. 89–145; Tsoukalis, *Politics and Economics of Monetary Integration,* pp. 126–129; Mourlon-Droul, *Europe Made of Money,* pp. 15–29; Eichengreen, *European Economy Since 1945,* pp. 246–251.

16. Commission, *Sixth Report on the General Activities of the European Communities* (Luxembourg: European Communities, 1973), pp. 6–9.

17. See Sir Con O'Neill, *Britain's Entry into the European Community: Report by Sir Con O'Neill on the Negotiations, 1970–1972* (London: Cass, 2000), p. 13.

18. Ibid., p. 60.

19. On the negotiations and accession treaty, see O'Neill, *Britain's Entry;* Stephen Wall, *The Official History of Britain and the European Community,* vol. 2, *From Rejection to Referendum, 1963–1975* (Abingdon: Routledge, 2012), pp. 332–404; Melissa Pine, *Harold Wilson and Europe: Pursuing Britain's Membership of the European Community* (London: Tauris, 2007); Michael J. Geary, *Enlarging the European Union: The Commission Seeking Influence, 1961–1973* (Basingstoke: Palgrave Macmillan, 2013), pp. 87–186.

20. O'Neill, *Britain's Entry,* p. 65.

21. See ibid., pp. 252–253.

22. Uwe Kitzinger, *Diplomacy and Persuasion* (London: Thames and Hudson, 1973), p. 129.

23. Quoted in O'Neill, *Britain's Entry,* pp. xii–xiii.

24. O'Neill, *Britain's Entry,* pp. 143–148, 174–175.

25. Quoted in Kitzinger, *Diplomacy and Persuasion,* p. 124.

26. White Paper, "The United Kingdom and the European Communities," July 1971.

27. See Kitzinger, *Diplomacy and Persuasion,* pp. 338–346.

28. See Michael J. Geary, *An Inconvenient Wait: Ireland's Quest for Membership of the EEC, 1957–1973* (Dublin: Institute of Public Administration, 2009).

29. See Lee Miles, *The European Union and the Nordic Countries* (London: Routledge, 1996), pp. 131–146.

30. See Lee Miles and Anders Wivel, *Denmark and the European Union* (Abingdon: Routledge, 2014), pp. 14–29.

31. See Simonian, *Privileged Partnership,* pp. 128–130.

32. Commission, *Sixth Report,* pp. 6–9.

33. See Simonian, *Privileged Partnership,* pp. 221–223.

34. Kitzinger, *Diplomacy and Persuasion,* p. 98.

35. O'Neill, *Britain's Entry,* p. 71.

36. Quoted in Commission, *Fifth Report,* p. x.

37. On harmonization, see Alan Dashwood, "Hastening Slowly: The Community's Path Towards Harmonization," in Helen Wallace, William Wallace, and Carole Webb, eds., *Policy-Making in the European Communities* (London: Wiley, 1977), pp. 278–279; Michelle Egan, *Constructing a European Market: Standards, Regulation, and Governance* (Oxford: Oxford University Press, 2001), pp. 67–81; Carol Cosgrove Twitchett, ed., *Harmonization in the EEC* (New York: St. Martin's, 1981).

38. Dashwood, "Hastening Slowly," p. 291.

39. Commission, *Seventh Report on the General Activities of the European Communities* (Luxembourg: European Communities, 1974), p. ix.

40. Commission, *Eight Report on the General Activities of the European Communities* (Luxembourg: European Communities, 1975), p. xxi.

41. See Eichengreen, *European Economy Since 1945,* pp. 246–251; James, *Making the European Monetary Union,* pp. 89–145; Mourlon-Droul, *Europe Made of Money,* pp. 15–29.

42. Commission, *Eighth Report on the General Activities of the European Communities* (Luxembourg: European Communities, 1975), pp. 297–304.

43. Tsoukalis, *Politics and Economics of Monetary Integration,* p. 154.

44. Commission, *Eleventh Report on the General Activities of the European Communities* (Luxembourg: European Communities, 1978), p. ix.

45. Commission, *Report of the Study Group "Economic and Monetary Union 1980"* (Marjolin report), Brussels, March 1975, p. 4.

46. On the relationship between EMU and regional policy, see Tsoukalis, *Politics and Economics of Monetary Integration,* pp. 121–122, 148.

47. Commission, *Sixth Report,* pp. 6–9.

48. Commission, *Eighth Report,* pp. 297–304.

49. Commission, *Sixth Report,* pp. 6–9.

50. Commission, *Eighth Report,* pp. 297–304.

51. Commission, *Sixth Report,* pp. 6–9.

52. See Robert A. Black, "Plus ça change, plus c'est la même chose: Nine Governments in Search of a Common Energy Policy," in Wallace, Wallace, and Webb, *Policy-Making in the European Communities,* pp. 165–196.

53. Commission, *Sixth Report,* pp. 6–9.

54. Simonian, *Privileged Partnership,* p. 213.

55. Commission, *Seventh Report,* pp. 489–491.

56. See Daniel Möckli, "Asserting Europe's Distinct Identity: The EC Nine and Kissinger's Year of Europe," in Matthias Schulz and Thomas A. Schwartz, eds., *The Strained Alliance: US-European Relations from Nixon to Carter* (Cambridge: Cambridge University Press, 2009), pp. 195–220.

57. Commission, *Eighth Report,* pp. 297–304.

58. See Frans A. M. Alting von Geusau, ed., *The Lomé Convention and the New International Economic Order* (Leiden: Sijthoff, 1977); Isebill V. Gruhn, "The Lomé Convention: Inching Towards Interdependence," *International Organization* 30, no. 2 (Spring 1976), pp. 241–262.

59. Garret FitzGerald, *All in a Life: An Autobiography* (Dublin: Gill and Macmillan, 1991), p. 151; see pp. 152–153 for an amusing account of the signing ceremony in Lomé.

60. On the British renegotiation and referendum, see David Butler and Uwe Kitzinger, *The 1975 Referendum* (London: Macmillan, 1976); Wall, *Official History,* vol. 2, pp. 511–590.

61. Commission, *Eighth Report,* pp. 297–304.

62. Dublin European Council, "Presidency Conclusions," March 10–11, 1975.

63. The question was: "Do you think that the United Kingdom should stay in the European Community (the Common Market)?" See Butler and Kitzinger, *1975 Referendum,* p. 1.

64. Speech to the House of Commons, June 9, 1975. Quoted in Butler and Kitzinger, *1975 Referendum,* p. 145.

65. Peter Ludlow, *The Making of the European Monetary System* (London: Butterworths, 1982), p. 27.

66. Quoted in *The Economist,* July 26, 1975, p. 6.

67. On the origins and development of the European Council, see Annette Morgan, *From Summit to Council: Evolution of the EEC* (London: Chatham, 1976); Jan Werts, *The European Council* (London: HarperCollins, 2008); Simon Bulmer and Wolfgang Wessels, *The European Council: Decision-Making in European Politics* (Basingstoke: Macmillan, 1987).

68. Commission, *Seventh Report,* pp. 487–491.

69. Commission, *Eighth Report,* pp. 297–304.

70. FitzGerald, *All in a Life,* p. 134.

71. Commission, *Eighth Report,* pp. 297–304.

72. FitzGerald, *All in a Life,* p. 148.

73. Ludlow, *Making of the European Monetary System,* p. 27.

74. Commission, *Ninth Report on the General Activities of the European Communities* (Luxembourg: European Communities, 1974), p. ix.

75. Ibid, p. viii.

76. Commission, *Sixth Report,* pp. 6–9.

77. FitzGerald, *All in a Life,* p. 132.

78. Commission, *Eighth Report,* pp. 297–304.

79. Leo Tindemans, *Report on European Union,* Bulletin EC S/1-1976.

80. The fate of the report can be traced in Commission, *Eleventh Report on the General Activities of the European Communities* (Luxembourg: European Communities, 1977).

5

Variable Weather

THE EARLY 1980S WAS ONE OF THE MOST DIFFICULT PERIODS IN the history of European integration. Events in Iran in 1978 triggered a second oil crisis in less than a decade, reversing Western Europe's fragile economic recovery. Growth ground to a halt, inflation soared, the balance of payments worsened, and unemployment crept stubbornly upward. There were wide variations in economic performance among the member states, with Germany faring best and Britain and Italy faring worst.

The international situation was tense. East-West relations were on a renewed collision course in the late 1970s following the Soviet Union's deployment in Eastern Europe of new, mobile, intermediate-range missiles capable of hitting targets in Western Europe. After much hand-wringing within NATO, the allies agreed to pursue a "dual track" approach to counter the Soviet threat: deploying intermediate-range missiles in Western Europe while negotiating an arms control agreement with the Soviet Union. Anxiety escalated following the Soviet invasion of Afghanistan in December 1979 and the imposition of martial law in Poland in December 1981. The impending deployment of NATO missiles in November 1983 increased tension not only between the Soviet Union and the alliance, but also within the alliance. Thousands of antinuclear demonstrators took to the streets in Western Europe, while some NATO governments accused Washington of wanting only to deploy new missiles, not to negotiate an arms control agreement.

Christopher Tugendhat, a commissioner at the time, predicted that "future historians will probably record that the way in which the achievements of the early years [of the European Community] were maintained and markets kept open during the successive oil shocks and the deep economic recession of the 1970s and early 1980s in itself constitutes a considerable success."[1] Yet appearances were deceptive. As this chapter shows, the real success of the EC in the early 1980s was to lay the foundation for the acceleration of integration that followed later in the decade. Responding to the challenges of renewed recession, declining global competitiveness (especially in the high-technology sector), and rising East-West tension, national leaders looked increasingly to the EC for solutions to their problems. Behind a facade of weak leadership, the Commission pursued an aggressive strategy to restructure European industry and complete the internal market. At the same time, the European Parliament exploited the fact that its membership was now directly elected, in order to strengthen its institutional position and advocate greater economic and political integration. Big business in Western Europe, reeling from recession and eager to benefit from an integrated, transnational market, supported the Commission's industrial strategy and urged governments to remove nontariff barriers to trade.

Interest in deepening integration, among member states, the Commission, the Parliament, and business, resulted in a series of initiatives that presaged the launch of the European Union in the early 1990s. Yet bitter battles over Britain's demand for a larger budget rebate and over the costs of the common agricultural policy overshadowed the EC's impending revival. Only when governments finally resolved their differences in June 1984 did the possibility of the EC's resurgence become apparent. The budgetary agreement paved the way for Portuguese and Spanish accession, an event of great importance for the EC. At the same time, by establishing a committee on institutional reform, which recommended an intergovernmental conference to revise the treaties, governments triggered a series of developments that culminated in the Single European Act of 1986, which presaged the transformation of the European Community.

Fair Winds

The setbacks in the early 1980s were all the more striking because the EC's situation appeared to be improving in the late 1970s. The EC's economic performance was mixed. On the one hand, there was progress in the fight against inflation and in efforts to restore balance-of-payments equilibrium; on the other hand, growth rates fell and unemployment rose. Despite continuing pressure on governments to protect home industries, the Commission detected in 1977 "a growing political interest in seeking Community solutions to common problems."[2] The Commission reported at the end of 1978 that "on the whole the economic outlook . . . [is] more promising, and the gradual recovery now underway gives reason to hope that the Community is beginning to emerge from the crisis."[3]

Before the second oil crisis triggered renewed recession in 1980, prospects for closer political integration also looked good. Roy Jenkins, a senior British politician, brought a breath of fresh air to Brussels when he became Commission president in January 1977. At the national level,

French president Valéry Giscard d'Estaing and German chancellor Helmut Schmidt collaborated closely on Community affairs. Both seemed eager to shake the EC out of its lethargy and get Western Europe moving again.

Two issues on the EC's agenda symbolized the endurance of European integration. One was the prospect of Greek accession; the other was direct elections to the EP. A new issue—the possibility of a European monetary system to help meet member states' monetary policy objectives—added to the impression that the EC was sailing satisfactorily ahead. Together, the situation in Greece, the inaugural direct elections, and what became the European Monetary System dominated EC affairs in the late 1970s.

Greek Accession

Greece returned to democracy in July 1974 when Constantine Karamanlis, a former prime minister and widely respected politician, formed a new center-right government after the collapse of the dictatorial colonels' regime. Bowing to deep-seated Greek resentment of the United States for its support of the colonels and backing of Turkey in the Cypriot conflict, Karamanlis pulled Greece out of NATO's military command. Yet he also pressed for quick accession to the EC. Due in no small part to his handling of foreign affairs, Karamanlis won the general election in November 1974.

Greece was then extremely poor, with a per capita income less than 25 percent of the EC average. Karamanlis saw EC entry as the key to his country's international rehabilitation, political stabilization, and economic modernization. He hoped that joining the EC would bolster Greek security vis-à-vis Turkey, with whom Greece endured a long-standing enmity and against whom Greece had nearly gone to war in 1974. But the prospect of EC accession was not universally popular in Greece. The Panhellenic Socialist Movement, a new political party founded by Andreas Papandreou, strongly opposed membership. Papandreou was a doctrinaire Socialist who saw the EC as a political arm of NATO and an instrument of capitalist exploitation.

Papandreou tapped latent Greek hostility toward the EC. The 1961 association agreement yielded few practical benefits for Greece before the EC "froze" it in 1967 in response to the military coup. Despite the EC's seemingly tough response to the coup, many Greeks resented what one academic called "the fundamentally pusillanimous attitude of the Community towards the Colonels' dictatorship."[4] Lingering Greek suspicion of the EC emboldened the Socialists' opposition to membership and strengthened Papandreou's position.

Greece applied to join the EC in June 1975. The Council responded positively. With European integration seemingly moribund, the prospect of Greek accession provided a welcome morale boost. The Commission took a more cautious approach in its opinion on Greece's application, published in January 1976. While welcoming the prospect of eventual Greek accession, the Commission pointed out several problems, especially in the areas of agriculture and Greek government support for favored industries. Given Greece's relative impoverishment and the likely impact of Greek accession on the EC's relations with Turkey, the Commission urged a lengthy "pre-accession period." That was a polite way of saying that Greece was not yet ready to join the EC.[5]

The Greek government reacted badly to the Commission's opinion. So did the Council, which endorsed Greece's application in February 1976. A statement by German foreign minister Hans-Dietrich Genscher typified the Council's attitude. Speaking from the heart rather than the head, Genscher declared that "Greece, only recently returned to the democratic fold, would march in future with the Community of European nations."[6] Exploiting such sentiments to the full, Greece began accession negotiations in July 1976. Despite the slow pace of the negotiations, Karamanlis received a strong mandate to press ahead when he won the November 1977 election. At the same time, the Socialists emerged as the largest opposition party.

The accession negotiations proceeded slowly because of inadequate information about economic conditions in Greece, due in large part to poor administrative capacity in Athens. Undoubtedly, attitudes in the Council changed during the negotiations, especially after Portugal and Spain applied to join the EC. Having paid little attention to the economic implications of Greek accession, the Council realized the potentially negative impact of large-scale Mediterranean enlargement. Member states feared that giving generous entry terms to Greece would set a bad precedent for the negotiations with Portugal and Spain.

Karamanlis's greatest concern was that the EC would lump together the Greek, Portuguese, and Spanish applications. The prime minister cited the 1961 accession agreement, which envisioned Greek entry by 1984, as proof that Greece was entitled to special treatment. He embarked on a tour of national capitals in early 1978 to press his case, warning of the negative consequences for Greek public opinion of protracted, joint accession negotiations. Because France was more concerned than other member states about the potential impact of Spanish accession, Giscard's attitude was crucial. Karamanlis, who had lived in exile in Paris during the colonels' regime, pulled out all the stops. Giscard received him warmly, urging the Council in February 1978 to allow Greece to join by 1980.

Although some hard bargaining lay ahead, the second stage of the negotiations, beginning in mid-1978, proceeded rapidly. The accession treaty, signed in Athens in May 1979, was a tribute to Karamanlis's acumen and skill. Ratification went smoothly, despite the Socialists' opposition to membership. Greece joined the EC, to great fanfare, in January 1981. The EC reveled in Greece's accession, especially in light of the budgetary dispute with Britain and the Community's slide once again into a political and economic quagmire.[7]

Direct Elections to the European Parliament

Whereas possible Greek accession was a cause of apprehension as well as expectation for advocates of deeper integration, direct elections to the EP seemed like a godsend. Fervent Eurofederalists, admittedly an endangered species by that time, hoped that direct elections would accelerate moves toward European union. Some member states, notably Britain, Denmark, and France, strongly opposed any increase in the EP's powers; others, such as Germany, Italy, and the Netherlands, favored a more influential EP but did not push the point. The Commission supported direct elections, hoping to enhance its own legitimacy and strengthen the supranational side of the Community system. The EP itself did not demand new powers at the time, lest it raise the hackles of unsympathetic member states.[8]

Yet the first direct elections, held in June 1979, failed to generate much interest or excitement throughout the EC. National political parties controlled the selection of candidates and ran the campaign. Many voters saw the elections as a referendum on the performance of their own governments. The overall turnout (63 percent) was low by the standard of national elections, although it varied from country to country. The results confirmed the dominance in the EP of the rival Social Democrats and Christian Democrats: the Socialist Group won 113 seats (27.5 percent); the European People's Party (the EC-wide political party established by the Christian Democrats in 1978 in anticipation of direct elections) won 110 seats (26.8 percent).[9]

Given the much larger size of the directly elected EP and the retirement of many sitting members, most of the members of the EP who were elected in 1979 were new to the job. Some, especially from Britain and Denmark, were Euroskeptics, but the vast majority favored deeper integration and wanted to enhance the EP's importance in the EC as a whole. A core group of Euro-enthusiasts filled leadership positions, ranging from the presidency and vice presidencies to the heads of the committees and party groups.

About 10 percent of the new MEPs held the dual mandate (they held seats in both a national parliament and the EP). Because the dual mandate formed a bridge between parliaments at the national level and at the European level, the Danish government wanted all MEPs to continue to hold the dual mandate after direct elections. Yet holders of the dual mandate tended to give priority to their national obligations, often neglecting EC affairs and further undermining public confidence in the EP. Although it was better institutionally for the EP not to have members who also held seats in national parliaments, the rapid demise after 1979 of the dual mandate weakened the link between the two levels of governance.[10]

The European Monetary System

The EMS was the second major monetary policy initiative undertaken in the EC, the first being the Werner Plan for economic and monetary union.[11] The abandonment of the Werner Plan in the mid-1970s hardly instilled confidence in another such initiative within a relatively short time. Indeed, uncomfortable memories of the EC's failure to achieve EMU by 1980 led governments to tone down their rhetoric about the EMS. Far from proclaiming the EMS as a step toward EMU, governments saw it for what it was: an effort to reduce exchange rate fluctuations among participating currencies in order to fight inflation, increase investment, and improve economic performance. Only the Commission claimed that the EMS aimed to promote deeper integration, although the relative success of the system, which nobody predicted at the time, undoubtedly contributed to the EC's revival later in the 1980s.

The birth of the EMS is generally associated with Giscard and Schmidt, but Commission president Roy Jenkins conceived the idea. He had a number of motives: to revitalize European integration, put himself and the Commission at the center of EC affairs, and help the Community cope with international exchange rate instability. Jenkins raised the idea in a lecture at the European University Institute in Florence in October 1977. He tried to interest Schmidt during a visit to Bonn in November 1977 but found the chancellor in a characteristically gloomy mood, preoccupied with an extreme-left-wing terrorist campaign and unwilling to take a lead in EC affairs.[12] The Commission issued a communication on EMU in November 1977, but the European Council paid little attention to it at a summit the following month.[13] Only perennially Eurofederal Belgium, then in the Council presidency, supported the Commission's position.

Schmidt had a sudden change of heart in early 1978, perhaps because of another drop in the dollar's value. Persistent depreciation of the dollar and a corresponding appreciation of the mark reduced the competitiveness of German exports and threatened German jobs. The United States appeared to be recovering economically at the expense of Germany's prudence and prosperity. Schmidt accused US president Jimmy Carter of taking a cavalier approach to international monetary matters. Schmidt wanted to cushion Germany from the impact of US action (or inaction) by establishing a European-wide monetary system and also demonstrate to the United States that Europeans were willing and able to respond to poor US leadership in international economic affairs.[14]

With the zeal of a convert, Schmidt championed a monetary policy initiative in the EC, relegating Jenkins and the Commission to the sidelines.[15] Instead, Schmidt chose Giscard as his main partner. The idea of the EMS appealed to Giscard intellectually and had far more weight coming from Schmidt than Jenkins. Giscard and his prime minister, Raymond Barre, author of the Commission's influential memorandum on EMU in 1969, embraced the proposal enthusiastically. The advantage to France of linking the weak franc to the strong mark was obvious, especially if Germany would bear the cost of maintaining parity between them.

From that time onward the EMS became a Franco-German initiative. Giscard and Schmidt unveiled an early version of it at the European Council in April 1978. Other national leaders resented this classic example of Franco-German high-handedness, but most wanted their currencies to participate in the proposed system. Only James Callaghan, Britain's prime minister, demurred, partly to protest Franco-German behavior but largely because of the negative reaction of Euroskeptics in the Labour Party and concerns about national sovereignty.

French and German officials had a free hand to work out the details of the EMS before presenting them at the next European Council, at the beginning of Germany's presidency in July 1978. Jenkins vividly described the British delegation's late arrival at the summit and indifference to the subject under discussion: "They marched [into the European Council] in single file like a jungle expedition into hostile territory, first Callaghan, then [foreign minister] Owen, then six or seven senior officials, then about fifteen bearers carrying about twice that amount of red despatch boxes, which must . . . have been more for show than use during a twenty-four hour period."[16] Callaghan's attitude once again demonstrated Britain's aversion to deeper European integration.

The Franco-German proposal called for an exchange rate mechanism using a parity grid and a divergence indicator based on an artificial unit of account made up of a basket of participating currencies, weighted according to their values. Currencies could fluctuate against each other within a band of plus or minus 2.5 percent of their value. Finance ministers and central bankers would have to agree to parity changes. Germany insisted that weak-currency countries (like France and Italy) take fiscal policy measures and not rely solely on intervention by strong-currency countries (notably Germany) to stay within the agreed-upon band (this was reminiscent of the debate between the "economists" and the "monetarists" during the EMU negotiations of the early 1970s).

Officials worked throughout 1978 to finalize details of the scheme. Prime Minister Giulio Andreotti wanted Italy to participate from the outset, although experts doubted whether the weak lire could stay in the exchange rate mechanism. Ireland wanted to join as well, despite its currency's parity with sterling, which would stay outside the mechanism. Both Ireland and Italy requested financial assistance from the EC in the form of larger allocations from the Regional Development Fund in order to cushion the impact of EMS participation. To complicate matters further, France and Britain insisted that their shares of the Regional Development Fund not diminish in relations to those of Ireland and Italy, and Germany balked at paying the extra cost.

National leaders thrashed out a final agreement at their summit in December 1979. Schmidt saved the day with an offer of extra financial assistance, thus ensuring that all member states except Britain would participate in the exchange rate mechanism. The EMS was to have started operating in January 1979, but a demand by Giscard for the abolition of monetary compensatory amounts, a device used since the early 1970s to cushion the common agricultural policy from exchange rate fluctuations, caused a delay. Because of the mark's tendency to rise against other currencies, the compensatory system helped prop up agricultural prices in Germany and was a source of resentment in France. Yet it was odd for Giscard to delay implementation of the EMS, a showpiece of Franco-German cooperation and leadership in the EC, for the sake of the compensatory system. He may have wanted to ingratiate himself with French farmers, always a worthwhile endeavor for French politicians. Giscard got his way when agriculture ministers agreed in March 1979 to abolish the compensatory system without specifying a timetable. The EMS then went into operation.

The EMS was highly unusual in the EC. Only member states could participate in it, although none was obliged to do so (Britain's opt-out proved the point). It was not based on the EC treaties, although closer monetary policy cooperation, culminating in EMU, was a cherished EC objective. It did not emerge from a formal Commission proposal, although two Community bodies, the Economic and Financial Affairs Council (Ecofin) and the Committee of Central Bank Governors, ran it. Ultimately, the EMS demonstrated the utility of institutionalized European integration: it could not have come into being had the EC not already existed.

In the Doldrums

Despite these promising developments, the EC sank into the doldrums in the early 1980s. The second oil shock of 1979 choked off the tentative economic recovery of the preceding two years. Beginning in 1980, growth stagnated, unemployment rose, and the balance of trade deteriorated. Only inflation began to fall, thanks in part to the success of the EMS. The Commission feared for the future of the common market, lamenting member states' tendencies "to resort to unilateral, national action which not only makes it harder to impose a common discipline but can also be the gradual undoing of what the Community has so far achieved."[17] The Commission warned in 1980 that "overt or covert protectionism" on the part of member states was fragmenting the internal market, damaging the EC's international credibility, and giving the EC's main trading partners an additional competitive advantage.[18]

The political situation was equally unpropitious. Giscard, unpopular and undermined by Jacques Chirac, his erstwhile prime minister, lost the French presidential election in May 1981. François Mitterrand, his successor, pursued a dash for growth that strained the country's public finances, put the franc under intense pressure, and called the future of the EMS into question. Schmidt lost office in 1982, when the Free Democrats, the minority party in the coalition government, jilted him in favor of Helmut Kohl and the Christian Democrats. Though he later became a founding father of the euro, during his first years in office Kohl devoted little time to the EC.

British prime minister Margaret Thatcher, by contrast, had a large majority in parliament and a definite domestic and international agenda. The EC did not loom large in her thinking, except as a source of resentment against Britain's excessive budgetary contribution. Her demand for a massive rebate both characterized and contributed to the EC's malaise in the early 1980s. Greek accession turned into a major political liability when Papandreou won the general election in 1981 and adopted a policy of obstruction toward the EC. To add insult to injury, Greenland voted in a referendum in February 1982 to leave "the geographical scope of the Treaties" (the remote country was a dependency of Denmark).

The twenty-fifth anniversary of the signing of the Rome Treaty was therefore a somber affair. Tugendhat, who represented the Commission at the commemoration ceremony in Brussels, painted an amusing portrait of it. Thatcher "wore black and looked forbidding"; Mitterrand, though still relatively new in office, "had already acquired that aura of unapproachability so characteristic of French presidents"; and Schmidt "was obviously impatient with all the fuss." Tugendhat wrote that after the lackluster speeches, "as we all trooped across the road to the Royal Palace for lunch, I could not help reflecting upon the uninspiring nature of the whole affair. The drizzle, which had replaced the fog, seemed to provide a fitting finale." The next day, news reached EC leaders at a dreary meeting of the European Council of the death of Walter Hallstein, the Commission's first president. "The symbolism inherent in the timing of Hallstein's death seemed unmistakable and attracted widespread comment. It was as if an ideal as well as a man was being declared dead."[19]

Institutional Inertia

Institutional inertia underlay the sense of drift. At the end of the 1970s the EC settled into a state best described by the French word *lourdeur* (heaviness or dullness). The Commission was a leaden bureaucracy, the Council lacked direction, and the Luxembourg Compromise (a government's right to veto) was an article of faith. The EC still suffered institutionally from the impact of the first enlargement. The Commission acquired four new commissioners without acquiring a greater range of responsibilities. Two of the new member states, Britain and Denmark, were avowedly intergovernmentalist and hostile to the Commission and the EP.

The prospect of renewed enlargement drew attention to the EC's institutional inadequacies. Some of the other member states suspected Britain of wanting enlargement in order to weaken the EC. A remark by

Prime Minister James Callaghan in October 1977 summed up Britain's position: "the dangers . . . of an over-centralized, over-bureaucratized and over-harmonized Community will be far less with twelve member states than with nine."[20] There was no question of radically redesigning the EC's institutional architecture in response to enlargement, only of streamlining the existing structure.

Ireland linked the use of qualified majority voting and enlargement in 1975, when Greece applied to join. The Benelux countries, Italy, and the Commission also questioned the institutional implications of enlargement, especially after Portugal and Spain submitted applications. France and Britain, and to a lesser extent Germany, seemed happy with the status quo. Nevertheless, the EC's manifest inefficiency in the late 1970s, when enlargement returned to the forefront of EC affairs, made it impossible for even the most sanguine of member states to ignore institutional reform.[21]

Giscard therefore suggested in 1978 that the European Council appoint a small committee of "wise men" to consider "adjustments to the machinery and procedures of the Community institutions" that would not necessitate formal treaty change.[22] Chosen after the usual haggling over nationality and political orientation, the group's chairman was Robert Marjolin (France), a former vice president of the Commission. The other members were Barend Biesheuvel (the Netherlands), a former prime minister, and Edmund Dell (Britain), a former government minister. Marjolin had no illusions about the job, remarking that "the wisdom with which [wise men] are credited vanishes the moment they hand in their conclusions."[23]

The wise men's conclusions, presented to the Council presidency in October 1979, painted an unflattering picture of the EC. Before addressing specific institutional issues, the wise men lamented the EC's poor progress in the 1970s, due to "substantive problems stemming from economic and political constraints." The wise men saw the member states' failure to sustain the EC's "integrative momentum" as "a sign of something fundamentally wrong," noting that "the role of the machinery and institutional procedures is a strictly secondary one."[24] Nevertheless it was on that secondary role, and especially on the functioning of the Council and Commission, that the wise men duly concentrated.

The European Commission. Roy Jenkins, who was Commission president when the wise men wrote their report, had arrived in Brussels in January 1977, hoping to breathe new life into the Commission. The horse-trading among governments over the allocation of Commission portfolios opened Jenkins's eyes to the reality of Brussels life. Tugendhat, who received one of the portfolios, recalled the "heated arguments round the Commission table and behind closed doors in the President's office, lasting in all for about twelve hours . . . as colleagues fought bitterly for position. This was despite the extensive preparatory talks conducted beforehand by Jenkins . . . with the individuals concerned and their governments."[25] Perceived national interest, even more than personal pride, accounted for what Jenkins called "the night of the long knives."[26]

Jolted by the experience, Jenkins got off to a slow start. His first six months as Commission president coincided with Britain's lackluster presidency of the Council. Jenkins fought a bitter battle with Giscard for the right to represent the Commission at the summit of the Group of Seven (G7) major industrialized countries in London in May 1977. Nothing would have come of Jenkins's idea for a monetary policy initiative in November 1977 had Schmidt not hijacked it. The prevailing political climate was simply not conducive to Commission activism. By 1978 it looked as if Jenkins's presidency would be as forgettable as any since Walter Hallstein's.

As the wise men pointed out in their report, the office of the president was politically and institutionally weak. There were too many commissioners and too few weighty portfolios. The Commission's directorates-general (departments) resented the size and influence of commissioners' *cabinets* (private offices). Promotion at the higher levels of the civil service depended on nationality and networking, not merit. Morale was low throughout the institution.

The relationship between Jenkins and Giscard, president of what was still the EC's most influential member state, epitomized the relationship between the Commission and the Council. So suspicious of Giscard was Jenkins that he detected in Giscard's proposal for a committee of wise men "a desire . . . to cut down the power of the Commission, to reduce or eliminate our political role, our connection with Parliament, and . . . to amalgamate us with the Council secretariat and with [the member states' permanent representatives], and thus to make us all servants of the European Council."[27]

Even if that was Giscard's intention, the wise men would never have condoned it. After all, Marjolin was a former commissioner who lamented the institution's current weakness. Thus the wise men recommended strengthening the powers of the Commission president, notably in the allocation and reshuffling of portfolios. Nevertheless, the committee deplored what it saw as "a lack of coherence, and increasing bureaucracy, in [the Commission's] own internal operations" and recommended reducing the number of commissioners to one per member state.[28]

The wise men's recommendations for Commission reform dovetailed with those of another report on the subject. That was by Dirk Spierenburg, a former member of the Coal and Steel Community's High Authority. At Jenkins's request, Spierenburg studied the Commission and submitted a series of proposed reforms in September 1979. They ranged from the role of the *cabinets* to recruitment, promotion, and other personnel problems. Spierenburg proposed the depoliticization and modernization of the institution through a radical program of internal reform.[29]

The Council of Ministers and the European Council. The Luxembourg Compromise continued to bedevil decisionmaking in the Council of Ministers in the late 1970s. According to the wise men's report, "an atmosphere has developed [in the Council] in which—even on minor issues and in quite humble forums [such as in working groups]—States can obstruct agreement for reasons which they know full well to be insufficient, but which are never brought into the open let alone seriously challenged by their colleagues." The wise men recommended greater use of qualified majority voting, as stipulated in the treaties. That would not necessarily mean a vote always being taken, as the mere prospect of voting would encourage governments to reach consensus. A government that nonetheless insisted on invoking the Luxembourg Compromise should say "clearly and explicitly . . . that very important interests are at stake."[30] The wise men recognized the importance of the European Council but did not see it as a panacea for the EC's problems, especially because decisions that should have been taken in the Council were being pushed up to the European Council.

Lack of action. Neither the wise men's report on general institutional reform nor the Spierenburg report on Commission reform was ever implemented. Jenkins lacked the necessary support in national capitals to act on them. The Spierenburg report achieved cult status among scholars of the Commission, because of its prescience and farsightedness. It was only in 2000, when the Commission undertook major internal reform in the wake of a resignation scandal, that some of the report's recommendations finally saw the light of day.

Giscard damned the wise men's report with faint praise at the European Council in November 1979. He noted with pleasure the report's criticism of the Commission and its endorsement, however tepid, of the European Council. Then he let the matter drop. After all, the report also criticized successive Council presidencies for lack of direction. The French presidency, in the first half of 1979, was particularly poor, with Giscard engaged in a procedural dispute with the EP and preoccupied with domestic political problems. After a perfunctory discussion of the wise men's report at the November 1979 summit, it sank into obscurity.

The British Budgetary Question

Whereas the EC's institutional problems percolated under the surface, the debilitating British budgetary question dominated meetings of the European Council between 1979 and 1984. No wonder that Roy Jenkins came to refer to it as the "bloody British question." At issue was not only the size of Britain's contribution but also the composition of the budget itself. The EC spent most of its money on agricultural subsidies and supports (the CAP devoured about 70 percent of the budget in 1980). Given the relentless increase in agricultural spending, the EC was bound to hit the limit of its own resources in the early to middle 1980s. Governments would then need to agree either to increase the size of their value-added tax contribution or to decrease spending on agriculture.

Britain never liked the CAP, not least because of its impact on the budget. Harold Wilson's Labour government had attempted to get a better deal for Britain as part of the renegotiation of accession terms in 1974–1975, but settled for relatively little. Only when Thatcher came to power in 1979 did Britain seriously address its budgetary imbalance in the EC. Thatcher knew instinctively that the British public would back her in a fight against Brussels to right such an obvious wrong.

Thatcher could not abide the CAP. Whereas French and German leaders saw it as part of the original bargain to bind their countries together after the war, she saw the CAP solely as a market-distorting mechanism. Thatcher viewed the EC as a collection of sovereign states cooperating closely for mutual economic gain. Other EC leaders, she suspected, aspired to an EC that was "interventionist, protectionist, and ultimately federalist." At the root of the CAP and the Community lay the Franco-German axis, which, Thatcher believed, "diminished Britain's capacity to influence events" and was "a factor to be reckoned with."[31]

Thatcher's approach to the CAP meshed with her domestic priorities. Being obsessed at home with cutting public spending, it would have been contrary to her nature and political instincts to allow the EC to spend public money profligately. Most other EC leaders saw things differently. They cared little about fiscal rectitude when it came to "Brussels money." Thatcher disliked the phrase "own resources," not only because of its inelegance but also because it disguised what for her was a fundamental truth: that money handed over to the EC was "ours," not "theirs," and that Britain contributed too much and was entitled to a generous rebate.

A visit by Schmidt to London in May 1979 gave Thatcher an early opportunity to make a case against the CAP and for a British rebate. Schmidt was one of the few foreigners, excluding Americans, whom Thatcher liked (although he was a Social Democrat, she admired his domestic economic policies and advocacy of EC financial reform). As Thatcher recalled, she told Schmidt "straight away that although Britain wanted to play a vigorous and influential role in the European Community, we could not do so until the problem of our grossly unfair budgetary contribution had been resolved."[32]

Schmidt's visit set the scene for Thatcher's first meeting of the European Council, in June 1979. Giscard and Schmidt were accustomed to dominating the European Council; Thatcher decided to shake things up. The first female member of the EC's most exclusive club, Thatcher was neither demure nor submissive. From then on, as Commissioner Tugendhat observed, the budgetary question "became inexorably caught up with the pride, prejudice and personalities of the heads of state and governments involved."[33] Giscard wanted to postpone discussion of the budget and instead celebrate the EP's first direct elections. "And so," as Thatcher recalled, "at my very first European Council I had to say no."[34] It was a word that her colleagues in the European Council would hear repeatedly in the years ahead.

The following summit, in November 1979, ended acrimoniously when Thatcher rejected a Commission analysis of the budgetary problem. A game of brinkmanship ensued. Thatcher implicitly threatened to withhold Britain's budgetary contribution (an illegal act), and Giscard and Schmidt speculated about relegating Britain to second-class EC membership (a legal impossibility). Foreign ministers searched for a solution while their agricultural counterparts agreed to yet another increase in CAP spending. Although the atmosphere at the next summit was much better, it was not good enough to facilitate a breakthrough. That came only after a marathon, eighteen-hour meeting of the Council of Ministers in May 1980 during which Britain was offered a two-thirds rebate covering a three-year period.

Thatcher reluctantly accepted. The European Council endorsed the agreement at the June 1980 summit, where Schmidt urged wider budgetary reform, especially in view of imminent Greek accession. That was easier said than done, not least because Germany's agriculture minister was among the most aggressive supporters of higher farm prices. Nevertheless, Thatcher succeeded in getting budget reform onto the EC's agenda and in temporarily resolving the question of Britain's contribution. As everybody knew, however, Thatcher would return to the charge in 1983 when the terms of the temporary agreement were due to expire.

The first round of the British budgetary question ended in victory for Thatcher, but Britain paid a high price. Other EC leaders had hoped that after the shilly-shallying of Wilson and the barely concealed hostility of Callaghan, British policy toward the EC would improve under Thatcher. Many recalled Thatcher's first political battle on becoming Conservative Party leader: campaigning for Britain's continued EC membership in the run-up to the 1975 referendum. They had hoped that Thatcher would contribute to the EC's development, as eventually she did by championing completion of the internal market. In the meantime, Thatcher's dogged pursuit of a budgetary rebate on terms acceptable only to Britain alienated her fellow EC leaders. Even Tugendhat, a sympathizer, observed that "the longer [the budgetary question] lasted, the more isolated Britain became and the more this single issue came to dominate British European policy."[35]

Obdurate though she was, other EC leaders preferred to deal with Thatcher than with her Labour Party opponents. At that time, the Labour Party was officially committed to pulling Britain out of the EC and repealing "those sections of Community law which have been imposed on the UK and which we do not find acceptable."[36] Despite their frustration with Thatcher, few of Britain's EC partners welcomed the prospect of conducting arduous withdrawal negotiations with a new British government. The contemporaneous negotiations on Greenland's withdrawal from the EC were difficult enough.

The Mediterranean Morass

Far from boosting the EC's fortunes, Brussels's involvement with Greece, Portugal, and Spain in the early 1980s was a source of considerable friction and mutual frustration. No sooner had Greece joined in January 1981 than the Socialists won the general election and Papandreou became prime minister. Despite having opposed EC membership, Papandreou decided not to take Greece out of the EC but to strike a better bargain for his country within it. No doubt impressed by Thatcher's antics, Papandreou demanded special concessions for Greece, ostensibly to help the country's economy adapt to membership. The Greek government sent Brussels a formal memorandum outlining its position on the economic impact of membership, in March 1981.

Negotiations on the Greek memorandum continued sporadically for the next four years. In a communication to the Council in March 1983, the Commission proposed that the EC assist Greece through regional policy and other redistributive measures, rather than through derogations to the treaties.[37] Most of the proposed special measures would be encapsulated in the so-called Integrated Mediterranean Programs. The European Council approved the Commission's approach in June 1983, but bad blood between Papandreou and other EC leaders delayed a final agreement and contributed to the collapse of the next summit, in Athens in December 1983, which ended without even a communiqué being issued.

The state of negotiations on the Greek memorandum mirrored the state of negotiations on Portuguese and Spanish accession, at least until a political breakthrough in 1982. Both Portugal and Spain embarked on the road to EC membership in the mid-1970s.[38] Portugal, following a period of turmoil in the aftermath of the revolution that ousted the country's authoritarian regime in April 1974, stabilized politically and applied to join the EC in March 1977. Public opinion and most political parties in Portugal strongly supported EC accession as a sure way to consolidate democracy and promote prosperity. Like Greece, Portugal wanted the EC to consider its application separately from Spain's. That proved impossible for the EC to do. In view of the two countries' propinquity and the timing of their applications (Spain applied four months after Portugal), the EC conducted parallel accession negotiations with them. Strong reservations in France and Italy about the economic implications of Spanish accession undoubtedly slowed the negotiations with Portugal.

In its opinion of May 1978 the Commission identified a number of impediments to early Portuguese accession, including agriculture, free movement of people, and textiles, which accounted for over 40 percent of Portugal's industrial output and 33 percent of its exports. Initially Portugal had hoped to join as early as January 1983. The delay in beginning substantive negotiations until 1980 convinced the Portuguese government of the unlikelihood of accession until at least the middle of the decade.

Like Portugal, Spain wanted to join for political and economic reasons. Politically, Spain wanted to regain international respectability after decades of authoritarian rule under General Francisco Franco. Economically, Spain wanted to accelerate the process of industrial and agricultural modernization begun in the later years of the Franco regime. A center-right government began the post-Franco transition and set Spain on the road to EC accession. Under the influence of former German chancellor Willy Brandt in the international socialist movement, the opposition Spanish Socialist Party transformed itself into a modern Social Democratic party. Unlike the Greek Socialists, the Spanish Socialists strongly supported EC membership.

France and Italy looked forward to the EC's post-accession center of gravity's tilting more toward southern Europe, but had serious reservations about the impact of Spanish accession on the CAP. By increasing the EC's agricultural area by 30 percent and its farming work force by 25 percent, Spain's entry would be a major drain on the budget. In addition, France, Italy, and Spain would compete directly in the production of fruit, vegetables, and olive oil. The ever-vigilant French agricultural lobby swung into action in the run-up to France's presidential election in May 1981, which Giscard lost, though for reasons unrelated to the EC.

The member states (and the rest of the world) were reminded of the political imperative of bringing Spain into the EC when a group of military officers attempted a coup in the Spanish parliament in January 1981. Despite the European Council's expression of support soon afterward for the consolidation of "a democratic Spain," the accession negotiations merely plodded along in 1981 and 1982.[39]

Mitterrand was as susceptible as were his predecessors to the French farmers' lobby. Fisheries and textiles remained major stumbling blocks in the accession negotiations with both countries. Apart from economic concerns, Mitterrand was not yet sufficiently interested in the EC's revival to see Mediterranean enlargement in a positive light. Nevertheless, the EC was not entirely to blame for the slow pace of the negotiations. The Spanish government seemed reluctant to accept all the obligations of membership, such as introducing a value-added tax and curtailing state subsidies. The European Council urged Spain in November 1981 to "make good use of the period until accession for careful preparations . . . by introducing the necessary reforms so that the potential benefits for both sides can be realized."[40]

Picking Up Speed

Notwithstanding the apparent impasse on enlargement and other contentious issues, reports of the EC's demise in the early 1980s were greatly exaggerated. The institutions continued to function and lay the groundwork for the EC's resurgence later in the decade. Despite weak leadership following Jenkins's departure, the Commission took important initiatives to restructure the steel industry, promote collaboration in the high-technology sector, and complete the internal market. Energized by the first direct elections, the EP reorganized itself internally and pushed for greater integration in a host of policy areas. The EMS was a surprising success and helped restore confidence in the utility of economic integration.

Perhaps the most striking change in the early 1980s was in the outlook of the member states. Reeling from renewed economic recession and frustrated with the EC's apparent stagnation during the preceding ten years, governments chafed at the constraint imposed by unanimity in the Council, swung toward support for deeper integration, and sought a stronger EC presence on the international stage. Nowhere was this more consequential than in France, where Mitterrand changed the direction of his economic policy in 1983 and became an advocate of deeper political and economic integration. The ongoing British budgetary question nevertheless obscured the EC's brightening prospects. Only when it was finally resolved in 1984 did the EC's fortunes suddenly look exceedingly bright.

Ending the Budgetary Battles

Thatcher was resoundingly reelected as Britain's prime minister in June 1983. She owed her success partly to the unelectability of the Labour Party, due in no small measure to its pledge to withdraw from the EC, and largely to the "Falklands factor," the victory dividend from the war against Argentina in the southern Atlantic for control of the disputed Falklands/Malvinas Islands. Flushed with success on the battlefield and at the ballot box, Thatcher returned to the fray in Europe. She demanded a permanent solution to the British budgetary question at the Stuttgart summit in June 1983.

By 1983, Thatcher was a veteran of the European Council and facing Mitterrand and Kohl, the relatively new leaders of France and Germany, who had not yet revived the Franco-German axis. Mitterrand and Kohl, weak domestically and uninterested in the minutiae of the EC budget, were no match for the experienced British prime minister. Kohl would have liked to resolve the issue during Germany's Council presidency, in early 1983, but the necessary groundwork had not been laid. EC leaders decided to postpone the matter until their meeting in Athens in December 1983.

The Athens summit was a disaster. The other EC leaders heartily disliked Papandreou, who made no secret of his determination to get as much as possible out of the EC while contributing as little as possible to its political or economic development. Usually EC leaders wanted the Council presidency to be able to proclaim a successful summit, regardless of the actual outcome. In this case the other EC leaders harbored such ill will toward Papandreou that they would not agree on a concluding communiqué and made no secret of the summit's failure. But poor preparation and Papandreou's presidency were not entirely to blame for lack of progress on the British budgetary question. Thatcher suspected that Mitterrand wanted to delay a settlement until France took over the presidency from Greece, so that he could then claim a diplomatic victory.[41]

Thatcher wanted a permanent British refund as part of a long-term reform of the EC's finances. By the end of 1983 the EC was approaching bankruptcy. The EC's inability to bring agricultural spending under control compounded the problem. In 1979 the Council introduced a modest change in the system of price guarantees and imposed a levy on dairy farmers to help meet the costs of storing or subsidizing exports of surplus produce. When this failed to curb excess output, the Commission proposed a production quota.

Negotiations on the proposed CAP reforms, on the terms of Britain's rebate, and on reconfiguring the size of the value-added tax contribution to the EC's budget were closely related. A comprehensive agreement seemed likely at the European Council in March 1984, held under the French presidency. A decision by agriculture ministers shortly before the meeting to curtail CAP spending by introducing milk quotas augured well for the outcome. But at the summit itself, Garret FitzGerald, Ireland's prime minister, rejected a draft agreement that, because of the structure of Irish agriculture, would have badly hurt the Irish economy (the dairy sector accounted for nearly 10 percent of Ireland's GDP). As Thatcher mischievously remarked, "we never seemed to get by [at a European Council] without a tear-jerking homily on the predicament of Ireland from . . . Garret FitzGerald, who was determined if he could to exempt his country from the disciplines on agricultural spending."[42] Ireland eventually got a special dispensation.

The summit failed not because of the dispute over milk quotas but because the participants were again unable to solve the British budgetary question. Disagreement centered on the basis as well as the size of Britain's rebate. France seemed to be steering the meeting to a successful conclusion when Kohl changed the dynamic of the negotiation by proposing an annual rebate for the next three years. Thatcher flatly rejected this, not only because she considered it insufficient (although by any measure it was a generous offer), but also because it was not a permanent solution. France and Italy's refusal after the summit to lift a veto on the payment of Britain's 1983 rebate further infuriated Thatcher.[43]

EC leaders finally resolved the long-standing British budgetary question at the final summit of the French presidency of the European Council, held in the splendid setting of Fontainebleau, outside Paris, in June 1984.

Eager for a settlement, Mitterrand and Kohl coordinated their positions before the summit began. Perhaps equally eager to put the issue behind her, Thatcher was surprisingly conciliatory.

All agreed at Fontainebleau on a permanent rebate in the form of a fixed percentage each year of the difference between Britain's value-added tax contribution to the EC and Britain's receipts from the EC. Thatcher worked down from an initial demand of 70 percent and the others worked up from an initial offer of 60 percent. Thatcher held out for 66 percent and Kohl for 65 percent. Mitterrand, the summit host, convinced Kohl to give Thatcher the extra 1 percent. Together with an agreement to raise the ceiling on value-added tax contributions to 1.4 percent and a vague commitment to curb CAP expenditure, this brought the budget saga to a close.

"In every negotiation," Thatcher wrote, "there comes the best possible time to settle: this was it."[44] She was as tired of the budgetary question as the others were. Thatcher was inclined to settle in mid-1984 also because of rising impatience at home with her obstructionism in Brussels. Her stridency in the European Council, initially a source of national pride, now embarrassed many Britons. More important politically was her declining support within the Conservative Party, which would eventually cost her the prime ministership.[45]

Mitterrand's renewed calls for a renegotiation of Britain's relationship with the EC may also have persuaded Thatcher to bring the dispute to an end. In a famous speech at the EP in May 1984, Mitterrand raised the prospect of a two-speed EC, with Britain relegated to the slow lane.[46] It seems unlikely, however, that Thatcher would have taken such threats seriously. She had her own understanding of what a two-speed EC meant: "Those who pay more are in the top group and those who pay less are not."[47] The most important factor in ending the dispute may have been simply that Thatcher, like her EC partners, wanted to move on. Resolution of the British budgetary question cleared the way not only for Portuguese and Spanish accession but also for a constructive debate about the EC's future.

Tugendhat, who sympathized with Thatcher, claimed that "no other European leader could have held out for so long nor secured so much against the opposition of all the rest."[48] Yet the dispute could have been resolved sooner, arguably to Britain's advantage. In monetary terms, Thatcher might have won greater or equal concessions at an earlier stage in the negotiations. Politically, by protracting the dispute, she forfeited whatever residual goodwill existed toward Britain in the EC.

Poor personal chemistry exacerbated the situation. Kohl detested Thatcher; Mitterrand found her oddly fascinating. Thatcher disliked both Kohl and Mitterrand. Such intense feelings mattered in the European Council, a highly intimate decisionmaking forum. By 1984, when the dispute finally ended, Thatcher was the second most unpopular member of the European Council (Papandreou was ahead of her by a long shot).

Resolution of the British budgetary question finally removed a persistent irritant in relations between Britain and the other member states. Resentment at the unfairness of its budgetary contribution was never far beneath the surface of British attitudes toward the EC. With the issue resolved, Britain could assess EC membership on its merits rather than on the basis of a budgetary quirk. Euroskeptics must have regretted the removal of an injustice that automatically engendered hostility in Britain toward Brussels, though there were plenty of other irritants in relations between the EC and the United Kingdom.

The long-running dispute at least instilled in other countries concern about excessive EC expenditure. As more of the original member states became net contributors to the budget, especially after the accession of Portugal and Spain, Thatcher's preoccupation with the EC's public finances became less peculiar. Yet the lure of a bountiful CAP was undiminished. Although the European Council agreed in Fontainebleau to cut spending on the CAP, it also agreed to increase the size of the EC's budget. As *The Economist* observed, "by agreeing to raise the EC's income, the Ten [member states] have removed the most direct pressure for reforming a runaway farm policy, namely the threat of running out of money."[49]

Portuguese and Spanish Accession

Resolution of the British budgetary question cleared the way for the accession of Portugal and Spain. Having reached a budgetary agreement, the Fontainebleau European Council set January 1986 as the date for the two countries to join the EC. In a move calculated to attract international attention, Mitterrand flew to Madrid immediately after the summit to report personally on the outcome.

Mitterrand's epiphany on enlargement coincided with important political changes in the candidate countries. In Portugal, the able and energetic Mario Soares formed a government in June 1983. Soares endeared himself to the EC when he introduced measures to reduce the country's substantial foreign debt and further restructure the economy. Soares cultivated close relations with Mitterrand, a fellow Socialist. During a tour of EC capitals later in 1983, Soares impressed his interlocutors with Portugal's determination to become a model member state. Rapid agreement on a number of outstanding issues quickly followed in the accession negotiations. Much to Soares's annoyance, however, the fate of Portugal's application hinged on the outcome of Spain's negotiations.

Following the landslide victory of Spain's Socialist Party in the 1982 general election, Felipe González reinvigorated the country's effort to join the EC. Young, personable, and passionately pro-European, González emulated Soares by visiting EC capitals and wooing national leaders. In anticipation of EC membership, González introduced badly needed but politically painful economic reforms. The accession negotiations proceeded well, although a number of tricky areas, notably agriculture and fisheries, became increasingly contentious. An informal summit of the prime ministers—all Socialists—of the EC's Mediterranean member states and applicant countries (France, Italy, Greece, Portugal, and Spain) in October 1983 paved the way for a breakthrough. At a meeting in Luxembourg only two days later, farm ministers approved rules to organize the EC's fruit, vegetable, and olive oil markets with a view to enlargement. Unencumbered by looming parliamentary or presidential elections, Mitterrand could afford to make concessions, although it was not until December 1984 that the EC resolved the remaining agricultural issues.[50]

Fisheries remained the final hurdle in the accession negotiations. The EC was reluctant to give Spain unrestricted access to its territorial waters: the Spanish fleet was larger than the combined Community fleet and had a notoriously insatiable appetite. Repeated clashes between Spanish trawlers and French and Irish naval vessels in 1984 emphasized the sensitivity of the issue. So did attacks by Spanish fishermen against trucks from EC member states, in protest against the seizure of Spanish trawlers, and retaliatory action by French truckers at the Spanish border. The two sides eventually concluded a fisheries agreement in early 1985, paving the way for Portuguese and Spanish accession in January 1986.

The negotiations with Portugal and Spain had taken six years to complete. Ratification of the accession agreements took another twelve months. Altogether, more than eight years elapsed between the two countries' applications to join and their entry into the EC. Portuguese and Spanish accession reinforced a lesson of the first enlargement: the road to EC membership was long and arduous for all concerned. Digesting the accession of Portugal and Spain would be equally challenging. Although the two countries were enthusiastic about European integration, they were much poorer than the existing member states, apart from Greece and Ireland. Yet they brought to the EC a new Mediterranean dimension and foreign policy orientation that led to the strengthening of economic and political relations with Latin America, a part of the world hitherto of little interest to the EC.

Commission Activism

The state of the Commission in the early 1980s mirrored that of the EC. Superficially, at least, the Commission was weak and demoralized. Jenkins, worn out after battling Thatcher on the budget and Giscard on the Commission's role and responsibilities, gladly returned to Britain at the end of his term in office, where he confronted Thatcher on surer ground. The European Council selected Gaston Thorn, a former prime minister of Luxembourg, to succeed Jenkins. Although thoroughly familiar with the EC, Thorn seemed detached and ill at ease in Brussels.

The Twelve Member States

Regardless of his personal shortcomings, Thorn was unfortunate to be selected at such a difficult time. The Commission president could be only as effective as the most influential national leaders wanted him to be. In Thorn's case, Giscard openly disdained the Commission, Schmidt was indifferent toward it, and Thatcher heartily disliked it. Although Mitterrand replaced Giscard early in Thorn's tenure and Kohl replaced Schmidt a year later, initially the new leaders of France and Germany showed little enthusiasm for European integration.

The Commission persevered, in the face of widespread public and political skepticism, in advocating deeper integration. Whereas Thorn soon faded into the background, some of the other commissioners relished the challenge of promoting integration at such a difficult time. Foremost among them was Commission vice president Étienne Davignon, a former Belgian diplomat who had also served in the Jenkins Commission. As the commissioner with responsibility for industrial affairs, Davignon sought to restructure old industries and encourage new ones while also pushing for completion of the internal market.

Steel. In October 1980 the Commission declared a "manifest crisis" in the EC's steel industry, under the terms of a hitherto-unused provision of the Coal and Steel Community. At Davignon's direction, the Commission imposed production quotas and other measures to give firms time to adjust to a massive slump in the steel market that brought the industry almost to its knees. The Commission's action required the unanimous approval of the Council, something notoriously difficult to obtain. The Commission's task was made more difficult by opposition in the steel industry from workers and employers, fearful for their livelihoods. In the end, even the fiercely anti-interventionist British government supported the Commission, because a Commission-imposed regime was preferable to a beggar-thy-neighbor policy of protectionist measures by individual member states. As it was, the Commission acted only after the collapse of the steel industry's voluntary crisis management plan. The Commission's action forced the European steel industry to restructure, albeit at a cost of lost jobs and closed plants. While blaming the Commission for imposing tough measures, national governments took credit for the industry's rescue.

High technology. In the early 1980s, industry, governments, and the Commission grew increasingly concerned about Western Europe's inadequacies in the high-technology sector, especially in view of intense competition from Asia and the United States. Davignon resolved to put the Commission at the forefront of efforts to improve European competitiveness by promoting collaboration among industries and universities. Davignon contacted the heads of major European manufacturers in the high-technology sector, urging them to consider the virtues of working together, something that the persistent economic recession in any case predisposed them to do. Not wanting to scare off European industrialists by raising the specter of Commission intrusiveness, Davignon kept discreetly in the background.

Davignon pushed through a reorganization of the Commission to bring under a single directorate-general all the departments responsible for research programs. The Commission then sent the Council a communication on the EC's research and development strategy for the 1980s, emphasizing the need to adopt a comprehensive approach by incorporating all EC research projects into a general framework program. The Council responded positively, noting that a broad consensus existed on the desirability of developing scientific research at the European level and improving the efficiency of the EC's research and development activities. The Council adopted the EC's first framework program for research and development in 1983, covering the period 1984–1987. The European Council encouraged greater EC involvement in research and development, especially during the French presidency in the first half of 1984. Resolution of the British budgetary question at the Fontainebleau summit in June 1984 facilitated funding of the new framework program, although not as generously as the Commission wanted.

The EC's renewed interest in research and development covered a range of issues but focused mostly on "industries of strategic importance." In 1982 the Council agreed on a pilot phase for the European Strategic Program for Research and Development in Information Technology (ESPRIT). This provided limited funding for collaborative research projects involving major manufacturers, small firms, and universities. ESPRIT proved extremely popular, although its impact was more symbolic than real. The research may not have produced scientific breakthroughs, but it bolstered confidence in the Commission's ability to advance the interests of European business.[51]

The internal market. As well as pursuing a bold industrial strategy, the Commission aggressively championed completion of the internal market. As early as 1979, the Commission signaled its determination to remove nontariff barriers and technical barriers to trade by following up on the landmark ruling by the Court of Justice in the *Cassis de Dijon* case, which arose out of a prohibition against the importation into Germany of Cassis, a French liqueur, on the grounds that it failed to meet Germany's alcohol-content standards. The Court ruled in February 1979 that because Cassis met French standards and did not pose a health risk, it could not be kept out of the German market.[52]

The Commission used the ruling to develop the principle of mutual recognition of national regulations and standards. Despite a general prohibition in the Rome Treaty on technical barriers to trade, governments frequently invoked an escape clause in the treaty allowing them to impose their own product standards for reasons of health and safety. In the event of differences among member states, the treaty provided for harmonization of standards, an arduous and politically sensitive process that caused a backlog of proposals in the Council. Building on the Cassis case, the Commission proposed that instead of trying to harmonize a potentially limitless number of product standards throughout the EC, member states should recognize and accept each other's standards as long as they satisfied certain health and safety concerns.[53]

On a broader front, the Commission continued in the early 1980s to outline the advantages to be gained from a fully functioning internal market. In June 1981 the Commission drafted a communication for the European Council on the importance of market integration. Meeting later that month, the European Council agreed that "a concerted effort must be made to strengthen and develop the free internal market, which lies at the very basis of the European Community."[54] Later in the year the Commission pressed the Council to pass a number of measures intended to simplify formalities at internal borders in the areas of customs, taxation, and statistics.[55]

The European Council devoted more attention in 1983 and 1984 to internal market issues, despite the distraction of the ongoing budgetary dispute. Sensing the imminent end of the protracted British budgetary question, the Commission prepared a detailed paper for the June 1984 Fontainebleau summit on a variety of internal market issues, ranging from the abolition of customs barriers to the free movement of people, capital, and services. In its postsummit communiqué, the European Council duly called for completion of the internal market.[56]

The Commission's industrial strategy and agitation for the internal market appealed to big business in Europe, which needed little prompting on the virtues of deeper integration. On the initiative of Guy Gyllenhammer, the head of Volvo, the leaders of some of Europe's biggest industries formed the European Round Table to lobby at the highest level for a single market. Although his own firm was located in Sweden, a nonmember state, Gyllenhammer appreciated the advantages for Volvo of a borderless EC, which he hoped that Sweden would join. Wisse Dekker, the head of Philips, the large Dutch electronics company, and a leading member of the European Round Table, published a pamphlet in 1984 calling for completion of the internal market by 1990.[57] Gyllenhammer and Dekker were in the vanguard of "an important and vocal constituency . . . impatient for an end to such things as customs delays at borders, conflicting national standards in data processing or arcane rules on property ownership . . . and pressing for the completion of the internal market."[58] Private-sector support for deeper economic integration quickly got the attention of European politicians.

European Parliament Activism

Less influential than the Commission and therefore of less interest to European business, the directly elected EP also pressed in the early 1980s for completion of the internal market. A number of members formed a cross-party "intergroup," known as the Kangaroo Group, to lobby for the removal of internal borders in the EC. Members of the group were strategically placed in the EP to advance various reports and resolutions calling for action on the internal market. Thus the EP asked two economists to write a report on the cost for European business of having to operate in an incomplete internal market. The ensuing report foreshadowed the Commission's more extensive and better-known study on "the cost of non-Europe" later in the decade.[59]

The EP suffered a political setback in 1980 when the Council refused to accept its amendments to the budget. Though imbued with a greater sense of purpose after the first direct elections, the EP wisely compromised in July 1980. At the other end of the budgetary procedure, the EP refused to grant discharge in November 1984 of the 1982 budget (in other words, the EP rejected the accuracy of the Commission's accounting for Community expenditure). The EP claimed that this amounted to censure of the Commission, which should have resulted in the Commission's resignation. Its credibility impaired, the Commission hung on until January 1985, when a new Commission was due in any case to take over.[60] The incident showed that the EP and the Commission, although institutional allies, were not destined always to get along. It also validated an observation by Roy Jenkins that direct elections produced "a potentially formidable new Parliament . . . which [the Commission] approached with a mixture of respect and apprehension."[61]

The EP aggressively exercised oversight of the Commission and, where possible, the Council in other areas as well. EP committees held more hearings, and MEPs tabled more questions on a variety of policy issues. For its part, the Commission introduced new procedures for dealing with the demands of EP plenary sessions and committee meetings. In 1981 the EP began the practice of voting on the incoming Commission, setting a precedent for the acquisition of formal investiture powers many years after.

It was in the legislative area above all that the EP sought to expand its limited role. At the time, the Rome Treaty provided for EP involvement in legislative decisionmaking only through the consultation procedure. Thus the EP could submit an opinion on a legislative proposal, which the Council generally ignored. In an effort to assert its authority, the directly elected EP challenged the validity of a Council directive on the grounds that the Council had acted before receiving the EP's opinion. The Court of Justice supported the EP and struck down the directive, proclaiming that the consultation procedure "reflects at Community level the fundamental principle that the peoples [of the EC] should take part in the exercise of power through the intermediary of an elected assembly."[62]

The Court's ruling strengthened the EP politically. The EP, by threatening to delay its opinion and thereby delay the enactment of legislation, leveraged its position in the legislative process. Moreover, the ruling enhanced the EP's claim to be the institution best placed to close the so-called democratic deficit, a term first used in the 1970s to describe the apparent gap between the governed and the governing in the EC. The EP used the Court's ruling in support of an elected assembly like a battering ram over the years to extend its legislative decisionmaking role.

The EP was particularly active in promoting European union. The wise men remarked in their report in 1979 that the term "European union" had recently been "the subject of much empty talk." Their most encouraging prognosis was that "everything [that] strengthens the Community's internal unity . . . and that of the Nine in dealings with the rest of the world, constitutes progress towards European Union."[63] The Commission's annual reports on the subject held out little hope in the early 1980s for a political breakthrough. Nevertheless, some of the newly elected MEPs saw themselves as the vanguard of a movement to recast the EC in a federal direction and achieve European union. A group of them, led by Altiero Spinelli, the irrepressible Eurofederalist and former commissioner, decided to use the EP as a constitutional convention and draft a treaty on European union.

In July 1980, Spinelli invited like-minded MEPs, from all political parties, to the Crocodile restaurant in Strasbourg. By the end of the year the "Crocodile club" had grown from ten to seventy members. Dedicated to reviving the EC, the club's proposals ranged from completion of the single market to replacing the EC with a federal European Union. Thanks to the work of the Crocodile club, between 1980 and 1982 the EP passed numerous resolutions advocating institutional reform and deeper integration.

Too large to meet and eat in its favorite Strasbourg restaurant, the Crocodile club moved to Brussels, thereby inaugurating the EP's influential Committee on Institutional Affairs. With Spinelli in the pivotal role of rapporteur (report writer), the committee set out to draft a new treaty. Knowing that most governments were likely to dismiss Spinelli as naive and excessively ambitious, the committee proceeded cautiously and responsibly. With the help of some academic experts, subcommittees worked on issues such as the legal personality of the proposed union and its institutional structure, competence, and relationship with the member states. The Draft Treaty Establishing the European Union finally emerged. In one of the most famous votes ever taken in the EP, a large majority of members voted for the draft treaty in February 1984.[64]

Far from being an unrealistic call for a United States of Europe, the draft treaty was a blueprint for a more efficient, democratic, and far-reaching organization of European states along federal lines. Its preamble stated that the EU would be responsible only for tasks that could be undertaken better in common at the European level than by member states acting alone at the national level. This was an early articulation of the principle of "subsidiarity" (member states' rights) that came to the fore in the late 1980s.

Despite its moderation and the political support of some sympathetic governments, the draft treaty had little chance of being implemented. Nevertheless, its existence, and the attention lavished on it by Mitterrand during France's Council presidency in early 1984, contributed to the momentum developing in the mid-1980s in favor of treaty reform. The draft treaty certainly was prescient, with many of its features finding their way, in some form or other, into subsequent treaty reforms. But it would be an exaggeration to say that the draft treaty triggered the EC's revival later in the 1980s.

The EP scheduled its vote on the draft treaty to generate publicity in the run-up to the second direct elections, in June 1984. Yet the draft treaty received little media coverage, and the second direct elections were even more disappointing than the first (the turnout in the second was 2 percentage points lower than in June 1979). Once again, the European elections seemed to consist of little more than separate national elections (Luxembourg even held a general election on the same day).

Member State Activism

Although the EP's draft treaty was too ambitious for most member states, many governments in the early 1980s wanted the EC to regain momentum. European integration seemed more necessary than ever in the context of incipient globalization and heightened East-West tension. The Luxembourg Compromise continued to impede decisionmaking in the EC, prompting Belgium to insist on the use of qualified majority voting during its Council presidency in the first half of 1982. But that was a small step on the road to EC reform, to which governments devoted increasing time and attention.

The Stuttgart declaration. German foreign minister Hans-Dietrich Genscher, eager to reassert German leadership in the EC and eager also to assert the leadership of his Free Democratic Party within the coalition government, prepared an initiative to deepen European integration. Because Franco-German relations were slightly unsettled after Mitterrand's election victory, Genscher chose Emilio Colombo, his Italian counterpart, rather than the French foreign minister, to cosponsor the initiative. Perennially pro-EC, Italy was delighted to share the limelight with Germany, hoping both to raise its international profile and to intrude upon the traditional Franco-German axis.

Speaking at the EP in November 1981, Genscher and Colombo proposed a nonbinding European Act, which would include institutional improvements, such as greater use of qualified majority voting and more power for the EP, to enhance the EC's effectiveness and legitimacy. Their main policy focus was on external relations. European Political Cooperation, the existing mechanism for foreign policy coordination, was patently inadequate, as shown by the member states' response to the Soviet invasion of Afghanistan in 1979 and the imposition of martial law in Poland in 1981, despite subsequent procedural improvements.

Genscher and Colombo urged member states to bring security and defense issues into European Political Cooperation. Yet governments were far apart on such a sensitive question. Wanting to restrict discussions on security and defense to NATO, Thatcher opposed the idea. A number of other leaders were wary as well. Papandreou resisted deeper European integration in general and closer security cooperation in particular. As a matter of principle, Denmark did not want European integration to move into the security realm. Sensitivity to a vague but popular notion of neutrality caused the otherwise indifferent Irish government to object to any initiative that touched on security and defense in the EC.

Member states finally endorsed a watered-down version of the Genscher-Colombo proposals in the form of the Solemn Declaration on European Union, issued in Stuttgart in June 1983.[65] The declaration called for closer cooperation on foreign policy and security and deeper European integration. Thatcher, taking the view that she "could not quarrel with everything" and that "the document had no legal force," reluctantly went along with it, later regretting that the Stuttgart declaration turned out to be "the linguistic skeleton on which so much institutional flesh would grow."[66]

A British proposal. While dismissing the wooliness of the Stuttgart declaration, Thatcher was not against the idea of deeper integration. Her main interests were economics and international relations: completion of the internal market would benefit Britain economically, while foreign policy cooperation could help to promote British interests internationally. Accordingly, Thatcher brought to the Fontainebleau summit in June 1984 a paper proposing deeper market integration and better foreign policy cooperation.[67] She preferred informal institutional arrangements to formal treaty changes. Because unanimity hindered completion of the internal market, governments should agree among themselves to vote in the Council on internal market measures. Apart from its intrinsic merits, Thatcher wanted the proposal to signal her commitment to the EC and end Britain's isolation after the long-running British budgetary question.

Mitterrand leads the way. Of all the national leaders, it was Mitterrand who led the way in revitalizing the EC. Mitterrand had long supported European integration but had little experience of the EC before becoming president of France in May 1981. He fought the campaign on domestic issues, promising, if elected, to reform the economy radically along Socialist lines. Mitterrand's policy prescription differed widely from the prevailing economic orthodoxy not only in Britain and the United States but also in most European countries run by Social Democratic governments.

Once elected, Mitterrand instituted extensive social and economic reform in France. Banks and industries were nationalized, new labor laws enacted, and welfare benefits increased. Mitterrand tried to jump-start growth and cut unemployment through old-fashioned Keynesian reflationary policies. The consequences were unfortunate. Popular consumption increased, but not enough to make a dent on unemployment. Inflation rose, the trade balance worsened, and the budget deficit grew. "By mid-1982, it had become clear that Socialist economic policies had failed: the old taunts that the Left was synonymous with economic profligacy reappeared."[68]

Jacques Delors, Mitterrand's finance minister, urged an immediate retreat. Mitterrand hesitated, hoping to hold the line at temporary austerity measures introduced in June 1982. The decisive moment came in March 1983, on the question of continued participation in the exchange rate mechanism of the EMS. Keeping the franc in the mechanism required a reversal of economic policy; removing it would have meant risking a freefall in the franc's value and would have required France to turn its back on Germany and the EC. But continued participation in the mechanism was politically unpalatable, because it necessitated a devaluation of the franc and acceptance of a rigorous austerity plan involving large tax increases and major cuts in public spending. Although generally more susceptible to political than economic arguments, Mitterrand heeded the advice of financial experts rather than party hacks.[69]

Far from resenting the EMS for having forced a painful decision on him, Mitterrand embraced it as an instrument of French economic salvation. As the French economy improved (although unemployment remained stubbornly high), he switched his attention from the domestic to the European arena. Mitterrand became an avid champion of deeper integration and wide-ranging institutional reform. His newfound European vocation "combined a mixture of idealism, realism, and self-interest; regardless of his motives, for Mitterrand the EC became an intensely *personal* affair."[70] The president's pet projects ranged from closer collaboration in high technology to strengthening the EP's role in the Community system. Having greeted the Genscher-Colombo proposals with indifference in 1981, Mitterrand welcomed the EP's draft treaty enthusiastically in 1984.

Mitterrand's zest for European integration reached its zenith in the first half of 1984 during France's presidency of the Council. He wanted to resolve the debilitating British budgetary question in order to clear the decks for bold new initiatives. These included wide-ranging institutional reform and intensive Community involvement in a range of policy areas. On external relations, Mitterrand took a more traditional position, calling for a permanent secretariat for the conduct of foreign policy cooperation (an old Gaullist objective) and urging member states to make an effort on common defense.[71]

Mitterrand sought to assert French leadership of a revived EC and to reinvigorate the Franco-German axis. His relations with Kohl, who became chancellor a year after Mitterrand became president, were cordial but not close. Like Mitterrand, Kohl was immersed in domestic politics, attempting to consolidate his grip on government. Also like Mitterrand, Kohl did not have much experience of the EC before coming to power, although he had a keen sense of the EC's political importance for Germany and of its historical significance for Europe.

Thatcher detected what she called "a gush of Euro-idealism" at the European Council in March 1984, with Mitterrand and Kohl becoming "quite lyrical on the subject of getting rid of frontier controls, which they seemed to invest with a high symbolic significance."[72] The prime minister's dismissiveness of such talk and thoughts demonstrated the vast difference between her, on the one hand, and Mitterrand and Kohl, on the other. Shared idealism, rooted in an appreciation of the practical benefits for their countries of ever closer union, drew Mitterrand and Kohl together. Nothing symbolized the extent of their personal rapprochement more than the poignancy of Mitterrand and Kohl holding hands during a visit in September 1984 to the World War I battlefield of Verdun, as they listened to each other's national anthems. It was unimaginable that Thatcher and Kohl would have behaved similarly in such a setting.

Notes

1. Christopher Tugendhat, *Making Sense of Europe* (New York: Columbia University Press, 1988), pp. 43–44.

2. Commission, *Eleventh Report on the Activities of the European Communities* (Luxembourg: European Communities, 1978), p. 17.

3. Commission, *Twelfth Report on the Activities of the European Communities* (Luxembourg: European Communities, 1979), p. 18.

4. Richard Clogg, "The Greek Political Context," in Loukas Tsoukalis, ed., *Greece and the European Community* (Farnborough: Saxon, 1979), p. 119.

5. Commission, "Opinion on the Greek Application for Membership," Bulletin EC S-2/76.

6. Quoted in Werner Feld, *West Germany and the European Community: Changing Interests and Competing Policy Objectives* (New York: Praeger, 1981), p. 55.

7. William Wallace, "Grand Gestures and Second Thoughts: The Response of Member Countries to Greece's Application," in Tsoukalis, *Greece and the European Community*, pp. 21–38. On Greece's application and EC entry, see also Iacovos S. Tsalicoglou, *Negotiating for Entry: The Accession of Greece to the European Community* (Aldershot: Dartmouth Publishing Company Limited, 1995).

8. On direct elections, see Richard Corbett, *The European Parliament's Role in Closer EU Integration* (Basingstoke: Palgrave, 2002), pp. 46–65; Amie Kreppel, *The European Parliament and Supranational Party System: A Study in Institutional Development* (Cambridge: Cambridge University Press, 2002), pp. 71–77; Berthold Rittberger, *Building Europe's Parliament: Democratic Representation Beyond the Nation State* (Oxford: Oxford University Press, 2005).

9. Commission, *Thirteenth Report on the Activities of the European Communities* (Luxembourg: European Communities, 1980), p. 27.

10. See Corbett, *European Parliament's Role*, pp. 67–69.

11. For an account of the EMS, see Daniel Gros and Niels Thygesen, *European Monetary Integration: From the European Monetary System Towards Monetary Union*, 2nd ed. (London: Longman, 1999); Peter Ludlow, *The Making of the European Monetary System* (London: Butterworths, 1982); Andrew Moravcsik, *The Choice for Europe: Social*

Purpose and State Power from Messina to Maastricht (Ithaca: Cornell University Press, 1998), pp. 238–313; Robert Triffin, ed., *EMS: The Emerging European Monetary System* (Brussels: National Bank of Belgium, 1979); Barry Eichengreen, *Globalizing Capital: A History of the International Monetary System,* 2nd ed. (Princeton: Princeton University Press, 2008), pp. 157–164; Emmanuel Mourlon-Droul, *A Europe Made of Money: The Emergence of the European Monetary System* (Ithaca: Cornell University Press, 2012); Harold James, *Making the European Monetary Union* (Cambridge: Harvard University Press, 2012), pp. 146–180.

12. Roy Jenkins, *European Diary, 1977–1981* (London: Collins, 1989), pp. 168–169.

13. COM(77)620 final, November 1977.

14. See Mattias Schulz, "The Reluctant European: Helmut Schmidt, the European Community, and Transatlantic Relations," in Matthias Schulz and Thomas A. Schwartz, eds., *The Strained Alliance: US-European Relations from Nixon to Carter* (Cambridge: Cambridge University Press, 2009), pp. 279–308.

15. Roy Jenkins, *Life at the Center: Memoirs of a Radical Reformer* (New York: Random, 1991), pp. 470–471. See also Haig Simonian, *Privileged Partnership: Franco-German Relations in the European Community, 1969–1984* (Oxford: Clarendon, 1985), p. 277.

16. Jenkins, *Life at the Center,* p. 479.

17. Commission, *Fifteenth Report on the Activities of the European Communities* (Luxembourg: European Communities, 1982), p. 18.

18. Commission, *Sixteenth Report on the Activities of the European Communities* (Luxembourg: European Communities, 1983), p. 18.

19. Tugendhat, *Making Sense of Europe,* pp. 69–71.

20. Quoted in Wallace, "Grand Gestures," p. 38, n. 15.

21. See Loukas Tsoukalis, "Second Round of Enlargement and the Mediterranean," in Tsoukalis, *Greece and the European Community,* p. 162; Commission, "General Considerations on the Problems of Enlargement," COM(78)120 final, April 20, 1978.

22. Bulletin EC 12-1978.

23. Bulletin EC 11-1979.

24. Ibid.

25. Tugendhat, *Making Sense of Europe,* pp. 140–141.

26. Jenkins, *European Diary,* pp. 25–26.

27. Ibid., p. 311.

28. Bulletin EC 11-1979.

29. Dirk Spierenburg, "Proposals for Reform of the Commission of the European Communities and Its Services," Brussels, Commission, September 1979.

30. Commission, *Thirteenth Report,* pp. 211–224.

31. Margaret Thatcher, *Downing Street Years* (New York: HarperCollins, 1993), pp. 61–62.

32. Ibid., pp. 34–35.

33. Tugendhat, *Making Sense of Europe,* pp. 121–122.

34. Thatcher, *Downing Street Years,* p. 65.

35. Tugendhat, *Making Sense of Europe,* p. 123.

36. Quoted in John Palmer, "Britain and the EEC: The Withdrawal Option," *International Affairs* 58, no. 4 (Autumn 1982), p. 640.

37. Commission, "Greece in the Community: Assessment and Proposals," Bulletin EC-3, 1983.

38. On Portuguese and Spanish accession, see José Luis Sampedro and Juan Antonio Payno, eds., *The Enlargement of the European Community: Case Studies of Greece,*

Portugal, and Spain (London: Macmillan, 1984); Charles Powell, "The Long Road to Europe: Spain and the European Community, 1957–1986," in Joaquin Roy and Maria Lorca-Susino, eds., *Spain in the European Union: The First Twenty-five Years* (Miami: Miami-Florida European Union Center, 2011), pp. 21–44; Marina Costa Lobo, "Spaniards' Long March Towards Europe," in Sebastián Royo and Paul Christopher Manuel, eds., *Spain and Portugal in the European Union: The First Fifteen Years* (London: Routledge, 2004), pp. 99–122; Charles Powell, "Portugal's European Integration," in Royo and Manuel, *Spain and Portugal in the European Union,* pp. 140–161.

39. Bulletin EC 2-1981.

40. Bulletin EC 11-1981.

41. Thatcher, *Downing Street Years,* pp. 541–544.

42. Ibid., p. 337. For FitzGerald's account of what happened, see Garret FitzGerald, *All in a Life: An Autobiography* (Dublin: Gill and Macmillan, 1991), pp. 485–486.

43. See Thatcher, *Downing Street Years,* pp. 539–540; Stephen George, *An Awkward Partner: Britain in the European Community* (Oxford: Oxford University Press, 1998), p. 155.

44. Thatcher, *Downing Street Years,* p. 545.

45. See George, *Awkward Partner,* pp. 157–158.

46. François Mitterrand, "Speech to the European Parliament," May 24, 1984, reprinted in *Vital Speeches of the Day,* August 1, 1984, pp. 613–623.

47. Quoted in *Daily Express,* June 4, 1984, p. 4.

48. Tugendhat, *Making Sense of Europe,* p. 124.

49. *The Economist,* June 3, 1984, p. 38.

50. Bulletin EC 12-1984.

51. See Margaret Sharp, "Technology and the Dynamics of Integration," in Richard T. Griffiths, ed., *Economic Development of the EEC* (Cheltenham: Elgar, 1997), pp. 518–533; Wayne Sandholtz, *High-Tech Europe: The Politics of International Cooperation* (Berkeley: University of California Press, 1992).

52. For an assessment of the Cassis case, see Karen J. Alter and Sophie Meunier-Aitsahalia, "Judicial Politics in the European Community: European Integration and the Pathbreaking Cassis de Dijon Case," *Comparative Political Studies* 26, no. 4 (January 1994), pp. 535–560; Michelle Egan, *Constructing a European Market: Standards, Regulation, and Governance* (Oxford: Oxford University Press, 2001), pp. 94–104; G. Garrett and B. Weingast, "Ideas, Interests, and Institutions: Constructing the EC's Internal Market," in J. Goldstein and R. Keohane, eds., *Ideas and Foreign Policy: Beliefs, Institutions, and Political Change* (Ithaca: Cornell University Press, 1993).

53. Commission, *Fourteenth Report on the Activities of the European Communities* (Luxembourg: European Communities, 1981), pp. 85–86.

54. Bulletin EC 6-1981.

55. Commission, *Fifteenth Report,* pp. 78–79.

56. Bulletin EC 6-1984.

57. Wisse Dekker, *Europe 1990: An Agenda for Action* (Eindhoven: Philips, 1984).

58. Margaret Sharp, Christopher Freeman, and William Walker, *Technology and the Future of Europe: Global Competition and the Environment in the 1990s* (New York: Pinter, 1991), p. 73.

59. Michel Albert and Robert James Ball, *Toward European Economic Recovery in the 1980s: Report to the European Parliament* (New York: Praeger, 1984).

60. See Corbett, *European Parliament's Role,* pp. 98–99, 125.

61. Jenkins, *European Diary,* p. 375.

62. Isoglucose Cases 138/79 and 139/79 ECR (1980), pp. 333, 339.

63. Bulletin EC 11-1979.

64. For an account of the draft treaty, see Roland Bieber, Jean-Paul Jacqué, and Joseph Weiler, eds., *An Ever Closer Union: A Critical Analysis of the Draft Treaty Establishing the European Union,* European Perspectives Series (Luxembourg: Office of Official Publications of the European Community, 1985); Corbett, *European Parliament's Role,* pp. 142–172.

65. Council, *Solemn Declaration on European Union,* Stuttgart, June 19, 1983, in Bulletin EC 6-1983.

66. Thatcher, *Downing Street Years,* p. 314.

67. The British paper "Europe: The Future" is reproduced in *Journal of Common Market Studies* 23 (1984), pp. 74–81. See also George, *Awkward Partner,* pp. 158–159.

68. Alistair Cole, *François Mitterrand: A Study in Political Leadership* (London: Routledge, 1994), p. 35.

69. See ibid.; David J. Howarth, *The French Road to European Union* (Basingstoke: Palgrave, 2001), pp. 55–82.

70. Cole, *François Mitterrand,* p. 122; emphasis in original.

71. See Mitterrand, "Speech to the European Parliament."

72. Thatcher, *Downing Street Years,* p. 538.

6

Transformation

BY THE MID-1980S, THE EUROPEAN COMMUNITY WAS POISED FOR a great transformation. Rapid technological change and fierce international competition convinced Western European governments of the wisdom of deeper integration. The hugely successful single market program, largely a response to the challenge of incipient globalization, meant going back to the future: back to the untapped potential of the Rome Treaty in order to give the EC a competitive edge in the emerging global marketplace. The main achievement of the Single European Act, the treaty change that symbolized the EC's resurgence, was to facilitate the enactment of single market legislation by providing greater recourse to qualified majority voting in Council decisionmaking. Monetary union looked like a logical sequel to the single market program, but one that raised serious political questions and concerns.

The late 1980s was a period of major political as well as economic and technological change. Mikhail Gorbachev, who came to power in the Soviet Union in 1985, launched a program of openness and reform that unintentionally stoked independence movements in Soviet-controlled Central and Eastern Europe and unexpectedly raised the prospect of German unification. The EC accession in 1986 of Portugal and Spain, two former dictatorships, emphasized the Community's importance for countries in transition. French and German leaders saw developments in Central and Eastern Europe as an additional reason to deepen integration, thereby anchoring Germany even more firmly into the EC. British prime minister Margaret Thatcher had a different interpretation, seeing these developments as a victory for democracy and neoliberalism and a sign that centralization and political integration in Western Europe were bound to fail.

Jacques Delors, who became president of the Commission in January 1985, was fortunate to have assumed office at such an auspicious time. After more than a decade of poor performance, Europe's economy was on the upswing. Governments had already decided in principle to complete the internal market, exploit economies of scale, and confront together the challenge of globalization. By seizing the moment, crafting a program to establish a single market by the end of 1992, and spearheading the drive for economic and monetary union, Delors personified the EC's extraordinary transformation.

This chapter examines the negotiation of the Single European Act and implementation of the single market program. Given the high political stakes, the European Council played a crucial role. There Delors, though head of the Commission rather than a national government, was in his element. There also, Franco-German leadership, in the form of President François Mitterrand and Chancellor Helmut Kohl, proved decisive. Thatcher, a staunch advocate of the single market program, became increasingly isolated in the European Council as she opposed extending EC competence into other policy areas. Ultimately, opposition to deeper integration and to German unification proved her political undoing.

Outside the rarified atmosphere of the European Council and far from the Commission's headquarters in Brussels, ordinary Europeans became interested in and even enthusiastic about developments in the EC. The slogan "1992," the target date for completion of the single market and shorthand for the entire undertaking, caught people's attention. For a brief, shining moment, the EC was popular, even fashionable, before the launch of the European Union in the early 1990s caused many people to worry that political and economic integration may have been going too far and moving too fast.

The Single European Act

There was near unanimity among EC member states in the mid-1980s on the desirability of deeper market integration. Delors, who undertook a tour of national capitals in late 1984 as Commission president-designate, got the message loud and clear. His decision to champion the single market program may have been "a grudging compromise for a man who had greater ambitions for Europe," but it showed a pragmatic streak in an otherwise visionary leader.[1] By going back to basics and emphasizing one of the original objectives of the Rome Treaty, Delors could hardly be accused by wary national leaders of overweening ambition.

Delors made clear his decision to champion the internal market in his first address to the European Parliament as Commission president. He also mentioned "1992"—the end of two consecutive Commission mandates (the Commission's term in office was then four years)—as a possible deadline for its implementation.[2] Given the presumed link between market integration and other policy initiatives, Delors envisioned the internal market project not as an end in itself but as a means toward the greater goal of European union.

The key question was not whether but how to complete the single market. Governments agreed that the legislative steps necessary to liberalize the European marketplace could not be taken without recourse in the Council to qualified majority voting. They could either agree informally to use qualified majority voting without changing the treaty, or negotiate a legally binding commitment to use qualified majority voting and, possibly, introduce other institutional reforms, such as extending the legislative role of the EP. Negotiating treaty change would require holding an intergovernmental conference of national representatives.

Initially Delors doubted whether an intergovernmental conference was desirable, preferring that governments would agree informally among themselves to become more efficient decisionmakers. Simply put, they needed to wean themselves off the national veto. Impatient to achieve results as soon as possible, Delors also feared that a conference would prove too contentious and time-consuming to have much impact on the EC before the end of the decade. Thus, at the outset of his presidency, Delors did not advocate the negotiations on treaty reform on which he later built his formidable reputation.[3]

Removing the Mediterranean Roadblock

An important piece of unfinished business held up Portuguese and Spanish accession and other important initiatives. That was Greece's demand for financial assistance to meet the costs of the country's adjustment to EC membership and to compensate for the anticipated diversion of funds from the country as a result of impending enlargement. The other member states made some concessions in 1984 by providing assistance for various agricultural, social, and transport projects.[4] But an overall solution needed to be found within the framework of the Integrated Mediterranean Programs, an assistance package for the existing and prospective Mediterranean EC member states.

Andreas Papandreou, the Greek prime minister, threw the December 1984 European Council into disarray by demanding a generous agreement on the Mediterranean programs in return for allowing enlargement to proceed. Thatcher, although relieved for once not to be the odd person out, was outraged by Papandreou's behavior. As a staunch opponent of additional EC expenditure, she did not want to allocate more money to regional development. What irked her was "not just the fact that Greece was holding [the EC] to ransom, nor even the particular tactics used, but still more the fact that, though Greece had been accepted into the Community precisely to entrench its restored democracy, the Greeks would not now allow the Community to do exactly the same for the former dictatorships of Spain and Portugal."[5]

Realizing that the Greek problem had to be resolved before the EC could advance on other fronts, Delors threw himself into the fray with characteristic energy and resolve. He soon proposed a solution involving a seven-year program of grants and loans to help the EC's Mediterranean regions "adjust under the best conditions possible to the new situation created by enlargement."[6] On the eve of a meeting of the European Council in March 1985, foreign ministers agreed on the final points in the Portuguese and Spanish accession negotiations during forty hours of talks without a break for sleep (a Community record). Italian foreign minister Giulio Andreotti, when praised for his stamina, commented wryly that "after twenty-five years in Italian government, it's really not so difficult."[7]

Yet enlargement still depended on a resolution of the Mediterranean programs, which necessitated intense negotiations among EC leaders. Despite Thatcher's legendary intransigence and Papandreou's legendary obstructionism, the European Council eventually reached agreement. The outcome was a success for Italy's Council presidency and for Delors, who had staked his political reputation on ending the dispute. As Delors had taken responsibility for the issue, failure to reach a settlement would have undermined his credibility at the outset of his Commission presidency. After the summit, a relieved Delors declared in typical melodramatic fashion that "all the family quarrels have been sorted out. The family is now going to grow and we can think of the future."[8]

The Dooge and Adonnino Reports

Faced with pressure from business interests, the Commission, and the EP in favor of deeper European integration, the European Council decided in June 1984, at the Fontainebleau summit, to convene a high-level committee to ponder the EC's future. The Ad Hoc Committee on Institutional Affairs started work in the fall of 1984, under the chairmanship of Jim Dooge, an Irish senator and former foreign minister. Thatcher, distrustful of the committee, appointed to it Malcolm Rifkind, a junior foreign minister, vigorous advocate of deregulation and market integration, and staunch defender of national sovereignty. Mitterrand's appointee could not have been more different. He was Maurice Faure, a close associate of the president, signatory of the Rome Treaty, and lifelong champion of European union.

Opinion within the committee spanned the spectrum of national preferences. At one end, the Italian representative favored radical treaty reform along the lines of the EP's Draft Treaty Establishing the European Union; at the other end, Britain's representative wanted only an informal agreement among member states to complete the internal market and coordinate their foreign policies more closely. Committee members generally favored using qualified majority voting in the Council on most internal market issues, without necessarily renouncing a government's right to veto legislation by invoking the Luxembourg Compromise.

The committee's final report, presented to the European Council in March 1985, identified a number of priorities for the EC.[9] These included "a homogeneous internal economic area" (that is, a single market), greater use of voting in the Council, more power for the EP and the Commission, and new initiatives in selected areas, including foreign policy. Reflecting the diversity of opinion among the committee's members, inevitably the report included numerous reservations and minority opinions. In particular, the British, Danish, and Greek representatives dissented from one of the report's key conclusions, that the European Council convene an intergovernmental conference to negotiate treaty reform.

Following the Fontainebleau summit, the European Council had established another committee of national representatives to consider ways of boosting popular awareness of, and interest in, the EC. That was the Ad Hoc Committee on a Peoples' Europe, chaired by Pietro Adonnino, a former Italian member of the EP. The Adonnino committee discussed issues ranging from taxation, to freedom of movement, to mutual recognition of degrees and diplomas, as well as symbols of further integration, such as an EC flag. Its report was far less consequential than that of the Dooge committee, but led, among other things, to the adoption of Beethoven's "Ode to Joy" as the EC's anthem.[10]

The White Paper

At Delors's prompting, the European Council tasked the Commission in March 1985 with submitting a program for completing the internal market. Delors delegated the work of drafting the white paper, including a detailed set of policy proposals, to Lord Arthur Cockfield, the commissioner with responsibility for the internal market. Thatcher had nominated Cockfield, a former trade secretary in her government, to the Commission and insisted that he get the internal market portfolio. She wanted him not only to help remove barriers to trade but also to hold the line in Brussels against spillover into other policy areas. Cockfield met her expectations for the internal market but otherwise disappointed the prime minister. As she later lamented, Cockfield was "the prisoner as well as the master of his subject. It was all too easy for him . . . to go native and to move from deregulating the market to reregulating it under the rubric of harmonization. Alas, it was not long before my old friend and I were at odds."[11]

By contrast, Cockfield and Delors hit it off immediately, even though they could not have been more different. Cockfield was upper-class and conservative; Delors lower-middle-class and moderately left-wing. They had difficulty communicating directly, as Cockfield spoke little French and Delors spoke little English. But they understood each other well. Both were committed to drafting and implementing a program to liberalize the European market. They played to different galleries. Cockfield, a former businessman, was an ideal ambassador for the Commission to the business community; Delors, a former trade unionist, helped to reconcile organized labor to an initiative about which traditional trade unionists were instinctively suspicious.

Although relatively few people in the Commission were involved in drafting the white paper, the exercise reverberated throughout the institution. Commission officials, however far removed from the drafting process, sensed that the EC was about to turn a corner. Delors wanted to give the Commission new direction and strong leadership. For its part, the Commission looked forward to a fresh start and enhanced importance after nearly two decades of drift. A single market strategy suited both Delors's and the Commission's objectives of reinvigorating the Brussels bureaucracy and returning the Commission to center stage.

The white paper, perhaps the most famous policy prescription ever promulgated in European Union history, contained a compelling rationale for further economic integration. Cockfield later described it as "one of the best [ever] expositions of Community policy, Community philosophy and Community aspirations."[12] Its final paragraph explained the initiative's broader purpose:

> Just as the Customs Union had to precede Economic Integration, so Economic Integration had to precede European Union. What this White Paper proposes therefore is that the Community should now take a further step along the road so clearly delineated in the treaties. To do less would be to fall short of the ambitions of the founding fathers of the Community; . . . it would be to betray the trust invested in us; it would be to offer the peoples of Europe a narrower, less rewarding, less secure, less prosperous future than they could otherwise enjoy. That is the measure of the challenge that faces us. Let it never be said that we were incapable of rising to it.[13]

The white paper listed nearly 300 measures necessary to complete the internal market by the target date of December 31, 1992. The Commission finished the white paper in record time, because many of the measures listed in it were already on the drawing board, a legacy of the Commission's earlier internal market efforts. Cockfield organized the measures under three categories of barriers to integration: physical, technical, and fiscal. Intended to achieve the free movement of goods, people, capital, and services, the white paper constituted a detailed action plan against which Commission officials, politicians, and businesspeople could measure progress toward a single market.

The Milan Summit

The European Council endorsed the white paper without debate at the Milan summit in June 1985. Would the single market program ever be enacted and could it serve as a springboard for deeper European integration? The Commission's white paper, the Dooge report, the breakthrough on the Mediterranean programs, and the prospect of imminent enlargement buoyed the hopes of those who advocated "more Europe." Adding to their excitement, the Italian government hoped to crown its turn in the Council presidency with a decision in Milan to launch an intergovernmental conference on treaty reform. Delors fully supported Italy's efforts. Thatcher, once more on the defensive, opposed treaty reform, advocating instead an informal agreement (possibly a "Milan Compromise" in contradistinction to the Luxembourg Compromise) to improve decisionmaking in the Council and to coordinate member states' foreign policies more closely.

The outcome of the summit would depend not on the ambition of the Italian presidency, the opportunism of Delors, or the recalcitrance of Thatcher, but on the positions of the French and German leaders. Despite rumors of a strain in Franco-German relations, Kohl and Mitterrand pushed strongly at the summit for a decision to convene an intergovernmental conference. Thatcher was irate. Here was another example of the power and perfidy of the Franco-German axis. Italy's prime minister, Bettino Craxi, then set a precedent in the European Council by calling for a vote on the question. Following some procedural wrangling, national leaders voiced their opinions. The result was predictable: seven in favor, three (Britain, Denmark, and Greece) against.

The summit may have looked like a major breakthrough for European integration, but the opposition of three national leaders to holding an intergovernmental conference was worrisome. As governments could approve treaty changes only by unanimity, Britain, Denmark, and Greece would have every opportunity to block progress. Not that they would need to apply the brakes all the time: the other member states had so many competing preferences that unanimity would surely prove elusive. As long as Britain could keep its partners focused on market integration, and as long as the result of the conference did not threaten their core interests, the three minority member states were willing to participate, however reluctantly.

The Intergovernmental Conference

A major intergovernmental conference was a novel event in 1985. Previous conferences had focused on narrow objectives, such as budgetary reform in 1970 and 1975. The door was now open for broader reform on a range of policy and institutional issues. As Delors remarked at the opening session, "conferences like this one are not convened every five or ten years. There may not be another between now and 2000."[14] Another conference indeed took place in 2000, but Delors could not have foreseen that the 2000 conference, thanks largely to the success of the Single European Act, would be the fifth in fifteen years (there were two in 1990–1991 and there was one in 1996–1997).

The conference began in September 1985. Portugal and Spain, on the verge of joining the EC, observed the proceedings. Negotiations took place at a number of levels. Senior officials (mostly the permanent representatives to the EC) met regularly to negotiate changes to the existing treaty.

Political directors—senior foreign ministry officials based in the national capitals—met less often to negotiate changes to European Political Cooperation (the mechanism for foreign policy coordination). Both sets of negotiations took place in Brussels. The foreign ministers moved the negotiations along at their monthly Council meetings. Defending their turf, the economic and finance ministers discussed a possible treaty change on monetary policy cooperation at their own Council meetings. Finally, the European Council reached political agreement on the most contentious issues of the conference at its regularly scheduled summit in Luxembourg, in December 1985. As well as the formal negotiating sessions, negotiators at all levels participated in numerous informal bilateral and multilateral meetings where much of the real work was done.[15]

The Commission was not formally a party to the negotiations, but had a seat at the table. Delors took charge of the Commission's contribution to the conference, working with a small team of trusted officials and bypassing the commissioner responsible for institutional affairs. Delors's strategy was to link the goal of the internal market to progress on institutional reform and in selected policy areas, such as cohesion (regional economic development) and social affairs. Without a commitment to cohesion, Delors argued, the gap between rich and poor countries would become unacceptably wide. Similarly, without stronger labor legislation at the European level, workers would be disadvantaged by greater market integration and become alienated from the EC. Delors also pushed for a commitment to monetary policy cooperation, as a step closer to his cherished goal of economic and monetary union. How could the market be fully integrated without common monetary and macroeconomic policies? The political and economic logic of a large, vibrant internal market, Delors argued, pointed inexorably toward EMU.

The Commission submitted proposals in a variety of policy areas and got the negotiations going. So much so that, according to one observer, "the [conference] in its initial stages took the form of a dialogue between the Commission and member state governments."[16] Delors calibrated the Commission's proposals not only to extend the frontier of European integration but also to appeal to member states' interests and allay their concerns. Sensitive to the positions of the three recalcitrant countries, Delors emphasized the advantages of market integration for the British, of environmental policy for the Danes, and of cohesion policy for the Greeks.[17] Luxembourg, in the Council presidency, cooperated closely with the Commission but was careful not to antagonize the more reluctant member states.

Yet the Commission lost ground in the conference as the negotiations gathered momentum in late 1985. With agreement expected at the summit in December, governments began to assert their positions. There was little disagreement on the definition of the internal market ("an area without internal frontiers in which the free movement of goods, persons, services and capital is ensured") or on approving the Commission's recommended target date of 1992, but negotiators disagreed on the institutional steps necessary to bring it about. Following intensive negotiations, governments agreed to allow voting on harmonization, but only for approximately two-thirds of the measures identified in the Commission's white paper. The remainder, on sensitive issues such as indirect taxation, remained subject to unanimity.[18]

The possibility of enhancing the EC's democratic credentials by increasing the power of the EP was one of the most controversial issues of the conference. Most governments balked at giving the EP the power of legislative co-decision alongside the Council. National representatives agreed instead to increase the EP's authority through the so-called cooperation procedure (the right to a second reading) for certain single market measures and through a new power of assent for accession and association agreements. By contrast, there was general agreement on strengthening the Commission's executive powers, at least in principle.

Greece and Ireland, supported by the Commission and by conference observers Portugal and Spain, wanted a major increase in Community spending on poorer regions through a revitalized regional policy. In the face of British opposition, they could not have succeeded in getting a commitment in the SEA to cohesion policy without strong German support. Germany also favored the inclusion of environmental policy in the treaty, as did Denmark and other environmentally conscious member states. Most governments favored adding provisions to the treaty for cooperation in research and technology development, without agreeing on how much money should be allocated to it. Social policy, anathema to Thatcher's Conservative government, became one of the most difficult items as the conference proceeded.

The conference gave governments an opportunity to reform European Political Cooperation and bring it under the umbrella of the Rome Treaty. The political directors considered various submissions from national governments, notably Britain and, jointly, France and Germany. Governments generally agreed on the need to make the EC's external economic policy and their own foreign policies more consistent with each other. Neutral Ireland, pacifist Denmark (though a NATO member), and idiosyncratic Greece (though also a NATO member) succeeded in excluding any reference to defense policy from the clauses covering political cooperation, which continued to limit foreign policy discussions to "the political aspects of security" but included a number of useful procedural changes.

France and Germany, despite differences between them on many institutional and policy issues, occasionally joined forces to move matters along. Roland Dumas and Hans-Dietrich Genscher, the French and German foreign ministers, were exceedingly close; much closer than Mitterrand and Kohl. A joint intervention by them at a foreign ministers' meeting at the end of November 1985 neutralized the opposition of some of their colleagues to parts of the proposed agreement.

Delors, with the support of the Belgian government, pushed for a commitment to greater economic and monetary policy cooperation. Britain was adamantly opposed, France in favor, and Germany equivocal. For the sake of securing the bigger prize of deeper market integration, Thatcher accepted a reference in the treaty to the importance of economic and monetary policy cooperation "for the further development of the Community." A stipulation that further steps toward monetary union could be taken only in another intergovernmental conference, which Britain would surely veto, reassured Thatcher.[19]

Although EC leaders engaged in lengthy, detailed negotiations at the Luxembourg summit in December 1985, their exchanges were free of the rancor that had marred meetings of the European Council in the early 1980s. The difference this time was the convergence of interest among the main players in completing the single market. Thatcher, Mitterrand, and Kohl had a common goal. In order to achieve that goal, Thatcher uncharacteristically conceded that she "would have to seek alliances with other governments, accept compromises and use language which I did not find attractive."[20]

Thatcher's reasonableness surprised some members of her own government, notably the chancellor of the exchequer (finance minister), Nigel Lawson. Having urged her before going to Luxembourg not to allow any mention of monetary policy in the treaty, Lawson "was skeptical of the wisdom of the deal she had struck. I felt that we had embarked upon a dangerous slippery slope towards EMU; whereas the move to majority voting, which had been strongly urged by Delors as essential if Europe was to regain the momentum it had latterly lost, would have been agreed even without EMU."[21] Lawson's comments revealed growing discord within the British government, with ardent Euroskeptics doubting Thatcher's ability to hold the line against deeper European integration.

It was at the summit also that the European Council approved a Commission proposal to conclude a single agreement incorporating all treaty changes, rather than separate agreements on EC and foreign policy cooperation reform: hence the name *Single* European Act (it was called an "act" because the word "treaty" was too politically charged). Foreign ministers continued working on a few outstanding issues, including social policy, until the end of January 1986. Nine of the twelve foreign ministers then signed the act in Brussels in mid-February. Denmark delayed doing so until the (successful) outcome of a referendum on the act later in the month; Italy delayed in order to protest the agreement's seemingly limited extension of the EP's powers; and Greece delayed until certain that Denmark and Italy would sign. The three holdouts—Euro-enthusiastic Italy, Euroskeptical Denmark, and Euro-ambivalent Greece—finally signed the SEA at a special ceremony in The Hague at the end of February 1986.

Outcome

The SEA was a relatively short and seemingly innocuous document. It did not directly challenge the Luxembourg Compromise, but its extension of qualified majority voting to most single market measures was a significant chink in the armor of unanimity. Indeed, the link between the single market and qualified majority voting formed the core of the SEA. The extension of the EP's legislative authority was an important institutional innovation, although it did not go far enough to satisfy the EP and its supporters in the intergovernmental conference.

The SEA also linked completion to the single market with greater economic cohesion, on the one hand, and stronger social policy, on the other. As part of a tidying-up exercise, the SEA brought environmental policy and foreign policy cooperation into the Rome Treaty, while keeping foreign policy cooperation strictly on an intergovernmental basis. Mention of monetary policy in the SEA seemed no more than symbolic, but would soon prove highly important.

The SEA included various declarations dealing with specific national concerns. For instance, Ireland won a derogation (or exemption) from the single market for its fragile insurance industry, and Portugal insisted that changes in decisionmaking as a result of the SEA "must not damage sensitive and vital sectors of the country's economy."[22] Such declarations, an inevitable result of intergovernmental bargaining, were mostly for domestic political consumption.

The Commission and the more integration-minded member states were disappointed with the outcome of the conference, especially with the exclusion of key single market measures from qualified majority voting and the relatively limited increase in the EP's power. A despondent Delors wondered whether the SEA would suffice to bring about the internal market by 1992. He also regretted that France and Germany had not undertaken bold initiatives and that progress at the conference had been reduced to the level of the lowest common denominator.

By contrast, Thatcher was pleased, claiming to have held the line against the use of qualified majority voting on harmonization of taxation and the free movement of people, and to have conceded only minimal new powers to the EP. The SEA, she declared, was "good for British business."[23] Thatcher was right about the commercial benefits of the SEA, but wrong about its broader impact. She and Delors, and everybody else for that matter, greatly underestimated the significance of the treaty changes that emerged from the intergovernmental conference.

Ratification

Most national parliaments ratified the SEA without much difficulty. The Italian parliament was highly critical, complaining that the SEA did not go far enough to deepen European integration. Ratification in Germany fueled an ongoing debate about the role of the state governments in EC decisionmaking. The Danish government failed twice in late January 1986 to win parliamentary support for the SEA, being unable to allay parliamentarians' concerns about the presumed loss of sovereignty inherent in the greater use of qualified majority voting in Council decisionmaking. The Danish government then put the issue to a referendum in February 1986, in which 56 percent of voters (in a 74 percent turnout) supported the SEA. Despite the Greek government's complaints about the EC, the Greek parliament easily ratified it.

Failure to ratify the SEA in Ireland before the agreed deadline of December 1986 caused a delay in the act's implementation throughout the EC. The problem was due to a court case brought by a citizen concerned about the impact of the SEA's foreign policy provisions on Irish sovereignty. In a dramatic decision at the end of December 1986, Ireland's highest court agreed with the plaintiff and mandated a referendum in order to ratify the act. The government easily won the referendum (70 percent in favor, but in a turnout of only 45 percent), clearing the way for implementation of the SEA in July 1987.

Except in Denmark and Ireland, ratification did not attract much public attention. There was little public awareness that European integration was on the verge of a major breakthrough. Those who participated in the ratification debates had little inkling that the SEA would presage a rapid transformation of the EC. Like the national leaders who concluded the intergovernmental conference in December 1985, most national parliamentarians saw the SEA as a set of uninspiring treaty amendments rather than a harbinger of unprecedented economic and political change.

Implementing the Single Market Program

The SEA supplied the institutional machinery necessary to implement the single market program.[24] Although the SEA came into effect only in July 1987, the Council decided before then to enact single market measures as expeditiously as possible. The Commission fed the Council a steady stream of proposals, most of which went also to the EP under the new cooperation procedure. The Dutch presidency, in the first half of 1986, gave the EP a list of decisions taken by qualified majority vote to show that the taboo on voting in the Council was now broken.[25] The succeeding British presidency made completion of the single market its top priority.[26] Britain was unusually at ease in the EC at that time: 1986 was an interregnum for Britain between the budgetary battles of the early 1980s and the epic struggle over EMU in the late 1980s.

During negotiation of the SEA, some unsympathetic officials in national capitals and the Council secretariat complained that giving the EP the right to a second reading of draft legislation was a recipe for delay and disaster. Partly to prove them wrong but mostly to enhance its credibility as a legislative body, the EP reorganized its rules of procedure in 1986 and was ready to put cooperation into practice when the SEA finally came into effect in July 1987. Fearing the worst, the *Financial Times* wondered in April 1987 whether the SEA "will change anything in the real world, other than introduce complex new negotiations between the member states and the Parliament."[27] Indeed, there were teething troubles with the cooperation procedure, which took the remainder of the year to work out. On the whole, the EP made the most of the new procedure to complete the internal market and advance its own position in the EC system of governance.

It was in 1987 that the phrase "single market" became widely used instead of "internal market," largely because of the program's association with the Single European Act. This reflected the popularization of the program, which by the end of 1987 was a staple item in newspapers as well as radio and television programs throughout the EC. The slogan "1992" unexpectedly caught people's imaginations. For the first time in its history, the EC became a topic of general discussion among Europeans interested in current affairs. "Delors" became a household name.

Business opinion was ahead of that of the general public in its enthusiasm for European integration. Even before the SEA came into effect, European businesspeople immersed themselves in the single market program. The Commission, governments, and the private sector organized conferences and published newsletters on how to exploit a frontier-free Europe. Large enterprises were best positioned to do so. In 1987 and 1988, merger mania swept the EC as companies attempted to realize economies of scale and improve their cross-border distribution networks. Sixty-eight major mergers and acquisitions took place in the EC in 1987, followed by three hundred in 1988.[28]

A report on the benefits of the single market, titled *The Cost of Non-Europe,* stoked business and public interest in what soon became known as the "1992 program." The report was the result of a huge, Commission-funded research project led by Paolo Cecchini, a former Commission official and noted Italian economist. Cecchini drew on data from the four big member states and on a comparison with the United States to quantify the cost to the EC of maintaining a fragmented market. The report examined everything from the cost to firms of the administrative procedures and delays associated with customs formalities, to the opportunity cost of lost trade, to the costs of border controls. In early 1988, Cecchini released his findings in a massive, sixteen-volume publication as well as a condensed single-volume version.[29] Although later criticized for its methodology and shown to be overoptimistic in its conclusions, the Cecchini report contributed to the hype surrounding the single market program.[30]

Buoyed by the publication of the Cecchini report, the program came into its own in 1988. Resolution early in the year of a dispute over the budget (discussed later in the chapter) cleared the decks for the German presidency's determination to implement the single market. By the end of the German presidency, the Commission had submitted most of the proposals outlined in the white paper, and the Council had agreed on a common position (the first stage in the cooperation procedure) for over a hundred of them. Inevitably, the more difficult issues, such as tax harmonization, and the free movement of people, remained on the drawing board. In a move that had major implications for EMU, the European Council agreed in June 1988 to liberalize all capital movements as early as July 1990, with exceptions until December 1992 for Greece, Ireland, Portugal, and Spain. This was a major political turning point in the program and prompted the European Council to declare that achievement of the single market was now irreversible. Delors, cautious by nature, was less sanguine about the success of the program, although he conceded some months later that "we are almost on the threshold of the irreversible."[31]

A Hard Slog

Despite the euphoria surrounding the program, the work of enacting and implementing the necessary legislation was arduous, time-consuming, and unglamorous. The process involved hundreds of national, Commission, and EP officials; national politicians, commissioners, and MEPs; and lawyers and lobbyists. Draft legislation worked its way through dozens of committee meetings in national capitals, Commission and EP offices, and Council chambers before emerging in the pages of the *Official Journal* as full-fledged directives (legislative acts). Implementing the single market program was a Herculean bureaucratic task of which most consumers of EC legislation were mercifully unaware.

The greatest appeal of the program for many ordinary Europeans was the promised abolition of border posts. The white paper included numerous proposals to eliminate customs formalities, paperwork, and inspections. Accompanying measures included miscellaneous provisions such as duty-free admission for the fuel in the tanks of trucks, an end to routine checks on passenger-car documentation, and a new statistical system for tracking trade among member states once border posts were eliminated. Other steps to make possible the abolition of borders covered plant and animal health requirements, the livestock trade, and trade in agricultural products. The Council adopted almost all the necessary measures by the end of 1992.

The EC had less success liberalizing the movement of people. In order to pressure other governments to open their inner-EC borders, France, Germany, and the Benelux countries signed an agreement in Schengen, Luxembourg, in 1985 to eliminate all frontier formalities. Greece, Italy, Portugal, and Spain signed up to the agreement by the end of 1992, but Britain, Denmark, and Ireland, citing security and other concerns, remained outside the Schengen area. Administrative delays in implementing the complex provisions of the agreement meant that border posts remained in existence between signatory states after the stipulated achievement of the single market program.

The removal of fiscal barriers would also have an immediate and obvious impact on most Europeans. The white paper included an ambitious set of initiatives for harmonizing taxation, a prerequisite for eliminating borders (where many taxes were assessed), and also for reducing distortions and segmentation of the market through disparate tax practices. Thus the white paper called on member states to harmonize value-added tax rates and to develop a system for charging value-added tax on cross-border sales once border posts were eliminated. The Council eventually adopted a general framework for harmonization in October 1992, which set a standard rate of 15 percent or greater in each member state as of January 1993. The Council reached only a provisional agreement before 1992 on who should pay value-added tax and where they should pay it. Businesses complained vociferously about the complexity of the reporting system, smaller firms doubted the feasibility of shipping goods across borders, and consumers wondered about the supposed benefits of tax harmonization.

By contrast, consumers benefited immediately from a Council decision in March 1991 to eliminate restrictions on cross-border purchases of items subject to excise taxes—mainly fuels, liquor, and tobacco—for personal use. Consumers benefited as well from the pressure successfully exerted on governments by airport authorities and ferry operators not to end immediately duty-free sales for people traveling within the EC. Because many airports and ferry operators gathered a large part of their revenues from highly profitable duty-free sales, the Council agreed to delay the demise of duty-free shopping until 1999. Thus shrewd British shoppers, for instance, could buy duty-free drink and cigarettes while ferrying back and forth to buy a limitless supply of inexpensive wine in France.

The bulk of the single market program consisted of arcane measures to remove technical barriers to trade, covering product standards, testing, and certification; movement of capital; public procurement; free movement of labor and the professions; free movement of services; transport; new technologies; company law; intellectual property; and company taxation. Of these, standards, testing, and certification had the biggest impact on European business.[32] The white paper sought to maximize mutual recognition of national regulations and standards, not to abolish harmonization.

Where harmonization remained essential, the white paper proposed a two-track strategy. First, a new approach would limit legislative harmonization to essential health and safety requirements with which products had to conform. Governments would have to transpose those fundamental requirements into regulations applicable nationally, but could not impose further requirements on the products in question. Second, where the new approach was not appropriate, the old approach of developing a single, Community-wide, detailed set of technical specifications for a given product would remain in place. As a result, the single market program was not simply deregulatory. According to a contemporary assessment, "although the language [of the program] is borrowed from neoliberalism, the actual proposals often involve a high degree of regulation in terms of harmonization of basic standards. On balance . . . [the 1992 program] is less an exercise in deregulation than in regulatory reform."[33]

The new approach required the Commission to contract with the relevant European organizations to develop voluntary standards. Manufacturers adhering to those standards would be presumed to comply with the essential requirements set in the relevant directive, and their products would therefore be ensured free circulation throughout the EC.[34] But the European standards bodies were unable to keep up with the flow of the directives, covering a wide range of products. Because of the serious backlog in the development of standards in the EC by the end of 1992, manufacturers of products covered by the new directives faced uncertainty and disruption over the pace at which European standards could be developed and introduced.

Despite these and other imperfections, the single market program was a success. In general, the white paper functioned as intended. By tying so many elements to a politically coherent and attractive vision, the Commission managed to push the Council into adopting proposals that might not otherwise have generated much support. For its part, the SEA gave the Council the means to act. Implementation of the program created a climate in which individuals as well as firms could begin to identify themselves as European and look for opportunities beyond their own borders. It also restored the image of the EC as a vital and modern entity, not least in the eyes of the EC's neighbors and trading partners.

The International Impact

The single market program had an immediate and unexpected impact on the EC's external relations and role in the world. The slogan "1992," just as it had attracted the attention of businesspeople and ordinary citizens in the EC, quickly caught on outside the EC's borders. Foreign governments and enterprises took a keen interest in the program's development and implementation. To the Commission's surprise, external reaction to the EC's internal economic reorganization was not altogether favorable. "Fortress Europe" became a catchphrase in the United States to signal concern about the implications of the single market program for nonmember states. The Commission had given little thought to the external perception of the program and responded to international criticism by emphasizing its commitment to free trade and open markets. In an effort to allay concern beyond the EC's borders, the European Council declared in December 1988 that "the single market will be of benefit to Community and non-Community countries alike. . . . The internal market will not close in on itself. 1992 Europe will be a partner and not a fortress Europe."[35]

The phrase "Partner Europe" lacked the resonance and appeal of "Fortress Europe." The Community's main trading partners remained unconvinced that the post-1992 European market would be as accessible as the European Council promised. Exporters to the EC of textiles, bananas, and cars had legitimate concerns. In order to eliminate internal borders, the EC abolished many quotas and other restraints imposed by individual governments under the terms of the Rome Treaty, and replaced some of them with a set of EC-wide quotas or voluntary restraint agreements. The most egregious of these protected the EC's textile and car industries as well as banana producers in some member states' former colonies. The EC's post-1992 banana regime became a source of bitter contention between the EC and the United States, which championed the interests of so-called dollar bananas from Latin America.

The contemporaneous Uruguay Round of global trade liberalization talks, held under the auspices of the GATT, gave the EC's trading partners a fortuitous chance to test the Community's commitment to maintaining an open international regime. It also gave the EC an opportunity to leverage concessions from its trading partners based on the single market's purported benefits. At the same time, the EC launched a public relations campaign in the United States to persuade US businesspeople and politicians of the advantages of the program. Large US businesses that were already represented in Europe appreciated the advantages of an integrated European market. Others decided to locate operations there in order to ensure against exclusion. As the single market program progressed, US and other avid 1992-watchers lost their initial skepticism about the single market program. The Uruguay Round ran well beyond its scheduled deadline of December 1990, not because of disputes over market access for manufactured goods and services but because of the EC's refusal to concede larger cuts in agricultural subsidies, a subject beyond the scope of the 1992 program.

The European Economic Area
Concern about possible exclusion from the single market led some members of the European Free Trade Area (EFTA) to contemplate EC membership. The economic impetus for EC accession became so strong that neutral Austria applied to join in July 1989, despite the Soviet Union's disapproval (the Cold War was not yet over). Neutral Sweden, where Volvo and other economic interests pressed for EC entry, decided not to apply for membership until the geopolitical situation in Europe had sorted itself out.

Until it digested the accession of Portugal and Spain and implemented the single market program, the EC was not interested in acquiring new members. Hoping to fend off applications from the EFTA countries, in January 1989 Delors proposed "a new form of association [between the EC and EFTA], with common decision making and administrative institutions."[36] Austria's application spurred Delors to press ahead with this initiative, which became known as the European Economic Area. Thus began what one senior Commission official described as "the most complex negotiations [that] we have ever conducted on behalf of the EC."[37]

On the internal market alone, the EFTA countries had to adopt approximately 1,400 existing Community acts covering over 10,000 pages of legislation. Contentious issues included truck transit through Austria and Switzerland from EC countries, and access for Community fishing boats to Icelandic and Norwegian waters. Talks were particularly difficult over institutional arrangements, with the EC eventually offering to consult the EFTA countries on certain draft legislation and to establish a panel of EC and EFTA judges to adjudicate European Economic Area–related disputes. The proposed dispute-resolution mechanism triggered a ruling by the EC's Court of Justice against the draft European Economic Area agreement in December 1991. Renewed EC-EFTA negotiations settled the dispute-resolution issue and paved the way for an agreement in May 1992.

Yet the European Economic Area failed in its original aim of allowing the EFTA countries to enjoy the benefits of the single market without having them become members. By the time that the European Economic Area came into operation in January 1993, most of the EFTA countries saw it as a staging post, not an alternative, to EC membership. With the Cold War over, the Soviet Union gone, and Russia agreeable to the EFTA countries' accession, neutrality was no longer a reason for them not to apply to join the EC. Eager to enjoy the full economic benefits of EC membership as opposed to the limited economic advantage of European Economic Area membership, most of the EFTA countries applied to join the EC in 1991 and 1992.

Solidarity Through Cohesion and Social Policy

The SEA included an implicit bargain to share the wealth of the single market program among rich and poor member states and among all classes of society. Delors, given his background in the French labor movement and his strong social conscience, was deeply committed to the idea of solidarity in the EC. He had pushed hard to include a section on cohesion (the reduction of economic disparities between richer and poorer countries) and provisions for a stronger social policy in the SEA. The next step was to flesh out these provisions by reorganizing and allocating more money for the structural funds—the means by which the EC implemented cohesion policy—and developing a social policy program.

Any mention of money in the EC was bound to be contentious. It immediately put Thatcher, a foe of additional public spending, on the alert. Ideologically, Thatcher opposed cohesion and social policy because she believed that the economy should be allowed to function according to free-market principles, not state or EC rules. Other EU leaders, even nominally conservative ones, had no problem in principle with cohesion or social policy. Some were reluctant to allocate more money to the structural funds; others, notably from the poor member states, wanted a major increase in spending of structural funds. All were ambivalent about social policy, not wanting to offend employers by imposing strict rules in the workplace, or offend workers by seeming to neglect their interests.

Cohesion

The battle over cohesion began in February 1987 when Delors, following up on the still-unratified SEA, released a package of budgetary proposals.[38] These included major increases in funding for research and development, transport, environmental policy, and especially cohesion. Delors proposed a doubling of the structural funds, with a particular focus on regions with a per capita income below 75 percent of the EC average. That meant Greece, Ireland, Portugal, and Spain. To cover the increase in Community spending, Delors proposed a new budgetary resource, based on member states' GDP. At the same time, partly to allay Thatcher's concerns, Delors proposed less spending on agricultural policy and better budget discipline. The Delors package was spread over a five-year time frame (1988–1992) in order to avoid debilitating annual budgetary disputes.

Just as Delors used the voluminous Cecchini report to bolster his arguments in support of the single market, he cited a report by Tommaso Padoa-Schioppa to make a compelling case for reform of the structural funds. Published in April 1987, the report stressed "the serious risks of aggravated regional imbalances in the course of market liberalization." In a memorable rebuke of neoliberal assumptions, it warned that "any easy extrapolation of 'invisible hand' ideas into the real world of regional economics in the process of market opening would be unwarranted in the light of economic history and theory."[39]

The battle lines were now drawn between Thatcher and those who supported a massive increase in the size of the structural funds, notably Delors and Felipe González, the prime minister of Spain and unofficial leader of the four countries that would benefit most from the measure (the cohesion countries, including chilly Ireland, soon became known as "Club Med"). Thatcher dismissed Delors as an unelected Socialist spendthrift. She heaped scorn on González, another Socialist but, as an elected head of government, her peer in the European Council. Surely, she thought, "in the long term a proud, ancient nation like Spain would baulk at continued loss of national self-determination in exchange for German-financed subsidies."[40] Indeed, Germany, as the largest contributor to the budget, would determine the fate of cohesion policy. Kohl's position was therefore pivotal in the negotiations on the Delors package. In principle, Kohl supported cohesion, but in practice he did not want to increase the size of the budget. Nor did he want to antagonize German farmers by reducing Community spending on agricultural subsidies.

The dispute over the Delors package rumbled on through 1987, overshadowing implementation of the single market program. The Club Med countries were reluctant to legislate for market liberalization in Brussels as long as their demands for more spending on the structural funds were not met. Given the political sensitivity of the matter, inevitably discussion of the Delors package dominated the European Council. Summit meetings in 1987 resembled summits in the early 1980s, with Thatcher refusing to sanction more Community spending while tenaciously defending Britain's rebate, and most of the other leaders urging acceptance of the Delors proposals.

The Delors package was an unwelcome piece of unfinished business for the German presidency in early 1988. It placed Kohl in a dilemma: as chancellor he wanted to protect German farmers from cuts in subsidies and German taxpayers from a hike in Germany's contribution to the EC's budget; as president-in-office of the Council he wanted to resolve a festering dispute that threatened to delay implementation of the single market program, another German interest. At a special summit in Brussels in February 1988, Kohl compromised on the budget increase and Thatcher relaxed her demand for cuts in guaranteed prices for cereals. Britain's rebate remained intact, and German farmers continued to be subsidized at the high level to which they were accustomed. The cohesion countries got a doubling of the structural funds by 1992, and the German presidency won accolades for resolving the budgetary dispute. But the EC was the real winner: cohesion became a vital instrument of economic and political integration, and agreement on the Delors package removed a major obstacle on the road to 1992.

Following agreement on the Delors package, the Council adopted regulations in June and December 1988 reforming the EC's structural funds. These included concentrating structural funds on five major objectives. The first, covering "regions whose development is lagging behind," was the main source of funding for Club Med and, financially, the largest objective. Another reform introduced the partnership principle, through which the Commission involved regions, not just governments, in formulating and implementing structural policy. That gave the regions throughout the EC, which varied from relatively powerless entities in centralized countries (such as France) to powerful states in federal countries (such as Germany), a vested interest in European integration and an incentive to cultivate relations with Brussels. As a result, the Commission and the regions were complicit in a political process that sought to undermine the authority of national governments and devolve power from national capitals upward to the European and downward to the regional levels.[41]

Social Policy

From the beginning of his presidency, Delors expressed a keen interest in social policy, focusing on women's rights, workers' rights, and working conditions. One of his first acts as Commission president was to launch a dialogue between the "social partners"—representatives of employers and workers—at the European level. The European Union of Employers' Confederations was already well established in Brussels. Representing employers' organizations throughout the EC, it was a wealthy, influential interest group. By contrast, national trade unions were poorly organized transnationally in Brussels. Delors sought to rectify that by boosting the standing of the European Trade Union Confederation.

Big business in Europe was instinctively wary of the Commission. That was a legacy of the Jean Monnet and Walter Hallstein years and reflected also the private sector's general distrust of government. The Commission and big business reached a modus vivendi in the early 1980s when Commissioner Étienne Davignon collaborated with the European Round Table, the elite group of leading industrialists, on high-technology projects and on internal market issues. Delors's obvious trade union sympathies and keen interest in social policy once again raised big business's suspicion of the Commission. Big business watched with alarm as the Commission's social affairs directorate-general grew increasingly influential.

Like Monnet before him, Delors felt that big business had the resources and the connections to look after itself. By contrast, Delors was willing to reach out to small business, which risked being left behind in the scramble to gain commercial advantage from the single market program. A scheme to assist small and medium-sized enterprises therefore became an important flanking policy for the single market.

In a victory for Delors and the left-leaning national governments, the SEA introduced qualified majority voting for the "health and safety of workers." As the employers' federation feared that it would, this provision produced the largest and most important body of social policy legislation in the late 1980s, the high point of social policy in the history of the European Union. Moreover, the qualified majority voting provision for health and safety legislation opened a loophole through which the Commission tried to enact other social policy measures. It also emboldened Delors to explore the broader "social dimension" of the 1992 project. Most national leaders were willing to go along with him, the obvious exception being Thatcher. Despite her objections, the European Council noted in June 1988 that, as the internal market had to be conceived "in such a manner as to benefit all our people," it was necessary to improve working conditions, living standards, protection of health and safety, access to vocational training, and dialogue between the two sides of industry.[42]

The Commission developed the social dimension of the single market program in a paper in September 1988 that outlined the intellectual and economic rationale for a vigorous social policy. Delors then proposed a charter of basic social rights and asked the sleepy Economic and Social Committee, an institution that represented vocational interests in the EC, for an opinion. Roused from its slumber, the committee produced a report supporting Delors's initiative, despite the misgivings of its employers' representatives. Delors's main political support came from France, where Mitterrand, a Socialist, was happy to champion a European initiative that had a particular appeal to voters on the left. Mitterrand put social policy near the top of his agenda during France's Council presidency in the second half of 1989. Confident of French support, Delors produced a draft Community Charter of the Fundamental Social Rights of Workers, with an attached "action program" of nearly fifty measures, about half of which required legislation in Brussels. Thanks to Mitterrand's advocacy of it, eleven of the twelve national leaders adopted the social charter at meeting of the European Council in December 1989. Thatcher was the lone dissenter.

Like cohesion, social policy was a divisive issue between Britain and the other member states. Whereas Britain eventually accepted cohesion policy, it continued to resist social policy. The difference, perhaps, was that Britain's outright rejection of cohesion might have jeopardized implementation of the 1992 program, because Club Med and its supporters could have blocked the enactment of single market measures. Also, Britain stood to benefit from the proposed increase in spending on structural funds, as the new second objective included economic conversion and modernization in declining industrial regions. By contrast, social policy would not have benefited Britain directly and was not a make-or-break issue for the single market program.

Notes

1. Helen Drake, *Jacques Delors: Perspectives on a European Leader* (London: Routledge, 2000), p. 80.
2. Jacques Delors, "Speech to the European Parliament," Bulletin EC-S/1 1985.
3. Ibid. See also Ken Endo, *The Presidency of the European Commission Under Jacques Delors: The Politics of Shared Leadership* (New York: St. Martin's, 1999), p. 137.
4. See Commission, *Eighteenth Report on the Activities of the European Communities* (Luxembourg: European Communities, 1985), p. 27.
5. Margaret Thatcher, *Downing Street Years* (New York: HarperCollins, 1993), pp. 545–546.
6. Bulletin EC 2-1985.
7. Quoted in *Financial Times,* April 2, 1985, p. 3.
8. Quoted in *Le Monde,* April 2, 1985, p. 1.

9. Ad Hoc Committee for Institutional Affairs, *Report to the European Council* (Dooge report), Brussels, March 29–30, 1985.

10. Pietro Adonnino, *A People's Europe: Reports from the Ad Hoc Committee,* Bulletin ECS/7-85 (1985).

11. Thatcher, *Downing Street Years,* p. 545. See also Arthur Cockfield, *Creating the Internal Market* (London: Wiley Chancery Law, 1984).

12. Cockfield, *Creating the Internal Market,* p. 4.

13. Commission, "Completing the Internal Market," COM(85)310 final, March 1985.

14. Quoted in Marina Grazzo, ed., *Towards European Union,* vol. 2 (Brussels: Agence Europe, 1986), p. 23.

15. On the conference and its outcome, see David Cameron, "The 1992 Initiative: Causes and Consequences," in Albert Sbragia, ed., *Euro-Politics: Institutions and Policymaking in the "New" European Community* (Washington, DC: Brookings Institution, 1992), pp. 23–74; Desmond Dinan, "The Single European Act: Revitalizing European Integration," in Finn Laursen, ed., *Designing the European Union: From Paris to Lisbon* (Basingstoke: Palgrave Macmillan, 2012), pp. 124–146; Andrew Moravcsik, *The Choice for Europe: Social Purpose and State Power from Messina to Maastricht* (Ithaca: Cornell University Press, 1998), pp. 314–378; Wayne Sandholtz and John Zysman, "1992: Recasting the European Bargain," *World Politics* 42 (1989), pp. 95–128; Jean de Ruyt, *L'Acte unique européen: Commentaire,* 2nd ed. (Brussels: Editions de l'Université de Bruxelles, 1987).

16. Endo, *Presidency of the European Commission Under Jacques Delors,* p. 141.

17. See ibid., pp. 142–143.

18. Text for the Single European Act is available at http://www.europa.eu.int /abc/obj/treaties/en/entoc113.htm.

19. See Kenneth Dyson and Kevin Featherstone, *The Road to Maastricht: Negotiating Economic and Monetary Union* (Oxford: Oxford University Press, 1999), pp. 155–156.

20. Thatcher, *Downing Street Years,* p. 548.

21. Nigel Lawson, *The View from No. 11: Britain's Longest-Serving Cabinet Member Recalls the Triumphs and Disappointments of the Thatcher Era* (New York: Doubleday, 1993), pp. 893–894.

22. Text of the Single European Act is available at http://www.europa.eu.int /abc/obj/treaties/en/entoc113.htm.

23. Quoted in *Journal of Common Market Studies: 1985 Annual Review,* p. 337. See also Stephen George, *An Awkward Partner: Britain in the European Community* (Oxford: Oxford University Press, 1998), pp. 184–185.

24. On the single market program, see Barry Eichengreen, *The European Economy Since 1945: Coordinated Capitalism and Beyond* (Princeton: Princeton University Press, 2007), pp. 236–340; R. Bieber et al., *1992: One European Market* (Florence: European University Institute, 1988); Michelle Egan, *Constructing a European Market: Standards, Regulation, and Governance* (Oxford: Oxford University Press, 2001), pp. 109–132; Jacques Pelkmans and Alan Winters, *Europe's Domestic Market* (London: Routledge, 1988); Michael Calingaert, *The 1992 Challenge from Europe: Development of the European Community's Internal Market* (Washington, DC: National Planning Association, 1990).

25. See *Journal of Common Market Studies: 1986 Annual Review,* p. 339.

26. See Helen Wallace, "The British Presidency and the EC's Council of Ministers: The Opportunity to Persuade," *International Affairs* 62, no. 4 (Autumn 1986), pp. 583–599.

27. *Financial Times,* April 11, 1987, p. 2.

28. See *The Economist,* February 13, 1988, pp. 46–47, and July 9, 1988, p. 30. See also D. Mayes, ed., *The European Challenge: Industry's Response to the 1992 Programme* (Hemel Hempstead: Harvester Wheatsheaf, 1991).

29. Commission, *Research on the "Cost of Non-Europe": Basic Findings,* 16 vols. (Luxembourg: Office of Official Publications of the European Communities, 1988); Paolo Cecchini, *The European Challenge, 1992: The Benefits of the Single Market* (Aldershot: Wildwood, 1988). See also Michael Emerson et al., *The Economics of 1992: The EC's Assessment of the Economic Effects of Completing the Internal Market* (Oxford: Oxford University Press, 1988).

30. John Kay, ed., *1992: Myths and Realities* (London: London Business School, 1989).

31. Quoted in *The Times* (London), October 27, 1988, p. 6.

32. Egan, *Constructing a European Market,* pp. 52–58, 121–131.

33. Renaud Dehousse and Giandomenico Majone, "The Institutional Dynamics of European Integration: From the Single Act to the Maastricht Treaty," in Stephen Martin, ed., *The Construction of Europe: Essays in Honor of Emile Noël* (Dordrecht: Kluwer, 1994), p. 95.

34. See Egan, *Constructing a European Market,* pp. 133–165.

35. Bulletin EC 12-1988.

36. Bulletin EC S/1-1989.

37. Quoted in *International Herald Tribune,* February 15–16, 1992, p. 1.

38. Commission, "Making a Success of the Single European Act," COM(87)100, January 1987.

39. Tommaso Padoa-Schioppa et al., *Efficiency, Stability, and Equity: A Strategy for the Evolution of the Economic System of the European Community* (Oxford: Oxford University Press, 1987), p. 10.

40. Thatcher, *Downing Street Years,* p. 746.

41. See David Mayes, "Introduction: Conflict and Cohesion in the Single European Market: A Reflection," in Amin and Tomaney, eds., *Behind the Myth of European Union: Prospects for Cohesion* (Abingdon: Routledge, 1995), pp. 1–9; Liesbet Hooghe, "Reconciling EU-Wide Policy and National Diversity," in Hooghe, ed., *Cohesion Policy and European Integration: Building Multi-Level Governance* (Oxford: Oxford University Press, 1996), pp. 1–26.

42. Bulletin EC 6-1988.

7

Achieving
European Union

THE SUCCESS OF THE SINGLE MARKET PROGRAM IN THE LATE
1980s propelled European integration forward. Most national leaders rode a
wave of Europhoria. François Mitterrand in France, Helmut Kohl in Germany, and Felipe González in Spain were all reelected largely on the strength
of their Euro-credentials. Jacques Delors, reappointed in 1989 and again in
1993, became the most powerful Commission president due to his association
with the single market program. While supporting the single market, British
prime minister Margaret Thatcher strongly opposed deeper integration. That
brought her into conflict not only with Mitterrand and Kohl, but especially
with Delors, whom she saw as the root of all evil: a French Socialist determined to establish an undemocratic European superstate.

Thanks largely to the single market program, economic and monetary
union returned to the forefront of European Community affairs. EMU became the rallying cry for proponents of deeper integration and a bone of
contention between Thatcher and other national leaders. Developments in
Central and Eastern Europe, culminating in the fall of the Berlin Wall in
1989 and German unification less than a year later, gave extra impetus to
EMU. Efforts to liberalize the movement of people within the EC and concerns about possible mass migration from Central and Eastern Europe increased governments' interest in cooperating on asylum, immigration, and
policing under the rubric of justice and home affairs. The 1990 Gulf War
and the violent collapse of Yugoslavia in 1991 strengthened the momentum
already developing in the EC toward a common foreign and security policy,
and possibly a defense policy as well.

Eager to reform the EC institutionally and extend its policy scope into
new areas, governments agreed to launch two intergovernmental conferences at the end of 1990. A year of intensive negotiations on major treaty
change ended at a summit in Maastricht in December 1991. By that time,

219

Thatcher was out of office, having been ousted by the ruling Conservative Party partly because of her implacable opposition to EMU and unease with German unification.

The Maastricht Treaty, signed with great fanfare in February 1992, was the greatest milestone in the history of European integration. Apart from its many innovative institutional and policy provisions, the treaty proudly proclaimed the existence of the European Union. Yet protracted and contentious ratification debates, epitomized by the negative result of the Danish referendum in 1992, delayed implementation of the treaty and robbed the occasion of much of its luster. Within a short time, public and political attitudes toward European integration soured. Many Europeans, having looked favorably on the single market program, recoiled from the apparent complexity and incomprehensibility of the Maastricht Treaty and were highly ambivalent about EMU. The new EU's ineffectualness in Yugoslavia dented public confidence in the fledgling common foreign and security policy. Concerns about a democratic deficit in European-level governance resurfaced with a vengeance. An economic downturn in the early 1990s added to the gloom. Under the circumstances, the launch of the EU in November 1993—the high point of forty years of European integration—was anticlimactic.

Economic and Monetary Union

Apart from the single market program, the existence of the European Monetary System helped bring EMU back onto the EC's agenda in 1987 and 1988. Participation in the exchange rate mechanism of the EMS promoted a degree of economic convergence and facilitated exchange rate stability. The experience of working together in the exchange rate mechanism also reconciled many politicians and officials to the prospect of EMU. Ten years earlier, Leo Tindemans had reported regretfully that there was not enough trust between national governments to transfer responsibility for EMU to a central European authority.[1] By the late 1980s, the EMS had spawned a network of officials in the Commission and national capitals who were committed to close monetary policy cooperation.

Operational problems with the EMS led to calls for its reform and possible replacement by EMU. The German mark was the system's de facto anchor currency, and other central banks followed the monetary policy lead of the Bundesbank. Germany's partners disliked at the "asymmetry" of a system that was so obviously dominated by the mark and by German policy preferences. Pressure on the French franc triggered a revaluation of the stronger currencies in January 1987 and sharpened French criticism of the system. France pressed for better coordination of monetary policies and greater flexibility in exchange rate intervention. That resulted in the so-called Basle-Nyborg agreement of September 1987 (negotiated by the Committee of Central Bank

Governors, a key monetary policy body that met in Basle, and endorsed by the economic and finance ministers in Nyborg) to strengthen the EMS, notably by monitoring monetary developments and coordinating interest rate policies more closely, and by relaxing the rules on intervention.[2] The agreement helped the EMS to respond better to fluctuations in international currency markets, such as the upheaval after the Wall Street crash in October 1987, but did not address the underlying problem of asymmetry.

Chafing at the ascendancy of the Bundesbank while acknowledging the benefits of German-inspired monetary policy preferences, notably price stability, French officials warmed to the idea of a monetary union in which France would be on a par with Germany. At the same time, the single market program, which included proposals for the liberalization of capital movements, provided an increasing impetus toward EMU. The maintenance of exchange rates within the EC seemed inconsistent with and contradictory to the objectives of the single market. Already enthusiastic about the single market, business leaders began to take an interest in monetary union. Valéry Giscard d'Estaing and Helmut Schmidt, authors of the EMS, formed a high-level committee to lobby for it.

The relationship between the single market and the EMS provided an additional argument in favor of EMU. Tommaso Padoa-Schioppa developed the point in an influential report in early 1987 on the implications of the single market for the EC's economic system. "In a quite fundamental way," Padoa-Schioppa pointed out, "capital mobility and exchange rate fixity (in the exchange rate mechanism) together leave no room for independent [national] monetary policies." Because a unified market with a free flow of capital could put the EMS under great strain, Padoa-Schioppa recommended the establishment of a monetary union.[3]

The momentum of market integration, continuing asymmetry in the EMS, and the possible impact of free capital movements on the exchange rate mechanism prompted Edouard Balladur, France's finance minister, to draft a memorandum for the Economic and Financial Affairs Council in January 1988 titled "Europe's Monetary Construction." After reviewing the history of the EMS and the trajectory of the single market, Balladur concluded that the EC should adopt "a single currency . . . [and a] common central bank." The Balladur memorandum signaled France's dissatisfaction with the status quo and willingness to embrace EMU.[4]

A similar memorandum the following month by Hans-Dietrich Genscher, Germany's foreign minister, was even more significant, not least because Germany was then in the Council presidency. While writing in a personal capacity, Genscher endorsed the idea of a common currency and a European central bank, modeled of course on the Bundesbank. Genscher's initiative indicated Germany's growing openness to EMU, although the Bundesbank remained opposed to the idea.

Genscher's trial balloon emboldened Delors to advocate EMU more openly. Not wanting to detract attention from the single market program and stir up sentiment against EMU, Delors had so far moderated his public statements on the subject. With the single market well on track and the post–Single European Act budget package out of the way, Delors turned his attention squarely to EMU. As it was, Delors had responsibility within the Commission for economic and monetary affairs. Accordingly, he attended the monthly meetings of the Committee of Central Bank Governors at the headquarters of the Bank for International Settlements. Delors sought to ingratiate himself with the central bankers, a notoriously cliquish group. In particular, he cultivated relations with Karl-Otto Pöhl, president of the Bundesbank, one of the most influential members of the committee and a presumed opponent of EMU.[5]

Having responsibility in the Commission for monetary policy, Delors also attended meetings of Ecofin, which played an important role in the evolution of EMU. The General Affairs Council (of foreign ministers) was also influential and vied with Ecofin for supremacy in monetary policy matters. But the European Council was the most powerful body, not only because of the political sensitivity of EMU but also because, as stipulated in the Single European Act, any effort to establish EMU would require the convening of an intergovernmental conference, in which the European Council would negotiate the final deal.

Delors had the great advantage of being a member of the European Council, although officially, as Commission president, he carried less weight than the national leaders. Within the European Council, and on the question of EMU generally, Mitterrand and Kohl were the key players. Mitterrand, since his economic about-face in 1983, had openly espoused greater European integration and made "the construction of Europe" the leitmotif of his presidency.[6] He favored EMU and, in the mid-1980s, nudged Kohl to take a stronger stand on the issue. Mitterrand, during a visit to Aachen in October 1987, where he was seduced by the charm of the historic town hall and the spirit of Charlemagne, glowingly of a common Franco-German destiny. As the motor of European integration, France and Germany should spearhead closer cooperation in a range of areas, including monetary policy.[7]

Kohl, another lifetime advocate of European integration, was susceptible to arguments in favor of EMU. Yet Kohl faced strong resistance from the Bundesbank, which did not trust the political instincts and policy preferences of the French and Italian monetary authorities and did not want to lose its dominant position in the EMS. Germans deeply respected the Bundesbank, an independent body with an impeccable record of monetary policy management. As a cautious and astute politician, Kohl would not confront the Bundesbank on the question of EMU until and unless circumstances changed and German public opinion became more open to the idea.

Circumstances began to change in the late 1980s not only within the EC, where implementation of the single market program generated interest in EMU, but also in the Soviet Union, where Mikhail Gorbachev's policies of economic and political reform began to have an impact abroad. Developments in the Soviet Union raised the specter of the German question, which had haunted the early years of European integration. A visit to Moscow in July 1986 convinced Mitterrand of the importance of tying Germany more tightly into Europe should Gorbachev's reforms result in significant geopolitical change. Kohl, equally aware of what was happening in the Soviet Union and sensitive to French concerns, was happy to commit Germany unequivocally to deeper European integration. EMU would be a sure sign of Germany's intentions.[8]

Mitterrand and Kohl had ample opportunity to discuss EMU together. The close relationship between Roland Dumas and Genscher, the French and German foreign ministers, was equally important for the evolution of Franco-German thinking on the subject. Dumas was Mitterrand's most trusted interlocutor. He and Genscher spoke regularly on the telephone and met frequently in the Council and other forums. Genscher, the leader of the junior party in Kohl's coalition government, was not close to Kohl, but his position as foreign minister and coalition partner gave him considerable influence in Bonn.

The Delors Committee and Report

Following up on Genscher's memorandum, Delors and Genscher floated the idea of convening a special committee to chart the road to EMU. Mitterrand, who easily won reelection in May 1988, swung fully behind them. Kohl, reveling in the success of the Germany's Council presidency, especially after reaching agreement on a comprehensive budget package in February 1988, became increasingly assertive on EMU. He and Delors struck a deal in the run-up to the June 1988 summit: Kohl would propose to the European Council that the committee should consist mostly of the central bank governors, with Delors as the chair. The European Council's acceptance of Kohl's proposal and establishment of the Delors committee, consisting of twelve central bank governors, two commissioners (including Delors), and three independent experts, put EMU at the forefront of the EC's agenda.[9]

It was also at the June 1988 summit that the European Council reappointed Delors as Commission president. This may have seemed a foregone conclusion, but Thatcher's support was nonetheless surprising. In her memoirs, Thatcher claims that Delors's reappointment was virtually unstoppable and that, at the time, she was unaware of the extent of his Eurofederalism.[10] Neither claim rings true. Thatcher had withstood greater pressure in the European Council and could hardly have had any illusions about Delors's ideas. Nevertheless, it would have taken considerable daring to blackball

Delors's reappointment as Commission president, although she could more easily have prevented his appointment as chair of the committee on EMU. Thatcher may have presumed that Pöhl, president of the Bundesbank and a stout defender of national monetary policies, would hold the line against EMU in the committee.

According to the foremost chroniclers of EMU, "the decision to have Delors chairing the . . . committee and the remit given to it unleashed a powerful momentum behind EMU and a single currency."[11] Delors mastered complicated economic and monetary policy issues and tried not to dominate meetings, as he usually liked to do. Within the Commission, however, Delors was obsessive and secretive. He relied on a handful of trusted officials, mostly in his own *cabinet* (private office), and did not consult the other commissioners much. When challenged by them, Delors retorted disingenuously that, as chair of the committee on EMU, he was acting in a personal capacity on behalf of the European Council, not as president of the Commission.[12]

The committee's brief was to outline concrete steps for the realization of EMU. The committee met in Basle, at the end of regular meetings of the Committee of Central Bank Governors, on which most of its members served. It began deliberations in September 1988 and presented its report in April 1989. During that time, even the most reluctant committee members rose to the intellectual challenge of devising a strategy for EMU. Delors strove to keep everyone on board and produce a unanimous report without sacrificing key elements of a common policy. His success in doing so was a tribute to his negotiating and mediating skills and a good reflection on the committee's composition and operation.[13]

The Delors report identified four basic elements of economic union: the single market, competition policy and other market-strengthening mechanisms, cohesion, and macroeconomic policy coordination. It defined monetary union as "the assurance of full and irreversible convertibility of currencies; the complete liberalization of capital transactions and full integration of banking and other financial markets; and the elimination of margins of fluctuation and the irrevocable locking of exchange rate parities."[14] That would require a single monetary policy, although not necessarily a single currency. The committee proposed a European System of Central Banks, consisting of a central institution and constituent national central banks, to manage the single monetary policy. Participating national central banks would be independent and pursue price stability as their primary objective. Clearly, that was a concession to the Bundesbank and, more broadly, to German political and public opinion.

The report is best known for proposing a three-stage approach to EMU. During the first stage, capital movements would be fully liberalized and there would be closer macroeconomic policy cooperation among member states. The European System of Central Banks would be established in the second stage, and margins of fluctuation within the exchange rate mechanism would be progressively narrowed. Finally, the third stage would see the irrevocable fixing of exchange rates, with the transfer of full responsibility for monetary policy among participating countries to Community institutions.

Pessimistic by nature, Delors was disappointed with the committee's report. He regretted that it did not call emphatically for a single currency and that there were no deadlines or automatic mechanism for the transition from one stage to another. Nevertheless, the report stated that "the creation of [EMU] must be viewed as a single process" and that "the decision to enter upon the first stage should be a decision to embark on the entire process." The report also recommended that Stage One of EMU, which did not require treaty change, should start no later than July 1990, when capital movements were due to be liberalized as part of the single market program.[15]

The Delors report elicited a mixed response among national leaders. Thatcher was livid with the governor of the Bank of England for signing the report and felt betrayed by Pöhl as well. She was in no doubt about Delors's intentions and about the political importance of EMU for the EC's future. The British government was then in the midst of a furious debate about possibly joining the exchange rate mechanism of the EMS. Nigel Lawson, the chancellor of the exchequer (finance minister), urged British participation both for its own sake and in order to strengthen Britain's credibility in the EC. Far from wanting to establish EMU, Lawson wanted Britain to continue to oppose it, but from within the exchange rate mechanism. Geoffrey Howe, Britain's foreign secretary, also opposed EMU but favored a more positive British policy toward the EC. Thatcher's notorious intransigence on EC issues drove a wedge between her and the finance and foreign ministers. Division at home reduced the effectiveness of Britain's opposition abroad to EMU. It also drove Lawson, Howe, and eventually Thatcher from office.[16]

Momentum for EMU

The outcome of the next meeting of the European Council, in June 1989, would be decisive for the future of the Delors report and the fate of EMU. Spain, in the Council presidency for the first time, jumped on the EMU bandwagon as a means of establishing its European credentials and, possibly, leveraging more money for cohesion policy. González, the Spanish prime minister, was a close ally of Mitterrand's. With France due to succeed Spain in the Council presidency, Mitterrand and González closely coordinated their positions on EMU. Feeling more confident of his position vis-à-vis the Bundesbank after Pöhl signed on to the Delors report, and mindful of the changing strategic situation in Central and Eastern Europe, Kohl had no hesitation endorsing EMU fully.

The European Council accordingly agreed "progressively to achieve economic and monetary union as provided for in the [Single European Act]" and endorsed the Delors report as a blueprint for action.[17] The European Council decided that Stage One of EMU would begin in July 1990 and that an intergovernmental conference would be convened to decide when and how to move to the final stage. Thatcher was completely outflanked. Under pressure from her finance and foreign ministers, Thatcher reluctantly agreed at the summit that Britain would participate eventually in the exchange rate mechanism.

Mitterrand carried the momentum generated at the summit into the succeeding French presidency. The strategic dimension of EMU, looming in the background since Gorbachev's ascendancy in the Soviet Union, suddenly jumped to the forefront in the fall of 1989 as anti-Communist protests in East Germany grew increasingly vociferous. Instead of ordering military intervention, as Soviet leaders had done in similar situations in Hungary in 1956 and Prague in 1968, Gorbachev allowed the protesters to breach the Berlin Wall in November 1989.

With the sudden possibility of German unification, the geopolitical situation in Europe changed overnight. Clearly discomfited by the prospect of a united Germany, Mitterrand was more determined than ever to tie Germany tighter into the EC through the rapid achievement of EMU. He conveyed that message to Kohl and other Community leaders at an extraordinary summit in Paris only a week after the Berlin Wall came down. Mitterrand was alarmed when Kohl outlined a ten-point program for German and European unification, in a speech to the German parliament at the end of November 1989, without consulting Paris. Despite Kohl's commitment in the speech to deeper European integration, Mitterrand wanted proof of Kohl's intentions.[18]

Mitterrand's instinctive evocation of the German question strained relations between Paris and Bonn. Yet Kohl had no intention of changing the course of postwar German foreign policy. He was happy to cement the link between German unification and European integration. The next meeting of the European Council, in Strasbourg in December 1989, gave him an opportunity to do so. A key passage in the summit's conclusions proclaimed that German unification "should take place peacefully and democratically, in full respect of the relevant agreements and treaties . . . in a context of dialogue and East-West cooperation . . . [and] in the perspective of European integration."[19] More concretely, the connection between German unification and European integration manifested itself in the decision to hold an intergovernmental conference on EMU following the German elections in October 1990.[20]

The Commission maintained the momentum toward EMU throughout 1990 with a series of pronouncements on the subject. Foremost among these was the Commission's much-quoted cost-benefit analysis of EMU. The report's title, *One Market, One Money,* reinforced the link between the single market program and EMU and became a mantra for advocates of a single currency.[21]

EMU was therefore well on track in the run-up to German unification, which merely reinforced the member states' commitment to hold an intergovernmental conference on the subject. The European Council decided in June 1990 to launch the conference on EMU before the end of the year. In October 1990, the European Council agreed to begin the second stage of EMU in January 1994. Thatcher alone dissented. Thatcher's obstructionism, and her resistance throughout the year to German unification, weakened her position within the government to the point that her cabinet colleagues ousted her as prime minister the following month.[22] Far from Thatcher killing EMU, EMU contributed to killing Thatcher politically.

The Changing Political Context

Peaceful revolution in Central and Eastern Europe, German unification, and ultimately the collapse of the Soviet Union were the most obvious manifestations of the changing geopolitical context of European integration in the late 1980s and early 1990s. In addition, implementation of the single market program and the momentum behind EMU altered the political situation within the EC. Questions about the accountability and legitimacy of EC institutions that had been percolating beneath the surface for a number of years quickly came to the fore. Concern about the democratic deficit, initially expressed in the late 1970s at the time of the first direct elections to the European Parliament, became more common. The impact of market liberalization and integration on people's everyday lives, and the likely impact of EMU on national sovereignty, raised troubling questions about Community governance.

In Thatcher's view, democracy itself was at risk. The prime minister denounced what she saw as the increasing and excessive centralization of power in Brussels. The single market program was to have facilitated as much deregulation as possible at the national level and as much reregulation as necessary at the European level. Thatcher saw plenty of evidence of European reregulation but little evidence, outside Britain, of national deregulation. She loathed the Commission, with its unelected and barely accountable college and bloated bureaucracy, adrift from the member states. In her view, Delors personified all that was wrong with Brussels. She thought him duplicitous, overweening, and unbearable. As in her dealings with most continental leaders, personal antipathy clouded political judgment.

There is no doubt that Delors was indeed overbearing at times. He was openly ambitious for himself, the Commission, and the EC. Employing phrases frequently used in France but jarring to British ears, he advocated "the construction of Europe" and the creation of a "European social space." Delors announced as early as January 1985 that the Commission was "the engineer" of European integration.[23] He leveraged the single market program for political commitments to cohesion and social policy and made no secret of his ultimate objective: EMU. He was more influential than most national leaders at meetings of the European Council and acted at G7 summits as if he represented Europe.

Although the Commission's profile rose along with Delors's prominence, Delors's success cost the institution dearly. The college increased in size in January 1986, following the accession of Portugal and Spain. Complaining that the college was already too large, Delors turned his back on the expanded Commission. Although the first Delors Commission (1985–1989) is generally credited with being the most successful in the EU's history, Delors rarely worked with all its members. Pascal Lamy, "the most forceful and feared" *chef de cabinet,* protected Delors from other commissioners as well as from Commission officials, thereby allowing Delors to focus on "public relations, negotiations with governmental leaders, and the conceptualization of new policy initiatives."[24] Other commissioners and senior officials resented the power of Delors's clique. The Commission as a whole became fractious and unmanageable as its responsibilities grew without a commensurate increase in its resources and with poor direction from the top. Delors greatly exacerbated the Commission's management deficit, which became glaringly obvious after his departure (see Chapter 8).

Despite its internal problems, outsiders viewed the Commission as an institution on the rise, firmly at the center of EC decisionmaking. Delors famously declared in July 1988, a month after his reappointment as Commission president, that in ten years' time, "80 percent of our economic legislation, and perhaps even our fiscal and social legislation as well, will be of Community origin."[25] That was too much for Thatcher, who used the opportunity of an invitation to speak at the College of Europe in Bruges, a bastion of Eurofederalism, to deliver a blistering rejoinder. Thatcher articulated an intergovernmentalist view of the EC and defended Britain's role in it. She peppered her address with barbed attacks against Delors and the Commission. The most evocative of these was the best-remembered part of her speech: "We have not successfully rolled back the frontiers of the state in Britain only to see them reimposed at a European level with a European superstate exercising a new dominance from Brussels."[26]

Thatcher's speech was music to the ears of British Euroskeptics, who formed the Bruges Group think tank in her honor. The British tabloid press, staunchly conservative and generally Euroskeptical, had a field day. By contrast, Thatcher's antics embarrassed moderates in Britain. The Labour Party, committed until recently to pulling Britain out of the EC, swung back in favor of membership in response to Delors's social policy agenda and in reaction against Thatcher's denunciation of Brussels. The Conservative

Party, once a bastion of pro-Europeans, became increasingly divided between rabid Europhobes and traditional Europhiles.

Both Thatcher and Delors believed that history was on their side. Each of them interpreted events in Central and Eastern Europe in that light. For Thatcher, the collapse of communism and the Soviet system demonstrated the bankruptcy of Western European socialism and the futility of trying to centralize power in Brussels. For Delors, those events demonstrated the appeal of European integration and the importance of strengthening supranational institutions. In June 1989 the European Council, of which Thatcher and Delors were members, welcomed the "profound changes" sweeping the Central and Eastern Europe.[27] Delors was gratified when countries in the region expressed their eagerness for EC membership. Surely countries so conscious of their newfound sovereignty and independence would not want to join the EC if they thought that it resembled the Soviet bloc? Nevertheless, Thatcher increasingly compared the EC to the Soviet Union. Her only comment on the membership aspirations of the Central and Eastern European countries was to express hope that enlargement would weaken the EC politically and derail prospects for EMU.

Thatcher strongly opposed German unification and the de facto enlargement of the EC to incorporate East Germany. An infamous outburst by Nicholas Ridley, a close friend and cabinet member, reflected Thatcher's thinking. In an interview published in July 1990, Ridley not only regretted the emergence of an "uppity" Germany but also denounced EMU as "a German racket."[28] By contrast, Delors endorsed German unification early and wholeheartedly. Mitterrand was equivocal but soon accepted the inevitable. Kohl, with strong US support, seized the chance presented by Gorbachev's moderation and the breach of the Berlin Wall to unify Germany before a possible coup in the Soviet Union or other reactionary event could firmly shut an unexpectedly open door. What to Thatcher (and Mitterrand) looked like unseemly haste was to Kohl an opportunistic response to unexpected developments. Kohl interpreted the Christian Democrats' victory in the first free elections in East Germany, in March 1990, as a mandate for immediate unification. At breakneck speed and with a generous exchange rate for the East German mark, he launched German monetary union in July 1990. Full unification followed three months later.[29]

Having a larger, unified Germany on the edge of an independent Central and Eastern Europe would change the character of the EC. United Germany would account for 27 percent of the EC's GDP and, with 77 million people, 25 percent of the EC's population. If traditional European trade patterns, sundered throughout much of the twentieth century, reasserted themselves, Germany would become the hub of a vibrant, pan-European marketplace. Strategically, the center of gravity could shift within the EC from West to East, from France to Germany. The Franco-German motor would be hard-pressed to keep European integration moving in a direction fully congenial to France.

Events in Germany and farther east intensified member states' interest in institutional and policy reforms other than EMU. In a speech at the College of Europe in Bruges in October 1989, where Thatcher had issued her infamous antifederalist manifesto a year earlier, Delors linked the themes of reform in Central and Eastern Europe and reform in the EC. Calling for a huge "leap forward" to meet the economic and strategic challenges confronting the Community, Delors gave wholehearted support to the idea of political union. Specifically, Delors proposed greater competence for the EC in a range of areas, including foreign policy and security, more efficient decisionmaking, and more subsidiarity (decentralization of power). He also advocated greater power for the EP as a means of increasing the EC's legitimacy.[30]

Delors and other EC leaders pushed hard in early 1990 for reform of the EC's institutions and policies. Belgium was the first member state to submit a formal proposal for political union, in March 1990. It called for greater democracy and more efficiency in the EC and for a common foreign and security policy instead of the existing system of foreign policy cooperation.[31] The EP, which stood to gain from any effort to increase the EC's legitimacy, eagerly endorsed political union in a series of resolutions in 1990. The Italian government, traditionally a strong supporter of the EP and of deeper European integration, threw itself behind the idea. Only Britain and Denmark remained unconvinced of the need for an intergovernmental conference on political union.

As with EMU, the essential impetus for political union came from France and Germany. Following the East German elections of March 1990, it was obvious to Mitterrand that German unification was inevitable. Hoping to anchor Germany further in the EC and patch up his differences with Kohl, Mitterrand suggested a Franco-German initiative on political union. Accordingly, Mitterrand and Kohl requested an extraordinary meeting of the European Council to discuss the possibility of convening an intergovernmental conference on political union alongside the conference on EMU. Kohl and Mitterrand did not define political union, but identified four elements of it: greater democratic legitimacy, more efficient decisionmaking, coherent socioeconomic policies, and the development of a common foreign and security policy.[32]

Meeting in April 1990, the European Council endorsed the idea of a second intergovernmental conference but, in deference to Thatcher, did not set a date for it. The European Council again took up the issue in June 1990. This time the other EC leaders agreed without dissent to open two conferences, on EMU and political union, in Rome in December 1990. Thatcher, realizing the futility of objecting to the European Council's declared aim of transforming the EC "from an entity mainly based on economic integration and political cooperation into a union of a political nature, including a common foreign and security policy," reluctantly went along with it.[33] She wanted member states to have a stronger collective international presence and impact, but opposed further formal integration.

While Italy, in the Council presidency in the second half of 1990, laid the groundwork for the launch of the intergovernmental conferences, the EC confronted the administrative and economic challenges of incorporating East Germany into the fold. A special group of commissioners, led by Martin Bangemann, Germany's senior commissioner, met weekly to provide overall direction. The achievement of German unity, in October 1990, raised a host of legal, financial, institutional, and policy issues for the EC. Contrary to Mitterrand's expectation only one year previously, German unification preceded EMU. Nevertheless, Kohl, secure in office after winning the first all-German general election in October 1990, seemed more committed than ever to achieving not only EMU but political union as well.

Thatcher's ouster in November 1990, on the eve of the intergovernmental conferences, seemed a fitting prelude to a further acceleration of European integration. Delors was gleeful, although as *The Economist* noted, Thatcher's removal robbed the EC of "the grit around which the other eleven formed their Euro-pearl."[34] Delors need not have worried. John Major, Thatcher's successor, was every bit as intransigent as his illustrious predecessor, except that he obstructed Community business with a smile.

Thatcher's departure coincided with the high point of Delors's power. Far from growing more influential during the intergovernmental conferences that followed, Delors began to fall from grace in 1990. Other national leaders, not just Thatcher, resented his political ascendancy and high public profile. Even sympathetic governments felt that the Commission was exceeding its authority and getting too big for its boots. Although he remained an important player during the rest of his presidency, Delors must have sensed that the short era of unbridled Commission activism was at an end. Paradoxically, the Commission's power peaked just as the EC embarked on the road to European Union.

The Maastricht Treaty

In December 1990, EC leaders launched the intergovernmental conferences on EMU and political union.[35] The conferences concluded a year later, at the Maastricht summit, with agreement not only to revise the existing treaties but also to promulgate a new treaty on European Union. There was consensus at the outset on the meaning of EMU, but not on how to organize or achieve it. The subject of political union was more amorphous. Nobody thought that it meant the establishment of a unitary political system, a federal United States of Europe. The most that ardent Eurofederalists hoped for was a further transfer of responsibility for various policy areas from the national to the European level, more responsibility for the EP, and the extension of qualified majority voting in the Council. There was little doubt that the conferences would transform the European Community into the European Union, but the form and substance of the union remained elusive.

At the everyday working level, the foreign ministers' personal representatives (mostly the governments' permanent representatives in Brussels) negotiated political union, and senior officials from national central banks and finance ministries negotiated EMU. At the next level, the foreign and finance ministers, meeting on the margins of their respective councils, reviewed progress and negotiated some of the politically more sensitive issues. Finally, national leaders tackled the most difficult questions at meetings of the European Council. At all levels, negotiators met informally, bilaterally or multilaterally, on the margins of conference sessions or on other occasions to move the process along.

National leaders hoped to wrap up the conferences at their summit in Luxembourg in June 1991. In the event, the conferences continued for another six months. Apart from the ceremonial opening of the conferences in Rome in December 1990, conference sessions took place during the presidencies of Luxembourg and the Netherlands, the same countries that had presided over the conference that preceded the Single European Act. Many of the officials and politicians participating in the 1990–1991 conferences had participated also in the 1985–1986 conference, thus contributing to a strong esprit de corps among the negotiators. As in the earlier conference, the Commission participated at all levels but, unlike national governments, could not veto the outcome.

Procedurally, the 1990–1991 conferences differed from the earlier conference in one important respect. Whereas the Dooge committee had prepared the ground for the Single European Act and the Delors committee had prepared the ground for EMU, no preparatory committee prepared the ground for political union. That caused some confusion about the scope of political union and the precise agenda of the negotiations. It may also have resulted in the conference lasting longer than the negotiators intended it to.

Economic and Monetary Union

As Kenneth Dyson and Kevin Featherstone observed: "The Delors report provided a vital basis of technical legitimacy for EMU and set the key parameters for the subsequent treaty negotiations."[36] Nevertheless, there was much for the conference to decide. Sensitive to pressure from the Bundesbank, German negotiators insisted that responsibility for monetary policy at the European level reside in a single, independent institution with the unambiguous, statutory mandate of maintaining price stability. In other words, the European Central Bank (ECB) should replicate the German central bank. The Bundesbank also warned against establishing the ECB at the beginning of Stage Two of EMU, before the launch of the single currency. Finally, German negotiators insisted on the importance of economic convergence between prospective EMU participants, even if it meant that not every member state would be able to participate in Stage Three from the outset. Weary of battling Delors in Brussels and Kohl in Bonn, Bundesbank president Pöhl resigned in 1991, well before the end of his second term.

Hans Tietmeyer, his successor, was an equally aggressive defender of the Bundesbank's interests. Throughout 1991, Pöhl and Tietmeyer pressured the German government by alerting the public to the implications of EMU, pointing out that other European countries lacked Germany's historical fear of inflation and warning that the proposed ECB might not be as rigorously independent of political control as the Bundesbank was. The German government got the message and held the line in the conference, although the German public woke up to the far-reaching implications of EMU only on the eve of the Maastricht summit, due largely to a banner headline in the mass-circulation *Bild* newspaper that proclaimed "The End of the D-Mark."

France had different institutional and policy preferences for EMU. Lacking a tradition of central bank independence, France wanted to put the ECB under some form of political control but conceded the impossibility of doing so, well before the conference began. Indeed, as part of the bargain on EMU, France agreed to make its own central bank independent. France strongly urged the establishment of the ECB at the start of a relatively short Stage Two rather than at the start of Stage Three, as Germany advocated. According to the French, a functioning ECB and a strict timetable for the introduction of the single currency would encourage economic convergence among member states. As the ECB could not perform its main function until the beginning of Stage Three, the Germans feared that establishing the ECB sooner would undermine its purpose and prestige.

Luxembourg, in the Council presidency and therefore chairing the conference, submitted a draft treaty text on EMU in May 1991. This included a relatively insubstantial Stage Two, in which the Committee of Central Bank Governors would try to coordinate national monetary positions. The ECB would be established on the eve of Stage Three, but the European Monetary Institute, a forerunner of the ECB, would be established at the beginning of Stage Two. The purpose of the monetary institute, which would subsume the Committee of Central Bank Governors, was to facilitate monetary policy cooperation among member states and prepare procedurally for the launch of Stage Three.

Negotiators in the conference accepted that a degree of convergence in the economic performance of prospective EMU participants was imperative in order to launch Stage Three. That raised an obvious question: Should

Stage Three begin before all member states met the convergence criteria, thereby creating a two-tier EU? Moreover, should countries be allowed to opt out and not participate in Stage Three, even if they met the convergence criteria? Before the conference opened, it was widely accepted that, because all member states could not meet relatively strict convergence criteria in a timely fashion, Stage Three would indeed begin with less than a full complement of EU member states. The unspoken presumption was that Greece, Portugal, and Spain would be in the second tier, and maybe Italy as well. Potential second-tier countries fretted about the political impact of not participating in Stage Three from the outset. Fear of marginalization became a major inducement for Italy and Spain, two large and proud member states, to make the first cut for full EMU membership (see Chapter 8).

The finance ministers, who discussed the Luxembourg draft in May 1991, agreed that a two-tier system was inevitable. A general consensus emerged that any member state capable of meeting the convergence criteria but preferring not to participate in Stage Three would have the right to opt out. Just as no member state would be allowed to prevent others from moving to Stage Three, no member state would be forced to adopt the single currency. In concrete terms, this meant that Britain and Denmark would not block movement toward Stage Three, in which they would not be obliged to participate. John Major described the opt-out provision of the proposed treaty as "a clause that we have secured enabling us to opt-in. If we wish, when we wish, and in the conditions that we judge to be right."[37]

A formula emerged in the conference whereby Stage Three would be launched as early as January 1997 if a majority of member states met the convergence criteria; otherwise it would commence in January 1999 with however many member states met the criteria. There were intense negotiations about the criteria themselves. The other member states eventually went along with German demands for seemingly strict criteria: an average inflation rate not exceeding by more than 1.5 percent that of the three best-performing member states, a budget deficit of less than 3 percent of GDP and a public debt ratio not exceeding 60 percent of GDP, an annual nominal long-term interest rate not exceeding by more than 2 percent that of the three best-performing member states, and participation of a country's currency within the normal margins of the exchange rate mechanism for at least two years, without devaluations.

As envisioned in the Delors report, member states agreed in the conference that an independent European System of Central Banks, consisting of the ECB and national central banks, would be established on the eve of Stage Three. The ECB's governing council, made up of a six-member executive board (appointed by the European Council) and the governors of the national central banks, would be the highest decisionmaking body, with overall responsibility for monetary policy, foreign exchange operations, management of participating countries' official foreign reserves, and the smooth operation of the payments system. The main objective of the ECB, like that of the Bundesbank, was to maintain price stability (fight inflation).

The negotiations on EMU were mostly complete before the Maastricht summit, which dealt largely with contentious issues of political union. Nevertheless, a link existed between both sets of negotiations, especially for Germany, which had the most to lose from EMU and the most to gain from political union. By agreeing to EMU, Germany would be giving up its much-loved mark and surrendering control over national monetary policy and de facto control over European monetary policy through the European Monetary System. With political union, Germany stood to gain a familiar federal-like system of European governance in which controversial domestic issues, such as asylum policy and defense, might be resolved, and in which a more powerful EP, with a large German contingent, would play a leading role. Frustrated by the recalcitrance not only of Britain but also of France and other supposedly integrationist member states, Kohl threatened before the Maastricht summit to veto EMU without a far-reaching agreement on political union. Although it lacked credibility, Kohl's threat indicated the seriousness with which he took the negotiations on political union.

Political Union

Unlike economic and monetary union, political union covered a large number of disparate institutional and policy issues. They ranged from the extension of qualified majority voting in the Council, to the role of the EP, to social policy, to the transformation of European Political Cooperation into the common foreign and security policy. Member state positions varied widely. Britain was in a minority of one in a number of cases, but was by no means the only country that doggedly argued its case. Whereas the April 1991 Luxembourg draft text on EMU contained about 80 percent of the agreement eventually approved at the Maastricht summit in December, much of the agreement on political union was still undecided as the conference came to an end.

What kind of entity would the EU be? One of the most vexing questions was whether to describe it as a federation. The Luxembourg presidency included the phrase "federal goal" in its draft treaty, but Britain would have none of it. Douglas Hurd, the foreign secretary, rejected "the implications which, in the English language, the phrase 'federal goal' carries."[38] The English word "federal" was perfectly acceptable to Americans, but not to British conservatives, despite their close affinity with the United States. A British member of the EP explained the problem: "On the continent [federalism] is a harmless label, neither exciting nor controversial. In Britain, it carries connotations of unspeakable disloyalty and unmentionable perversity."[39]

At the Luxembourg summit in June 1991, Major denounced the draft treaty's reference to a "federal goal." To his intense annoyance, the incoming

Dutch presidency changed the phrase only to "federal vocation." As the conference intensified, Major escalated his campaign to excise the "F-word." The other Community leaders finally agreed shortly before the Maastricht summit to drop "federal" from the treaty in return for some British concessions in key policy areas. "What does the word matter, as long as we have the actual thing?" Delors wondered.[40] It mattered a lot to Major, because conservative Euroskeptics were watching his every move. Prominent among them was Thatcher, now a backbencher in the House of Commons and a bitter opponent of any concessions to federal-minded member states.

The row over the structure of the EU seemed equally arcane, yet it dominated the conference in mid-1991. Keenly aware of British and Danish determination to restrict the proposed CFSP and cooperation on justice and home affairs to intergovernmental decisionmaking, the Luxembourg presidency proposed that the edifice of the EU rest on three pillars: the Rome Treaty, the CFSP, and justice and home affairs. Governments were divided on the issue. Most wanted the EU to have a unitary structure, what the Belgian foreign minister later called a "tree with branches" rather than a "temple with pillars."[41] In their view, the Rome Treaty, which already included a variety of decisionmaking mechanisms, could incorporate the common foreign and security policy and justice and home affairs as well. Delors invested heavily in the discussion about the EU's architecture, fearing that the proposed pillar system would cut the Commission and the EP off from the CFSP and justice and home affairs, which is exactly what some governments wanted.

Despite an agreement at the Luxembourg summit in June 1991 to establish the three pillars, the new Dutch presidency attempted to restore the EU's unitary structure. Major traveled to The Hague in September 1991 to caution the Dutch to stick to the Luxembourg formula. Other governments sympathized with the Dutch position but were unwilling to engage in a pitched battle with Britain over the EU's architecture. The Dutch went ahead anyway and produced a new draft treaty with a unitary structure. At a foreign ministers' meeting at the end of September, only Belgium and the Commission supported the text that the Dutch prime minister had earlier proclaimed "acceptable to all our partners."[42] The near-unanimous rejection of the new draft treaty on "Black Monday" was a serious setback for the Dutch presidency and its supporters. It put an end to debate at the conference about the EU's structure and ensured that the treaty agreed to in Maastricht included the three pillars.

The first pillar. In addition to its provisions on EMU, the Maastricht Treaty included a number of important changes to the Rome Treaty that fell under the EU's first pillar. The treaty's main institutional reforms involved a modest extension of qualified majority voting in the Council and a major extension of the EP's legislative authority. The aim was to increase decisionmaking efficiency while enhancing the new EU's democratic legitimacy. Member states were well aware that the Single European Act had deepened the democratic deficit, despite its extension of the EP's legislative role under the cooperation procedure. In a measure of public dissatisfaction with the EC and lack of enthusiasm for the EP, the turnout in the elections of June 1989 was smaller than in the previous elections, in 1984 and 1979. Nevertheless, the EP and its supporters, notably Belgium, Germany, and Italy, lobbied during the intergovernmental conference to increase the EP's legislative power.

Concern about a widening democratic deficit undermined the resistance of governments unsympathetic to the EP. These ranged from Britain, which opposed extending the EP's power for reasons of national sovereignty, to Ireland, which was unenthusiastic about the EP because of the country's small representation there. Following protracted negotiations, governments agreed to extend the EP's power considerably, but not as much as the EP wanted. Thus the Maastricht Treaty switched the decision-making basis of a number of policy areas from the original consultation procedure to cooperation (right to a second reading) and switched some others, notably relating to the internal market, from cooperation to the new co-decision procedure (shared legislative authority with the Council). As a result, cooperation became the most important procedure used in EU legislative decisionmaking, although the co-decision procedure was the most extensive in terms of the EP's powers.

The co-decision procedure elevated the EP almost to the legislative equal of the Council. Through an extremely complicated mechanism, it gave the EP the right to a third reading of draft legislation and established a conciliation committee in which representatives of the Council and the EP could attempt to agree on a compromise text at the final stage. Many members of the EP complained that co-decision gave their institution only a limited right of rejection rather than a positive right of approval, whereas many ministers in the Council and officials in the Council secretariat complained that the procedure was too complicated for the EP to master. Just as it amended its rules of procedure in 1986 to make the most of the cooperation procedure, however, the EP soon introduced procedural changes to exploit the potential of co-decision without further impairing the efficiency of the EU's notoriously cumbersome decisionmaking apparatus.

The outcome of the conference was satisfactory for the EP in other respects as well. For instance, the Maastricht Treaty extended the assent procedure to all international agreements that set up institutions or had major financial implications. Although excluded from the treaty's intergovernmental pillars, the EP exploited its enhanced power of assent to play a limited role in the conduct of the CFSP. The treaty also introduced the assent procedure into a number of internal EU affairs, and extended significantly the EP's oversight role by giving Parliament a right of inquiry, a more formal right of petition, and the right to appoint an ombudsman to field complaints about maladministration in the EU's institutions. Finally, the treaty obliged governments to consult the EP before nominating a new Commission president, and obliged a new Commission to win a vote of approval in the EP.

Despite complaining about the outcome, the EP emerged from the conference a major institutional winner. By contrast, the Commission was lucky not to have had its formal powers seriously curtailed. In a sign of the backlash against the Commission, a number of governments raised the possibility of ending the Commission's exclusive right to initiate legislation and allowing the Council to amend Commission proposals by qualified majority instead of unanimity. As Delors told the EP in April 1991, changes of that kind would have gravely undermined supranationalism and turned the Commission into "a sort of general secretariat" for the Council.[43]

Apart from institutional reforms intended to increase accountability and legitimacy, governments added a number of treaty provisions to assuage popular concerns and give the EU wide appeal. Chief among these was a clause enshrining the principle of subsidiarity, which stated that the EU should involve itself only in issues that could best be dealt with at the European rather than the national level. Precisely because it was a statement of principle, subsidiarity was notoriously difficult to define in practice, as the EU would discover in due course. The Commission interpreted subsidiarity as a self-denying ordinance, whereas the less integration-minded member states used it as an opportunity to try to roll back intrusive or expensive Community policies.

The Maastricht Treaty redefined or expanded Community involvement in a number of policy areas, such as education, culture, the environment, and consumer protection. Felipe González wanted to leave his mark on the negotiations by including in the new treaty the concept of EU citizenship. Other leaders agreed on condition that it not conflict in any way with national citizenship.[44]

As in the conference that led to the Single European Act, González championed the cause of cohesion, this time arguing that moves toward EMU justified an additional redistribution of money to the poorer member states. Once again he succeeded. As a result, cohesion became a major objective of the EU, and member states promised to set up a Cohesion Fund by the end of December 1993 to contribute to environmental and transport projects, mostly in countries with a per capita GDP less than 90 percent of the Community average, and a program designed to achieve convergence in preparation for Stage Three of EMU.

Social policy was the final stumbling block at the Maastricht summit. Delors and eleven national leaders wanted a package of social policy provisions called the "social chapter" included in the treaty. This would have extended qualified majority voting to social policy and given a greater role to the "social partners" (employers' and employees' representatives). John Major adamantly refused. The issue almost derailed the conference and was resolved only late in the summit when the eleven agreed to remove the contentious chapter from the treaty. Instead, they attached a protocol to the treaty along the lines of the proposed chapter, allowing them to use EU institutions and decisionmaking procedures to develop social policy without British participation.

The second pillar. The CFSP was one of the trickiest issues in the conference. Foreign and security policy was at the core of national sovereignty. Whereas member states were willing to pool responsibility for monetary policy, they were not about to establish a truly *common* foreign and security policy, let alone a truly *common* defense policy. There was no impetus to share sovereignty on security and foreign policy as there was on economic and monetary policy. Member states had markedly different foreign policy interests, orientations, and traditions. The most that they could aspire to achieve was a high degree of coordination.

As the EC's international profile rose, thanks to the single market program and moves toward EMU, the gap between external economic and political influence widened. For instance, events in Central and Eastern Europe called for a concerted Community response. At the July 1989 G7 summit in Paris, the United States asked the Commission to orchestrate Western aid to Hungary and Poland and later to all of Central and Eastern Europe. The Commission happily obliged, but the EC did not have a common foreign policy toward the region. Governments coordinated their positions through European Political Cooperation but lacked joint instruments of diplomatic persuasion.

The discrepancy between the EC's external economic policy and traditional foreign policy became even more apparent in the run-up to the conference, following the Iraqi invasion of Kuwait in August 1990. The EC reacted promptly and forcefully: within two days it embargoed oil from Iraq and Iraqi-occupied Kuwait. Governments used European Political Cooperation to issue a joint condemnation of Iraq's action. Beyond that, they could do little together. France convened a meeting of the Western European Union, an organization that included most of the EC's member states that were also members of NATO, in Paris on August 1990 to discuss a possible military response. Precisely because the Western European Union did not include every EC member state, Italy reached the obvious conclusion and called for a merger of the Western European Union and the EC. Meeting in Rome in October 1990, the European Council "noted a consensus to go beyond the present limits in regard to security," but could not agree on the scope, content, and procedure of the CFSP or the Western European Union's relationship with the putative EU.[45]

Any discussion of defense inevitably led to a discussion of NATO. France wanted to develop an EU defense capability in part to strengthen the European pillar of NATO; Britain was more sensitive to US concerns; and Germany leaned intellectually toward the French position but politically toward the British position. The United States made its disapproval of a European defense identity or capability known early in the conference, thereby nixing discussion of the issue. Denmark, Greece, and Ireland, all opposed to the militarization of the EU, breathed a sigh of relief. US concern about the impact of a European defense policy on NATO, or on US hegemony in NATO, got the EU off the hook. Even without US interference, governments would have had difficulty agreeing on such sweeping changes.[46]

The formula eventually included in the Maastricht Treaty allowed for "the eventual framing of a common defense policy, which might in time lead to a common defense." The treaty also recognized the Western European Union as "an integral part of the development" of the EU. Moreover, the EU could ask the Western European Union "to elaborate and implement the [EU's] decisions and actions . . . [that] have defense implications."[47] At the same time, the more Atlanticist member states were careful to reassure the United States that nothing in the treaty could be construed as undermining NATO. In a separate development, the Western European Union agreed to admit Greece. Although not specifically an EC issue, Greece had made this one of its main objectives during the conference in an effort to distinguish itself further from fellow NATO member but non–Western European Union member Turkey.

The disintegration of Yugoslavia, which began in mid-1991, further demonstrated the difficulty of devising joint EU positions on tricky international issues. Like the United States, EC member states initially cautioned secessionist states not to break away from the Yugoslav federation. When Slovenia did so anyway and the Yugoslav army intervened, the EC immediately sent a mission to mediate between both sides. Hostilities broke out just as the European Council was convening in Luxembourg in June 1991. The troika of EC foreign ministers (from the current, preceding, and succeeding presidencies) left Luxembourg for a dramatic overnight peace mission to Belgrade. Reflecting the EC's self-confidence and naiveté at that stage of the Yugoslav conflict, one member of the troika observed that "when we went on this mission . . . [we] really had the feeling that the Yugoslav authorities thought that they were talking to Europe, not just to a country incidentally coming by but to an entity whose voice counts."[48] Commenting on the EC's apparent coming-of-age, the foreign minister of Luxembourg, then in the Council presidency, declared that "this is the hour of Europe, not of the Americans."[49]

The foreign ministers soon regretted their statements. The fighting in Slovenia ended quickly with the withdrawal of the Yugoslav army. But a savage war broke out in Croatia as the Serb-dominated federal forces attempted to bring the breakaway republic to heel. The new round of hostilities unleashed a level of brutality not seen in Europe since World War II.[50]

The EC had a limited array of instruments at its disposal to try to end the fighting, including economic sanctions and inducements, and diplomatic recognition or isolation of the warring parties. The EC was not in a position to take military action, although individual member states could do so either on their own, under United Nations auspices, or as part of a NATO or Western European Union operation. Even if the EC had had the authority to act militarily, member states would have been able to undertake only limited peacekeeping operations.

The EC convened a peace conference in The Hague in September 1991 for leaders of the warring factions. But the EC was unable to exert much pressure on either side. The EC's potential diplomatic leverage was undermined when Germany began to press for recognition of Croatia and Slovenia in the fall of 1991. Other governments fretted about Germany's newfound international assertiveness and feared that diplomatic recognition of the breakaway republics would inflame the situation. Matters came to a head at a Council meeting in mid-December. After ten hours of fierce debate, the foreign ministers agreed to draw up criteria for recognition of new states in Yugoslavia and the disintegrating Soviet Union. The other member states succumbed to German pressure and recognized Croatia and Slovenia in January 1992.

The row within the EC about diplomatic recognition of breakaway states coincided with the Maastricht summit. Despite the clear need for a robust foreign and security policy, governments approached the subject guardedly in light of events in Yugoslavia. Germany's support for Croatian independence jogged memories of the Nazi regime's support for the Croatian Fascists fifty years earlier and sparked an ugly media frenzy in France. The mood during the closing stages of the negotiations on political union was not conducive to the development of an EC defense identity, let alone a fully functioning CFSP.

The section of the Maastricht Treaty dealing with foreign and security policy was therefore relatively restrained. It outlined the policy's objectives, called for "systematic cooperation" between member states, and provided for "joint action" by the EU in the foreign and security policy realm. The treaty allowed for majority voting to implement joint actions, but only if governments first agreed unanimously on the principle of joint action. That clumsy compromise undermined the effectiveness of joint actions and reflected continuing unease among governments about the CFSP. Aware of the unsatisfactory nature of the new arrangement, negotiators agreed in Maastricht to convene another intergovernmental conference in five years' time to review progress on foreign, security, and defense policy cooperation.

The third pillar. Because of the provisions in the single market program for the free movement of people and fears in Western Europe that the end of the Cold War would trigger a huge influx of migrants from Central and

Eastern Europe, issues such as immigration, asylum, and control of cross-border crime were high on the agenda of the intergovernmental conference on political union. Governments were already addressing these issues in a number of ways. As far back as the mid-1970s, for instance, justice ministers and officials had formed the so-called Trevi Group to facilitate cooperation on terrorism and cross-border crime.

As discussed in the previous chapter, in 1985 the original member states, minus Italy, had reached agreement in Schengen, a small town in Luxembourg, on steps to expedite the removal of border checkpoints. The so-called Schengen regime became a laboratory for the eventual abolition of barriers to cross-border travel within the EC. It covered everything from police cooperation, to the rights of "guestworkers" (long-term workers in the EC, mostly from Turkey and North Africa), to fiscal fraud. Most of the other member states subsequently signed on to the Schengen agreement, but Britain and Ireland remained resolutely aloof (Britain because it wanted to retain complete control of its own borders, Ireland because it formed part of a free travel zone with Britain).

Responding to a rise in the numbers of immigrants and asylum seekers in Western Europe in the early 1980s, justice ministers established the Ad Hoc Immigration Group of Senior Officials in 1986. Although restricted to EC member states and served by the Council secretariat, the immigration group operated on an informal, intergovernmental basis. Its most notable accomplishment was to draft the 1990 Dublin Convention, on the handling of asylum applications submitted in the EC.

The negotiations on political union gave governments an opportunity to bring immigration and asylum, and police and judicial cooperation, into the putative EU. Given national sensitivities on internal security issues, however, they decided to confine justice and home affairs to a separate, intergovernmental pillar, with minimum involvement by the Commission, Court of Justice, or Parliament.[51]

Thus the treaty's third pillar would cover a number of areas of common interest, such as asylum, immigration, control of external borders, cooperation in combating drugs and fraud, judicial cooperation in civil and criminal matters, and police cooperation. The treaty included a provision making it possible eventually to move some of these areas into the first (supranational) pillar. For the time being, the Schengen regime remained outside, but closely related to, the treaty's provisions on justice and home affairs.

Outcome

Whereas in 1985–1986 there was one intergovernmental conference but talk of two final acts (one on regular treaty reform and the other on foreign policy cooperation), in 1990–1991 there were two conferences but agreement from the outset to have only one treaty. The treaty, worked out in the waning hours of the Maastricht summit, was a notable achievement. Within four years of reemerging on the agenda of European integration, EMU was front and center of the new EU. Governments committed themselves to striving for a single monetary policy and a single currency, although not all of them would participate in it.

The treaty's intergovernmental pillar on the CFSP was less a radical departure than a continuation of the member states' efforts since the early 1970s to coordinate their foreign policies. The change of name from "European Political Cooperation" to "common foreign and security policy" was more portentous than the likely impact of the new instruments outlined in the second pillar. The third pillar, on justice and home affairs, also reflected continuity rather than change, although member states promised in the treaty to cooperate more closely than hitherto on immigration, asylum, policing, and judicial affairs.

The treaty's extension of Community competence into several new areas, increase in the scope of qualified majority voting, expansion of the cooperation procedure, and introduction of co-decision had major implications for the EU. The European level of governance became increasingly entrenched, with the Council and the EP playing key legislative roles. Despite its political problems, the Commission remained at the core of the EU. The establishment of a Committee of the Regions symbolized the member states' recognition of another level of governance in the EU system—the subnational level.

The treaty included another important innovation: the institutionalization of differentiated integration. Social policy included an opt-out for Britain. Not every country would participate in Stage Three of EMU, at least at the outset, and Britain could choose not to participate at all. Differentiated integration had long been mooted as a solution to the recalcitrant member states' unwillingness to go along with new policy initiatives. Now, for the first time, the EU enshrined the principle and endorsed the practice of countries either choosing or not being obliged to participate in core activities.

There were no absolute winners or losers in the intergovernmental conferences. The appeal of the final agreement was that each government could claim victory even though no member state got everything that it wanted. France was happy to have EMU but disliked many of its characteristics. Germany would have preferred stronger provisions on political union. Denmark favored the EU's emphasis on environmental policy but felt that other provisions encroached too much on national sovereignty. Ireland was happy to dip into the promised Cohesion Fund but worried about the domestic political implications of the CFSP. Although disliking most of the treaty, John Major could claim on returning from the summit that last-minute agreement on the social protocol represented victory for Britain.[52] The other EU leaders made similar claims to their home audiences about the significance of the treaty, but with less fanfare.

Ratification

The Maastricht Treaty engendered greater public interest than did the Single European Act, not least because European integration had progressed so far and so fast during the intervening years. Inevitably, EMU was the main thing on people's minds. Europeans were generally uneasy about the prospect of losing their national currencies and adopting a common currency. Nevertheless, governments were confident that ratification would proceed smoothly. When they signed the treaty at a special ceremony in Maastricht in February 1992, foreign ministers confidently predicted that the treaty would be ratified in time to come into force in January 1993.

Denmark and Ireland were the only two countries constitutionally obliged to hold a referendum on ratification. The Danish vote was scheduled first, in June 1992. Danes were notoriously ambivalent about the EC. Despite rumblings of discontent in the run-up to the referendum, most observers, in Denmark and abroad, presumed that the result would be positive. To everybody's surprise, Danes voted by a narrow margin—50.7 to 49.3 percent—to reject the treaty. The result sent shock waves throughout the Community.

There were many reasons why a majority of Danes voted against the Maastricht Treaty. Some reasons were specific to the treaty, while others pertained to the EC generally. Some were rational, and others not. They ranged from vague concerns about EMU, to fear of united Germany's influence in the putative EU, to worries about the erosion of Denmark's high environmental standards. Many Danes rightly complained about the incomprehensibility of the treaty, although few of them tried to read it. Despite serious dissatisfaction throughout Denmark with the country's EC membership and with the terms of the treaty, the result could have gone either way. After all, fewer than 30,000 votes separated the two sides.

The fact that the Maastricht Treaty was only narrowly rejected presented the EC's leadership with a serious problem. Unless ratified in all member states, the treaty could not be implemented. Governments were loath to renegotiate the treaty but realized that they would have to offer special concessions to the Danish electorate in order to secure a positive result in a second referendum. More broadly, Community leaders grasped that Denmark's rejection of the treaty was symptomatic of widespread popular dissatisfaction with the institutions and procedures of European integration. Ireland's resounding endorsement of the Maastricht Treaty in a referendum held only two weeks later was cold comfort for EC leaders, who presumed that Ireland's support for European integration was unwavering.

Meeting in Lisbon at the end of June 1992, EC leaders sought to appease Danish voters and reassure European citizens by fleshing out the principle of subsidiarity. The Commission immediately dropped a number of proposals that it now decided did not warrant legislation at the European level. EC leaders also redoubled their efforts to make the EC's operations more open, accessible, and comprehensible.

A major test of the treaty's survivability came in September 1992, when France held a referendum. The French parliament had already ratified the treaty, but Mitterrand called for a popular endorsement of it nonetheless. Mitterrand was certain of a positive result, hoping thereby to turn the tide against Euroskepticism. He also had domestic political motives (he wanted to deepen divisions in the conservative opposition over the treaty).

Mitterrand miscalculated badly. He split his own Socialist Party as much as he did the conservatives and almost caused a rejection of the treaty in France. Taking victory for granted, the government did not begin to campaign in earnest until after the sacrosanct August holidays, whereas the opposition mobilized early against the treaty. Those who advocated rejection of the treaty exploited popular concerns about German unification, monetary union, and the EC's lamentable efforts to halt the fighting in Bosnia, the latest and most violent Balkan battleground. Having staked the reputation of his presidency on achieving deeper European integration, Mitterrand risked a humiliating repudiation by an electorate disgruntled with his domestic policies and unimpressed by his international escapades.

In the final, desperate days of the campaign, both sides used outlandish arguments to try to win over wavering voters. The normally staid *Le Monde* warned on the eve of the referendum that a vote against the treaty would "be for France and for Europe the greatest catastrophe since Hitler's coming to power."[53] Opponents characterized the treaty as a sellout to Germany, a surrender of sovereignty, and the end of *grandeur* (French greatness). Both sides invoked the legacy of de Gaulle. It was easier for opponents than proponents of the treaty to do so, but the government's point man in the campaign managed to claim that rejection of the treaty "would destroy the collective work of Charles de Gaulle, Georges Pompidou, Valéry Giscard d'Estaing, and François Mitterrand."[54]

The result of the French referendum was a small majority in favor of ratification: the vote was 51.05 percent for and 48.95 percent against, with a turnout of 70 percent. As a seasoned politician, Mitterrand knew that the fact of a majority mattered more than its size. But his domestic and European strategy backfired. The French referendum brought the Maastricht Treaty into further disrepute. There could be no doubt now about the extent of public dissatisfaction with the treaty in France and in other member states.

The Danish and French results emboldened Euroskeptics in Britain, whose influence in the governing Conservative Party was disproportionate to their numbers. John Major won the general election of April 1992 not on the strength of the government's record but because a majority of the electorate still distrusted the Labour Party to form a government. Faced with a virulent Euroskeptical wing in his party and a rabidly anti-EU popular press, Major procrastinated. The currency crisis of September 1992, which lost the Bank of England billions of pounds and prompted the government to pull sterling out of the exchange rate mechanism of the EMS (discussed in Chapter 8), soured British opinion on the treaty, and especially on EMU. Instead of bringing it up for ratification in the House of Commons before the stipulated deadline of December 1992, Major decided to wait until after the second Danish referendum, scheduled for May 1993.

Ironically, Britain was in the Council presidency in the second half of 1992 when the ratification crisis was at its height. Other leaders despaired of Major's political acumen and ability to steer the EC out of its current plight. Earlier, the Danish government had produced a lengthy white paper outlining various options for a solution to the ratification crisis. That formed the basis for a number of Danish opt-outs from the terms of the Maastricht Treaty, which the European Council approved in Edinburgh in December 1992. Chief among these were Danish nonparticipation in the third stage of EMU and in foreign policy decisions that held defense implications.

Also in Edinburgh, the European Council discussed subsidiarity on the basis of reports from the Council and the Commission. Thus the summit's conclusions contained a lengthy section providing guidelines for the application of subsidiarity and giving examples of legislative proposals that met the key criteria of "need for action and intensity (proportionality) of action" at the European level. The European Council called for an interinstitutional agreement (among the Council, Commission, and Parliament) on the concrete application of subsidiarity. In a related move, the European Council adopted a number of specific measures to promote transparency and openness. The most significant of these was a decision to publish the record of formal votes taken in the Council.[55]

The European Council's decisions demonstrated the profound political impact of the ratification crisis. Governments had been aware since the mid-1980s of the existence of a democratic deficit, but had addressed the problem only in piecemeal fashion. The ratification crisis, and later the accession of Nordic countries with a strong tradition of open government, finally forced them to tackle the problem, going beyond merely increasing the power of the EP. By then it may have been too late, as the democratic deficit had become ingrained in public perceptions of the EC. "Subsidiarity," a word and a concept that few people understood, seemed to accentuate rather than alleviate the situation.

Buoyed by the Edinburgh agreement, a new Danish government succeeded in convincing a majority of the electorate to ratify the Maastricht Treaty in the May 1993 referendum. The result was a comfortable majority of 56.8 percent in favor. Buoyed in turn by the Danish vote, but dogged by conservative Euroskeptics, Major brought the treaty up for ratification in the British parliament in August 1993. In the meantime, ratification proceeded smoothly in most other member states. The exception was Germany, where, despite large majorities in favor of the treaty in both houses of parliament, a legal challenge to the treaty's constitutionality held up ratification until the outcome of a court case.

Passage of the ratification legislation in the British parliament and the ruling of the German constitutional court on the compatibility of the treaty with German law removed the last hurdles impeding implementation of the Maastricht Treaty, which finally came into effect in November 1993. Governments, institutions, and other actors quickly mastered the treaty's provisions. EMU was already on track, the CFSP was being implemented, and member states began to cooperate more closely on justice and home affairs. The name "European Union" caught on quickly. Yet the ratification crisis spoiled the celebration of the EU's birth and presaged serious political problems for the fledgling entity.

Notes

1. Leo Tindemans, *Report on European Union,* Bulletin EC S/1-1976, p. 20.

2. On the origins and development of the EMS, see Horst Ungerer, *From EPU to EMU: A Concise History of European Monetary Integration* (Westport: Quorum, 1997), pp. 338–347; Daniel Gros and Niels Thygesen, *European Monetary Integration: From the European Monetary System Towards Monetary Union,* 2nd ed. (London: Longman, 1999); Barry Eichengreen, *Globalizing Capital: A History of the International Monetary System,* 2nd ed. (Princeton: Princeton University Press, 2008), pp. 157–164; Emmanuel Mourlon-Droul, *A Europe Made of Money: The Emergence of the European Monetary System* (Ithaca: Cornell University Press, 2012); Harold James, *Making the European Monetary Union* (Cambridge: Harvard University Press, 2012), pp. 146–180.

3. Tommaso Padoa-Schioppa et al., *Efficiency, Stability, and Equity: A Strategy for the Evolution of the Economic System of the European Community* (Oxford: Oxford University Press, 1987), pp. 3, 13.

4. Kenneth Dyson and Kevin Featherstone, *The Road to Maastricht: Negotiating Economic and Monetary Union* (Oxford: Oxford University Press, 1999), pp. 162, 164–165.

5. Ibid., p. 708.

6. See Alistair Cole, *François Mitterrand: A Study in Political Leadership* (London: Routledge, 1994), p. 122.

7. Ibid., p. 162; Dyson and Featherstone, *Road to Maastricht,* p. 130.

8. Dyson and Featherstone, *Road to Maastricht,* pp. 166–167.

9. On the Delors committee, see ibid., pp. 702–705, 770–773, 741–742; Eichengreen, *Globalizing Capital,* pp. 219–225; James, *Making the European Monetary Union,* pp. 210–264; Niels Thygesen, "The Delors Report and European Economic and Monetary Union," *International Affairs* 65, no. 4 (Autumn 1989), pp. 637–652.

10. Margaret Thatcher, *Downing Street Years* (New York: HarperCollins, 1993), p. 740.

11. Dyson and Featherstone, *Road to Maastricht,* pp. 604–605.

12. Ibid., p. 705.

13. See Ken Endo, *The Presidency of the European Commission Under Jacques Delors: The Politics of Shared Leadership* (New York: St. Martin's, 1999); Charles Grant, *Delors: Inside the House That Jacques Built* (London: Brealey, 1994), pp. 119–123.

14. Committee for the Study of Economic and Monetary Union, *Report on Economic and Monetary Union in the European Community* (Delors report) (Luxembourg: Office of Official Publications of the European Communities, 1989), pp. 18–19.

15. Ibid., pp. 34–40.

16. Nigel Lawson, *The View from No. 11: Britain's Longest-Serving Cabinet Member Recalls the Triumphs and Disappointments of the Thatcher Era* (New York: Doubleday, 1993), pp. 893–894; Thatcher, *Downing Street Years,* p. 660; Geoffrey Howe, *Conflict of Loyalty* (New York: St. Martin's, 1994); Dyson and Featherstone, *Road to Maastricht,* pp. 601–612.

17. Bulletin EC 6-1989.

18. On the relationship between German unification and EMU, see Jonathan R. Zatlin, "Rethinking Reunification: German Monetary Union and European Integration," in Peter C. Caldwell and Robert R. Shandley, eds., *German Unification: Expectations and Outcomes* (Basingstoke: Palgrave Macmillan, 2011), pp. 61–98.

19. Bulletin EC 12-1989.

20. Ibid.

21. Commission, *One Market, One Money: An Evaluation of the Potential Benefits and Costs of Forming an Economic and Monetary Union* (Luxembourg: Office of Official Publications, 1990).

22. Thatcher, *Downing Street Years,* pp. 839–862.

23. Bulletin EC S/1-1985.

24. Endo, *Presidency of the European Commission Under Jacques Delors,* p. 47.

25. Jacques Delors, "Speech to the Parliament," July 6, 1988; OJ-EP, 2-367, July 6, 1988, p. 140.

26. Margaret Thatcher, *Britain in the European Community* (London: Conservative Party Center, 1988), p. 6. Thatcher's description of this speech and denunciation of Delors in her memoirs convey the depth of her feeling on the matter. See Thatcher, *Downing Street Years,* pp. 742–746.

27. Bulletin EC 6-1989.

28. *The Spectator,* July 1990, p. 24.

29. On German unification, see Philip Zelikow and Condoleezza Rice, *Germany Unified and Europe Transformed: A Study in Statecraft* (Cambridge: Harvard University Press, 1995); Stephen F. Szabo, *The Diplomacy of German Unification* (New York: St. Martin's, 1992).

30. Jacques Delors, "Address at the College of Europe," October 19, 1989.

31. The Belgian proposal is reproduced in Finn Laursen and Sophie Vanhoonacker, *The Intergovernmental Conference on Political Union: Institutional Reforms, New Policies, and International Identity of the European Community* (Dordrecht: Nijhoff, 1992), pp. 269–275.

32. The letter is reproduced in Laursen and Vanhoonacker, *Intergovernmental Conference,* pp. 276–277.

33. Bulletin EC 6-1990.

34. *The Economist,* March 23, 1991, p. 15.

35. On the negotiation of the Maastricht Treaty, see Michael J. Baun, *An Imperfect Union: The Maastricht Treaty and the New Politics of European Integration* (Boulder: Westview, 1996); J. Cloos, *Le traité de Maastricht: Genèse, analyse, commentaires* (Brussels: Bruylant, 1993); Dyson and Featherstone, *Road to Maastricht;* Laursen and Vanhoonacker, *Intergovernmental Conference;* Colette Mazzucelli, *France and Ger-*

many at Maastricht: Politics and Negotiations to Create the European Union (New York: Garland, 1997); Kathleen McNamara, *The Currency of Ideas: Monetary Politics in the European Union* (Ithaca: Cornell University Press, 1997); Moravcsik, *Choice for Europe,* pp. 379–471; George Ross, *Jacques Delors and European Integration* (Oxford: Oxford University Press, 1995); James, *Making the European Monetary Union,* pp. 264–323.

36. Dyson and Featherstone, *Road to Maastricht,* p. 691.

37. Quoted in Laursen and Vanhoonacker, *Intergovernmental Conference,* pp. 419–428.

38. Quoted in *Financial Times,* June 18, 1991, p. 1.

39. Quoted in *The Guardian,* July 7, 1991, p. 12.

40. Quoted in *Agence Europe,* December 6, 1991, p. 1.

41. Quoted in *Agence Europe,* June 4, 1991, p. 1.

42. Quoted in *Financial Times,* September 21–22, 1991, p. 3.

43. Quoted in *Agence Europe,* April 18, 1991, p. 1.

44. On EU citizenship, see Cris Shore, *Building Europe: The Cultural Politics of European Integration* (London: Routledge, 2000), pp. 66–112.

45. See Trevor C. Salmon, "Testing Times for European Political Cooperation: The Gulf and Yugoslavia, 1990–1992," *International Affairs* 68, no. 2 (April 1992), pp. 233–253.

46. On the US démarche, see Sophie Vanhoonacker, *The Bush Administration and the Development of a European Security Identity* (Aldershot: Ashgate, 2001), pp. 106–108.

47. Treaty on European Union, available at http://www.europa.eu.int/abc/obj/treaties /en/entoc01.htm.

48. Quoted in *International Herald Tribune,* July 1, 1991, p. 2.

49. Quoted in *Financial Times,* July 1, 1991, p. 1.

50. See Misha Glenny, *The Third Balkan War,* 3rd rev. ed. (New York: Penguin, 1996).

51. On the development of immigration and asylum policy in the EU, see Andrew Geddes, *Immigration and European Integration: Towards Fortress Europe?* (Manchester: Manchester University Press, 2000); Sharon Stanton Russell, Charles B. Keely, and Bryan P. Christian, *Multilateral Diplomacy to Harmonize Asylum Policy in Europe, 1984–1993* (Washington, DC: Institute for the Study of International Migration, 2000).

52. Quoted in *Financial Times,* December 12, 1992, p. 3.

53. *Le Monde,* September 20–21, 1992, p. 1.

54. Jack Lang, quoted in *Le Monde,* "L'Europe de Maastricht," special supplement, August–September 1992, p. 2.

55. Bulletin EC 12-1992.

8

The Triumphs
and Tribulations of
European Union

THE EUROPEAN UNION ACHIEVED TWO MONUMENTAL TASKS IN
the long decade following implementation of the Maastricht Treaty: implementation of the third stage of economic and monetary union in 1999, resulting in the launch of the euro; and enlargement to include eight Central
and Eastern European countries (plus Cyprus and Malta) in 2004. Both
developments irrevocably changed the EU's character and composition.

Enlargement had an important geopolitical dimension reminiscent of
the early days of European integration. Both the EU and the candidate
countries saw it as a means of strengthening European stability and security
after decades of Cold War division. Nevertheless, the prospect of enlargement on such a scale, involving so many different countries, discomfited
the EU. The road to accession proved arduous for all concerned. Yet the accomplishment was immense. Within little more than a decade, the EU had
increased in size from fifteen to twenty-five member states, spanning almost the entire continent.

Launching the third stage of EMU was no less impressive. Despite unfavorable economic circumstances in the mid-1990s, a majority of the EU's
then fifteen member states met the Maastricht Treaty's convergence criteria
and adopted a common monetary policy. Though the euro came into being
as a virtual currency in 1999, it was the introduction of notes and coins in
2002 that brought home the enormity of the undertaking.

The launch of the third stage owed a great deal to German chancellor
Helmut Kohl, who single-mindedly pushed for it despite domestic doubts
and EU-wide difficulties. Kohl was not in office when EMU came to
fruition, having lost the general election of October 1998. Nor was Jacques
Delors, Commission president at the time of the Maastricht Treaty and
Kohl's helpmate in the quest for EMU (he retired in 1995).

A new crop of leaders came to prominence in the late 1990s. Jacques Chirac, who won the French presidential election in May 1995, was a veteran politician. In Britain, Tony Blair, who refashioned the Labour Party and won the general election in May 1997, was a relative neophyte. Gerhard Schröder, leader of the Social Democratic Party, was mostly unknown outside Germany when he replaced Kohl as chancellor. Jacques Santer, Delors's successor, was well known in European political circles, having been prime minister of Luxembourg for many years, but was little known to most Europeans. The Commission's political influence, having peaked during the Delors years, was on the wane. Making matters worse, the Commission's enforced resignation in 1999 severely dented the institution's image.

As this chapter shows, the EU faced a host of challenges other than enlargement and EMU in the 1990s: completing and consolidating the single market, promoting employment, protecting the environment, and reforming the common agricultural policy and cohesion policy. The EU's record was mixed: the single market remained a work in progress; unemployment stayed stubbornly high; sustainable development, the leitmotif of environmental policy, was easier to proclaim than to achieve; and agriculture and cohesion seemed impervious to reform. Cooperation on justice and home affairs, ranging from immigration and asylum to policing, became increasingly necessary and complicated in view of the growing North-South global divide and the international war against terrorism.

The EU struggled to develop a common foreign and security policy, let alone a common defense policy, in a new global system characterized by intense economic interdependence and dominated by the United States. Despite its economic heft, the EU was not a global power. The extent of the EU's weakness became apparent first in the Balkan wars of the 1990s, then during the Iraq crisis of 2003. Structural changes in the international system, together with US unilateralism, posed a particular challenge for the management of US-EU relations.

In an effort to meet an array of internal and external challenges, governments revised the EU's founding treaties in 1997 (with the Amsterdam Treaty) and 2001 (the Nice Treaty). The two rounds of treaty change were intended in part to allay public concerns about accountability and transparency in the EU while improving efficiency in anticipation of enlargement. Widespread dissatisfaction with the Amsterdam and Nice treaties, and with the method of treaty change, prompted the launch of the Convention on the Future of Europe in 2002, which resulted in the Constitutional Treaty of 2004. The promulgation of a *constitutional* treaty suggested that the EU was on the verge of a major political breakthrough. Yet the convention and its outcome could not disguise a high degree of public estrangement from the EU, which became a cause of growing concern in the years ahead.

Enlargement

The end of the Cold War raised the prospect of EU enlargement on an unprecedented scale and scope. Three categories of countries sought membership: neutral countries no longer constrained by the Cold War (Austria, Finland, Malta, and Sweden), nonneutral and in some cases NATO members submitting or reactivating membership applications because of altered international circumstances (Cyprus, Norway, and Turkey), and newly independent Central and Eastern European countries (Bulgaria, Czechoslovakia, Estonia, Hungary, Latvia, Lithuania, Poland, Romania, and Slovenia).

Although each country's circumstances were different, there were sufficient similarities between some of the applicants to warrant a common approach by the EU toward them. Austria and the Scandinavian countries were clearly a group apart: economically advanced, politically stable, and well acquainted with the EU's policies and procedures. The Central and Eastern European countries were an equally obvious group: economically underdeveloped, politically fragile, and unfamiliar with the EU's policies and procedures. Cyprus and Turkey differed from each other economically and politically but were linked because of Turkey's occupation of the northern part of Cyprus. Malta, a Mediterranean microstate, was a case apart.

As discussed in Chapter 7, the EC was preoccupied with internal developments, notably German unification, EMU, and completion of the single market, as the Cold War came to an end. The Commission and most member states were equivocal about the prospect of enlargement. France feared a diminution of its influence in the EU. Due to previous enlargements and to German unification, France's traditional role in the EU already seemed under threat. The accession of numerous Central and Eastern European countries would likely shift the political focus of the EU firmly toward Germany. Britain and Denmark, historically Euroskeptical, supported enlargement partly in the hope that it would slow the momentum toward political union. Denmark had a particular interest in restoring Scandinavian solidarity by bringing Finland, Norway, and Sweden into the EU. The poorer member states welcomed the prospect of contributions to the EU budget from wealthy countries such as Austria, Finland, Norway, and Sweden, but did not relish the prospect of the Central and Eastern European countries staking a claim to the EU's redistributive funds.

Regardless of their initial impressions, the Commission and the member states soon realized that enlargement was inevitable. With the Cold War over, the EU could not restrict itself to Western Europe. Other European countries had every right to seek membership in an association that claimed to be open to all the countries of Europe. When the newly independent countries proclaimed their eagerness to rejoin "Europe," they meant joining the EU. For them, membership in the EU was a badge of honor, a stamp of political approval, and a path to prosperity. The EU's preoccupation with internal affairs and concern about the costs of enlargement seemed selfish by comparison.

Austria, Finland, Sweden

As discussed in Chapter 6, the purpose of the European Economic Area, an association of the EU and European Free Trade Association members, was to extend the benefits of the single market to many more consumers and manufacturers and in the process satisfy some of the EFTA countries' main economic reasons for wanting to join the EU. Dissatisfied with what was on offer, most of the EFTA countries applied to join the EU even before concluding negotiations for the European Economic Area in December 1992.[1]

Motivated entirely by economic considerations, Switzerland applied to join the EU in May 1992, but rejection by Swiss voters of membership in the European Economic Area, in a referendum in December 1992, doomed the country's EU application. Norway also sought EU accession purely on economic grounds, but many interest groups and a large percentage of the population opposed membership for a variety of reasons. Accession was much less contentious in Austria, Finland, and Sweden, where, following the end of the Cold War, neutrality was no longer seen as an obstacle to EU membership. Indeed, the applicants were at pains to point out that neutrality would not affect their participation in the evolving common foreign and security policy.

Resolution of the Maastricht ratification crisis, agreement on the post-Maastricht budgetary package, and the applicants' insistence on early membership led to the opening of accession negotiations with Austria, Finland, Norway, and Sweden in 1993. Compared to earlier and later rounds of enlargement, the accession process was relatively swift. After all, many of the "chapters" into which the negotiations were broken down were already included in the European Economic Area. But problems pertaining to social policy, energy, the environment, agriculture, and fisheries still had to be resolved.

Social and environmental standards and agricultural subsidies were generally higher in the applicant countries. Norway did not want to relinquish control over its vast reserves of oil and natural gas or over its rich fishing grounds. Other difficulties arose on specific issues such as support for remote and sparsely populated parts of Finland, Norway, and Sweden; truck transit through Austria; the EU's ban on the sale of snuff, to which many Swedes were addicted; and Sweden's state monopoly on the sale of alcohol, which Swedes consumed in great quantity but at considerable expense.

The accession agreements, concluded in mid-1994 after months of hard negotiations, included transitional arrangements for certain regulatory matters, a new category of structural funds for Arctic areas, special measures to maintain farmers' incomes in the new member states following the alignment of agricultural prices in the enlarged EU, and the maintenance of higher environmental standards in the applicant countries after their accession. The EU's concessions to Norway failed to tip the balance in favor of membership: in the November 1994 referendum, 53 percent voted against joining. By contrast, Austria endorsed accession by a majority of 66 percent, Finland by a majority of 60 percent, and Sweden by a majority of 52 percent.

Ratification of the accession treaties was much easier on the EU side, although the European Parliament kicked up a fuss because the member states would not countenance major institutional reform in light of enlargement. Indeed, the only institutional change agreed to by the Council in order to facilitate enlargement was the so-called Ioannina Compromise of March 1994, a concession to British and Spanish demands to raise the threshold for a qualified majority.[2] Though the EP denounced the Ioannina Compromise, which would make decisionmaking in the Council even less efficient, it had little choice but to approve enlargement, which took place in January 1995.

This was the easiest enlargement for the EU to manage. The three new member states were small demographically and well-off economically. Sweden was somewhat Euroskeptical (the results of the country's first elections to the EP in September 1995 revealed widespread dissatisfaction with EU membership), but Austria and Finland were relatively enthusiastic. The EU's arcane legislative system and alien administrative culture shocked Finnish and Swedish politicians and civil servants, who zealously advocated openness and transparency in EU decisionmaking. Finland and Sweden championed higher EU social and environmental standards and a more liberal EU trade policy. They also promoted a "northern dimension" for the EU, including engagement with Russia and early accession for Estonia, Latvia, and Lithuania, their neighbors across the Baltic Sea.

Far from whetting the EU's appetite for further enlargement, the accession of Austria, Finland, and Sweden highlighted the difficulties that lay ahead. Even with the advantage of the European Economic Area, the accession negotiations with Austria, Finland, and Sweden had been arduous. How much longer and more difficult would the Central and Eastern European negotiations be? The dispute over the threshold for a qualified majority that resulted in the Ioannina Compromise was a harbinger of future disputes over the institutional implications of Central and Eastern European enlargement, which were bound to be considerable.

The Central and Eastern European Countries

The road to accession for the Central and Eastern European countries was largely uncharted. Member states and the Commission groped for the right path to take. Despite an awareness of the historic importance of the project, there were major misunderstandings and recriminations between the EU and the applicant states. The applicants accused the EU of foot-dragging;

The Fifteen Member States

the EU accused the applicants of grandstanding. The public on both sides began to tire of the process, wondering if the means were worth the end and even if the end was worth having.[3]

Various European summits provided milestones along the way. Some member states, more interested in enlargement than others, sought to accelerate the process while in the Council presidency. They could do so because enlargement was primarily an intergovernmental activity, with the presidency leading the negotiations and coordinating member states' positions.

The Commission had an important supporting role: providing information, drafting progress reports, making recommendations, and acting as honest broker. The EP was a cheerleader for enlargement, engaging in lofty rhetoric about the sacredness of European unification.

From assistance to association. Eastern Europe might as well have been on another planet during most of the history of the European Community.[4] The existence of the Cold War and the hostility of the Soviet Union toward Western Europe helped cement European integration. The Soviet Union did not allow the EC to establish diplomatic relations with the countries of Central and Eastern Europe, insisting instead that it deal with the Council for Mutual Economic Assistance, the Soviet bloc's supposed equivalent to the EC.

In 1989, as the Cold War came to an end, the Commission assumed responsibility for coordinating Western assistance to Central and Eastern Europe. The EC launched its own aid program, known as Phare, to complement the member states' assistance efforts in the region. As well as providing humanitarian assistance, the Phare program helped recipients develop social-market economies and establish democratic institutions. A separate, French initiative resulted in the establishment of the European Bank for Reconstruction and Development. With the EC and its member states as majority shareholders (the United States and other non-EU members were the other shareholders), the bank became a major provider of loans to promote economic development in the former Soviet bloc.

Financial and technical assistance was a necessary first step for the modernization of Central and Eastern Europe. It complemented a series of bilateral trade and cooperation agreements between the EC and the Central and Eastern European countries. Intended primarily to provide market access to the EC for Central and Eastern European products, the trade and cooperation agreements pitted the member states' protectionist proclivities against the rhetoric of pan-European integration. When it came to concrete market access measures, the EC refused to make generous concessions for agriculture, textiles, and steel, highly sensitive sectors politically for the EC and highly important sectors economically for the Central and Eastern European countries.

Pressure for a more generous EC approach led to offers of association with selected countries of the former Soviet bloc. Pushed by Helmut Kohl, whose country had so much to gain from a successful transition in Central and Eastern Europe, in August 1990 the Commission proposed association agreements with Czechoslovakia, Hungary, and Poland, the most economically advanced and strategically important countries in the region. These "Europe agreements" would include free trade, intensive economic cooperation, and an institutionalized political relationship. Member states acknowledged that the "final objective" for the new associates was to join the EU.

The Commission eventually opened negotiations for Europe agreements with ten countries in the region, including the Czech Republic and Slovakia following the breakup of Czechoslovakia in January 1993. Negotiation and ratification of the agreements took several years, with the EU driving a hard bargain on market access and the free movement of people. Here was a further example of the EU's seeming inability to deal expeditiously and generously with its neighbors to the east.

From Copenhagen to Copenhagen. It was only after ratification of the Maastricht Treaty that the EU began to turn its attention fully to the challenge of Central and Eastern European enlargement. Spurred by Denmark, which strongly supported enlargement, the European Council declared unequivocally in Copenhagen in June 1993 that "the associated countries in Central and Eastern Europe which so desire shall become members of the European Union." The European Council also endorsed conditions drawn up by the Commission for the accession of new member states. These were the so-called Copenhagen criteria:

- Stability of institutions guaranteeing democracy, the rule of law, human rights, and respect for and protection of minorities.
- Existence of a functioning market economy, as well as the capacity to cope with competitive pressures and market forces in the EU.
- Ability to take on the obligations of membership, including adherence to the aims of political, economic, and monetary union.[5]

Delors, who was lukewarm about enlargement, finally accepted that it was unavoidable. By then his days as Commission president were numbered. His successor, Jacques Santer, was more amenable to enlargement, which, along with EMU, became a priority of his generally lackluster Commission presidency. Kohl supported enlargement wholeheartedly. Jacques Chirac, the new French president, was even less keen on enlargement than François Mitterrand had been. British prime minister John Major supported enlargement in the hope that widening would weaken the EU, a position that hardly endeared him to the Central and Eastern Europeans, who wanted to join a strong EU that would enhance their security and provide considerable economic opportunities.

Between 1994 and 1996, as the Europe agreements came into effect, the ten Central and Eastern European countries lodged applications for membership. By that time, neither they nor the EU were in any doubt about the difficulties ahead. Five years after the fall of the Berlin Wall, Central and Eastern Europe was in bad shape administratively, economically, and environmentally. Countries in the region still faced the daunting legacy of several decades of Communist mismanagement. Although conditions varied from country to country, all struggled with the transition from communism to capitalism and from dictatorship to democracy. The lengthy process of reconstruction and rehabilitation involved an array of legal, banking, and business reforms; the privatization of state-owned companies; agricultural and industrial modernization; major social welfare reform; massive environmental improvement; a revolution in public administration; a new educational system; and a major overhaul of physical plant and infrastructure. The prospect of EU membership provided an incentive for the aspiring member states to persist with painful reforms that were mostly necessary in any case.

The EU stepped up its efforts in 1994 to prepare the applicant countries for accession. Based on a Commission report and prodded by the German presidency in the second half of the year, the European Council agreed to launch a "structured dialogue" between the EU and the applicants. Covering most EU policy areas, the structured dialogue involved regular ministerial meetings between both sides as well as annual meetings of the national leaders of current and prospective member states on the margins of the European Council.[6]

The EU also began the process of integrating the candidate countries economically into the EU. In June 1995 the European Council approved a Commission white paper on how to prepare the candidate countries, sector by sector, for full participation in the single market.[7] The specificity of the white paper left neither side in any doubt about the complexity and enormity of the task ahead. Far from simply promulgating new laws, the candidates would have to overhaul their entire administrative, legal, and economic structures. The EU reformed the Phare program and launched other initiatives in order to help the candidate countries adhere to the EU's regulatory standards.

Guided by the white paper and assisted by the EU, most of the candidates adopted detailed pre-accession plans as part of their overall accession strategies. At the same time, the Commission began to gather information and conduct analysis for its formal opinions on the candidates' suitability for EU membership. Published in July 1997 as part of the *Agenda 2000* package, the Commission's opinions reached the following conclusions about the applicants:

- *Democracy and the rule of law:* All had adequate constitutional and institutional arrangements and practices, except Slovakia, which seemed to be sliding back toward authoritarian rule.
- *Functioning market economy:* All had made good progress, but structural reforms were still necessary, especially in the financial sector and in social security.
- *EU rules and regulations:* All were in the process of absorbing EU rules and regulations, but all had a long way yet to go.[8]

The most difficult and controversial task for the Commission was to decide which of the candidates to recommend to the European Council for the opening of accession negotiations. The ten candidates were at different levels of development. Some had reformed more thoroughly than others. None wanted to be relegated to a second division of countries slated to join later. The EU viewed each candidate differently. Poland, because of its size, location, and economic importance, was at the top of the accession queue. The Czech Republic and Hungary, relatively well developed economically, strategically located, and culturally attuned to Western Europe, were well placed for early accession. The Baltic states had strong support from the EU's Scandinavian members, but their history of having been part of the Soviet Union posed a special challenge. Slovenia, a prosperous and stable former Yugoslav republic, was culturally, economically, politically, and geographically close to Austria, which championed its early accession. Bulgaria and Romania were farther away in every sense from the EU.

The Commission recommended that the EU begin accession negotiations with five countries: the Czech Republic, Hungary, Poland, Estonia, and Slovenia. The choice of the first three was unsurprising. The Commission decided to add Estonia and Slovenia not only on the merits of their cases but also because it wanted to make a sharp distinction between EU and NATO enlargement. Just a week before the Commission released *Agenda 2000,* NATO announced that the Czech Republic, Hungary, and Poland would join the military alliance in 1999. Largely to assuage Russian concerns, the Commission sought to show that EU and NATO enlargements were not congruent. Accordingly, it added Estonia and Slovenia, at opposite ends of Eastern Europe, to the list.

The Commission consulted closely with the member states while drafting its opinions and making its recommendations. It was no surprise, therefore, that the European Council endorsed the Commission's findings in December 1997.[9] The other candidates felt slighted and feared the emergence in post–Cold War Europe of a new dividing line between them and the enlarged EU. Latvia and Lithuania were peeved by Estonia's selection for early accession negotiations. The shock of exclusion may have helped them, and the other candidates that were initially relegated to the second division, to redouble their reform efforts in order to join the first division as soon as possible.

The EU began accession negotiations with the first five countries in March 1998. The initial stage consisted of a "screening process" to examine in minute detail the extent to which the candidates already met the rules and obligations of EU membership. Substantive negotiations began in November 1998. The EU organized the vast agenda of the negotiations into about thirty chapters corresponding to the EU's policies and programs. Inevitably, negotiators closed the least-contentious of them first. As the negotiations progressed, negotiators checked more and more chapters off an accession negotiation scorecard.

In October 1999 the Commission recommended that the EU begin negotiations with the five remaining candidates. Although the recommendation was supposedly based on objective analysis, undoubtedly the Commission had succumbed to pressure not only from the candidates, whose leverage was relatively weak, but also from member states that were advocating a full round of enlargement primarily for strategic reasons. The five remaining candidates had made important strides toward meeting the requirements for accession, although Bulgaria and Romania accepted that they were still a long way behind the others. Slovakia, now under democratic government, made rapid economic progress in the late 1990s. The European Council endorsed the Commission's recommendations in December 1999, paving the way for the opening of accession negotiations with Latvia, Lithuania, Slovakia, Bulgaria, and Romania in February 2000.

Despite their late start, the second group of candidates (with the exception of Bulgaria and Romania) soon caught up with the first group in the negotiations. Each country progressed at its own speed, depending on the degree of difficulty of particular chapters of the negotiation process. Although the EU negotiated separately with each country, the relative transparency of the process and publication of the negotiation scorecard pressured the candidates to make progress. None of them wanted to top the list of incomplete chapters. By the end of 2002, only the most contentious issues, such as agriculture and the budget, remained unresolved. Institutional issues (notably the prospective member states' representation in EU institutions) were not included in the accession negotiations but were decided by the existing member states in the intergovernmental conference of 2000 that resulted in the Nice Treaty.

The EU was always wary of declaring a date for enlargement. The more assertive of the candidates had set their sights on the year 2000. EU politicians often encouraged them by proclaiming during visits to the capitals of candidate countries their hopes of seeing the EU expand by that time. When 2000 came and went, the candidates hoped to be able to join by 2002 at the latest. Meeting in June 2001 at the end of the strongly pro-enlargement Swedish presidency, the European Council finally decided that countries whose negotiations ended successfully by December 2002 could join in early 2004. That would give both sides a year to ratify the accession treaties and allow the candidates to join in time to participate in the June 2004 elections to the EP (thereby possibly increasing the overall turnout for the first time since the original direct elections in 1979).

In a report on enlargement in October 2002, the Commission recommended accession by 2004 for eight of the Central and Eastern European candidates, the exceptions being Bulgaria and Romania, which the Commission recommended for membership in 2007. Nevertheless, the Commission pointed out that most of the candidates had continuing problems with corruption, lack of independence of the judiciary, and gaps in implementing the EU's rules and regulations. Although a number of chapters remained to be closed, the Commission was optimistic that the prospective member states would soon be ready for membership.

An agreement on funding the common agricultural policy during the next budgetary cycle (2007–2013), reached by the European Council in October 2002, removed the last obstacle on the EU's side to conclusion of the negotiations. Despite their dissatisfaction with the EU's offer of smaller agricultural subsidies than farmers in the existing member states would receive, the candidates accepted the EU's terms at the Copenhagen summit in December 2002.[10] Except for Bulgaria and Romania, this closed the circle of Central and European enlargement "from Copenhagen to Copenhagen": from the European Council's approval of the EU accession criteria in June 1993 to the European Council's endorsement of the accession agreements almost ten years later.

The EU and the successful candidate countries signed the accession treaties in a splendid ceremony in Athens in April 2003. All of the Central and Eastern European candidates ratified the treaties by referendum. Although the turnout and the margin of victory varied significantly, the referendum results amounted to an impressive endorsement of accession. Ratification of the accession treaties proceeded equally smoothly on the EU side, paving the way for enlargement in May 2004.

The long, hard slog to accession risked obscuring the significance of the occasion. Despite the difficulties along the way, the 2004 enlargement represented an extraordinary transformation for Central and Eastern Europe, for Europe as a whole, and for the EU as an entity. The prospect of EU membership had helped most of the candidates undertake necessary political and economic reforms. The EU was immensely influential in strengthening democracy and fundamental rights throughout Central and Eastern Europe. Without EU conditionality, countries in the region might not have moved as swiftly and successfully out of the communist past.[11]

The 2004 enlargement demonstrated the EU's ability to extend a zone of economic and political stability well beyond Western Europe, thereby achieving one of the elemental objectives of European integration. Henceforth, the EU would be European not only in name, but also in geographical scope. Yet the adjustment to enlargement was bound to be painful. The process of acquiring so many new member states produced "enlargement fatigue" well before the first candidates joined. Public opinion in the EU seemed long ago to have lost whatever enthusiasm for enlargement it originally possessed. Opinion in the candidate countries, where many people associated enlargement with enduring social dislocation and economic hardship in the hopes of a brighter future, seemed equally skittish. Though differences would persist between the eastern and western parts of the EU, however, few people anywhere on the Continent wanted Europe to remain divided, the fault line this time being membership of the EU.

Cyprus and Malta

Cyprus. Cyprus applied to join the EU in July 1990. The Commission issued a favorable opinion in June 1993. The EU could have negotiated accession with Cyprus at the same time that it negotiated with Austria and the Scandinavian applicants, but chose to wait. The EU had an understandable reason: the division of the island into the Turkish-occupied north and the Greek

The Twenty-Five Member States

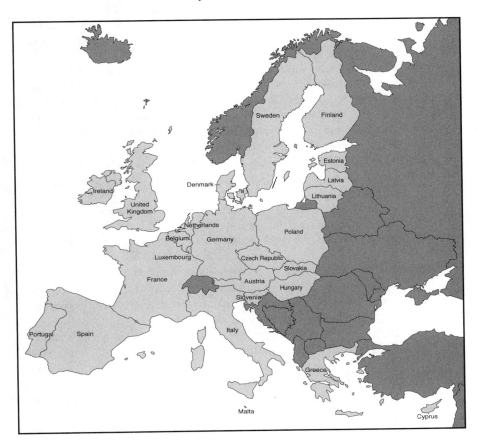

Cypriot south turned the Cypriot application into a poisoned chalice. The EU could be forgiven for wanting to deal with it later rather than sooner.[12]

But the EU could not keep Cyprus on the back burner forever. The European Council's decision in December 1997 to open negotiations with five of the Central and Eastern European candidates plus Cyprus (the so-called 5 + 1 arrangement) incensed Turkey, which disputed the right of the Greek Cypriot government to negotiate on behalf of the entire island. As the sole sponsor of the separatist regime in Northern Cyprus, Turkey was in a position to facilitate reunification, subject to the Cypriot government guaranteeing the rights of what would become a large Turkish minority. Because both Cyprus and Turkey wanted to join, the EU had leverage over both governments.

Apart from the fraught problem of partition, the EU's negotiations with Cyprus were relatively straightforward. Although most member states were reluctant to bring a divided Cyprus into the EU, Greece threatened to veto the entire enlargement if Cyprus was not admitted alongside the first wave of Central and Eastern European candidates. Making the best of a bad situation, the EU sought to appease Turkey with additional economic assistance and the promise of eventual accession and appease Greece with the promise of Cypriot accession.

At the Copenhagen summit in December 2002, the European Council therefore endorsed the Commission's recommendation that the EU admit Cyprus along with the eight Central and Eastern European countries (plus Malta). The European Council's decision at the same time not to give Turkey a date for the start of accession negotiations further strained EU-Turkey relations and damaged prospects for the reunification of Cyprus. Giving the green light to Cypriot accession also robbed the EU of leverage over the Cypriot government to make concessions to the Turkish community in Northern Cyprus.

The extent to which the EU lost influence over the Cypriot government became apparent only a week before Cyprus joined, when a large majority of Greek Cypriots rejected, in a referendum, the UN-sponsored "Annan Plan" to reunite the island. By contrast, a large majority of Turkish Cypriots endorsed the plan in a referendum held simultaneously in the north of the island. The accession of a divided Cyprus represented a setback for EU foreign policy and a blot on the otherwise impressive achievement of the 2004 enlargement.

Malta. The ruling conservative Nationalist Party submitted Malta's application to join the EC in 1990. Deeply attached to the country's status as a nonaligned country since independence from Britain, Malta's opposition Labour Party opposed membership. After winning the country's general election in October 1996, Labour promptly canceled Malta's application. The EU was relieved to have one less application to deal with. The EU was equally nonchalant when the conservatives returned to power in September

1998 and reactivated Malta's application. The EU agreed in 1999 that Malta could begin accession negotiation.

The only problem for the EU was Malta's size: the EU did not relish having another member state approximately the same size as Luxembourg, but without Luxembourg's international standing or long involvement in European integration. Nevertheless, Malta moved easily toward EU entry, completing its accession negotiations at the end of 2002. Although a majority approved Malta's membership in a referendum in March 2003, the fiercely anti-EU opposition Labour Party insisted that the issue be decided in the forthcoming general election, to be held only a week before the signing of the accession treaty in April 2003. The governing conservatives easily won reelection, thus ensuring that Malta joined the EU in May 2004.

Treaty Reform

Enlargement—whether from six member states to nine in 1973 or from fifteen to twenty-five in 2004—has had a profound institutional impact. Numerous memorandums and reports, stretching back to the 1960s, advocated treaty-based institutional reform in light of imminent enlargement. Yet enlargement was never an impetus for treaty reform. That changed in the mid-1990s, when the EU received applications from ten Central and Eastern European countries.

The Amsterdam Treaty

As it happened, the Maastricht Treaty mandated that an intergovernmental conference begin in 1996, in order possibly to improve the functioning of the common foreign and security policy. By the time that the conference was due to take place, the likely institutional implications of the next round of enlargement were becoming apparent. An EU of twenty-five or more member states seemed unworkable without major institutional reform. Although not convened for that purpose, the upcoming intergovernmental conferences gave member states an ideal opportunity to act. When asked to explain why the conference was taking place, EU officials and politicians usually gave institutional reform as the reason.[13]

The Reflection Group. Mindful of the fallout from the Maastricht ratification crisis, EU leaders established the Reflection Group, a high-level committee to prepare the conference. The Reflection Group met for the first time in Messina, Sicily, in June 1995. The fact that the original Messina conference forty years earlier had paved the way for the Rome Treaty seemed auspicious for the group's deliberations.

The group's remit was to draw up the agenda for the conference, which would go beyond institutional reform, and identify areas of likely agreement. Governments' different approaches and preferences were evident from the outset, with the more integration-minded countries (notably Belgium, Germany, Italy, Luxembourg, and the Netherlands) ranged against those less inclined toward supranational solutions, especially Britain. Indeed, the growing Euroskepticism of Britain's Conservative government overshadowed the group's work, just as it would overshadow all but the final stage of the conference itself.

The possibility of differentiated integration (closer cooperation in selected policy areas among like-minded member states) emerged during the group's deliberations as a subject likely to dominate the forthcoming conference. The subject had burst into the open in September 1994 when the parties in Germany's conservative coalition government published a paper claiming that "the existing hard core of countries oriented to greater integration and closer cooperation must be further strengthened" and that "the EU's institutions must combine coherence and consistency with elasticity and flexibility." The authors identified the core group as Germany, France, Belgium, Luxembourg, and the Netherlands—in other words, the original member states minus Italy. As for Britain, the authors argued that "determined efforts to spur on the further development of Europe are the best means of exerting a positive influence on the clarification of Britain's relationship to Europe and on its willingness to participate in further steps toward integration."[14]

Italy, already sensitive to criticism of its seeming inability to meet the EMU convergence criteria and embroiled in post–Cold War political upheavals, was deeply offended. The smaller member states, even the three Benelux countries included in the putative hard core, shared Italy's fear of a possible Franco-German scheme to pursue closer integration outside the EU system. Nor was the main thrust of the paper lost on the British government. For some time, Prime Minister Major had been talking cavalierly about flexibility, by which he meant an à la carte, pick-and-choose EU. In response to the German paper, Major rejected the idea of an EU "in which some [countries] would be more equal than others." By arguing against a two-tier EU and advocating instead a system in which countries could opt in and out of certain policies, Major drew one of the most important battle lines of the impending negotiations.[15]

In its report to the European Council, the Reflection Group reviewed the debate on differentiated integration without making a specific recommendation. In general, the report identified three main areas for reform: making the EU more relevant to its citizens; improving the EU's efficiency and accountability; and improving the EU's ability to act internationally. In all cases, the report emphasized the likely impact of enlargement.[16]

The intergovernmental conference. The intergovernmental conference began at a special summit in Turin in March 1996. Participants dragged out the proceedings for over a year, largely because of the timing of the British general election, which was due to take place no later than May 1997. Britain's partners hoped that the election would see off Major's Conservative government, which was holding up progress on a range of issues. Tony Blair, the Labour Party leader, was an unknown quantity, but he seemed refreshingly pro-EU. Much to the relief of other EU leaders, Labour swept the Conservatives from office in the May 1997 election.

With the British Conservatives out of power, the question of differentiated integration lost its sense of urgency. Indeed, the subject aroused more academic interest than political passion during the intergovernmental conference. Although some countries remained wary, a consensus emerged that, in principle, differentiated integration should be included in the treaty as long as it was limited, in practice, to precisely defined conditions that would not endanger the existing corpus of EU rules and regulations. Governments eventually agreed to a compromise that included both general "enabling" clauses for countries wishing to cooperate more closely, and particular provisions governing the use of flexibility in certain policy areas. Hedged with qualifications and safeguards, flexibility would be difficult to put into practice. What emerged in the treaty was a far cry from what some countries favored and others feared: a two-tier EU.[17]

Institutional affairs turned out to be the most contentious issues in the intergovernmental conference. Questions relating to the EP—its size, location, and legislative powers—proved relatively easy to resolve. Governments accepted the EP's own proposal to set a ceiling of 700 members and agreed to enshrine in the treaty an earlier political agreement to hold the bulk of the EP's plenary session in Strasbourg (a persistent French demand). Following the change of government in Britain, the conference agreed to revise the co-decision procedure in a way that would greatly enhance the EP's legislative power.

Most governments favored extending qualified majority voting to additional policy areas. This became bound up with the technical but highly sensitive question of the reweighting of Council votes, which would dominate the debate on institutional reform for the next ten years. The big countries favored either an increase in the number of their votes or the introduction of a double majority, combining the traditional requirement of a qualified majority with a new demographic criterion. Without such a change, they argued, a qualified majority could be formed following the next round of enlargement by a group of countries that together did not represent a majority of the EU's population.

Negotiations about the reweighting of votes inevitably touched on another highly controversial issue: the size and composition of the Commission. Nearly every government conceded that the Commission was too large, but few would countenance a Commission with fewer representatives than the number of EU member states. Not least because the big countries wanted to increase their relative weight in Council voting, most small countries adamantly opposed the idea of radically reducing the Commission's size, possibly resulting in a loss of "their" commissioner. With varying degrees of enthusiasm, big member states expressed a willingness to give up at least their second commissioner, but only in return for a reweighting of votes in the Council.

Meeting in Amsterdam in June 1997, the European Council negotiated far into the night to conclude the intergovernmental conference, but failed to reach a comprehensive agreement on institutional reform. EU leaders settled on a temporary solution: a protocol attached to the treaty stipulating that the Commission would comprise one representative per member state as soon as the next enlargement took place, provided that Council votes were reweighted in order to compensate the big countries for the loss of a second commissioner. The protocol also stated that the EU would hold another intergovernmental conference before the next round of enlargement in order to settle the outstanding institutional issues.

The ensuing Amsterdam Treaty was a disappointment. Giving more power to the EP and extending the range of qualified majority voting were not insignificant changes, but were unlikely greatly to enhance the EU's efficiency, credibility, or legitimacy. Nevertheless, the treaty was noteworthy for a number of important changes of a constitutional kind, such as imbuing the EU with core political values and allowing the EU to sanction any member state that deviated from them. Given the origin of the conference and the fact that the negotiations took place in the shadow of the Yugoslav wars, the Amsterdam Treaty included significant changes to the common foreign and security policy. At the same time, rising public concern about the internal security implications of external instability emboldened governments to strengthen treaty provisions relating to justice and home affairs.

A treaty intended in part to make the EU more intelligible to its citizens was almost unintelligible even to experts. Overall, the Amsterdam Treaty was a fitting testimonial to the impossibility of reconciling the complexity of EU governance with citizens' demands for greater simplicity and comprehensibility, a difficulty that would become more acute in the years ahead. Unlike the Maastricht Treaty before it and the Nice and Lisbon treaties to follow, at least the Amsterdam Treaty was easily ratified. In both Denmark and Ireland, the only countries to hold a referendum, large majorities endorsed the Amsterdam Treaty, which came into effect in May 1999.

The Nice Treaty
The EU embarked on another intergovernmental conference in February 2000 to tackle the so-called Amsterdam leftovers (the weighting of Council votes and size and composition of the Commission).[18] As part of a general

institutional reshuffle, governments also addressed the number of EP seats and Council votes for the prospective new member states.

The narrowness of the conference agenda was inherently unsatisfactory, leaving little room for side bargains or trade-offs among participants. As expected, the negotiations on voting weights in the Council and the Commission's size opened a can of worms. These issues were all about the power of governments to shape EU decisions. A split soon emerged, with the big member states wanting to increase their share of Council votes and reduce the size of the Commission, and the small member states mostly wanting to keep their share of Council votes and maintain representation in the Commission.

A spectacular row broke out among EU leaders at an informal summit in October 2000, their first discussion of institutional reform since the rancorous Amsterdam summit in June 1997. Chirac irritated many of his counterparts by proposing a radical reduction in the size of the Commission while promising a system for the selection of a smaller group of commissioners that would ensure equality among member states. The small countries were unimpressed, distrusting France and fearing that the big countries would skew the proposed new system against them. Chirac claimed that the sharp exchange over the Commission's size cleared the air in the conference. In fact, it led the small countries to dig in their heels and set the stage for a bruising battle at the Nice summit in December 2000.

The discussion of voting weights was equally acrimonious. France was determined to keep the same number of Council votes as Germany, a far more populous country. Chirac, a Gaullist, even cited Jean Monnet to bolster his claim that equality between France and Germany was an inviolable part of the original Franco-German bargain. German chancellor Gerhard Schröder, participating in his first intergovernmental conference, conceded the point in return for the addition of a demographic criterion for qualified majority voting. At the same time, the Netherlands exasperated Belgium, its less populous neighbor, by demanding more Council votes, thereby ending the traditional parity between the two countries.

When they convened in Nice, EU leaders were so far apart on the main agenda items that it looked to two officials involved in the conference "as if eighteen months of preparation had been thrown out of the window and the negotiations [were restarting] from scratch."[19] After spending two days on other EU business, the European Council spent two more days concluding the conference, making the Nice summit the longest in EU history. Yet the length of the summit hardly justified the effort. EU leaders haggled until the final minutes over the reallocation of Council votes. Belgium, still refusing to accept fewer votes than the Netherlands, was finally bought off with the promise of hosting all meetings of the European Council in Brussels. France managed to keep parity with Germany, but the addition of a demographic criterion gave Germany extra voting weight. The deal eventually struck on Council decisionmaking was especially inglorious. Far from making voting simpler and easier to understand, it changed the system in a way that seemed unnecessarily convoluted.

As for the future of the Commission, the agreement called for the big member states to give up their second commissioner when the next Commission took office, and for the number of commissioners to be reduced to fewer than the number of member states when the EU reached twenty-seven members (a number based on the existing fifteen plus the twelve candidates). At that time, governments would rotate Commission appointments according to a system yet to be worked out.

Rarely had national leaders devoted so much time to so few issues with so little to show for their efforts. Signed without much fanfare in February 2001, the Nice Treaty barely succeeded in preparing the EU institutionally for enlargement. Arguably the treaty's most significant innovation was to ease the criteria under which differentiated integration could come into effect, with governments having agreed to remove the veto on its use and reduce the number of member states allowed to initiate the procedure.

When Irish voters rejected the treaty in June 2001, it was difficult to regret the result. The European Council announced only a week later that the EU would enlarge regardless. In February 2002, the Convention on the Future of Europe, intended to prepare a more far-reaching round of treaty reform, held its inaugural meeting in Brussels. As the purpose of the convention was to help reform the EU in anticipation of enlargement, it was hard to understand why the EU put such emphasis on ratifying the Nice Treaty. Clearly, EU leaders felt strongly that, once negotiated, the treaty had to be implemented. Pressed by other governments and by the Commission, the Irish government badgered voters to approve the treaty in a second referendum, in October 2002. To the relief of the EU establishment and the candidate countries, the Irish endorsed the treaty in the second attempt, thanks to a much higher turnout.

The political legacy of Nice was more enduring than the treaty's institutional provisions. The conduct of the conference turned opinion against the negotiation of treaty reform using the traditional method. Small member states resented what they saw as the emergence of a more intergovernmental EU dominated by the big member states. Further reform, though necessary, would be even more difficult to achieve.

The Constitutional Treaty

In May 2000, Joschka Fischer, Germany's foreign minister, made a speech in Berlin about the nature, organizing principles, and institutional structure of the enlarging EU. Speaking in a personal capacity, although with great authority as foreign minister of the EU's largest member state, Fischer called for a more federal European Union.[20] Jacques Chirac issued a rejoinder in a historic address to the German parliament in Berlin in September 2001, supporting greater European integration while defending the primacy of national governments. Thus began a debate on the future of the EU to which numerous politicians in the member states and candidate countries contributed.[21]

The launch of what came to be called the "post-Nice debate" in the pre-Nice period indicated widespread disillusionment with the narrow focus of the intergovernmental conference then in progress. Anticipating the inadequacy of the Nice Treaty, EU leaders included in it a declaration calling for yet another intergovernmental conference to deal with a range of issues such as the democratic deficit, the effectiveness of particular policies, and the status of the Charter of Fundamental Rights, a nonbinding document that EU leaders had endorsed at the Nice summit in December 2000.[22]

A growing awareness of the enormity of enlargement and of the extent of public alienation from the EU convinced EU leaders that the next intergovernmental conference could not be conducted like previous ones. The European Council therefore agreed at a meeting in Laeken, Belgium, in December 2001, not only to widen the agenda of the next conference but also to prepare for it in a novel way. Drawing on the method used to draft the Charter of Fundamental Rights, the European Council announced that representatives of national governments, national parliaments, the Commission, and the EP would meet in a convention to prepare the conference "as broadly and openly as possible." The composition of the convention reflected a consensus on the need to diversify participation in the process of EU treaty reform. The candidate countries would be represented in the same way as the member states, but would not have a decisionmaking role.[23]

The Constitutional Convention. The convention was to have a chair and two vice chairs. The European Council selected them in the usual way. Chirac announced that either the chair would be French or the convention would not take place, and proposed Valéry Giscard d'Estaing, a former president of France. The small member states remembered Giscard's disinterest in them and disdain for the Commission but felt powerless to block the appointment. And so the septuagenarian Giscard, an arch-defender of the interests of big member states, came to personify the future of Europe.

The convention opened in Brussels in February 2002.[24] It soon became known as the Constitutional Convention because of Giscard's intention to draft not simply a new treaty but a constitution for the EU. In reality, the convention could only propose a constitutional treaty (an agreement among sovereign states with constitutional characteristics). The decision to draft a constitutional treaty was mainly symbolic, given that the Court of Justice already interpreted the existing treaties as constitutional texts. Nevertheless incorporating the Charter of Fundamental Rights into the treaty would give the EU the equivalent of a Bill of Rights, an important constitutional attribute. Moreover, using the word "constitutional" emphasized the political nature of the EU project.

Plenary sessions were large and unwieldy affairs. Their most striking feature was a palpable sense of Euro-enthusiasm. Delegates drafted hundreds of proposals and amendments on a wide range of policy and institutional issues. Governments nonetheless controlled the agenda. Although the purpose of the convention was partly to curb governments' monopoly on treaty reform, discussions in the plenary sessions and in the convention's governing body increasingly reflected national positions as the deadline approached.

The big country–small country divide was bound to resurface in any forum that addressed touchy institutional questions. A proposal by France and Germany, submitted in January 2003 on the fortieth anniversary of the Franco-German Elysée Treaty, brought the divide starkly to the fore. It endorsed a call already made by Britain, France, and Spain for an elected president of the European Council to replace the rotating presidency. Many of the small member states (plus the Commission) immediately cried foul. They feared that the standing president would always come from a big country and that the proposed new position would undermine the influence of the Commission president, traditionally a champion of the small countries.

There was general agreement among all governments that an EU foreign minister should combine the recently established position of High Representative for the Common Foreign and Security Policy with that of commissioner for external relations. The same person would chair meetings of a newly configured Foreign Affairs Council and coordinate the Commission's external relations responsibilities. The advent of an elected European Council president and an EU foreign minister would downgrade the rotating presidency, which would be restricted to chairing the other Council configurations.

In return, many of the small countries mounted a fierce rearguard action to scrap the provision in the Nice Treaty that broke the link between the number of member states and the number of commissioners, asserting their right always to nominate a commissioner. With the support of the big countries, however, Giscard pushed through a provision for a college of thirteen commissioners, selected on the basis of equal rotation among member states, plus the Commission president and the combined position of EU foreign minister and Commission vice president.

One of the most heated issues in the convention concerned the modalities of qualified majority voting in the Council. Keenly aware of their relative loss of power as a result of enlargement, which had brought and would bring into the EU many more small member states, France and Germany pressed for a new system based on the double majority principle. In future, half the number of member states representing at least 60 percent of the EU's total population would constitute a qualified majority. Such a proposal, coming so soon after the redistribution of votes agreed to at the Nice summit, was further evidence of deep dissatisfaction with the Nice Treaty's institutional reforms. Using their considerable powers of political persuasion, France and Germany succeeded in having the new voting formula included in the convention's Draft Constitutional Treaty.

As the convention proceeded, a noticeable divide emerged between the original Six (the founding member states) and the rest, particularly those about to join in 2004. French and German representatives worked closely together in the convention, despite their differences on a range of issues. Although often on the defensive, the British government's representative was rarely isolated. Nevertheless, Britain stuck rigidly to a number of positions, such as refusing the use of the word "federal" in the draft treaty.

Institutional issues were by no means the only sticking points. The question of EU competences preoccupied delegates in early 2003 and demonstrated the difficulty of demarcating EU-level and national powers in a process as politically and historically muddled as European integration. The convention eventually agreed on a short list of exclusive responsibilities (such as monetary policy and trade policy) and a long but not exclusive list of responsibilities shared between the EU and national levels of governance (ranging from agricultural policy to economic and social cohesion). The EU could take supporting, coordinating, or complementary action in areas such as industry, culture, and civil protection. The limits of EU competences were governed by the principle of conferral by the member states, and the use of competences was governed by the principles of subsidiarity and proportionality.

Reaching agreement on the values and objectives of the EU was relatively easy, apart from an impassioned discussion about whether and how to recognize the EU's religious heritage. It did not go unnoticed that mention of an explicit Christian heritage would hinder (if not prevent) Turkish accession to the EU. In the end, the preamble merely included a reference to Europe's religious "inheritance." Membership in the EU would be open to all European states that respected the EU's values and were committed to promoting them together—hardly clear-cut criteria, either geographically or normatively.

Most delegates wanted to include the Charter of Fundamental Rights in the Constitutional Treaty in order to emphasize the EU's values and possibly increase the EU's appeal to citizens. The British and Irish governments were unenthusiastic, doubting that it would have any effect on public opinion (except perhaps to provide more ammunition to Euroskeptics) and fearing that strict adherence to it would increase business costs.

Bringing the various bits and pieces together and concluding the Draft Constitutional Treaty was a daunting task. Undoubtedly democratic, the convention method was unavoidably awkward. It needed strong leadership to succeed. Giscard was determined to produce a single draft text instead of alternative versions of controversial provisions. He could not hope for unanimity, only for majority support. By emphasizing the convention's historic importance, Giscard won the approval, grudging or otherwise, of most of the delegates for the final text.

The convention succeeded in producing, by the stipulated deadline of June 2003, a single, reasonably understandable (although long) document. In one important respect, however, the convention was a failure: ordinary Europeans seemed to know little and care less about it. Media coverage was sparse, apart from a flurry of alarming articles in the British tabloid press. Even under the best of circumstances, it would have been difficult to interest most citizens in the vagaries of majority voting or other arcane institutional issues. If anything, the convention reinforced a widespread public perception that European integration was driven entirely by elites, for elites.

Negotiating the Constitutional Treaty. The Constitutional Convention had been convened because of dissatisfaction with the traditional method of treaty reform. Yet under the terms of the existing treaties, governments had to convene an intergovernmental conference in order to reform the treaties. Far from merely rubber-stamping the convention's draft treaty, most governments were determined to use the intergovernmental conference to get a better deal in the definitive Constitutional Treaty. For many small countries, especially those about to join the EU, the conference was a chance to try to reclaim the right to representation in the Commission. For Spain and Poland, it was a chance to try to preserve the Nice agreement on voting weights, which was extremely advantageous to them. France and Germany, for their part, were determined to scrap the Nice arrangement in favor of the proposed new double majority system.

The intergovernmental conference began in late 2003. The depth of French and Spanish feelings—on opposite sides of the issue—with respect to qualified majority voting, together with poor conduct of Italy's Council presidency, under the leadership of the mercurial Silvio Berlusconi, caused a breakdown of negotiations in December 2003. France and Germany threatened to link the outcome of the conference to the upcoming budget negotiations (by implication cutting funds to Spain and Poland) and to forge ahead with a "core" or "pioneer" group of member states (by implication excluding Spain and Poland).

The incoming Irish presidency lost little time in early 2004 quietly getting the negotiations going again. Changes of government in Spain and Poland (for reasons unrelated to the conference) improved the chances of success. Wanting to signal a more accommodating policy toward the EU, the two countries' new governments were willing to reach a compromise on the proposed new voting system. Although other issues remained on the table, an agreement on the Constitutional Treaty seemed possible by June 2004.

Altogether, the conference approved eighty amendments to the convention's draft treaty. The small countries eventually agreed to a Commission reduced in size, but beginning only in 2014. The new double majority was set at 55 percent of the member states and 65 percent of the population, making it easier for countries to form a blocking minority but without allowing the three biggest to do so by themselves. Overall, the Constitutional Treaty looked much like the convention's draft document, though advocates of deeper integration complained that many of the changes were retrograde steps.

Given the strength of Euroskepticism, or simply of indifference toward the EU, the fate of the Constitutional Treaty was highly uncertain. Ratification by each member state, especially by those countries holding referendums, could not be taken for granted. Not that the EU was in danger of falling apart without it. Strictly speaking, the Constitutional Treaty was desirable but not essential. Even with the Constitutional Treaty in place, strong national interests, a willful EP, and a weak Commission would continue to impede the EU's effectiveness.

Launching the Euro

The road to the third stage of EMU was bumpy even before ratification of the Maastricht Treaty.[25] Rising German interest rates pushed up the value of the mark and down the value of other currencies in the exchange rate mechanism of the European Monetary System. What mushroomed into a major EMS crisis began in August 1992, outside the mechanism, with the currencies unofficially linked to it. First the Finnish markka, then the Swedish krone, collapsed under pressure from massive speculative attacks.

The situation seemed to warrant a general realignment within the exchange rate mechanism. But there had not been a realignment since 1987, giving the EMS the appearance by 1992 of a quasi–currency union. Although governments associated devaluation with political and economic weakness, Italy swallowed its pride and devalued the lire by 7 percent in early September 1992. The British authorities struggled to maintain the value of the pound, which entered the exchange rate mechanism in October 1990 at too high of a rate against the mark. Much to Britain's chagrin, the Bundesbank refused to intervene in the currency markets to help sterling. Unable any longer to prop up the pound, a chastened chancellor of the British exchequer pulled sterling out of the exchange rate mechanism on "black Wednesday," September 16, 1992.

Predictions of a vote against the Maastricht Treaty in the French referendum in September 1992, or of a narrow result in favor, intensified pressure on the franc. In a move that revealed Germany's much closer relationship with France than with any other member state, Germany bolstered French efforts to avert a disaster in late September and keep the franc within its exchange rate band. The franc survived; other weak currencies, such as the Spanish peseta, Portuguese escudo, Irish pound, and Italian lire, were devalued in late 1992 and early 1993.

The currency crisis escalated in July 1993 when the Bundesbank decided not to make an eagerly awaited cut in interest rates. With international currency transactions increasing at a rapid rate and vast amounts of capital moving freely throughout the EU, the Germans felt unable any longer to support the franc. At an emergency meeting in August 1993, finance ministers decided to relieve pressure by allowing currencies in the exchange rate mechanism to move within a 15 percent band (instead of a 2.5 percent band) around their parity with the German mark.

Some central banks lost vast amounts of money during the currency crisis; some speculators, such as international financier George Soros, made a fortune. People wondered how EMU, given its close relation to the EMS, could succeed under such inauspicious circumstances. The crisis had a devastating impact in Britain, because the EMS, and by implication EMU, became associated with currency turmoil and national humiliation. Yet the currency crisis strengthened the conviction of most EU politicians and officials to press ahead with EMU. The Bundesbank, whose high interest rates exacerbated the crisis, acted only in Germany's interest. The European Central Bank, by contrast, would act in the interest of all EMU members. Nor would there be separate currencies for speculators to attack in a monetary union with a single currency.

The second stage of EMU began without fanfare in July 1994, with the establishment in Frankfurt of the European Monetary Institute, forerunner of the ECB. The institute's purpose was to make technical preparations for the third stage and help coordinate member states' monetary policies. Its tasks included specifying the regulatory, organizational, and logistical framework for the proposed European System of Central Banks, including the ECB; drafting a "changeover scenario" from national currencies to the single currency; devising monetary policy instruments and procedures; preparing a cross-border payments system; and compiling reliable statistics.

The Maastricht Treaty stipulated that Stage Three could begin in January 1997 if a majority of member states met the convergence criteria. It looked in the mid-1990s as if the deadline could not possibly be met. The EU was in recession. High interest rates in Germany pushed up interest rates throughout the EU, increasing the cost of borrowing money and reducing investment. As unemployment rose and consumer spending fell, governments took in less revenue but spent more on welfare benefits. It was impossible under these circumstances for governments to reduce their deficits and debts to the levels required for participation in Stage Three. Most member states' inflation rates were outside the targeted band of not more than 1.5 percent of the EU's three best performers.

With member states thus diverging from, rather than converging on, the EMU criteria, it was unsurprising that the European Council, meeting in December 1995, abandoned the goal of launching Stage Three in 1997. The European Council's decision instead to aim for the 1999 deadline also seemed unrealistic. As if to emphasize its resolve, the European Council decided to name the new currency the "euro" and adopted the changeover scenario prepared by the European Monetary Institute on introducing the currency as legal tender throughout the eurozone. What some dismissed at the time as a foolish act of faith looked to others like a bold assertion of political will.

Indeed, the success of EMU only a few years later owed much to the determination of a handful of political leaders, notably Chancellor Kohl and Commission president Santer. Both were in relatively weak positions (Kohl narrowly won the October 1994 elections and lacked a majority in the upper house of parliament, and Santer was perceived from the beginning of his presidency as a political lightweight) and ended their careers ignominiously (with Kohl accused of accepting illegal party contributions, and Santer forced to resign amid allegations of corruption in the Commission). Yet in the mid-1990s, Kohl pursued EMU with a passion, arguing relentlessly that it was essential for Germany's and Europe's well-being. Santer, though far less influential than Kohl, spearheaded the Commission's commitment to EMU and orchestrated the technical measures necessary to ensure the successful launch of the euro.

At first, Jacques Chirac was equivocal about deeper European integration and especially about EMU. Violent demonstrations in Paris in December 1995 against government austerity measures were a reminder to the newly elected president of the risks involved in bringing France's public finances into line with EMU standards. Yet the division of authority between the president and prime minister in the French political system allowed Chirac to appear to be above the fray while his prime minister took the heat for unpopular economic reforms. Chirac soon realized that France had little choice but to press ahead with EMU. Making a virtue of necessity and wanting to be seen as a leader of European stature, Chirac jettisoned his earlier misgivings and wholeheartedly endorsed EMU.

The Stability and Growth Pact

In December 1995 the European Council asked the Economic and Financial Affairs Council to study a question raised by Germany that was central to EMU's success: how to ensure the sustainability of monetary union through the continuation of fiscal discipline after the launch of the third stage of EMU. In due course, Ecofin proposed a "stability pact." Bearing an obvious German imprint, the pact included automatic penalties for eurozone members running excessive budget deficits, defined, as was the deficit criterion in the Maastricht Treaty, as above 3 percent of GDP. By 1996, when the proposal was being debated, governments were cutting budgets in order to bring deficits below the 3 percent ceiling. As the effects of budget cuts rippled through the economy, unemployment increased and generous social welfare programs came under financial pressure. These developments reinforced a growing perception that EMU itself exacerbated unemployment and worsened the plight of the unemployed.

Nowhere was this perception stronger, and nowhere was a government more sensitive to its political repercussions, than in France. In deference to French sensitivity, Germany watered down the terms of the proposed pact, making fines not automatic but subject to approval by governments. Also in deference to the perception that EMU was imposing a fiscal straitjacket and destroying jobs, Ecofin renamed the proposed agreement, which the European Council adopted in December 1996, as the Stability and *Growth* Pact.

In March 1997, France entered a period of cohabitation (the presidency and the prime minister came from opposing political parties). Lionel Jospin, leader of the Socialist Party and the new prime minister, was outspoken in his criticism of EMU. One of Jospin's first steps was to demand a renegotiation of the Stability and Growth Pact, which Germany flatly rejected. Jospin succeeded only in having the European Council adopt a resolution on growth and employment that stressed governments' determination to keep employment firmly at the top of the political agenda. A call by Jospin for an "economic government" to watch over the supposedly independent ECB caused even greater alarm in Berlin. Germany and like-minded member states had no intention of undermining the ECB's independence or commitment to price stability, but agreed to establish a forum for discussions among governments in the eurozone about such key issues as maintaining fiscal discipline, coordinating taxation policy, and setting the euro's exchange rate. Accordingly, the European Council decided in December 1997 to establish the Eurogroup, consisting of finance ministers of countries in the eurozone.[26]

Reaching Stage Three

The controversy surrounding the Stability and Growth Pact and the Eurogroup demonstrated both the increasing politicization of EMU and the probability that it would indeed come to fruition. French and German efforts to meet the convergence criteria by engaging in what some critics derided as "creative accounting" reinforced the impression that that the third stage of EMU would be launched at all costs. France's creative accounting was successful, Germany's was a failure. The Commission allowed France to apply a huge onetime payment from France Telecom in 1997 against the country's deficit. However, the Bundesbank rejected the German finance minister's effort to revalue Germany's gold reserves in May 1997 and apply the proceeds against the country's deficit.

Even with recourse to such measures, neither France nor Germany seemed likely in early 1997 to come under the 3 percent ceiling. If one or both of them proved unable to participate in EMU, the entire project would collapse. Within a few months, however, Europe's economic recovery began to fill national exchequers. It looked as if France, Germany, and most other countries would confound the skeptics and meet the 3 percent criterion. The Commission's autumn 1997 economic forecast bore out this rosy scenario and strengthened the growing conviction that EMU would start in 1999 with a large majority of member states.[27]

Most surprising of all was the likelihood that Portugal, Spain, and Italy, countries notorious for loose fiscal discipline, would make the first cut. Even strong supporters of EMU dismissed the possibility of the Mediterranean countries' participation in it. Snide comments by German officials about Italy's ineligibility for EMU strained relations between the two countries. Yet Italy's center-left coalition government took such politically courageous steps as introducing tough austerity measures and levying a special tax to help cut the budget deficit. For Italy, then in the throes of post–Cold War political upheaval, failure to make the EMU grade came to be seen as a potential national disaster.

Germany's concerns about Italy, shared by most northern EU countries, pertained especially to sustainability. Even if Italy met the convergence criteria, would it sustain the 3 percent budget deficit ceiling after 1999? Opponents of Italy's participation may have had legitimate concerns, but attempting to keep Italy out of Stage Three on grounds of nonsustainability would have implicitly acknowledged the weakness of the Stability and Growth Pact, which the European Council had recently adopted to deal with this issue.

The Maastricht ratification crisis had exposed a high degree of public concern about deeper integration, which many observers expected to crystallize around EMU. In the event, the pain of meeting the convergence criteria was unevenly spread, and reaction to EMU differed widely among aspiring participants. Luxembourg was a model of fiscal rectitude. Belgium considered that EMU membership was its birthright, despite having a bloated public debt. Alone among the Nordic member states, Finland was highly motivated to participate in EMU. The convergence criteria caused little pain in Ireland and the Netherlands, which had embarked on structural reform and were enjoying strong economic growth, but caused considerable pain in Italy, Portugal, Spain, and Greece, countries that badly needed to put their public finances in order and at the same time feared the humiliation of not meeting the EMU standard.

Only in France and Germany, the EU's core countries, might hostile public opinion have jeopardized EMU. France seemed especially vulnerable because of its tradition of government surrender in the face of violent political protest. In the event, economic recovery made it possible for Jospin to square the circle of EMU-inspired austerity and traditional Socialist largesse. Anti-EMU protests never materialized, and the government did not have to put its commitment to the Maastricht criteria to the ultimate political test of facing down demonstrators.

Germany's political tradition was one of public obedience to authority. That may explain why, despite numerous polls showing how unhappy the majority of Germans were about giving up the mark, a powerful anti-EMU movement did not develop. Germans confined their protests to writing letters to the editor and bringing a case before the constitutional court. Most Germans reckoned that the political consequences of abandoning EMU were potentially more destabilizing than the economic consequences of staying the course.

With the realization by late 1997 that opposition to EMU was muted and that most countries would meet the convergence criteria, the procedure for selecting participants in Stage Three lost its political edge. In February 1998, governments released data showing a high degree of nominal convergence. Only Greece failed to qualify, because its budget deficit was a full percentage point above the reference point. Britain, Denmark, and Sweden, which had decided not to adopt the single currency, came in well under the 3 percent ceiling. By contrast, France reported a deficit of 3.02 percent. Because the treaty included some wiggle room, the French figure was deemed acceptable. The figures on national debt were less impressive, with Belgium, Italy, and Greece coming in well above 100 percent. Fortunately for them, the treaty allowed countries to exceed the 60 percent reference point if "the ratio [of debt to GDP] is sufficiently diminishing and approaching [60 percent] at a satisfactory pace."[28]

In their reports on economic convergence, the Commission and the European Monetary Institute therefore recommended that eleven member states begin Stage Three in January 1999. The European Council endorsed these recommendations in Brussels in March 1998, thereby avoiding what could have been a bruising political battle over the composition of the eurozone. Instead, the Brussels summit became infamous for a sharp encounter between Chirac and Kohl on a related matter: the presidency of the ECB. Chirac insisted that its first president be French, and pushed Jean-Claude Trichet, governor of the French central bank, for the job. Kohl supported Wim Duisenberg, head of the Dutch central bank, who also had the support of the governors of the national central banks. The bitter dispute ended with a compromise: Duisenberg would be appointed ECB president, but would step down sometime after mid-2002. Trichet would then succeed Duisenberg for the remainder of the president's eight-year term in office.[29]

The row over Duisenberg's appointment brought out the worst in Chirac and soured his relationship with Kohl. It also raised questions about possible French interference in the operation of the ECB. Yet the members of the ECB's governing board, appointed at the same meeting of the European Council, were experienced, independent-minded central bankers. Duisenberg himself gave a spirited display of independence at a hearing in the EP only a week after the summit.

Stage Three

The third stage of EMU began in January 1999 when exchange rates between participating currencies were locked in place and the ECB assumed responsibility for monetary policy in the eurozone. The euro itself existed only notionally; notes and coins did not begin to circulate for another three years. In the meantime, the ECB, the Commission, and national authorities tackled the immense logistical challenge of introducing the new currency and withdrawing the old ones. According to the Maastricht Treaty, the new and old currencies could have circulated alongside each other for up to six months. In the event, national authorities were eager to minimize possible confusion by withdrawing the old currencies almost immediately.

The introduction of the single currency went remarkably smoothly. People snapped up euros from cash machines and banks and exchanged their national currencies more quickly and with far less fuss than expected. There were complaints in some countries of price increases by retailers. Otherwise, people easily accepted the euro, without ever loving it, being concerned more about the soundness than the color and design of the money in their pockets. Those who traveled across national borders were happy not to have to go to the trouble and expense of changing money.

The euro began life at an exchange rate of 1.18 to the US dollar. Its value dropped steadily until rebounding in late 2002, soon after which it regained its original level. Some saw in the decline of the euro evidence that EMU was on shaky ground; others saw it as the market's reaction to initial over-valuation and a reflection of economic fundamentals on both sides of the Atlantic. For EU officials and politicians, the drop in the euro's external value was a disappointment. For manufacturers, it meant that exports from the eurozone were more competitive. For tourists visiting the eurozone, it meant a relatively inexpensive vacation.

European Commission/P-002627/00-1

The ECB faced a difficult task managing monetary policy for a large and disparate economic zone. As anticipated, a "one size fits all" monetary policy was far from ideal for a region that included a booming economy such as Ireland's and a stagnant economy such as Germany's. Given the vast difference in size between the two countries, inevitably the ECB set interest rates that were more appropriate to Germany's than to Ireland's circumstances, thereby unintentionally contributing to a property bubble in the booming Celtic Tiger. Constitutionally obliged to fight inflation, the ECB faced an unexpected risk of deflation in 2002 and 2003 as prices dropped and economic performance faltered in the eurozone as a whole.

Faced with declining revenues and increasing expenditure at a time of renewed recession, a number of countries failed to keep their deficits within the 3 percent target, as stipulated by the Stability and Growth Pact. To the undisguised delight of its EU partners, Germany was one of the offenders. Gerhard Schröder, Kohl's successor, seemed unwilling to do much about it. France, another transgressor, was unapologetic about its persistently high budget deficit.

It was difficult for the Commission, the guardian of EU orthodoxy, to uphold the Stability and Growth Pact after the Council blocked its effort in February 2002 to issue a formal "early warning" to Germany and after Commission president Romano Prodi announced in October 2002 that the pact was "stupid."[30] Called to account before the EP, Prodi explained that the pact seemed unsuited to the straitened economic circumstances of the time. With falling growth and rising unemployment, governments should be in a position to raise spending and borrow money rather than having to abide by the strictures of the pact. Prodi's pronouncement, as well as French and German disregard for the pact, undermined the credibility of EMU and offended countries that had taken painful political steps in the 1990s to impose fiscal discipline.

EMU was never intended to be an end in itself but a means toward the greater end of increasing productivity and growth, and providing more jobs. By the early 2000s those objectives seemed elusive. Recession in the United States and uncertainty following the September 2001 terrorist attacks contributed to a gloomy economic outlook. Nevertheless, Germany availed itself of the opportunity presented by EMU to undertake badly needed labor-market reforms, which began to pay off later in the decade. As the engine of the eurozone's economy, only Germany had the potential to drive the region out of recession.

Britain remained outside the eurozone, despite Blair's hopes of bringing it in. Apart from no longer being in the exchange rate mechanism, Britain easily met the criteria for membership. Gordon Brown, Britain's chancellor of the exchequer and Blair's rival within the Labour Party, set criteria of his own for the British economy to meet before accepting the euro, and the government promised to hold a referendum before entering Stage Three of EMU. Although Blair argued the case for EMU on economic grounds, he had a compelling political reason to support it: only by adopting the euro, Blair believed, would Britain ever punch with its full weight in the EU.

Internal Affairs

The launch of the EU in 1993 represented continuity as well as change. Work continued in a variety of policy areas, many of which faced new challenges arising from a host of internal and external developments. Governments and EU institutions grappled with important administrative issues separate from the treaty-based reforms negotiated in the years following implementation of the Maastricht Treaty.

Policies

Though preoccupied with EMU and enlargement, governments and EU institutions in the post-Maastricht period were immersed in a host of policy initiatives, such as strengthening the single market program, promoting economic modernization and reform, bolstering the CAP and cohesion policy, and intensifying cooperation in the area of justice and home affairs.

Economic integration, modernization, and employment. EMU was one element of a multifaceted approach to promoting growth and employment. Other elements included the single market program, a revamped social policy, and coordination of member states' employment policies.

Consolidating the single market was a fundamental objective of the new EU and a cornerstone of the EU's approach to economic modernization. Important breakthroughs in the 1990s involved existing and new proposals, including legislation in the areas of product standards, innovative technologies, and intellectual property rights. Liberalization of the energy and telecommunications sectors, excluded from the original single market program, finally came onto the agenda.

The success of the single market depended in large part on the transposition of EU directives into national law within a prescribed period, and the enforcement of them by national authorities. Without transposition and enforcement, the single market meant little in practice. Regardless of its waning political influence, the Commission pressed governments to improve their mixed records of transposition and enforcement. France, Greece, Italy, and Portugal were consistently among the laggards, with Euroskeptical Britain, Denmark, and Sweden steadfastly at the top of the league.

The Commission was equally forceful in the pursuit of competition policy, a necessary corollary to the single market program. Despite the Commission's vigilance, the problem of national subsidies (state aid) remained acute and continued to distort the single market. Although appreciating that subsidies were expensive, wasteful, and generally unavailing, national governments found it impossible to give them up. It was also difficult for the Commission to stamp them out, as legal action proved time-consuming and provoked a strong reaction from national capitals.

The Commission's antitrust authority stepped up its investigations into allegations of market abuses and restrictive practices by enterprises operating in the EU. As the number of mergers increased in the early 2000s following the introduction of the euro, the Commission's merger task force became more prominent and powerful. Although it blocked only a small number of mergers, the task force came under severe criticism from certain governments, multinationals, and outside governments for acting hastily and seemingly arbitrarily. The EU's lower court delivered a devastating blow against the Commission in October 2002 when, twice within a week, it overruled Commission decisions to block major mergers. While putting the Commission on the defensive, the court's rulings addressed procedural problems and did not question the importance of merger control for market integration in the EU.

Despite the EU's impressive record of staying the course on EMU and consolidating the single market, productivity in the EU remained relatively low and unemployment stubbornly high. Responding to rising concerns throughout the EU and eager to increase the Commission's role in coordinating economic policy, President Santer proposed in January 1996 a "confidence pact on employment." The purpose of the pact was to boost jobs by strengthening the single market, curbing state aid, improving vocational training, helping small and medium-sized enterprises, and funding trans-European networks (transport, telecommunications, and energy infrastructures).[31]

Unemployment rose higher on the EU's agenda when the Socialists in France and Labour in Britain won the elections of May 1997. At the insistence of the new French government, the European Council held a special summit on employment in November 1997, and agreed to a procedure whereby governments would submit national employment action plans for annual peer review. The European Council evaluated governments' annual employment plans for the first time at its summit in June 1998. A year later, the European Council adopted the European Employment Pact, which brought together efforts to coordinate economic policy and employment strategy, and to improve implementation of the single market program.

The EU's increasing emphasis on employment cast social policy in a new light. Support for old-fashioned social policy, with its intrusive legislation on the workplace, was already on the wane when eleven of the then twelve member states (Britain was the exception) added the social protocol to the Maastricht Treaty. With unemployment high throughout the EU, by the end of the 1990s the social protocol seemed a luxury that European business simply could not afford. Governments, including the French government, quietly acknowledged that the provisions of the social protocol risked making European business uncompetitive in the global economy, thereby undermining one of the core objectives of the single market. Even when Labour came to power in Britain in May 1997 and agreed to bring the protocol squarely into the EU, via the Amsterdam Treaty, governments continued to recast social policy as a means of promoting employment rather than making jobs more costly.

At a special summit in Lisbon in March 2000, the European Council sought to inject new life into economic reform and modernization in the face of intense global competition. Declaring that by 2010 the EU should become "the most competitive and dynamic knowledge-based economy in the world, capable of sustainable economic growth and more and better jobs and greater social cohesion," EU leaders set an ambitious goal of a 3 percent rate of annual growth and 20 million new jobs within a decade.[32] The so-called Lisbon strategy drew on a number of existing initiatives, ranging from completion of the single market, especially for telecommunications and financial services, to better education and training, to exploiting fully the economic potential of the Internet. Emulating the original single market program, the strategy set target dates for many of its objectives, and was to be implemented through a combination of legislation, benchmarking, and peer pressure. The European Council pledged to meet annually in the spring specifically to keep up the political pressure necessary to implement the strategy.

Yet the Lisbon strategy and other initiatives succeeded mostly in focusing political attention on the EU's economic problems without providing adequate solutions. Despite the single market and EMU, the EU and the eurozone remained a collection of separate and often dissimilar economies. Growth and job creation varied widely among member states. Some governments were more willing than others to undertake the painful steps necessary to improve economic performance. The situation in the EU as a whole did not seem conducive to achieving the laudable Lisbon goals.

Agriculture and cohesion. The CAP and cohesion policy continued to account for the bulk of EU expenditure. The prospect of Central and Eastern European enlargement affected both directly. Because the candidate countries were poor and had relatively large agricultural sectors, their participation in the CAP and cohesion policy on the same terms as those of the existing member states could have bankrupted the EU. Enlargement presented an opportunity for radical CAP and cohesion reform, although recipients of generous financial transfers from Brussels wanted to protect their share as much as possible.

Agriculture. Under pressure to curb surpluses and reduce trade-distorting subsidies in order to complete the Uruguay Round of the GATT, the Council agreed to major reform in May 1992. The MacSharry reforms, named after agriculture commissioner Ray MacSharry, broke the link between guaranteed prices and overproduction by shifting the basis of subsidies to direct payments to farmers. Ironically, the reformed CAP cost more than the original version, because of generous compensation offered to big farmers who otherwise would have experienced a sharp drop in income.

Widespread concern about food safety, following a number of scares in the mid-1990s, led to pressure for further CAP reform. At the same time, people became more critical of an agricultural policy that encouraged farmers to overproduce, regardless of the environmental consequences. Sensitive to consumer concerns and obliged under the terms of the Amsterdam Treaty to incorporate environmental protection "into the definition and implementation of Community policies and activities . . . with a view to promoting sustainable development," the EU sought to cast the CAP in a better light. The main thrust of the agricultural provisions of *Agenda 2000*, the proposed EU budget for the period 2000–2006, was to continue the MacSharry reforms by shifting the basis of subsidies from price supports to direct payments. Under the aegis of *Agenda 2000*, which the European Council approved in March 1999, the EU also began to emphasize the importance of organic farming, agri-environmentalism, and rural development.[33]

The accession of ten predominantly agricultural Central and Eastern European countries in the middle of this century's first decade was bound to put the CAP under enormous financial pressure. Without a substantial budget increase, which was politically impossible, existing member states would see their share of CAP spending drop dramatically as funds flowed to the new member states. The response of the existing member states was to insist in the accession negotiations that the new member states should accept substantially smaller subsidies during a lengthy transition period. The rationale for this position was that a sudden influx of agricultural subsidies as high as those in Western Europe would cause massive economic dislocation and social resentment in the new member states. That may have been a legitimate concern, but the EU simply did not have enough money to subsidize Central and Eastern European farmers at a level to which Western European farmers had become accustomed. Led by Poland, the candidate countries resisted the EU's discriminatory position on the CAP. A tense standoff at the December 2002 Copenhagen summit ended when the Council presidency managed to eke out a little extra money for Central and Eastern European farmers, thereby bringing the accession negotiations definitively to an end.[34]

Regardless of changing preferences and priorities in Europe, and the impact of enlargement, the CAP survived in large part because of its mythical importance in the history of European integration. It was in the interest of France to cast the CAP as a fundamental element of the original Franco-German bargain for the European Community and as a symbol of enduring Franco-German rapprochement.[35] Sensitive as ever to French concerns,

Germany agreed to play along. At the same time, the domestic politics of the CAP made it impossible for France and difficult for Germany to countenance radical reform. Despite their declining numbers, farmers were too influential politically for either government to confront. External pressure for CAP reform, emanating from agricultural free-traders and the developing world, especially within the World Trade Organization (WTO), was insufficient to overcome the entrenched interests of EU farmers or jeopardize the deep-rooted relationship between France and Germany.

Cohesion. The Maastricht Treaty included a number of provisions that strengthened the EU's commitment to reducing social and economic disparities between richer and poorer countries and regions. The most important of these mandated a Cohesion Fund by the end of December 1993 to contribute to projects on the environment and transportation in member states with a per capita GDP of less than 90 percent of the EU average, and a program designed to achieve the EMU convergence criteria. Specifically, the Cohesion Fund was intended to help Greece, Ireland, Portugal, and Spain. Together with the existing structural funds, the Cohesion Fund represented a considerable commitment on the part of the EU's net contributors to the less developed member states.

The post-Maastricht budgetary package, which included a generous allocation for cohesion policy, covered the period 1993–1999. The battle for cohesion funding in the next multiannual financial framework, covering 2000–2006, was overshadowed by the needs of the candidate countries in Central and Eastern Europe and by developments within the EU. Having transformed itself into the Celtic Tiger, Ireland no longer qualified for generous cohesion funding. At the other end of the spectrum, Greece remained relatively impoverished despite having received massive financial assistance from the EU over a period of nearly twenty years. The net contributors to the budget did not want to continue subsidizing a country like Ireland, which was rapidly acquiring one of the highest rates of per capita GDP in the EU, and a country like Greece, which was notorious for squandering its share of the structural funds. With governments tightening their belts for monetary union, and ten needy Central and Eastern European countries knocking at the door, cohesion policy seemed ripe for reappraisal.

In its proposals for *Agenda 2000,* the Commission called for limited reform of cohesion policy but not for a significant cut in spending.[36] The proposed reforms included reducing the structural-fund objectives to three, covering low-income countries (where the bulk of the spending would go), declining industrial regions, and the development of human resources. In general, the Commission recommended reducing the proportion of the EU population covered by the structural funds from 51 percent to less than 40 percent. At the crucial European Council meeting on *Agenda 2000,* in

March 1999, EU leaders accepted most of the Commission's proposals. With enlargement still some time off, EU leaders deferred difficult budgetary decisions until the negotiations for the next financial framework, which would cover the period 2007–2013, when the demands of the new Central and Eastern European member states would be more pressing.[37]

The principle of cohesion policy remained uncontested in the enlarging EU. The problem was how to put that principle into practice. Despite bickering over the budget, a consensus emerged in the early 2000s that a combination of sound macroeconomic policies, a favorable international economic climate, generous financial transfers from Brussels, and closer coordination in the formulation and implementation of regional policy at the national and European levels was essential for economic development in the poor member states. Cohesion policy covered some of these elements; other EU policies touched on the rest.

An area of freedom, security, and justice. Responding to public concern about the security implications of deeper integration and accelerating globalization, governments strengthened their cooperation in the area of justice and home affairs. The Amsterdam Treaty contained a number of noteworthy developments in that regard. Thus member states agreed to shift all but police and judicial cooperation out of the intergovernmental pillar on justice and home affairs established by the Maastricht Treaty. They also agreed to bring the Schengen regime, the set of rules and regulations that facilitated unhindered cross-border travel among most member states, into the EU's legal framework. A protocol attached to the treaty provided for Schengen's incorporation into EU law, with special provisions for non-Schengen members Britain, Denmark, and Ireland.

In an effort to make the EU more responsive to citizens' concerns, member states pledged in the Amsterdam Treaty that, by 2004 at the latest, they would create "an area of freedom, security and justice, in which the free movement of persons is assured in conjunction with appropriate measures with respect to external border controls, asylum, immigration and the prevention and combating of crime."[38] In December 1998 the Council adopted an action plan to bring the area of freedom, security, and justice into existence. Finland identified justice and home affairs as a priority for its presidency during the second half of 1999 and organized a special summit on the subject in Tampere, in October. The summit produced a set of steps to give concrete meaning to the area of freedom, security, and justice. These included a common asylum and immigration policy; better administrative, judicial, and police cooperation to fight organized crime; and fair treatment of resident third-country nationals.[39]

Drawing on the experience of the single market, in March 2000 the Commission launched the first in a series of biannual "scoreboards" to monitor progress on the creation of the area of freedom, security, and justice and to pressure governments to act. A year later the Commission suggested supplementing EU legislation with a system of peer review for immigration and asylum policy, whereby the Council would adopt multiannual guidelines to be implemented through national action plans and monitored by the Commission. The launch in March 2001 of Eurojust, the EU body for criminal justice cooperation and coordination, was another example of the impetus provided by Tampere.

Nevertheless, progress on justice and home affairs was extremely mixed, given differences of political interest and administrative capacity in the enactment and implementation of relevant measures across the EU. The Belgian presidency produced a scathing progress report on the Tampere agenda in December 2001, especially in the area of immigration and asylum.[40] By that time, interest in the internal and international dimensions of justice and home affairs focused squarely on global terrorism, following the attacks on the United States in September 2001.

Although the atrocities of September 11 were directed against the United States, they were mostly planned in Europe. Indeed, Europeans appreciated that the new wave of global terrorism was as much a threat to their own countries and societies as it was to the United States. There was an obvious need for close cooperation among member states and other like-minded governments on antiterrorism measures. The most immediate impact was to boost cooperation within the EU and between the EU and the United States on issues such as extradition and arrest warrants.[41]

Economic insecurity in the form of rising unemployment caused further disquiet. It was easy for right-wing demagogues to blame the situation partly on illegal immigration. The success of far-right parties in Austria, Belgium, Denmark, and France in the early 2000s showed that their message resonated among the electorate. Enlargement was a predictable target, as it was easy to exploit popular fears of unrestricted flows into Western Europe of allegedly impoverished and unscrupulous Central and Eastern Europeans. The well-publicized activities of organized criminals made Europeans feel increasingly insecure in the first decade of the 2000s.

Responding to such concerns, the EU allowed the existing member states, under the terms of the accession treaties, to impose a delay of seven years on the applicability to the new member states of the provisions for the free movement of people, a cornerstone of the single market and a basic objective of the EU itself. The EU also worked with the candidate countries to shore up the security of their eastern borders in order to ensure the integrity of the EU's external frontiers.

Insofar as Europeans were amenable to deeper integration in the early 2000s, it was certainly in the area of internal security. Accordingly, the EU emphasized security more than freedom and justice in its pursuit of the Amsterdam objectives for justice and home affairs. Even so, many Europeans saw the EU as a poor provider of security or even as a cause of insecurity, for the simple reason that the process of European integration undermined member states' abilities to act independently. Here was a vivid example of the difficulty that the EU faced in meeting popular expectations and communicating undoubted achievements of collective action.

Institutional Arrangements

At the same time that governments were deeply engaged in the protracted process of treaty change throughout the late 1990s and early 2000s, the Commission, the Council, and the Parliament undertook considerable internal reform. This was partly a response to the anticipated impact of enlargement, but was also the result of intra-institutional problems and interinstitutional conflicts.

The Commission

Jacques Delors was the most successful Commission president in EU history. By the end of his tenure, however, the Commission was in disarray. Delors's disregard for fellow commissioners, disdain for many senior officials, and aggrandizement of power in his *cabinet* (private office) fueled resentment within the ranks. With the sudden rise in the Commission's responsibilities and no commensurate increase in its size or efficiency, many officials feared that the institution would self-destruct. During the Maastricht ratification crisis, when the Commission unfairly came under widespread attack, the institution's morale reached rock-bottom.

The Commission's organizational problems were rooted in the national governments' determination to retain as much control as possible over the Commission and were compounded by successive enlargements, the proliferation of portfolios for new commissioners, and the excessive power of the *cabinets*. Delors made a belated effort to streamline the Commission, but his management style only made matters worse. As a result, Jacques Santer, Delors's successor, put internal reform at the top of his agenda, and launched a series of programs for organizational change in the late 1990s.

The resignation crisis. Ironically for a president genuinely interested in internal reform, Santer will forever be associated with the Commission's enforced resignation in March 1999, a piece of political theater that drew massive media attention.[42] At issue was not just alleged corruption and maladministration, but an intense struggle between the Commission and the EP, which profoundly recast their relationship with each other. The Commission was always accountable to the EP, which could vote the college out of office by a two-thirds majority of its total membership. Such a high threshold reflected the seriousness of the censure procedure, long known as the "nuclear option" in Commission-EP relations. In keeping with the doctrine of mutual assured destruction, the Commission presumed that the EP would never press the button.

The increasingly powerful EP was not spoiling for a fight with the Commission, but would not back down should a confrontation occur. The conflict came in early 1999, following a series of skirmishes during the previous twelve months, with the EP increasingly critical of the Commission's management of the budget and at one point threatened the Commission with censure. The EP held its fire, but MEPs became angrier throughout the year as additional allegations emerged of fraud and financial mismanagement in the Commission.

Santer was never accused of financial impropriety, but he failed to act decisively against the commissioners who were. The most conspicuous was Edith Cresson, a former prime minister of France who allegedly awarded a contract to a friend who was unqualified to carry out the work. The EP demanded Cresson's resignation. Cresson refused to step down, with the French government backing her to the end and Santer lacking the authority to dismiss her.

The prospect of a Commission-EP showdown kept Brussels in a tizzy. There was little public sympathy for either of the protagonists, although the EP held the moral high ground against an apparently feckless and wasteful Commission. Santer, lacking flair and largely unknown outside Brussels, was an easy target for media and public scorn. Some national politicians, eager to avoid an interinstitutional confrontation, urged MEPs to drop the matter. Center-right politicians were especially concerned about the vulnerability of Santer, a Christian Democrat, to partisan attacks from the Socialist Group. By late 1998, however, the issue transcended party politics. Regardless of party affiliation, most MEPs were too incensed to back down and wanted to put the Commission in its place.

Nevertheless, the Commission escaped censure in January 1999 when the EP failed to muster the necessary two-thirds majority. The EP decided instead, with the Commission's agreement, to establish a committee of independent experts to investigate the allegations. The committee's report, published in March 1999, was damning. One widely reported verdict could not have been more injurious: "It is becoming difficult to find anyone [in the Commission] who has even the slightest sense of responsibility."[43] Once the EP made it clear that the Commission would not survive another censure motion, Santer accepted the inevitable and the Commission resigned as a body.

Far from being the result of a calculated parliamentary maneuver, the Commission's collapse was the culmination of a series of mistakes and misjudgments on both sides. But the widespread perception was that the EP, acting strategically, had finally come of age and asserted its authority over the feckless Commission. As perception shapes political reality, the events of early 1999 represented a major advance for the EP. In principle, the Commission was always accountable to the Parliament; in practice, it now had to behave accordingly.

The confrontation between the Commission and the EP may have strengthened the EU political system by striking a new institutional balance and forcing the Commission to undertake serious internal reform. Yet it weakened public support for the EU as a whole. However entertaining, interinstitutional squabbles in Brussels and Strasbourg seemed irrelevant to the real concerns of most Europeans. Certainly, the EP did not reap the reward for its victory that it most coveted: a large turnout in the June 1999 elections.

Postresignation reform. Building on work begun by the old Commission, Romano Prodi, the new president, launched a "root and branch" overhaul of the Brussels bureaucracy. His goal was to alter not only administrative procedures and practices but also the culture of the Commission itself. The Prodi reformation included strengthening the recently approved codes of conduct for commissioners and senior officials, launching a major shakeup of the directorates-general, and radically reorganizing the commissioners' portfolios.[44] One seemingly unimportant but highly symbolic change was that directorates-general, instead of being known by number, as had been the case throughout the EU's history, henceforth became known by function (thus "DG VI" became "DG Agriculture").

Prodi chose Neil Kinnock, ironically a holdover from the Santer Commission, to head a new reform portfolio. Kinnock, a loquacious former leader of the British Labour Party, threw himself into a difficult task. Following widespread consultations, Kinnock released a white paper on administrative reform in March 2000, on the basis of which the Commission adopted a detailed "roadmap."[45] This included new methods of auditing and financial control; a system of activity-based management (intended to match responsibilities and resources); and new recruitment, promotion, and disciplinary procedures.

Prodi's efforts to reform the Commission were urgent and important, but not entirely successful. Although they moved the Commission in the right direction, the Prodi reforms faced several entrenched obstacles. One was the inertia and even outright opposition of some parts of the bureaucracy. Prodi and Kinnock dared to question EU officials' generous pay and pensions and to link remuneration to performance. That stirred up a hornets' nest and provoked a number of work stoppages and strikes. Another, more serious consideration was governments' reluctance to give up their stranglehold on key aspects of the Commission's staff policy. Despite rhetorical flourishes to the contrary, governments jealously guarded what they saw as their right to influence the appointment of senior officials, a not-so-subtle way of pushing national interests in the EU.

The Prodi reforms, like the Santer reforms before them, drew on British and Scandinavian models of public administration, in contrast to the French model on which the Commission had largely been built. The French government and many French nationals in the Commission disliked the reform strategy's implicit rejection of the Commission's original organizational principles and ethos, which accentuated a general unease in France about the direction of European integration and the apparent decline of French influence in the EU.[46]

The Commission's reform strategy was a long-term undertaking driven by the EP's exposure of corruption and maladministration rather than by anticipation of the disruptive impact of enlargement. Indeed, the white paper on reform hardly mentioned enlargement. Nevertheless, the post-resignation reform effort helped prepare the Commission for what lay ahead.

The Council

Governments began a less far-reaching reform of the Council at about the same time as the Commission's resignation, based a report from the Council secretariat.[47] The report's recommendations, which the European Council approved, included strengthening the coordinating role of the foreign ministers, reducing the number of Council configurations, streamlining legislative procedures, and improving preparatory work at all levels. The feasibility of the rotating presidency came increasingly into question as enlargement loomed, but that was an issue requiring treaty change. The EU acquired a standing presidency of the European Council and of the Foreign Affairs Council in December 2009, when the Lisbon Treaty entered into force (see Chapter 9).

The Parliament

Despite having encouraged both the Commission and the Council to undertake reform, the Parliament was slow to put its own house in order. MEPs acknowledged the need for reform, including better organization of plenary sessions, livelier debates, rationalization of voting procedures, and a reduction in the number of amendments to draft legislation, but were reluctant to do anything about it. Only on the eve of enlargement did the EP launch a serious reform program. Thereafter it raced against time to meet the administrative and organizational challenge of accommodating 162 new members, who arrived first as observers, then (in May 2004) as MEPs.

External Challenges

The EU was a major actor on the world stage. Its weight and stature as an international economic entity were striking. Together with the United States, the EU dominated the WTO. Just as the conclusion of the Uruguay Round of the GATT in the early 1990s depended on the United States and the EU reaching a deal on agriculture, the launch of the Doha Round of the WTO a decade later hinged on the United States and the EU reaching agreement on the agenda. The United States and the EU were also the principal parties in most of the cases brought before the WTO dispute-settlement body.

The EU extended its global economic reach by negotiating or renegotiating a variety of trade and aid pacts. These ranged from the Cotonou agreement of June 2000 with over eighty African, Caribbean, and Pacific countries, which replaced the long-standing (and thrice-revised) Lomé agreement, to a free trade agreement with Mexico, which came into effect in March 2001. The EU institutionalized its relationship with the United States first with the Transatlantic Declaration of 1990, then with the New Transatlantic Agenda of December 1995. EU competition policy had a significant international impact. As well as affecting large foreign companies operating, or hoping to operate, in the EU, it was an integral part of many EU trade agreements. The EU became a leading player in international environmental policy, especially after the United States abandoned the field by abruptly rejecting the Kyoto Protocol in 2001. Finally, the euro added luster to the EU's international image, at least before the onset of the eurozone crisis.

Common Foreign and Security Policy

In the realm of foreign policy, security, and defense, by contrast, the EU remained relatively weak.[48] The common foreign and security policy, an important innovation in the Maastricht Treaty, got off to a slow start. The treaty provided for common positions and joint actions that could be implemented by qualified majority voting if adopted first by unanimity. The distinction between common positions and joint actions was unclear, and the decisionmaking process was confusing. The Council found it difficult to break the habit of deciding everything by unanimity.

These procedural problems disguised deep differences among governments on a number of foreign policy issues, the most important of which in the 1990s was the series of wars in the former Yugoslavia. Serbia's belligerence undermined the EU's early mediation efforts. With few powers of persuasion and with member states unwilling to intervene militarily, EU involvement was reduced to providing humanitarian assistance, although individual countries sent troops under UN auspices to protect so-called safe areas.

The inadequacy of the recently launched CFSP became obvious in April 1994 with the establishment of a Contact Group, consisting of Britain, France, Germany, Russia, and the United States, to "manage" the Yugoslav situation. Although the three EU countries in the group (later joined by Italy) supposedly represented the EU as a whole, in fact they were included because of their size and influence and represented only themselves. The establishment of the Contact Group engendered resentment among other member states, especially those (such as the Netherlands) with sizable contingents of troops in Bosnia.

The war in Bosnia reached its denouement in the summer and fall of 1995, when Serbian atrocities in Sarajevo and Srebrenica finally compelled the United States to act militarily. Heavy NATO bombardment of Serbian positions brought the Serbs to their senses. The United States followed up diplomatically by convening a peace conference in Dayton, Ohio, at which a settlement was hammered out. In order to emphasize the transatlantic nature of the peace initiative, the Dayton Accords were formally signed in Paris in November 1995. Yet this move could not disguise the predominantly US stamp on the peace process and the failure of EU efforts to end the fighting in the former Yugoslavia during the preceding four years.

Public frustration with the EU's ineffectualness in Bosnia focused the EU's attention on the need to develop a more effective means of acting outside its borders. As a result, governments revised procedural aspects of the CFSP in the Amsterdam Treaty. Though an improvement, the changes were not as far-reaching as the EU's supranational institutions and more federal-minded member states had hoped. They included new policy instruments, greater use of qualified majority voting, agreement on "constructive abstention" (by member states not wanting to participate in a particular initiative), and the establishment of a Policy Planning and Early Warning Unit in the Council secretariat. The treaty also established the position of High Representative for the Common Foreign and Security Policy, to represent the EU externally.

In an inspired move, in June 1999 the European Council appointed Javier Solana the first High Representative. Solana's experience as secretary-general of NATO, which brought him into close contact with makers of US foreign and defense policy, was an invaluable asset for the EU. As intended, Solana personified EU foreign and defense policy cooperation. Yet his authority was moral rather than real. Procedural weaknesses continued to undermine the effectiveness of the EU's external action: Solana was the servant of the presidency; as a senior official he was inferior in rank to the foreign minister of even the smallest member state; and the relationship between his position and that of the commissioner for external relations was unclear.

Military Capability

Chastened by the EU's experience in Yugoslavia and aware of the waning interest of the United States in European security, British prime minister Tony Blair proposed developing an EU military capability in discussions with Jacques Chirac at a bilateral summit in St. Malo in December 1998. With Britain having opted out of the euro, Blair saw defense cooperation as a means of giving Britain a leadership role in the EU. Chirac was happy to collaborate with Britain on the pursuit of what was, after all, a long-standing French objective: a European military force.[49]

Kosovo. The need for such a capability became painfully clear the following year, when the EU was unable to act swiftly and effectively to halt Serbian assaults on the Muslim population in Kosovo. The Serbs ended their aggression only when confronted by a sustained NATO bombardment and the threat of a NATO invasion. Although many EU member states participated in the NATO action and in peacekeeping operations in postwar Kosovo, the EU had neither the means nor the will to act decisively during the Kosovo crisis.

The short war over Kosovo was decisive in pushing the EU to develop the military means to conduct peacekeeping operations, albeit along intergovernmental lines. Meeting in Cologne in June 1999, the European Council therefore launched the European security and defense policy, under the auspices of the CFSP. According to the Cologne Declaration, this would represent "a new step in the construction of the European Union."[50]

Six months later, at the Helsinki summit in December 1999, the European Council specified what the EU's military capacity would be: a force of up to 60,000 personnel, with the necessary command, control, and intelligence capabilities, able to deploy within sixty days and stay in the field for at least a year.[51] The EU established a number of institutions to manage its emerging security and defense policy: the Political and Security Committee, the Military Committee, and the Military Staff. In November 2000, member states held a conference on commitment capabilities at which they pledged resources to meet the "headline goals" agreed to at the Helsinki summit. At the same time, the EU effectively took over the structure and responsibilities of the Western European Union, the long-standing organization for intra-European defense cooperation.

The development of a security and defense policy, with an operational arm, preoccupied the EU in the early 2000s. Despite NATO's support of the initiative, the EU and NATO had difficulty sorting out a political-military relationship. Reconciling Turkey, a large NATO member and EU candidate, to the new arrangement was also tricky politically. The biggest challenge, however, was matching the rhetoric of closer security and defense cooperation with the reality of strained member state budgets. Despite their pledges at the capability conference, governments generally reduced military spending during the straitened economic circumstances of the early 2000s.

The terrorist attacks on the United States in September 2001 gave a tremendous boost to the CFSP and to military and defense cooperation in the EU. The EU immediately issued a declaration under the CFSP condemning the attacks and held an extraordinary meeting of the European Council to express solidarity with the United States. More concretely, the EU was instrumental, through the CFSP, in helping to broker the UN-backed agreement on political transition in Afghanistan, signed in Bonn in December 2001.

The United States did not seek European military assistance immediately after the September 2001 attacks. Nevertheless, the EU continued to develop a military identity and capacity, taking over most of the functions and bodies of the Western European Union in 2002. At the same time, EU defense ministers began to meet regularly on the margins of the Council of Ministers.

Iraq. Even as they called for closer defense cooperation within the EU, Britain and France differed sharply over how to deal with Iraq. Anglo-French tension escalated in late of 2002, as the United States prepared openly to invade the country. Blair backed the United States unreservedly; Chirac and Gerhard Schröder, who exploited the issue for electoral gain in September 2002, opposed it wholeheartedly. That divergence set the stage for a bitter altercation among member states (and soon-to-be member states) that jeopardized recent progress on security and defense policy cooperation.

Efforts by EU leaders to show unity at an extraordinary meeting of the European Council in February 2003, on the eve of the US invasion, failed spectacularly. The Panglossian statements of Romano Prodi, who declared after the summit that "Europe is united and its voice must be heard," could not disguise the extent of the EU's disarray.[52] Solana was more realistic, observing that "the EU still does not have a genuine common external policy, it has several. One day there is an agreement and the next day this is torn to shreds."[53] Soon after the US invasion, the leaders of France, Germany, Belgium, and Luxembourg, in a fit of pique, held a summit among themselves on defense cooperation, to which Britain and other pro-US member states were pointedly not invited. The EU's fledgling security and defense policy appeared to be in tatters.

Appalled by this turn of events, Solana struggled in the aftermath of the invasion to repair the damage within the EU and between leading EU member states and the United States. This was the background to the European Security Strategy, which Solana presented to the European Council in June 2003. The strategy, which EU leaders endorsed six months later, called for an assertive EU foreign and security policy, including the possible use of military force, and identified three main threats to European and global security: terrorism, weapons of mass destruction, and the consequences of failed states.[54] The new strategy veered toward the US view of post–September 11 security challenges, although it strongly endorsed the multilateral international system and the fundamental role of the UN. Therefore, it helped to reconcile divergent views within the EU and among the Europeans and Americans while salvaging the EU's incipient security and defense policy.

Even as the fallout from Iraq unfolded, the EU began to conduct a number of significant peacekeeping operations. It launched a police mission in Bosnia in January 2003 and undertook its first military operation in

March 2003, taking over from a NATO force in neighboring Macedonia. In June 2003 the EU deployed a French-led peacekeeping mission, authorized by the UN Security Council, in the Democratic Republic of Congo. The following year, the EU launched a military mission, its biggest to date, with over 7,000 troops, to replace NATO's Stabilization Force in Bosnia. All of these operations took place despite the highly visible sniping among national leaders over the invasion of Iraq.

Nevertheless the experience of Iraq, and of Yugoslavia before it, demonstrated the limits to establishing a truly effective EU security and defense policy. Member states had relatively limited military capabilities, and many were reluctant to use whatever military force they possessed. Few governments seriously considered handing over responsibility for defense policy to a European supranational authority.

A Highly Political Union

In the decade following implementation of the Maastricht Treaty, the EU became a highly political entity, both in substance and in the way that citizens perceived and responded to it. The Maastricht Treaty endowed the EU with political objectives and constitutional characteristics, such as the concept of EU citizenship; the upholding of democracy, human rights, and national identities; and the federal principle of subsidiarity. The Amsterdam Treaty went further. It included a key provision stating that the "Union is founded on the principles of liberty, democracy, respect for human rights and fundamental freedoms, and the rule of law, principles which are common to the member states."[55] That short treaty change was highly significant. Whereas the EU and the communities that preceded it were political constructions, governments had not explicitly imbued them with core political values. The Amsterdam Treaty clearly stated what those values were.

The treaty also included a provision to sanction member states that deviated from the EU's core values. Should it determine "the existence of a serious and persistent breach . . . of principles mentioned [in the treaty]," the European Council could decide by a qualified majority "to suspend certain of the rights deriving from the application of [the treaty] to the Member State in question, including the voting right of the government of that Member State in the Council."[56] Governments drafted this provision with the Central and Eastern European applicants in mind. Indeed, it was one of the few provisions of the Amsterdam Treaty that owed its origin to impending enlargement.

Not long after the Amsterdam Treaty came into effect, in Austria the Christian Democratic Party and the far-right Freedom Party opened negotiations to form a government. Jörg Haider, leader of the Freedom Party, was a demagogue who exploited racism and xenophobia, especially in the context of EU enlargement. Appalled by the prospect of having Haider's party in the Austrian government and emboldened by the Amsterdam Treaty, most of the other governments threatened unspecified action if the Christian Democrats and the Freedom Party formed a coalition. When the parties went ahead regardless, the other governments introduced mild political sanctions against Austria.

What began with great fanfare in February 2000 when the new Austrian government was formed, ended in embarrassment in September 2000 when the other governments let the matter drop. It was obvious even at the beginning of the imbroglio that Haider was not Hitler and that Austria at the dawn of the twenty-first century could not be compared with Austria in the 1930s. More to the point, it was also obvious that the new Austrian government was not endangering the principles of liberty, democracy, and respect for fundamental human rights. Soon after coming to power, the Austrian government published a program unequivocally endorsing European integration and condemning racism. A committee of "wise men," appointed by the other governments to investigate the political situation in Austria, reported in the summer of 2000 that minority, immigrant, and refugee rights were as well protected there as anywhere in the EU.[57]

As the situation in Austria unfolded, representatives of EU and national institutions negotiated the Charter of Fundamental Rights, a catalog of EU civil and economic rights proposed by the German government in 1999 during the celebrations for the fiftieth anniversary of the German constitution.[58] Negotiations on the charter proceeded swiftly and relatively smoothly in 2000. The charter was generally uncontroversial, although the British government and some business interests objected to the inclusion of some social rights that could increase labor costs. The European Council "solemnly proclaimed" adoption of the charter in Nice in December 2000 but deferred discussion of its constitutional status until the next intergovernmental conference.

Public Reaction

As the Austrian case showed, by the early 2000s the EU had become pervasive in the lives of ordinary Europeans, politically as well as economically. The launch of the third stage of EMU in January 1999 was an event of profound political and not just economic importance, which many people came to appreciate only when the new currency began to circulate in January 2002. Despite the successful launch of the euro, many people regretted the loss of their national currencies. At the same time, EU regulatory policies seemed to cause greater public irritation, which unsympathetic media sources eagerly exploited.

Alongside a growing reaction against the EU's rising political profile and way of doing business, there was continuing concern about the supposed democratic deficit. Strictly speaking, the EU's institutions were accountable: people could vote directly for national governments, which formed the Council of Ministers and European Council (of national leaders), and for the EP, which had considerable budgetary and decisionmaking power as well as oversight authority. Though unelected, the Commission was accountable to the EP, as the Commission's enforced resignation demonstrated. The European Court and the ECB were unelected, independent, and powerful, but that was the norm for supreme courts and central banks in most liberal democracies. Moreover, in response to the enduring democratic deficit (or to people's perception of it), governments included provisions in the Amsterdam Treaty to strengthen subsidiarity, increase openness and transparency, and increase involvement of national parliaments in EU affairs.

Such measures, which may have improved the quality of EU governance, failed to overcome public unease about the EU itself. The Commission's resignation merely reaffirmed the public's low opinion of the EU's executive body. Whereas the EP trumpeted the outcome as evidence of its ability to hold the Commission to account, most Europeans were unimpressed. For many of them, the EP epitomized all that was wrong with the EU. MEPs' peripatetic existence, moving them monthly between Brussels and Strasbourg, and their reportedly lavish lifestyles, brought the EP and the EU as a whole into disrepute. Far from flocking to the polls in the aftermath of the Commission's censure, even fewer voters (49.9 percent) turned out in the June 1999 EP elections than in any of the four previous direct elections.[59] The disgraced Commission's continuation in office for a further six months, until a new Commission finally took over, increased public cynicism about the EU.

Besides disliking the EU's institutions, many Europeans resented what they saw as the EU's intrusiveness and heavy-handedness. However exceptional, the situation in Austria added fuel to the fire. Although not an official EU act, the decision to impose sanctions deeply offended many people. Some countries were more zealous than others in denouncing the new Austrian government. The governments of Belgium and France, countries with popular far-right parties of their own, seized on the situation in Austria for domestic political purposes. Most Europeans despised Haider and his ilk, but many disapproved of what looked like unwarranted interference in Austrian politics and an exploitation of the situation there by some member states.

Fear of Referendums

The Austrian affair demonstrated a regrettable consequence of the popular backlash against the EU: governments' fear of holding referendums on EU-related issues. When the Austrian government announced in May 2000 that it would hold a referendum on EU participation unless the other member states came up with a concrete proposal to lift the sanctions, Austria's EU partners soon backed down. As the Austrian government and others knew full well, the outcome of the referendum could have been a major embarrassment for the EU. The German government, which in its 1998 election manifesto called for more referendums as a matter of principle, shied away from a suggestion that it hold a referendum on enlargement, because it feared that the result would be negative. While striving to improve the EU's accountability in so many other ways, national leaders knew that rampant public unease, combined with enlargement fatigue and incipient "Euro-fatigue," made it risky for them to hold referendums on the EU.[60]

The result of the Irish referendum on the Nice Treaty in June 2001 reinforced the point. There were many non-EU-related reasons why Irish voters rejected the treaty, but the result buttressed the perception of declining popular support throughout the EU for initiatives of a quasi-constitutional kind. The Irish government gave the electorate a chance to redeem itself in a second referendum in October 2002. The government characterized the question as a simple choice between opposing or supporting enlargement, and EU institutions and governments castigated the Irish as ingrates. Whether out of conviction or contrition, more people turned out to vote, and a majority endorsed the treaty.

EU leaders had argued that it was undemocratic for Ireland's electorate to torpedo a treaty already ratified by the other member states, especially as the turnout in the first referendum was a paltry 35 percent. Many Irish people, regardless of their position on the treaty, thought that it was undemocratic of the Irish and other EU governments to disregard the result of the first referendum and insist on holding a second. The EU's handling of the issue reinforced a popular perception in Ireland and abroad of the EU as arrogant and high-handed.

As noted earlier, the Constitutional Convention of 2002–2003 sought not only to improve the EU's effectiveness but also to strengthen its political character. The Constitutional Treaty, which came out of the convention and the subsequent intergovernmental conference, emphasized and enhanced the EU's political nature. The recent history of treaty reform had alerted governments to the risks of entrusting ratification to ordinary Europeans. The fate of the Constitutional Treaty would confirm their fears.

Notes

1. On the 1995 enlargement, see Günter Bischof, Anton Pelinka, and Michael Gehler, eds., *Austria in the European Union* (New York: Transaction, 2002); Max Jacobson, *Finland in the New Europe* (Westport: Praeger, 1998); Lene Hansen and Ole Waever, *European Integration and National Identity: The Challenge of the Nordic States* (London: Routledge, 2002); Sieglinde Gstöhl, *Reluctant Europeans: Norway, Sweden, and Switzerland in the Process of Integration* (Boulder: Lynne Rienner, 2002); John Redmond, *The 1995 Enlargement of the European Union* (Aldershot: Ashgate, 1997).

2. See *Agence Europe,* March 30, 1994, pp. 1–2.

3. On Central and Eastern European enlargement, see Graham Avery and Fraser Cameron, *The Enlargement of the European Union* (Sheffield: Sheffield University Press, 1998); Stuart Croft, John Redmond, G. Wyn Rees, and Mark Webber, *The Enlargement of Europe* (Manchester: Manchester University Press, 1999); Michael J. Baun, *A Wider Europe: The Process and Politics of European Union Enlargement* (Lanham: Rowman and Littlefield, 2000); Alan Mayhew, *Recreating Europe: The European Union's Policy Towards Central and Eastern Europe,* 2nd ed. (Cambridge: Cambridge University Press, 2014).

4. See, for instance, Robert Cutler, "Harmonizing EEC-CMEA Relations: Never the Twain Shall Meet?" *International Affairs* 63, no. 2 (Spring 1987), pp. 259–270.

5. Bulletin EC 6-1993.

6. Bulletin EU 12-1994.

7. Cannes European Council, June 26–27, 1995, Presidency Conclusions.

8. Commission, *Agenda 2000: For a Stronger and Wider Union* (Brussels, August 1997).

9. Bulletin EU 12-1997.

10. Bulletin EU 12-2002.

11. On the impact of EU conditionality, see Heather Grabbe, *The EU's Transformative Power: Europeanization Through Conditionality in Central and Eastern Europe* (Basingstoke: Palgrave Macmillan, 2006); Milada Anna Vachudova, *Europe Undivided: Democracy, Leverage, and Integration After Communism* (Oxford: Oxford University Press, 2005).

12. See Angelos Sepos, *The Europeanization of Cyprus: Polity, Policies, and Politics* (Basingstoke: Palgrave Macmillan, 2008), pp. 34–46.

13. On the Amsterdam intergovernmental conference and treaty, see Geoffrey Edwards and Alfred Pijpers, *The Politics of European Treaty Reform: The 1996 Intergovernmental Conference and Beyond* (London: Pinter, 1997); Anna-Carin Svensson, *In the Service of the European Union: The Role of the Presidency in Negotiating the Amsterdam Treaty, 1995–1997* (Uppsala: Acta Universitatis, 2000); Jörg Monar and Wolfgang Wessels, eds., *The European Union After the Treaty of Amsterdam* (London: Continuum, 2001); Finn Laursen, ed., *The Amsterdam Treaty: National Preference Formation, Interstate Bargaining, and Outcome* (Odense: Odense University Press, 2002); Bobby McDonagh, *Original Sin in a Brave New World: The Paradox of Europe—An Account of the Negotiation of the Treaty of Amsterdam* (Dublin: Institute for European Affairs, 1998).

14. Christian Democratic Union/Christian Social Union Group in the Lower House, "Reflections on European Policy," Bonn, September 1, 1994.

15. John Major, "Europe: A Future That Works," William and Mary Lecture, Leiden University, September 7, 1994.

16. Report of the Reflection Group, "A Strategy for Europe: An Annotated Agenda," Brussels, December 5, 1995.

17. See Alexander Stubb, *Negotiating Flexibility in the European Union: Amsterdam, Nice, and Beyond* (Basingstoke: Palgrave Macmillan, 2003), pp. 58–105.

18. On the intergovernmental conference and the ensuing Nice Treaty, see M. Andenas and J. A. Usher, *The Treaty of Nice and Beyond: Enlargement and Constitutional Reform* (Portland: Hart, 2003); D. Galloway, *The Treaty of Nice and Beyond: Reality and Illusions of Power in the EU* (Sheffield: Sheffield Academic, 2001); Finn Laursen, ed., *The Treaty of Nice: Actor Preferences, Bargaining, and Institutional Choice* (Leiden: Brill, 2006).

19. Mark Gray and Alexander Stubb, "The Treaty of Nice: Negotiating a Poisoned Chalice?" in *Journal of Common Market Studies: Annual Review of the European Union 2000–2001,* p. 13.

20. Joschka Fischer, "From Confederacy to Federation: Thoughts on the Finality of European Integration," speech at Humboldt University, Berlin, May 12, 2000.

21. For an assessment of national contributions to the debate, see Simon Serfaty, ed., *The Finality Debate and Its National Dimensions* (Washington, DC: Center for Strategic and International Studies, 2002).

22. Bulletin EU 12-2000.

23. Laeken Declaration, Bulletin EU 12-2001.

24. On the conduct and outcome of the convention, see Erik Oddvar Eriksen, John Erik Fossum, and Agustín José Meníndez, eds., *Developing a Constitution for Europe* (London: Routledge, 2004); Finn Laursen, ed., *The Rise and Fall of the EU's Constitutional Treaty* (Leiden: Brill, 2008); Peter Norman, *Accidental Constitution: The Making of Europe's Constitutional Treaty,* 2nd ed. (Brussels: EuroComment, 2005).

25. See Peter B. Kenen, *Economic and Monetary Union in Europe: Moving Beyond Maastricht* (Cambridge: Cambridge University Press, 1995).

26. Amsterdam European Council, "Presidency Conclusions," Bulletin EC 6-1997, point 1.1.10.

27. Commission, *European Economy,* supp. A, no. 10 (October 1997).

28. Treaty on European Union, available at http://www.europa.eu.int/abc/obj /treaties/en/entoc01.htm.

29. See Lionel Barber, "The Euro: Single Currency, Multiple Injuries," *Financial Times,* June 10, 1999, p. 10.

30. See *Financial Times,* October 10, 2002, p. 1.

31. Philippe Pochet, Jo Antoons, and Cécil Barbier, "European Briefing: Employment," *Journal of European Social Policy* 6, no. 4 (1996), pp. 329–335.

32. Bulletin EU 3-2000.

33. Bulletin EU 3-1999.

34. Bulletin EU 12-2002. See also Derek Baker, "Agriculture in the EU's Eastern Enlargement: The Current Status for CEECs," *Intereconomics,* January–February 2003, pp. 19–30.

35. See John T. S. Keeler, "Agricultural Power in the European Community: Explaining the Fate of CAP and GATT Negotiations," *Comparative Politics* 28, no. 2 (January 1996), pp. 127–150.

36. Commission, *Agenda 2000.*

37. Bulletin EU 3-1999.

38. Amsterdam Treaty, available at http://europa.eu.int/scadplus/leg/en/s50000.htm.

39. Bulletin EC 10-1999.

40. Council Document 14926/01.

41. See Monica den Boer and Jörg Monar, "11 September and the Challenge of Global Terrorism to the EU as a Security Actor," in Geoffrey Edwards and Georg Wiessala, eds., *The European Union: Annual Review of the EU 2001/2002* (Oxford: Blackwell, 2002), pp. 11–28; John Occhipinti, *The Politics of EU Police Cooperation: Toward a European FBI?* (Boulder: Lynne Rienner, 2003).

42. See Desmond Dinan, "Governance and Institutions 1999: Resignation, Reform, and Renewal," in *Journal of Common Market Studies: Annual Review of the European Union 1999–2000,* pp. 27–30; Julian Priestley, *Six Battles That Shaped Europe's Parliament* (London: John Harper, 2008), pp. 210–246.

43. Committee of Independent Experts, "First Report on Allegations Regarding Fraud, Mismanagement, and Nepotism in the European Commission," Brussels, March 1999, point 1.6.2.

44. On Commission reform, see Neill Nugent, *The European Commission* (Basingstoke: Palgrave, 2001).

45. Commission, "Reforming the Commission: A White Paper—Part 1," Brussels, 2000; Commission, "Reforming the Commission: A White Paper—Part 2, Action Plan," Brussels, 2000.

46. See Desmond Dinan, "Governance and Institutions 2000: Edging Toward Enlargement," in *Journal of Common Market Studies: Annual Review of the European Union 2000,* pp. 25–41.

47. Council, *Operation of the Council with an Enlarged Union in Prospect: Report by the Working Party Set Up by the Secretary General of the Council* (Trumpf-Piris report), Brussels, March 10, 1999.

48. See Jolyon Howorth, *Security and Defense Policy in the European Union* (Basingstoke: Palgrave Macmillan, 2005).

49. See Seth G. Jones, *The Rise of European Security Cooperation* (Cambridge: Cambridge University Press, 2007); Panos Koutrakos, *The EU Common Security and Defense Policy* (New York: Oxford University Press, 2013).

50. Bulletin EU 6-1999.

51. Bulletin EU 12-1999.

52. Quoted in *European Report,* February 19, 2003, p. 15.

53. Ibid.

54. Council, *A Secure Europe in a Better World: European Security Strategy,* Brussels, December 12, 2003.

55. Amsterdam Treaty, available at http://europa.eu.int/scadplus/leg/en/s50000.htm.

56. Ibid.

57. On the Austrian situation, see Gerda Falkner, "The EU14's 'Sanctions' Against Austria: Sense and Nonsense," *ECSA Review* 14, no. 1 (Winter 2001), pp. 14–15.

58. See Ricardo Alonsa Garcia, "The General Provisions of the Charter of Fundamental Rights of the European Union," Jean Monnet Working Paper no. 4/02, http://www.jeanmonnetprogram.org/papers.

59. See Juliet Lodge, ed., *The 1999 Elections to the European Parliament* (Basingstoke: Palgrave, 2001).

60. On the EU and referendums, see Simon Hug, *Voices of Europe: Citizens, Referendums, and European Integration* (Boulder: Rowman and Littlefield, 2003); Sara Binzer Hobolt, *Europe in Question: Referendums on European Integration* (Oxford: Oxford University Press, 2009).

9

The Limits of
European Union

THE REJECTION BY FRENCH AND DUTCH VOTERS OF THE CONSTI-
tutional Treaty in 2005, though not unexpected, was a serious blow to the EU.
Inevitably the word "crisis," liberally bandied about in the history of European integration, was used to describe the situation in which the EU found itself. As crises go, the demise of the Constitutional Treaty was relatively mild.
The EU was not in danger of collapsing, the institutions continued to function, and there were no economic repercussions. Nevertheless, rejection of a
treaty that had emerged out of a broadly based convention, and that specifically addressed citizens' complaints about how the EU operated, was a cause
of deep concern. Clearly, the EU faced a growing and potentially debilitating
gap between the governed and the governing, and between those who benefited most and those who benefited least from the rapid economic and social
changes associated with globalization and deeper integration.

National leaders were determined to save the treaty, without which they
believed the recently enlarged EU could not function adequately or achieve
its full potential. Their solution was to reconfigure the treaty, to rescue as
much of its substance as possible while sacrificing as much of its symbolism
as necessary. Nowhere was this more striking than in the change of name.
Gone was the adjective "constitutional," with the substitute treaty being
known simply as the Lisbon Treaty, after the name of the city where it was
signed. Inevitably, the Lisbon Treaty had its own ratification problems. Voters in Ireland, the only country to ratify by referendum, rejected it in June
2008. Only after a second referendum, in October 2009, could the treaty
come into effect.

The accession of Bulgaria and Romania in 2007, while discussions
about a new treaty were taking place, accentuated the enlargement fatigue
prevalent in the EU. So did the prospect of acquiring more member states in
southeastern Europe, notably the countries of the Western Balkans and

305

Turkey. Croatia, which joined in 2013, was the exception that proved the rule, having distanced itself during the accession process from the shadow of the Balkans. Because enlargement was not a feasible option, at least for the foreseeable future, EU influence in the Western Balkans greatly diminished. The same was true with respect to Turkey. As a result, EU conditionality, the key to understanding the success of enlargement policy in Central and Eastern Europe, lost its utility. By the mid-2010s it seemed as if the EU had reached the limits of enlargement as a foreign policy tool.

Enlargement fatigue and discontent with treaty reform coincided with the onset of the global financial crisis, which triggered the great recession. Though the crisis originated outside the EU, its effects were magnified within by the structural weaknesses and unintended consequences of economic and monetary union. The situation in the eurozone grew dire, with low or negative economic growth and soaring unemployment. The eurozone crisis was several crises rolled into one: a banking crisis, a sovereign debt crisis, a competitiveness crisis, a political crisis, and a crisis of confidence. Material aspects of the crisis affected different parts of the EU in different ways at different times. The cumulative effect was to threaten the survival of the euro and the stability of the eurozone. Here was a crisis worthy of the name.

Coping with the eurozone crisis put EU institutions and governments under enormous stress. Germany emerged as the EU's undisputed, albeit reluctant, hegemon. Angela Merkel, chancellor since 2005, became the most powerful politician in Europe. Though criticized for a seemingly tentative leadership style, Merkel insisted on a policy of austerity for the eurozone, especially for countries in receipt of EU assistance. The severity, dubious economic benefit, and high social costs of national austerity programs generated a backlash against Germany. François Hollande won the French presidential election in May 2012 partly because of his opposition to austerity and open criticism of Merkel. His victory caused a chill in the bilateral relationship at the tip of the EU political pyramid.

The frosty personal relationship between Hollande and Merkel reflected a growing and seemingly irreversible divergence in French and German perceptions of the EU. France and Germany had always had different institutional and policy preferences, which they somehow managed to reconcile. The difference now was that the EU increasingly suited France less and Germany more. The 2004 enlargement, which shifted the EU's center of gravity farther to the east, and the eurozone crisis, which highlighted French economic weakness and German economic strength, exposed the stark differences in each country's fundamental bond with Brussels.

For Britain, by contrast, the EU seemed an alien place. David Cameron, who became prime minister in May 2010, responded to pressure from the strongly Euroskeptical wing of his Conservative Party, and to concern about the rise of the ultranationalist United Kingdom Independence Party, by promising, if reelected, to hold a referendum on continued EU membership. Britain's nonmembership in the eurozone, semidetachment from other policy areas, and flirtation with exiting the EU greatly diminished Cameron's potential influence in Brussels. It also demonstrated the depth of unease within the EU, at the highest political levels as well as among ordinary Europeans.

This chapter explores the limits of European union in an era of global economic uncertainty and political insecurity. It focuses on three key developments. First, the Lisbon Treaty, as the culmination of a wrenching period of treaty reform that lasted more than a decade; second, enlargement, which effectively reached its limits following the accession of twelve member states in 2004–2007; third, the eurozone crisis, the greatest calamity ever in the history of European integration.

The Lisbon Treaty

The road to Lisbon began with the defeat of the Constitutional Treaty in the 2005 French and Dutch referendums.[1] France could have ratified the treaty on the basis of a vote in parliament, but President Jacques Chirac called for a nonbinding yet politically crucial referendum, which took place in late May 2005. Like French presidents before him, Chirac thought that a successful referendum on a key EU issue would bolster his standing among other leaders and provide domestic political dividends. Yet by opposing a directive for the liberalization of services in the EU, which was then being discussed in Brussels, Chirac played into the hands of the treaty's opponents, who stoked fears of rising unemployment due to the "nearshoring" of jobs to the new member states and an influx of cheap labor. The Constitutional Treaty became a proxy in France for the economic disruption associated with deeper integration and globalization. Nor did the possibility of Turkish accession, hugely unpopular in France, help the treaty's chances. In the event, a majority of voters (55 percent) rejected the treaty.

The outcome of the referendum in the Netherlands four days later was 62 percent against. Opposition in Holland, which had never held a national referendum on any issue, had crystallized around the unpopularity of the government, resentment of the country's large contribution to the EU budget, and vague concerns about the loss of national identity. In Holland as in France, most of the dissatisfaction had little to do with the treaty itself. Instead, the referendums provided an opportunity for voters to express deep dissatisfaction with developments primarily in their own countries and, secondarily, in the EU.

Although several other countries had already ratified the treaty, the French and Dutch results were devastating. Instead of wrapping up EU-wide ratification by the end of 2006, as had been planned, the European

Council reluctantly agreed in June 2005 to consign the Constitutional Treaty to a year-long "period of reflection."[2]

Despite the fate of the Constitutional Treaty, the EU was hardly in crisis. Day-to-day decisionmaking continued unabated, and breakthroughs on big issues still proved possible. Rejection of the treaty nevertheless represented a setback for the EU. Yet the results of the referendums were a symptom, not a cause, of the EU's underlying problem: growing public dissatisfaction, compounded by governments that were apt to exonerate themselves and blame "Brussels" for everything from the fiscal constraints imposed by EMU to tough competition rules, regardless of the reasons for those policy measures. To the extent that the EU was handicapped operationally during this time, the underlying cause was political posturing on the part of governments rather than the treaty's demise.

Rescuing the Constitutional Treaty

Most politicians and officials involved in EU affairs were loath to let the Constitutional Treaty die. Their best hope was to dress it up differently and present it again for ratification. First they would need to call it something else. For Finland's foreign minister, changing the name would be a "minor point," as "everyone agrees it was a mistake to call it a constitution."[3] The European Council agreed in June 2006 to explore the possibility of saving parts of the treaty under a new name, initially the "Reform Treaty." This was part of a "twin track" approach, the other part being to assuage the EU's critics by delivering a "Europe of results."[4] Hopes for a successful rescue of the treaty rose toward the end of 2006, thanks to the eagerness of newly elected chancellor Angela Merkel to make an impact on the European stage, especially during Germany's Council presidency in the first half of 2007.

Despite some misgivings, no government stood in the way of relaunching the negotiations on treaty reform. Moreover, all agreed that the obligatory intergovernmental conference should be as short and swift as possible. To that end, Germany decided in effect to conduct the bulk of the negotiations during its Council presidency, leaving the intergovernmental conference proper, which would begin later in the year under the Portuguese presidency, to wrap up the technical details. Apart from diplomatic heft, the key to Germany's success was secrecy and speed. German officials sounded out opinion in other national capitals and ascertained the limits of each country's negotiating position, while Merkel held bilateral meetings with fellow leaders.

The British, Dutch, and French governments wanted to change the treaty only in ways that would avoid having to hold new referendums. Their solution was to amend the existing treaties on the basis of most of the changes introduced in the Constitutional Treaty, not replace them with an entirely new treaty. Governments could therefore claim that a referendum was unnecessary, given that changes to the existing treaties had happened in the past without recourse to a referendum.

In view of the virulence of Euroskepticism in the United Kingdom, Prime Minister Tony Blair felt it necessary to declare a number of "red lines" or unalterable demands. These included removing the Charter of Fundamental Rights from the treaty text; dropping the title "foreign minister"; and retaining national control of foreign policy, defense policy, social security, and civil law. In general, Britain wanted the revised treaties to give the EU an appearance that was as unconstitutional and unstatelike as possible.

The presidential election campaign in France coincided with the beginning of the informal treaty renegotiations. Nicolas Sarkozy, the leading contender in the race, declared that he would not put a revised treaty to a second referendum. Elected in May 2007, Sarkozy signaled a vigorous approach to the constitutional question and to a variety of policy issues, announcing in his first speech as president-elect that "France is back in Europe."[5]

For Poland's government, led by the Euroskeptic Jarosław Kaczyński, a new intergovernmental conference held out the prospect of reopening negotiations on the "double majority" formula for qualified majority voting contained in the Constitutional Treaty. Understandably, Poland wanted to retain the Nice arrangement whereby Poland's share of the total number of Council votes almost equaled Germany's. This became a major sticking point at the June 2007 summit, where EU leaders hoped to reach agreement on key changes to the treaty. Other outstanding issues included "European symbols" (whether the new treaty should retain references to the EU flag and anthem, and celebration of Schuman Day); acknowledgment of the primacy of EU law, which Britain found objectionable but most other governments thought commonplace; where to put the Charter of Fundamental Rights; precise language on the delimitation of competences; and the exact role of national parliaments.

The June 2007 summit—Blair's last, after ten years in office—was a fractious affair. Countries that had ratified the Constitutional Treaty tried to hold the line; the referendum-constrained countries pushed for cosmetic more than substantive changes; and Poland stuck to its guns on majority voting. Defenders of the Constitutional Treaty made many concessions to accommodate the others, including protecting Britain's red lines. As the summit came to an end, only the issue of majority voting remained unresolved. Under intense pressure from almost every national leader, Prime Minister Kaczy ski and his twin, Polish president Lech Kaczyński, finally dropped their opposition to the double majority system in return for an agreement to delay its entry into force until 2014.[6]

Procedurally, the ensuing intergovernmental conference resembled any other. In fact, it was unprecedented in that the work of the conference fell mostly on the shoulders of a technical group of legal experts, who went through the Council presidency's draft treaty article by article, line by line, eventually producing a definitive version. Their work was uncontroversial but highly complicated, especially because of the need to accommodate various opt-outs and opt-ins.

Though it seemed as if all the difficulties had been resolved, a summit held in October 2007 formally to conclude the intergovernmental conference was not without drama. A number of touchy issues had arisen since the previous summit. Foremost among them was yet another Polish demand for clarification of the provisions on majority voting. Eventually the European Council found a form of words with which everyone could live.[7] With an election scheduled for the weekend of the summit, and public opinion turning strongly against the Kaczyński twins, the Polish government was disinclined to put up its usual fight. Fundamentally, Poland was and would remain deeply attached to the EU. "Solidarity," a word with special resonance in Polish history, had become a codeword used by EU politicians and officials to alert Warsaw to the danger of alienating other member states. The resounding victory in the election of the opposition and strongly pro-EU Civic Platform, under the leadership of Donald Tusk, bore out the point.

Ratifying the Lisbon Treaty

National leaders signed the new treaty at a subdued ceremony in Lisbon, in December 2007. Other than in Ireland, whose constitution mandated a referendum on EU treaty change, there would not be any referendums on the Lisbon Treaty. Much to the dismay of those who had labored to rescue the Constitutional Treaty, the result of the Irish referendum, held in June 2008, was 54 percent against. There were several reasons for the outcome, including lack of knowledge or understanding of the treaty; nebulous concerns about Irish identity; apprehension that the alleged militarization of the EU would put an end to Irish neutrality; and fear that the EU would somehow undermine Ireland's constitutional prohibition of abortion. Another concern was loss of influence and representation in Brussels because of a reduction in the Commission's size—a reduction already mandated by the Nice Treaty. Underlying everything was the government's unpopularity. Moreover, it was far harder to argue for than against the Lisbon Treaty, especially in short sound-bites. Under the circumstances, "If in doubt, vote no" seemed like good advice.[8]

For most EU leaders, the Irish result was yet another obstacle to a treaty reform that they were determined to implement. They would have to find a way to remove the Irish obstacle; prevent contagion to other "high risk" countries; and ensure implementation of the treaty as soon as possible. EU leaders were careful to say that they would not press the Irish government to find a solution, but behind the scenes the Irish government faced unrelenting pressure.

A growing realization among political and business elites that the referendum result was a disaster for Ireland's image helped concentrate the government's mind. Spurious though many of the arguments against Lisbon appeared to be, the Irish government had no choice but to attempt to change the opinions of as many naysayers as possible by getting guarantees from the EU to allay their concerns. If the European Council would assuage some of Ireland's concerns and agree also to retain one commissioner per member state, the government would hold a second referendum.

Thus the European Council announced in December 2008 that it would decide in due course, "provided the Lisbon Treaty enters into force," to retain the Commission's size at one commissioner per member state.[9] Six months later, the European Council reached agreement on the "special protocol" for Ireland, a largely meaningless form of words intended to facilitate the holding of a second referendum—and ensure a successful outcome.[10]

By that time, prospects for a favorable outcome had improved considerably, due in part to the global financial crisis, which hit Ireland particularly hard. Although ratifying the Lisbon Treaty would not make a material difference to Ireland's plight, it would provide some comfort by affirming the country's good fortune to be in a relatively safe port—the EU—during a fierce financial storm. As expected, the Lisbon Treaty passed, by a majority of 67 percent, with a 59 percent turnout, in October 2009.

Ireland was not the only country not to have ratified the treaty. Despite approval of the treaty by the Czech parliament, President Václav Klaus, an ardent Euroskeptic, refused to sign the instrument of ratification until the last possible moment. Klaus raised an implausible eleventh-hour concern that the treaty could open the way for property claims by ethnic Germans expelled from Czechoslovakia after World War II. EU leaders appeased Klaus by giving the Czech Republic an opt-out from the Charter of Fundamental Rights. Klaus, having milked the ratification procedure for all it was worth, finally signed in November 2009, allowing the treaty to come into effect the following month.

Germany's parliament had voted in good time to ratify the treaty, but the president was unable to sign the instrument of ratification pending a ruling by the country's constitutional court on the compatibility of the treaty with Germany's Basic Law. The court finally ruled in June 2009 that the Lisbon Treaty was indeed compatible, subject to a change in German law on the role of parliament in EU decisionmaking. Although proponents of the treaty breathed a sigh of relief, a closer look at the lengthy court ruling revealed that it raised several concerns about the direction of European integration. In particular, the court emphasized the limits of EU competence and the existence of a "structured democratic deficit" that only national parliaments, not the European Parliament, could possibly close.[11] If anything, the ruling should have reassured Euroskeptics as to the limits of the Lisbon Treaty and the process of European integration.

Implementing the Lisbon Treaty

The Lisbon Treaty included a host of changes to EU institutions and policies. Some were easier to effect than others; a few could not be implemented immediately. For instance, the double majority system for Council voting, one of the treaty's most important innovations, was due to take effect only in 2014. In most cases, however, governments and EU institutions lost little time availing themselves of the improvements offered by the new treaty.

The EP, a winner once again in the treaty reform process, quickly made the most of its additional budgetary authority and greater legislative power. Yet the most visible institutional changes concerned the European Council, the Council of Ministers (now officially called the Council of the European Union), and the Commission. Two changes stood out: the election of a president for the European Council, and the appointment of a High Representative for Foreign Affairs and Security Policy.

The European Council presidency. Instead of being chaired by the leader of the country in the rotating Council presidency, the European Council would have its own, full-time president, elected for a period of two and a half years, renewable once. During the Constitutional Convention, there was speculation that the first incumbent would be an EU heavyweight, a former leader of a big member state. In the event, Sarkozy and Merkel, the potential kingmakers, decided that the inaugural office holder should be a less forceful and less famous person. They opted for Herman Van Rompuy, the little-known, unassuming prime minister of Belgium, who was duly elected by the European Council in November 2009.[12]

Van Rompuy had no intention of turning the European Council presidency into a platform for forceful EU leadership, even if he could have. He focused squarely on improving the European Council procedurally by tightening its agenda; restricting participation in its meetings to the principals and inviting government ministers on an ad hoc basis only; shortening and sharpening summit conclusions; and ensuring better follow-through.[13]

The escalation of the eurozone crisis raised the political profile and importance of the European Council at precisely the time when the new presidency system came into operation. As a result, the European Council met more often—in regular and special sessions—during Van Rompuy's five years in office than in the fifteen years before then. In addition, the leaders of the eurozone countries began to meet frequently early in the crisis, with Van Rompuy as the chair. In October 2010, eurozone leaders decided that a "Euro Summit" would take place regularly, entirely apart from meetings of the European Council. When they renewed Van Rompuy's term as president of the European Council, in March 2012, national leaders decided also to formalize his position as president of the Euro Summit.

As the full-time European Council president, Van Rompuy had an obvious advantage over national leaders with a presidency tenure of only six months: an ability to focus exclusively on EU business. Van Rompuy had the time to travel throughout the EU in order to consult constantly, between meetings, with national leaders and other key interlocutors. Van Rompuy was confident that having a standing president benefited the EU. "Thanks to the new continuity of my function," he wrote in 2011, "[the European Council] is better equipped to steer change, to give orientations or quite practically to follow-up earlier decisions."[14]

The Council of the European Union. The Lisbon Treaty affected the configuration and operation of the Council in a number of ways. One was the establishment of the Foreign Affairs Council, chaired by the High Representative for Foreign Affairs and Security Policy. A key issue in the run-up to implementation of the Lisbon Treaty therefore became the selection of the High Representative, who would also be vice president of the Commission with responsibility for external relations. The politics of high-level appointments in any international organization are usually arcane and contentious. In the case of the EU, such appointments needed to respect balance between northern and southern, eastern and western, big and small member states; between political groups (notably Socialist and Christian Democratic); and, ideally, between men and women.

Van Rompuy had been selected president of the European Council precisely because he came from a small member state, in this case a northern one. José Manuel Barroso, the Commission president, also came from a small member state, a southern one (Portugal). For reasons of balance, the High Representative would therefore have to come from a big member state. By common consent it was Britain's turn to make such an appointment. As the Labour Party was in power, the appointee would come from the center-left (Van Rompuy and Barroso were center-right). To meet the other, informal criterion for balance, the nominee would be a woman. Gordon Brown, who had replaced Blair as prime minister in June 2007, chose Catherine Ashton, who had been in government for only a short time and had been a substitute commissioner in Brussels for only one year. That was the extent of her international experience.

National leaders were well aware of Ashton's background and qualifications when they appointed her in November 2009. Though some may have had misgivings, all acquiesced in the British government's decision. A number of members of the EP questioned Ashton's suitability at the time of her approval hearing as commissioner-designate in January 2010, but the EP as a whole did not object to her appointment.

Not surprisingly, Ashton soon faltered. Her new position was unusually onerous. In some cases it required her, literally, to be in more than one place at the same time. Ashton's early performance cast doubt on the soundness of combining the positions of High Representative and Commission vice president, as provided in the Lisbon Treaty, and again on her suitability for the job. Despite such legitimate concerns, it was hard to avoid the conclusion that many national leaders and foreign ministers were pleased to see Ashton flounder, not least because they feared that a strong incumbent would threaten the preponderance of national players or become too influential on the European and global stages. Ashton's performance gradually improved, though she never enjoyed positive media coverage or uniformly strong support from national capitals and from the Brussels establishment.

The European External Action Service. The idea of establishing an EU diplomatic service emerged in the Constitutional Convention and survived in the Lisbon Treaty. Yet there was little discussion of it until after the successful Irish referendum on the treaty, the terms of which required the Council to consult the EP about establishing the diplomatic service. Experience should have taught the Council that the EP would play its part to the full. In this case, the EP had considerable leverage, because the budget for the service was subject to its approval. Whereas the Council viewed the budget as a mere technicality, the EP was determined to influence the shape and structure of the new service.

The ensuing interinstitutional battle lasted almost a year. The eventual agreement included a number of demands by the EP relating to the political accountability of the service and an equal distribution of posts among the three constituencies identified in the relevant treaty article—the Council secretariat, the Commission, and national diplomatic services. The EP insisted as well on respect for geographical balance, meaning that the new member states should be fairly represented in the service. The latter point was especially important for EP president Jerzy Buzek, a former Polish prime minister.

The European External Action Service finally came into existence in December 2010, exactly a year after implementation of the Lisbon Treaty. The service was an institution in the political sense, but not within the meaning of the Lisbon Treaty; nor was it analogous to a Commission service, the Council secretariat, the Committee of Permanent Representatives, or an EU agency. Rather, it was something new entirely.[15]

The establishment of the service saw the usual jockeying over appointments in the upper echelons of the organization. Some politicians complained that Ashton, lacking foreign policy experience, depended too much on the British foreign office. Others complained that the management system of the service, with a secretary-general under the High Representative, favored the French administrative model. Indeed, Pierre Vimont, previously the French ambassador to the United States, became the first secretary-general. His two deputies were a German and, much to EP president Buzek's delight, a Pole. The fourth member of the top leadership team was Irish but, more important for the future of the service, was a former secretary-general of the Commission.

Initially, over 1,600 permanent officials were transferred from the Commission and the Council secretariat to the service. These included a majority of staff from the Commission's directorate-general for external relations, which then ceased to exist. National diplomats who joined the service brought their own cultures and styles, but these were too numerous and too disparate to have a decisive impact on the culture of the service itself. In keeping with their institution's ethos, officials of the Council secretariat were too self-effacing to put their stamp on the service. That left the field open to the former Commission officials in the new service, whose working methods remained firmly set in the mold of their home institution.

The External Action Service, with its large Brussels headquarters directly opposite the Commission's flagship Berlaymont building, and approximately 130 delegations (or embassies) in countries outside the EU or accredited to international organizations, took several years to become fully staffed and operational. Ashton's inexperience and initial missteps, together with the delay in getting the service off the ground, may have impaired the effectiveness of EU diplomacy in the early 2010s. At a time of turmoil in nearby North Africa and the Middle East, this was particularly unfortunate. Once the External Action Service was up and running, however, and Ashton gained confidence and experience on the international stage, EU diplomacy noticeably improved. Nowhere was this more evident than in its dealings with Iran.

The Commission

Barroso, who became Commission president in 2004, was reappointed in 2009, while the Lisbon Treaty was being ratified. In an effort to strengthen the weak legitimacy of the Commission—and of the Commission president—the Lisbon Treaty required the European Council to take "into account" the outcome of the elections to the EP and to hold "appropriate consultations" between the two institutions before designating the candidate for Commission president. Although the treaty was not yet in force when it was time to appoint a new Commission president, the ever-assertive EP pressed the European Council for a political agreement to abide by the rules of the Lisbon Treaty. Given that the European People's Party, to which Barroso belonged, won the largest number of seats in the June 2009 EP elections, the European Council could fairly claim to have taken into account the outcome of the elections.

That did not satisfy some MEPs, especially among the socialist and green parties, who opposed Barroso for his liberal economic philosophy and his alleged coziness with big business. They claimed that pushing through Barroso's candidacy without due consultation with the EP was a violation of democratic principles. In the event, Barroso convincingly won the vote on his reappointment, in September 2009, although by a smaller margin than in 2004.

Having a standing European Council president inherently weakened the position of the Commission president. Much to Barroso's dismay, the European Council presidency soon upstaged the Commission presidency. Van Rompuy did not feel threatened by Barroso, because Van Rompuy knew that he himself was in the ascendant. At Van Rompuy's suggestion, the two presidents agreed to meet once a week to discuss EU affairs. They also agreed on a set of arrangements between themselves regarding external representation of the EU at presidential level. These referred specifically to participation in international summits such as the Group of Eight (G8) and the Group of 20 (G-20): both presidents would participate but, depending on the topic, only one would "state the position of the EU."[16] This appeared to fly in the face of the Lisbon Treaty's goal of streamlining the EU's external representation, and occasionally bemused or befuddled the EU's international interlocutors.

The problem of Barroso's limited influence within the EU, as emphasized by his playing second fiddle to Van Rompuy, was not new. Ever since the presidency of Jacques Delors (1985–1993), successive Commission presidents had become less prominent and influential. Barroso tried valiantly to restore the institution's political position. He was adept at presiding over a fractious Commission consisting of one commissioner per member state. Under his presidency, the Commission became more accountable and open, and more responsive to the needs of citizens. It also became more pragmatic in highlighting selective policy objectives rather than launching grand political initiatives. Aware of the constraints facing the Commission, Barroso was not inclined to tilt at windmills and challenge the predominance of national capitals, especially Berlin and Paris. Supranationalists were disappointed with what they saw as Barroso's subservience to national leaders and unwillingness to reassert the Commission's authority. Arguably, Barroso did as much as he could at a time of resurgent intergovernmentalism, compounded by economic uncertainty and grandstanding by the EP.

The Declining Utility of Enlargement

Croatia's accession to the EU, in July 2013, was a shot in the arm for Brussels. At a time when the EU's image at home and abroad was reeling from the eurozone crisis, the fact that the EU acquired a new member state was a cause of some satisfaction. Substantively, however, Croatia's accession did not amount to much, at least for the EU. As a small member state (twenty-first out of twenty-eight in both population and GDP), Croatia would hardly make a splash in the newly enlarged EU. Croatia would be in neither the eurozone nor the Schengen area for some time to come.

Paradoxically, Croatia's accession accentuated the declining utility of enlargement. Far from heralding the entry of several other candidates in southeastern Europe, Croatia's accession highlighted the challenges facing many Balkan countries on the way to EU membership. For the EU, the sense of accomplishment accompanying Central and Eastern European enlargement had given way to a sense of dread about the prospect of large-scale Balkan enlargement, let alone Turkish accession. The EU's receding interest in further enlargement, in turn, undermined the effectiveness of conditionality—the EU's ability to leverage reform in candidate countries in return for impending accession.

Completing Central and Eastern European Enlargement

Enlargement is a long-term process that does not end when a country joins the EU. Post-accession assimilation, which affects the new member state as well as the newly expanded EU, is part and parcel of enlargement. The 2004 enlargement brought eight Central and Eastern European countries into the EU, leaving Bulgaria and Romania outside. Yet the EU could not keep the two laggards out indefinitely, as that would have further weakened its leverage and tarnished the international image of its enlargement policy.[17] Accordingly, the EU included in the accession agreement provisions to sanction the two countries should they fail to carry through administrative and legal reforms or fail to combat corruption and organized crime. In particular, the Commission could halt financial transfers to Bulgaria and Romania, notably agricultural subsidies and regional development funds. Nevertheless, there was little enthusiasm for the entrance of these two countries into the EU. The signing ceremony for the Bulgarian and Romanian accession treaties, held in Luxembourg in April 2005, was decidedly less glamorous than the ceremony for the other Central and Eastern European countries, held in Athens two years previously.

In contrast to public attitudes throughout the EU, most Bulgarians and Romanians could hardly wait to join. The vote in the Romanian parliament on ratification of the accession treaty was unanimous. In the equivalent vote in the Bulgarian parliament, only one member dissented. National parliaments within the EU were decidedly less enthusiastic, but none blocked accession. Nor did the EP. That paved the way for Bulgaria and Romania to join the EU in January 2007.[18]

Adjusting to Enlargement

Enlargement fatigue became widespread in the EU even before the first group of Central and Eastern European countries joined. Enlargement was brought to people's attention in a wholly negative way, through horror stories, real and imagined, of Romanian migrants in Italy; fears about Polish plumbers undercutting their competitors in France; and rumors about lawless Lithuanian migrants in Ireland. Unease in Western Europe about the labor and social consequences of enlargement became magnified many times over when the country in question was Turkey.

Opposition to enlargement accounted in part for the resurgence of the far right in Western Europe, beginning in the late 1990s. Ireland's rejection of the Nice Treaty in June 2001 looked like a manifestation of anti-enlargement feeling, though the referendum registered general dissatisfaction with the EU and with the Irish government. France's rejection of the Constitutional Treaty in the May 2005 referendum owed much to fears of companies relocating to the new member states and a possible influx of cheap labor.

The likely consequences of enlargement for the institutions, policies, and politics of the EU had gradually sunk in among the existing member states. Despite doubts about the institutional capacity of the enlarging EU, and the inadequacy of treaty reform before enlargement took place, existing institutional arrangements, notably those for qualified majority voting that came into effect under the Nice Treaty, worked much better than expected. Post-enlargement legislative gridlock in Brussels failed to materialize. Nor, in the legislative arena, did a split emerge between the old and the new member states. Coalitions remained fluid, their composition depending on the issue. The new member states had good records for implementing EU legislation, often better than those of the older member states.

A more noticeable divide emerged on external relations, with the new countries generally advocating a harsher approach toward Russia and a friendlier approach toward the United States. Differing attitudes toward the United States became obvious in the run-up to the war in Iraq, a year before the 2004 enlargement. Whereas most Western European governments strongly condemned the US invasion, most Eastern European governments supported or condoned it. Even more striking were differences in public opinion, with Western Europeans almost uniformly opposing the invasion, regardless of their governments' positions, and Eastern Europeans almost uniformly supporting or at least excusing it.

On economic policy, the new members tended to be more liberal than many of the older member states. Membership or nonmembership in the eurozone became the most significant fault-line within the enlarged EU. Ten years after the 2004 accession, only four Central and Eastern European member states were also eurozone members (Slovakia joined in 2007, Slovenia in 2009, Estonia in 2011, and Latvia in 2014). The others complained that, because of the crisis, the EMU convergence criteria were being applied more strictly to them. Given the political as well as the economic significance of eurozone membership, some of the new member states felt deliberately excluded from the EU's inner sanctum.

Concerns about the porousness of the Central and Eastern European countries' eastern borders triggered an acceleration among member states of cooperation on asylum and immigration policy. It was not until December 2007 that the 2004 EU entrants (minus Cyprus) joined the Schengen regime. By contrast, Bulgaria and Romania had little prospect of joining Schengen for many years after they joined the EU. Similarly, concern about relations between the enlarged EU and its new neighbors in Eastern Europe, and about neglect of the Southern Mediterranean, led the EU to launch the European Neighborhood Policy, an all-encompassing approach to the countries of the "wider Europe"—running in an arc from North Africa to the former Soviet Union.

Politically, the EU's adaptation to enlargement was strained. It was difficult for some of the old member states to adjust to the new reality. France seemed especially ill at ease, as the center of gravity in the enlarged EU shifted in Germany's direction. France appeared to resent the arrival of so many new countries around the table. This was most noticeable in the French-inspired European Council, which, in 2004, ballooned in membership from fifteen to twenty-five national leaders.

Even before the new member states formally acceded, Chirac lashed out at leaders of the Central and Eastern European countries, who had been invited to attend an EU summit in February 2003, for daring to take a position on Iraq that was contrary to his own.[19] Nicolas Sarkozy, Chirac's successor, was notorious in the European Council for being impatient with interventions from Central and Eastern European leaders. François Hollande, Sarkozy's successor, was more restrained, but was no less discomfited by the size of the European Council and, more to the point, the size of the EU itself.

Managing the impact of enlargement within the EU's institutions was bound to be difficult, not least because of the profusion of official languages. Politicians and officials, accustomed to the relative coziness of the old EU, were inclined to scorn their counterparts from the east. Undoubtedly, some officials feared the impact of enlargement on their promotion prospects, given that their counterparts from the new member states would have to be accommodated at all levels in the Brussels bureaucracy. Yet many of new Central and Eastern European officials were thoroughly familiar with the functioning of EU institutions, having studied the EU or served it through internships in Brussels. As with previous enlargement, but on a greater scale, it took some time for officials from the new countries to settle into their posts.

The accession of Bulgaria and Romania greatly exacerbated enlargement fatigue. Not surprisingly, given the reason for their late admission, the two countries had great difficulty adapting to the norms and standards of membership. This was especially the case with policing, judicial behavior, and governance at the local and national levels. Every six months, under the Cooperation and Verification Mechanism, the Commission reported on progress in Bulgaria and Romania in the areas of judicial reform and anti-corruption and, in the case of Bulgaria, the fight against organized crime. The Commission withheld funding for EU programs in both countries following negative reports, but without any noticeable effect.

The Western Balkans

The mixed experience of enlargement in 2004, and especially in 2007, soured the EU on further expansion. Critics of enlargement worried about the EU's "absorption capacity," an imprecise term suggesting that the EU's institutions and policies could cope with only a finite number of member states. It was impossible to know what that number could be, although some people had a definite idea of what it should be—no more than the size of the existing EU.

The fact that Bulgaria, Romania, and Greece, generally viewed as the EU's problem children, were all Balkan states, added to the general lack of interest within the EU for expansion into the Western Balkans, an artificial region encompassing Albania, Bosnia and Herzegovina, Croatia, Kosovo, Macedonia, Montenegro, and Serbia. With the exception of Albania, all were part of the former Yugoslavia.

Haunted by its failure in the 1990s to stop the wars in the former Yugoslavia, the EU became extremely active in military and civilian peace-keeping operations in the Western Balkans. The EU was also the largest donor of development aid in the region. The EU saw the situation in the Western Balkans after the recent wars as being similar to the situation in Europe after World War II. Not surprisingly, the EU advocated economic and political integration as the best means of promoting peace, stability, and prosperity.[20]

The EU and the countries of the Western Balkans launched the Stabilization and Association Process at a summit in Zagreb, Croatia, in November 2000. At a follow-on summit in Thessaloniki, Greece, in June 2003, the EU declared that all of the Western Balkan countries were potential member states. The EU promoted economic, political, judicial, and administrative reform through the Stabilization and Association Process, and provided financial aid, trade preferences, technical advice, and development assistance.

The "Thessaloniki agenda" also helped the countries of the Western Balkans meet the Copenhagen criteria for eventual EU membership. As part of the pre-accession process, the EU concluded stabilization and association agreements with each country (except Kosovo). These agreements were analogous to the "Europe agreements" that the EU signed with the countries of Central and Eastern Europe in the 1990s, and they held out the same prospect of EU membership.

In addition to the myriad challenges of economic and political reform, the countries of the Western Balkans were hobbled by entrenched corruption and organized crime. Albania was the most obvious example. The countries of the former Yugoslavia had made an easier transition from communism, but corruption was just as deep-rooted there as well. The wars of the 1990s were a gift to organized crime, which burrowed deep into the administrative apparatus in most of Yugoslavia's successor states.[21]

The EU's financial largesse and the lure of possible membership had some effect on the conduct of the countries concerned. The EU was able to help Albania, which was a highly repressed, almost completely isolated communist country during the Cold War, make considerable progress after an extremely difficult period of postcommunist transition. Albania applied for EU membership in April 2009, and received a positive recommendation from the Commission in 2012. However, the European Council was reluctant to give the country candidate status, officially designating Albania a "potential candidate." Like Turkey, Albania was a majority-Muslim country; unlike Turkey, its population was small (just over 3 million).

Slovenia, a former Yugoslav republic, joined the EU in 2004. Of the remaining states of the former Yugoslavia, Croatia had the best prospect of joining next. Nevertheless, it was another nine years before Croatia reached its goal. As with Slovenia, success for Croatia depended in part on the country distancing itself from the image of the Balkans, a region with negative historical connotations for many Europeans.

Croatia became a candidate country in June 2004 and began accession negotiations the following year. Because of Croatia's economic situation and relatively successful transition to democracy, the accession process was reasonably smooth, the most difficult issue being the question of Croatia's relations with the International Criminal Tribunal for the former Yugoslavia (Croatia was sheltering a number of indicted war criminals). Under intense pressure from the EU and the United States, Croatia finally cooperated with the tribunal. In the meantime, a maritime border dispute with neighboring Slovenia threatened Croatia's accession. Having only a small coastline, Slovenia demanded use of part of a disputed bay so that it could access international waters. The dispute ended only when the Croatian parliament approved a deal between the two countries to bring the issue before an impartial international mediator, paving the way for Croatia's EU membership in July 2013.

Macedonia, which escaped the kind of violence that tore through other parts of the former Yugoslavia, applied for EU membership in March 2004. Following a positive report by the Commission, the European Council granted Macedonia candidate status in December 2005, largely in recognition of its avoidance of civil war. Yet Macedonia was a long way from membership, largely because of a bitter bilateral dispute with Greece, which has a province called Macedonia and, therefore, insisted that the EU refer to its neighbor as the "former Yugoslav Republic of Macedonia." Macedonia's refusal to change its name ensured a standing Greek veto on the opening of ac-

The Twenty-Eight Member States

cession negotiations. Macedonia also had a dispute with Bulgaria over contending interpretations of nineteenth- and twentieth-century history. As for the early twenty-first century, EU concerns about political and economic stability in Macedonia precluded accession in the near future.

Montenegro, which became independent of Serbia only in June 2006, seemed to have a relatively rapid trajectory toward EU membership. Montenegro applied to join in 2008 and became a candidate in 2010. Negotiations, which started in 2012, proceeded well, but the Commission emphasized the need for more progress by Montenegro in the areas of judicial, police, and human rights reforms. Given the shallowness in the region of judicial independence, police accountability, and respect for fundamental rights, the Commission proceeded warily.

Bosnia-Herzegovina was also a constituent republic of the old Yugoslavia until it declared independence in 1992. The war that followed was the bloodiest in the region. The December 1995 Dayton Accords included a new constitution that organized the country along ethnic lines (Bosniac, Croat, and Serb). The agreement ended the war but failed to provide a framework for lasting peace and stability. Two decades after the Dayton peace agreement, Bosnia-Herzegovina remained mired in ethnic, religious, and political disputes. As a highly dysfunctional state, Bosnia-Herzegovina had little prospect of joining the EU.

Kosovo was part of Serbia before breaking away, with NATO help, in 1999, in response to the ethnic cleansing of Kosovo's Muslim majority by Serbian security forces. It then became a United Nations protectorate, before declaring independence in February 2008. Serbia's continuing claim to Kosovo, and support for militant Serbs living in the northern part of the state, undermined EU efforts to stabilize the country. The EU secured a breakthrough when it brokered a deal between Kosovo and Serbia in April 2013 to normalize relations between them. Although the EU saw Kosovo as a potential candidate with "a clear European perspective," membership remained notional rather than possible.[22]

The April 2013 Kosovo agreement was a reminder that the situation in the Western Balkans would never be normal until Serbia, historically the regional power and still a cultural beacon in southeastern Europe, was in a position to join the EU. Serbia's prospects improved when the pro-EU coalition won the Serbian general election of May 2008, leading to an application for EU membership in December 2009. Progress depended on Serbia's full cooperation with the International Criminal Tribunal. Following the resolution of a number of high-profile cases, the EU granted Serbia candidate status in March 2012.

Nevertheless, Serbs remained deeply divided on the issue of EU membership. Many continued to see the EU as an enemy that had facilitated the breakup of the former Yugoslavia and supported NATO in its war against Serb forces in 1995 and again in 1999. In addition, Serbs harbored a grudge against EU countries that recognized the independence of Kosovo, which the vast majority of Serbs still considered to be an integral part of their country. Before it could hope to join the EU, Serbia and all of the EU's member states would have to accept Kosovo's independence. More fundamentally, Serbia would have to come to terms with its recent past and adopt a policy of reconciliation toward its neighbors, an important element of the integration process but one that was difficult to pursue in an atmosphere of unreconstructed Serbian nationalism.

Overall, the picture in the Western Balkans was bleak in the mid-2010s. The global economic recession hit the region hard. Corruption and organized crime flourished. EU conditionality lost its utility as the countries' accession prospects stalled or faded. Serbia and Montenegro still had a chance of joining the EU within a few years; Albania, Bosnia-Herzegovina, Macedonia, and Kosovo did not. The EU could not refrain from making a rhetorical commitment to further enlargement, sooner rather than later. For many countries of the Western Balkans, such rhetoric sounded hollow. Not surprisingly, EU policies aimed at promoting economic reform and good governance were becoming less and less effective.

Turkey

In no country was disillusionment with the EU greater than in Turkey in the mid-2010s. And in no other country, even in the Western Balkans, had EU enlargement policy reached its limits.[23] Having applied for membership far earlier than any of the existing candidates, and having already signed an agreement for a customs union with the EU, Turkey pressed for participation in the round of accession negotiations with the Central and Eastern European countries that began in 1998. The EU was in a quandary. On the one hand, Turkey was economically underdeveloped, had fragile political institutions, and had a questionable human rights record. On the other hand,

The Candidate and Potential Candidate Countries

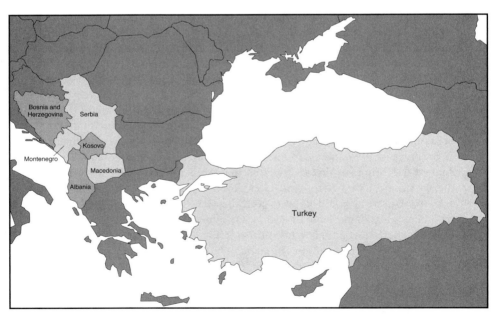

Notes: The candidate countries are Serbia, Montenegro, Macedonia, and Turkey. The potential candidate countries are Bosnia and Herzegovina, Kosovo, and Albania.

Turkey was a big emerging market and was strategically important with respect to the Balkans, the Middle East, and parts of the former Soviet Union. Although there were legitimate economic and political reasons to doubt Turkey's suitability for membership in the foreseeable future, many opponents were motivated primarily by anti-Muslim prejudice and were fearful of the consequences of admitting a country whose population of over 70 million people would make it the EU's second largest member state.

Having decided in 1997 not to invite Turkey to participate in accession negotiations, the European Council sought to reassure Ankara that the EU's door was still open. Turkey protested so vehemently and strove so hard to improve its membership prospects that the European Council officially recognized it as a candidate country in December 1999. Yet Turkey was again rebuffed in October 2002 when the Commission recommended that the EU admit ten countries by 2004, while in Turkey's case offering merely to increase pre-accession assistance.

A change of government in Turkey in November 2002 greatly improved the country's prospects. The new government of Prime Minister Recep Tayyip Erdoğan pushed through numerous economic and social reforms, improved relations with Greece, and moderated Turkey's position on Cyprus. Nevertheless, Turkey opposed the accession of a divided Cyprus to the EU, fearing, rightly, that the Greek-Cypriot regime, representing only the southern part of the island, would be an impediment within the EU to harmonious relations with Turkey.

The Commission rewarded Erdoğan's reform and reconciliation efforts with a recommendation in October 2004 that the European Council agree to open accession negotiations with Turkey. The Commission did not suggest that the negotiations would be short or trouble-free; on the contrary, it held out little hope of Turkish accession for the foreseeable future. France took a particularly hard line, acknowledging that negotiations would probably have to begin but pointing out that they might not necessarily end in full membership. The political climate at the time was soured by growing tension over the assimilation (or nonassimilation) of Muslim minorities in Europe. Lurking behind the rhetoric of many conservative politicians in the EU was deep-seated concern about the social and cultural impact of Turkish membership, even if Turkey were to meet the political and economic criteria.

The European Council nevertheless agreed in December 2004 that accession negotiations would begin. After much preliminary posturing, the talks opened in October 2005. Yet the framework for the negotiations reflected the EU's doubts about Turkey's readiness for membership: "in the case of a serious and persistent breach in Turkey of the principles of liberty, democracy, respect for human rights and fundamental freedoms and the rule of law on which the Union is founded, the Commission will, on its own initiative or on the request of one-third of the Member States, recommend the suspension of the negotiations and propose the conditions for eventual resumption."[24]

It was hardly surprising that the negotiations did not go well. Turkey's refusal to open its ports and airports to traffic from Cyprus, a basic EU demand, became a main stumbling block. In December 2006, at the behest of the Cypriot government, the EU blocked the opening of additional chapters in the negotiations because of the Cyprus issue. For its part, Turkey complained that the EU had not fulfilled its promise to end the trade embargo on the self-styled Turkish Republic of Northern Cyprus. In the second half of 2012, when Cyprus was in the rotating Council presidency, Turkey refused to recognize the presidency and to cooperate with the Council during the six-month period.[25]

In its annual reviews of Turkey's candidacy, the Commission acknowledged that Turkey was a functioning market economy that would be able to cope with competitive pressure and market forces within the EU, and that Turkey had made progress in aligning itself with the EU's legal order. Indeed, Turkey made great strides forward. The process of Europeanization helped the country move in a direction that it wanted to go in any case, despite the considerable adjustment costs. Yet the political price of domestic reform was high, especially for Erdoğan's Islamist-leaning government, which Turkey's fiercely secular military and judiciary deeply distrusted.

The coming to power of Sarkozy in France and Merkel in Germany, both of whom were adamantly opposed to Turkish accession, represented a major setback for Ankara. Instead of full accession, Merkel and Sarkozy proposed a "privileged partnership" with Turkey. In light of such posturing, public opinion in Turkey turned decisively against the EU. Even strongly secular, pro-Western Turks, once reliably enthusiastic about the EU, lost interest in reaching a goal that seemed increasingly unattainable. More troubling was a nationalist backlash against the EU, which many Turks began to see as an anti-Turkish entity biased in favor of Greece and the Greek Cypriots.

For their part, many EU citizens rejected the idea of Turkish membership, reflecting deep-rooted anti-Turkish and anti-Muslim prejudice. Some claimed that Turkey was not even European, as only a small part of the country was on the western side of the Bosporus, traditionally the dividing line between Europe and Asia Minor. Yet the European Council had rejected this argument when it decided in 1999 to grant Turkey candidate status. In effect, the European Council decided that the answer to the question about a country's Europeanness was political, not geographical.

Regardless of Turkey's candidate status, many EU citizens saw Turkey as culturally and religiously distinct; unstable and impoverished; and a potential drain on the EU budget. Turkey was indeed a poor country. Despite remarkable economic growth, Turkey's per capita GDP remained less than one-third that of the EU average. Given the prevailing mood of Euro-pessimism and the persistence of enlargement fatigue, few were willing to argue the case for Turkey: that its accession could benefit the EU by bringing in a rapidly developing economy; would remove a roadblock in EU-NATO relations, which Turkey was impeding because of its dispute with Cyprus; would enhance EU energy security; would add greatly to the EU's military capacity; would strengthen EU influence in the volatile Middle East; and would show the world that the EU was an open, pluralistic entity and not a closed Christian club.

Governments were divided on the question of Turkish accession, between and sometimes within themselves (in the case of ruling coalitions). An unofficial collection of anti-Turkish states, led by Austria and Germany, remained adamantly opposed to Turkish accession. François Hollande sought to mend fences with Turkey, though sentiment in France continued to run against Turkish entry into the EU. By contrast, Britain consistently supported Turkey, a position that fueled suspicion in other member states that what Britain really wanted was a wider and weaker EU.

By the mid-2010s, most EU governments, even those led by anti-Turkish politicians, seemed satisfied with the status quo, which meant keeping the accession negotiations going but without making much progress. The EU could claim that it was not against Turkish accession, secure in the knowledge that Turkey would never join. The EU did not want to push Turkey away from the table, preferring that Turkey take the initiative and withdraw its membership application.

The people and government of Turkey knew that there was little chance of accession. As a result, the EU's ability to leverage reform in Turkey became almost nonexistent. Given statements by prominent national leaders to the effect that Turkey did not belong in the EU, the Commission's official commitment to enlargement lost credibility. The case of Turkey, though exceptional in many respects, demonstrated the limits of EU conditionality, in contrast to the earlier success of enlargement policy in Central and Eastern Europe.

The Eastern Partnership

In principle, every European country has the possibility of joining the EU. In practice, economic, political, and strategic factors—let alone uncertainty about what constitutes being European—determine a putative member's prospects. A number of countries in Eastern Europe and the southern Caucasus have little hope of ever joining the EU. Nevertheless the EU is eager to cultivate a special relationship with them. Accordingly, in 2009 the EU launched the Eastern Partnership with Armenia, Azerbaijan, Belarus, Georgia, the Republic of Moldova and Ukraine, with a view to promoting economic development and boosting political stability in each partner country.

Lithuania, in the Council presidency, hosted an Eastern Partnership summit in Vilnius in November 2013, at which the signing of an EU-Ukraine association agreement was to have been the highlight. Under pressure from

Russian President Vladimir Putin, who feared that Ukraine was slipping out of Russia's self-proclaimed sphere of influence, Ukraine president Viktor Yanukovych rejected the agreement only days before the summit. This sparked massive demonstrations in Kyiv, which drove Yanukovych from power in February 2014. Yanukovych's ignominious ouster, in turn, triggered Russia's annexation of Crimea the following month.

The Crimea crisis caused a deep rift in relations between Russia and the West, reviving memories of the Cold War. Initially flattered by the public reaction in Kyiv against Yanukovych's rejection of the association agreement, the EU quickly realized the limits of its influence in the region. Member states disagreed on the extent to which the EU should sanction Russia, which openly disdained the EU's capacity for effective external action. While eager to revive the association agreement with the new Ukrainian regime, the EU had little else to offer a country in dire economic and political straits, and that was bitterly divided between the largely pro-European west and the pro-Russian east. Far from acting as a catalyst for a more coherent and effective EU policy toward non-member countries in Eastern Europe, Russia's annexation of Crimea and destabilization of Ukraine demonstrated the difficulty of forging a common foreign and security policy among twenty-eight countries and of honing an instrument as blunt as the Eastern Partnership.

The Eurozone Crisis

In the summer of 2007, as the EU completed the process of Central and Eastern European enlargement and grappled with the future of the Constitutional Treaty, the economic situation seemed to be sound. Performance varied greatly from country to country, ranging from tigerlike growth in Ireland and Estonia, to solid growth in Sweden, to respectable growth in Germany. In general, productivity was rising, GDP was growing, and unemployment was falling throughout the EU. The combined economic growth of the eurozone was set to surpass that of the United States.

The financial news from across the Atlantic, where severe problems with mortgage-backed securities were beginning to cause major anxieties in money and credit markets, added to the sense of satisfaction enveloping many Europeans. So-called subprime mortgages—property loans given to applicants who had little or no creditworthiness—were at the heart of the looming US crisis. Most Europeans considered such loans reckless and quintessentially American. The prevailing European attitude was one of *Schadenfreude:* malicious pleasure in someone else's misfortune.

Given the interconnectedness of global financial markets, however, Europe could hardly emerge unscathed from developments in the United States. Even if US "casino capitalism" was squarely to blame and European banks were beyond reproach, the EU was bound to suffer some side effects.

In fact, many European banks had also been handing out easy loans and had participated enthusiastically in the global market for mortgage-backed securities. German banks, it soon transpired, were among the worst offenders.

Calm Before the Storm

The years immediately preceding the onset of the global financial crisis and, later, the eurozone crisis, were deceptively calm.[26] The European Central Bank operated quietly in Frankfurt. Jean Claude Trichet, a former head of the French central bank, became its president in 2003. Although France's President Chirac had insisted that the successor to Wim Duisenberg, the first ECB president, be French, Trichet was not susceptible to national political pressure.

True to its mandate and to the predominant position of Germany in the Maastricht Treaty negotiations, from the outset the ECB pursued a monetary policy aimed exclusively at maintaining price stability (defined as an inflation rate below but close to 2 percent). Initially, there was little inflationary pressure throughout the eurozone, apart from some hot spots such as Ireland. The disparity in economic performance and inflationary pressures between Ireland and Germany, the weightiest economy in the eurozone, highlighted a concern about EMU: the suitability of a "one size fits all" monetary policy for national economies that were diverging rather than converging, contrary to a basic assumption underlying EMU. The unsuitability of relatively low interest rates for Ireland, set by the ECB in faraway Frankfurt, contributed to the property bubble of the middle first decade of this century, which, when it burst, threw Ireland into an economic tailspin and aggravated the eurozone crisis.

Diverging economic performance among eurozone members and fragmented financial and banking markets within the eurozone revealed the extent to which "economic and monetary union" was a misnomer. The EU had a monetary union, but not an economic union. Economic integration in the EU had not reached a level comparable to that of a national economy. Governments of eurozone members controlled fiscal policy (taxation and spending), and the single market was still a work in progress, especially for financial services. Banking supervision remained a national responsibility; its effectiveness varied greatly from country to country.

The Stability and Growth Pact was intended to keep national budgets within certain bounds. Governments agreed to participate in a surveillance process, coordinated by the Commission, to help ensure that they did not run excessive deficits (defined as greater than 3 percent of GDP). France and Germany exceeded the 3 percent limit in 2002 and 2003. Both complained about the illogicality of sticking rigidly to an arbitrarily chosen indicator for fiscal management regardless of prevailing economic circumstances. At first the Commission insisted on sanctioning the EU's two leading member states, but soon bowed to political reality and agreed to revise the pact. The changes eventually approved by the European Council, in

March 2005, kept the 3 percent reference point for budget deficits but gave members of the eurozone ample room for maneuver.

France and Germany's disregard of the Stability and Growth Pact raised concerns about the credibility and viability of EMU. So did revelations in November 2004 that Greece had misled the EU about the state of its public finances in 2000, when it had applied to participate in the third stage of EMU. By 2005, however, the EU economy was generally buoyant. Germany had emerged from its slump earlier in the decade and attained a respectable growth rate. Budget deficits dipped below the 3 percent threshold, though in many countries debt remained stubbornly above the widely disregarded threshold of 60 percent of GDP.

The economic improvement led to complacency, and the high value of the euro contributed to the overall sense of satisfaction. Having dropped against the dollar in its early years, the euro recovered strongly in the middle of the first decade of the twenty-first century. European exporters, who had enjoyed the advantages of a weak euro, now paid the price (fewer foreign sales) of a strong euro. Politicians and officials saw the rising value of the euro as validation of the euro itself. For residents of the eurozone, at least, the reversal in the euro's fortunes had a silver lining: vacations and shopping expeditions in the United States became extremely affordable.

Enlargement of the eurozone was another source of satisfaction with EMU. Though Swedish voters decisively rejected eurozone membership in a referendum in September 2003, most of the countries that joined the EU in 2004 and 2007 were eager to adopt the euro as soon as possible. Despite marked variations in economic performance among the new member states, meeting the criteria for monetary union initially seemed possible in most cases. Slovakia was the first to join, in January 2007; Malta and Cyprus, the smallest of the new member states, followed in January 2008; and Slovenia joined in January 2009. By that time, the remaining new member states were having difficulty meeting the convergence criteria, because of poor public finances, high inflation, or both. For many of them, not being in the eurozone during the crisis may have been a blessing in disguise, though Estonia joined in 2011 and Latvia in 2014.

Onset of the Crisis

The first major manifestation in Europe of the global financial crisis came in September 2007, in Britain, where a major mortgage lender called on the Bank of England (the central bank) to provide emergency lending. As Britain's economic model resembled that of the United States more closely than those of continental European countries, initially most EU leaders seemed unconcerned. The European Council discussed the situation in December 2007, and concluded optimistically "that macroeconomic fundamentals in the EU are strong and that sustained economic growth is expected."[27]

British prime minister Gordon Brown was far from sanguine and called for a summit of Britain, France, Italy, and Germany to take place at the end of January 2008. Opinions differed over how to respond to the escalating crisis. Sarkozy wanted coordinated government intervention in EU financial markets, with better regulation and stronger supervision of financial institutions. He also wanted the EU's leading member states to take the lead in reshaping the international financial architecture. Brown acknowledged the need for greater intervention and supervision, but not to the extent that Sarkozy desired. Believing that Germany could weather the storm, Merkel was disinclined to adopt an ambitious agenda.

There was no coordinated follow-up. Instead, as the crisis intensified in the United States and began to spread from Britain to continental Europe, national governments acted largely alone. The main instruments at their disposal were bank bailouts, recapitalization schemes, and fiscal stimulus packages. All were expensive and, if implemented separately in a space as tightly integrated as the EU, were unlikely to be fully effective. There was a glaring need for coordination, which the Commission seemed unwilling and the Council presidency (Slovenia in the first half of 2008) seemed unable to provide.

Complacency gave way to alarm in summer 2008, as the extent of the damage in Europe became more apparent. Britain, with a large, lightly regulated financial sector and a recent housing boom, was in dire economic straits. The housing bubbles burst in Ireland, Latvia, and Spain. Hungary, burdened by a big budget deficit, was another early victim. Even Germany was not immune from the global financial crisis. German banks had invested heavily in risky subprime products, while German manufacturers were losing export orders. Because exports rather than domestic consumption drove the German economy, which in turn drove the eurozone economy, this was a potentially disastrous development. France, by contrast, with a comparatively small export sector, strong banks, and robust domestic demand, was still relatively unscathed.

The enormity of the crisis became fully apparent in September 2008 with the sudden collapse of Lehman Brothers, the giant US-based global financial services firm. Its fall spread a wave of panic and caused a drastic drop in the value of stocks that reached far beyond Wall Street. When the crisis hit Ireland, the Irish government guaranteed the liabilities of the country's banks. But with its economy already in recession, revenues from its property boom a thing of the past, and the cost of its bank guarantee rapidly mounting, Ireland saw its budget surplus soon become a whopping deficit.

The European Recovery Plan. European governments' piecemeal approach to the escalating crisis, now spreading rapidly into the real economy, was unsustainable. Sarkozy, in the presidency of the European Council in the second half of 2008, took the lead. Here was a chance to restructure the

EU's financial framework, showcase the French economic model, and put France (and himself) at the forefront of international affairs. What followed was one of the most intensive periods of high-level diplomacy in the history of the EU, with a host of summits among various combinations of national leaders, plus an informal EU-US summit, in the month of October 2008 alone. The summits showed clearly that the differences between the EU's top three national leaders were still unresolved.

Sarkozy wanted a European fund to rescue failing banks; Merkel was skeptical, knowing that Germany would be expected to foot the bill. Sarkozy pressed the ECB to lower interest rates (a matter over which national governments had no control) and reiterated his wish for some form of economic government for the eurozone; Merkel preferred high interest rates if the alternative risked stoking inflation, but respected the independence of the ECB. Sarkozy again emphasized the importance of tough regulation of financial markets; Brown conceded that regulations would have to be tightened but wanted national bodies, not European institutions, to do the tightening.

Having responsibility for policing the single market and for monitoring the Stability and Growth Pact, the Commission wanted to hold the line against governments that might be tempted to skirt the rules. Yet by sticking to the letter of the law, the Commission risked alienating governments that were disregarding competition policy rules or running an excessive budget deficit because of dire economic circumstances. The Commission would need to strike a balance between enforcement and leniency, compassion and credibility. In other words, it would need to be flexible.

The Commission, availing itself of the consensus among governments on the need to improve financial controls and banking supervision in the EU, proposed a number of new measures, such as strengthening capital requirements for banks and regulating credit-rating agencies. The Commission also looked into the activities of hedge funds and private equity, which were accused of contributing to the crisis. Barroso established a high-level group to review the crisis more broadly and recommend more effective European and global supervision of financial institutions.

The Commission also coordinated work on a plan for growth and jobs. Announced in late November 2008, the European Recovery Plan was really a repackaging of existing EU measures, such as more lending, especially to small and medium-sized businesses, by the European Investment Bank, and quicker disbursement to the poorer member states of social and regional policy funds. Existing and new measures would amount to 1.5 percent of the member states' combined GDP over a two-year period (about €200 billion). This was a substantial sum by any standard, but far less than US stimulus spending (5.5 percent of GDP). While continuing to disagree on how to respond to the deepening economic crisis, Sarkozy and Merkel endorsed the plan, ushering it through the European Council in December 2008.

The G-20. Internationally, the crisis presented an opportunity to cast the EU as a leader of the global reform effort and savior of the rickety financial system. In global financial circles, Brown was better known than Sarkozy, having already become a key participant in discussions about global financial reform. Sarkozy, however, being in the Council presidency, had a powerful platform. In October 2008, Sarkozy, with Barroso in tow, visited the United States to confer with President George W. Bush on resolving the global crisis and redesigning the international financial system. Reporting to the EP on his return, an exuberant Sarkozy described his visit as a triumph for the EU and as evidence of the EU's ability to shape the international system: "Europe must uphold the idea of recasting international capitalism. . . . The world needs Europe to be proactive. If it has things to say, it should say so."[28]

The international track of the EU's reform efforts bore fruit in November 2008 in the first meeting of the Group of 20, representing the world's major economies, at the level of national leaders. Going beyond the G8, which included only the developed countries, the G-20 encompassed important emerging economies such as China and India and included the EU as an entity, represented by the Commission.

The Central and Eastern European countries. The launch of the Economic Recovery Plan and, to a lesser extent, the G-20 process, seemed to indicate the effectiveness of the EU in the face of a withering financial crisis. Yet the EU was by no means out of the woods. The extent of the downturn became even more apparent in early 2009 and put EU solidarity sorely to the test. Hard-hit countries in Central and Eastern Europe, with little money to spend on economic recovery and no prospect in the near future of entering the eurozone, felt increasingly isolated. Sarkozy's threat to support French car-makers only on condition that they repatriate their manufacturing plants from the Czech Republic was an egregious example of economic nationalism that deeply offended the new member states.[29]

Acutely aware of rising resentment among the new member states, the Polish prime minister invited the leaders of the Central and Eastern European countries to meet just before the opening of yet another extraordinary EU summit, in early March 2009, to discuss the deteriorating financial and economic situation. This was the only time during the crisis when the Central and Eastern European countries met as a bloc in the EU. They quickly realized that they had little in common. Some, like Poland and the Czech Republic, were riding out the economic crisis; others were floundering (by March 2009 the danger of financial collapse in Hungary and Latvia was acute). It was not in the interests of the better-off countries to be lumped together with the worst cases.

In March 2009, Hungary called on the European Council for massive financial assistance to recapitalize banks in Central and Eastern Europe and reschedule foreign currency debt. Merkel, to whom the appeal was primarily addressed, was not amused. Rather than establish a new EU fund to help countries that were in trouble partly because of their own irresponsibility, she favored IMF intervention and using an existing EU instrument to provide balance-of-payments support on a case-by-case basis to eligible non-eurozone countries.

The deepening financial crisis increased the eagerness of the Central and Eastern European member states to enter the eurozone as soon as possible. Only Estonia and Latvia qualified for membership, joining in 2011 and 2014 (Slovakia and Slovenia had joined earlier). Lithuania struggled with deteriorating economic and financial conditions. Hungary's disastrous financial situation put eurozone membership well out of reach. Poland, despite faring comparatively well during the crisis, increased public borrowing beyond the threshold for adopting the euro. Faced in any case with a difficult political situation—entry would require a constitutional amendment—Poland deferred for several years its planned entry into the eurozone. Similarly, the financial crisis damaged the Czech Republic's prospects of imminent eurozone entry, though the country's economic fundamentals were sound. Bulgaria and Romania, late EU entrants, were not serious candidates for eurozone membership.

Despite their straitened circumstances, some of the Central and Eastern European outsiders were irate that the Commission held so rigidly to the convergence criteria, not least because the Commission had relaxed the rules on budget deficits for existing eurozone members. Moreover, the criteria seemed less and less relevant to the situation facing the EU by 2010. Nor did it seem fair to base the inflation criterion on the performance of the three EU countries with the lowest inflation rates, when some of those countries, such as Britain and Sweden, were outside the eurozone. In the event, inflation became less of a concern during the recession, whereas budget deficits assumed greater importance.

Muddling through. January 2009 was an inauspicious time to commemorate the tenth anniversary of the euro. Understandably, the celebrations were muted, though EU leaders noted the apparent resilience of monetary union. At another extraordinary EU summit, in March 2009, EU leaders again pledged "to act together in a coordinated manner, within the framework of the single market and EMU."[30] Meeting later that month at their regular summit, they agreed to contribute an additional €75 billion to the IMF; increase to €50 billion the size of the EU instrument for balance-of-payments support; and allocate an additional €5 billion from unused money in the current EU budget to energy and infrastructure projects. The decision to spend the unused €5 billion, instead of returning it to the member states, did not sit well with the net contributors to the EU budget, including Germany. This was fur-

The Eurozone

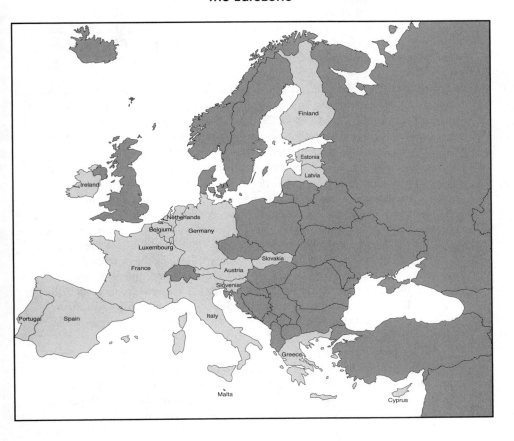

ther evidence of the bitterness of budgetary discussions within the EU as well as the parsimoniousness of Germany and other wealthy states when it came to helping less well-off countries during the economic downturn.

By mid-2009, the global financial system was stabilizing and the rate of economic decline was slowing. With the economic clouds still dark but not as ominous as three months earlier, national leaders made a special effort at the June 2009 summit to present a united front. They endorsed a report on financial supervision in the EU that called for a new regulatory agenda, stronger supervision, and effective crisis management procedures. Specifically, the report recommended setting up two new bodies at the EU level, the European Systemic Risk Council, under the auspices of the ECB, and the European System of Financial Supervisors. Despite approving the report, Brown, highly protective of British prerogatives in the areas of

banking and finance, made it clear that it would be difficult to reach consensus on detailed plans to flesh out the new bodies. Nevertheless, by the
end of 2009, national leaders were closer to agreement on the broad out-
lines of the financial and economic challenges facing the EU than at any
time in the previous two years.

ECB response. At the outset of the crisis the European Central Bank in-
jected almost €95 billion in overnight funds into the financial system in
order to ease credit flows. The ECB's action caught other central banks by
surprise and signaled an aggressive approach to combating the crisis. The
ECB's strategy of "enhanced credit support" provided additional liquidity
by giving emergency help to eurozone banks. In May 2009 the ECB decided to buy over €60 billion worth of covered bonds, high-quality securities that were a major source of mortgage finance in Europe. The move was
controversial. Within the ECB, a number of governing council members, including the head of the Bundesbank, reportedly objected strenuously to
what they saw as an unconventional operation that would inflate the money
supply. The action brought a swift and highly unusual rebuke from Merkel,
who claimed that the ECB was caving in to international pressure and con-
forming to the irresponsible practices of the US Federal Reserve and the
Bank of England. "We must return to independent and sensible monetary
policies," Merkel proclaimed, "otherwise we will be back to where we are
now in ten years' time."[31]

While infusing the financial system with liquidity, initially the ECB
was reluctant to lower interest rates, a conventional way of dealing with an
economic slowdown. In that respect, the ECB acted differently from its
leading international counterparts. Concerned about inflation, which peaked
at over 4 percent in mid-2008 (well above the 2 percent reference point and
the highest in eurozone history), the ECB raised interest rates in July of that
year to 4.25 percent. At a time when the rapidly deteriorating economic situation called for a substantial cut in interest rates, the ECB was moving in
the opposite direction. Critics (though not Merkel) claimed that the bank
was blinded by its obsession with price stability. The ECB began cutting interest rates only in October 2008. By May 2009 the main rate was 1 percent, after seven cuts in eight months. By that time also, inflation had fallen
to zero. It turned negative—stoking fears of deflation—in July 2009.

The Eurozone Under Threat

One of the most striking manifestations of economic disunion in the eurozone was the existence of separate, national bond markets (one for each of
the eurozone's members). In the early years of monetary union, the yield on
government bonds did not diverge appreciably throughout the eurozone, despite the distinctly different reputations of its members for fiscal responsi-

bility. Being in the eurozone made it easier for a country like Greece to borrow, and the presumption that a eurozone member would never default—or be allowed to default—greatly reduced Greek borrowing costs. With seemingly unlimited access to cheap loans, successive Greek governments went on a borrowing binge and a spending spree to fund public-sector jobs (many of them for political patronage), generous state pensions, welfare programs, and the like.

By the end of 2009, the global financial crisis was making international lenders jittery about the extent of the Greek deficit and debt. As the crisis deepened, a large spread began to open between the yield on German government bonds, which the market perceived as safe, and the yield on Greek bonds, which looked increasingly risky. What would happen if Greece—or one of the other heavily indebted eurozone members—was unable to repay its debts? The EU treaty did not allow the ECB to bail out a eurozone member, and countries were not allowed to assume the debts of others in the eurozone (even if they wanted to). Would Germany nonetheless intervene to prevent a potentially disastrous financial collapse in a eurozone member? What would the ECB do? The question became urgent in early 2010 when Greece, running a budget deficit of over 13 percent of GDP and facing entrenched public resistance to government-imposed austerity measures, teetered on the brink of bankruptcy. Thus began the second, most acute phase of the financial crisis, which threatened not only the stability but also the survival of the eurozone.

Crisis management. The European Council exists in part as a crisis management mechanism. That was its original purpose. If the European Council had not existed in 2010—a fanciful notion, given the development of European integration since the origin of the European Council in the mid-1970s—it would had to have been invented. Who else but the national leaders had the stature and authority to confront a crisis of this magnitude?

It was difficult for Van Rompuy, the newly elected European Council president, to conduct the European Council successfully in the presence of two headstrong soloists, Merkel and Sarkozy, who seemed far apart on how to deal with the Greek debacle. Initially Merkel had a hands-off approach. She seemed stunned by the enormity of Greece's deficit and unaware of its implications for German creditors as well as for the stability of the eurozone. Merkel was well attuned to domestic opinion, which was extremely censorious of Greece. She was equally concerned about the constitutionality of a bailout, given the critical tone of recent EU-related rulings by the German constitutional court.

Merkel's position struck many EU leaders as excessively cautious and even irresponsible. When, eventually, she decided to act, Merkel insisted on IMF involvement in any bailout, on assistance to Greece only as a last resort, and on reform of the Stability and Growth Pact. Merkel was in a strong position to get her way: without Germany, Europe's largest contributor to any potential EU rescue fund, a bailout would be impossible.

The way that Merkel pushed her proposal typified the dynamics of the Franco-German relationship and of the European Council. First she convinced Sarkozy, who had opposed IMF involvement because it appeared to imply that the EU was unable to act independently and because it would boost the profile of IMF director Dominique Strauss-Kahn, a potential rival in the 2012 French presidential election. She and Sarkozy then presented their plan, drawn in part from ideas already floated by others but repackaged as an exclusively Franco-German initiative, at a summit of eurozone leaders in March 2010. Finally, the European Council approved what was, in effect, the already agreed proposal of the eurozone leaders for a Greek rescue package.

The Greek bailout came in May 2010, in the form of a €110 billion EU-IMF package. In return, Greece agreed to impose draconian cuts in public expenditure and to increase state revenue. Realizing the extent of the Greek debacle and the possible need for intervention also in Ireland and Portugal, later in May 2010 the European Council agreed to establish, for a limited time, the European Financial Stability Facility. The purpose of the facility was to bail out insolvent eurozone members, on condition that they implement macroeconomic adjustment programs—in other words, severe budget cuts. Initially, the facility was woefully underfunded.

Though Merkel and Sarkozy had come together in response to the situation in Greece, they still seemed far apart on the broader eurozone crisis. Concerned about the differences between them, Valéry Giscard d'Estaing and Helmut Schmidt, nostalgic about the early days of the European Council, publicly appealed to Merkel and Sarkozy in May 2010 to strengthen Franco-German ties and "pursue the direction taken by their predecessors to preserve the security of the euro."[32] Perhaps mindful of the elder statesmen's appeal, but more likely because of political expediency, Merkel and Sarkozy developed a joint approach.

Increasingly alarmed about the precarious state of public finances in the eurozone, Merkel personified Germany's unyielding stance on imposing austerity programs and cutting budget deficits. She persuaded Sarkozy of the wisdom of these measures, thereby allowing her to present German preferences in a Franco-German framework. Sarkozy acquiesced partly because of ideological affinity (both leaders were on the center-right), and partly because of the preponderance of German power, which he hoped to exercise vicariously. Despite the personal and policy differences between them, by late 2010 Merkel and Sarkozy were united in their main approach to resolving the crisis: imposing tough austerity measures. Their close collaboration signaled the centrality of France and Germany in eurozone emergency management and crisis decisionmaking.

Merkel's preponderant influence, initial indecisiveness, and subsequent assertiveness rubbed other leaders the wrong way. So did the newly strengthened Franco-German axis. British prime minister David Cameron, who attended his first meeting of the European Council in June 2010, hoped to cultivate a close relationship with Merkel. Yet Britain's troubled history of EU involvement and position outside the eurozone precluded the possibility of a vibrant Anglo-German axis rivaling, let alone supplanting, the Franco-German axis.

Nevertheless, Merkel and Sarkozy did not always get things entirely their own way. Shortly before a meeting of the European Council in October 2010, they met in the French town of Deauville and issued a declaration on reform of the Stability and Growth Pact, which they fully expected the European Council to endorse. The declaration included a call for pact offenders to lose their voting rights in the Council. This was unlikely to win the support of leaders whose countries were most likely to be sanctioned.

Merkel therefore dropped her demand concerning the loss of voting rights, but won agreement in the European Council in December 2010 to include a minor change to the Lisbon Treaty authorizing the establishment of a permanent bailout fund, the European Stability Mechanism, to replace the European Financial Stability Facility, which was due to expire in 2013. The thought of changing the Lisbon Treaty and fighting new ratification battles, even for such an apparently benign purpose, had little appeal for most EU leaders. Nonetheless, Merkel was adamant: given the treaty's no-bailout for eurozone members, a treaty amendment authorizing a permanent bailout mechanism was essential in order to assuage German public opinion and prevent an unfavorable ruling from the ever-vigilant constitutional court. Eurozone leaders duly signed a treaty establishing the mechanism in February 2012. With total subscribed capital of €700 billion, it came into operation in October 2012.

The need for a large, permanent rescue fund became apparent in November 2010, when Ireland requested emergency assistance. Due to the open-ended bailout of its banks, Ireland's deficit rose to a stratospheric 32.3 percent of GDP in 2010, making it impossible for the government to borrow. In response, the IMF and the EU agreed to a rescue package of €85 billion, with strict conditions attached.

In the maelstrom. The years 2011–2013 were tumultuous for the EU. The escalating crisis resembled an ocean storm crashing toward shore. EU leaders responded by building an ever-higher seawall as ever-larger waves—in the form of rapidly deteriorating public finances in Greece, Ireland, Portugal, Spain, and Italy—risked inundating the eurozone. The seawall consisted of various measures thrown together in haste: the European Stability Mechanism, the European Semester, the Six-Pack, the Euro Plus Pact, the

Fiscal Compact, and the Compact for Growth and Jobs. The seawall appeared sufficiently sturdy by mid-2012, though the prospect of a rogue wave, capable of breaching the eurozone's defenses, remained acute. Only when ECB president Mario Draghi pledged, in July 2012, to do whatever was needed within the institution's mandate to save the euro—in other words, the ECB would act as a lender of last resort—did the high water finally recede. Nevertheless, the crisis remained acute, as events in Cyprus in early 2013 demonstrated dramatically.

A surfeit of summits. The intensity and duration of the crisis increased the frequency of EU summits and the level of media interest in them. National leaders, the key political decisionmakers, met almost continuously to address the crisis, either in the European Council, the Euro Summit (the subset of the European Council consisting of the leaders of eurozone members), or in other forums, such as bilateral summits or on the margins of other international events.

As the crisis deepened, each summit assumed a make-or-break aspect, despite Van Rompuy's stricture that "raising expectation of a solve-it-all summit is not helpful."[33] Nevertheless, summits were essential for containing the crisis at crucial stages. Key meetings included the Euro Summit in July 2011, where leaders approved a second assistance program for Greece, including voluntary private-sector involvement; the series of EU and eurozone summits in October 2011, where leaders agreed on measures to maximize the capacity of the European Financial Stability Facility, and on bank recapitalization and funding; the EU and eurozone summits in December 2011, where leaders decided to conclude a fiscal compact to require balanced national budgets; the European Council in June 2012, where leaders approved the Compact for Growth and Jobs to address unemployment and the social costs of the crisis; and the European Council in December 2012, where leaders endorsed a version of Van Rompuy's "roadmap" for a fundamental overhaul of EMU.

As Van Rompuy observed with respect to the crisis, "markets have the luxury of moving with the speed of the click of a mouse; political processes . . . cannot deliver so quickly."[34] Having so many people sharing responsibility for managing the eurozone inevitably made matters worse. "There are 17 governments sitting at the table in the Eurogroup, representing a total of more than 40 political parties," Eurogroup president Jean-Claude Juncker pointed out in early 2011, observing that "it's no wonder that there are occasional difficulties with coordinating things."[35] At the highest political level, EU summits faced a similar constraint. Given the eurozone's political character and institutional architecture, EU leaders were simply unable to respond rapidly, no matter how urgent the situation became.

The endless round of summits, each one followed by a grandiose declaration that appeared to do little to stem the crisis, fueled intense criticism of EU summitry. Martin Schulz, who became EP president in January 2012, was among the most vociferous critics. As soon as he took office, Schulz began to fashion a new, overtly political model for the EP presidency. Thriving on confrontation, Schulz denounced the excessive role of the European Council in the crisis, which, he claimed, accentuated intergovernmentalism, undermined parliamentary scrutiny, and weakened the legitimacy of EU governance.[36] Schulz's forcefulness, acumen, nationality (German), and ambition for higher EU office enhanced his public profile and political stature.

Restricted as EP president to delivering a speech to national leaders immediately before the official opening of each European Council, Schulz demanded full membership in the EU's most exclusive club. At issue was not only Schulz's eagerness to be at the center of EU decisionmaking, but also a growing rivalry between the European Council and the EP, due in part to the Lisbon Treaty, which had elevated the importance of both institutions. Schulz's election as EP president brought latent tension to the fore.

The meetings that Schulz criticized but that he so desperately wanted to attend were lengthy and lively affairs, characterized by intense discussions and often testy exchanges. Sarkozy was notoriously impulsive and unrestrained. Silvio Berlusconi, Italy's mercurial prime minister, added spice to the proceedings. With Berlusconi's departure in December 2011, and Sarkozy's in May 2012, EU summits became less dramatic and more businesslike, which suited most of the other participants but did not necessarily improve the quality of decisionmaking.

As in years past, only more so, Sarkozy and Merkel dominated. Invariably, the French leader and the German leader met to thrash out their differences and agree on a proposal for presentation at the next summit. Without prior Franco-German agreement, Sarkozy was sure that key decisions of EU leaders would not have been possible.[37] He may have been right, but Van Rompuy put it slightly differently when he wrote that agreement between France and Germany was "necessary, but not sufficient" to ensure agreement among EU leaders.[38]

Despite the appearance of equality between France and Germany, the balance of influence between both countries changed appreciably during the height of the eurozone crisis. Germany, for a long time the most powerful economic player in the EU, became unquestionably the most influential politically as well.[39] With Germany contributing most to the bailout funds, German politicians were not shy about advancing German interests.

Increasingly, political leadership to resolve the crisis seemed to rest on Merkel's shoulders. Understated by nature, Merkel faced criticism at home and abroad for not grasping the seriousness of the crisis, for responding too slowly, and for advocating austerity *über alles*. By the end of 2011, however, her increasingly alarmist statements about the implications of the crisis for the survival of the eurozone and the future of the EU suggested that she understood the gravity, if not yet the complexity, of the situation.

The "Six-Pack." In December 2010, the European Council endorsed a report, submitted by Van Rompuy, on ways to reinforce fiscal discipline, improve economic coordination and surveillance, and strengthen eurozone institutions. In particular, the report recommended reform of the Stability and Growth Pact.[40] Even before the European Council endorsed the report, the Commission introduced six legislative proposals (the so-called Six-Pack), partly for that purpose.

Given the importance and complexity of the proposals, the legislative procedure was bound to be fraught. Providing overall political direction, the European Council urged the Council and EP to reach agreement in the first reading stage, with a view to having the legislation enacted by the end of 2011. This put considerable pressure on the EP and, in the view of many of its members, lessened the value of parliamentary deliberation.

The most consequential issue concerned the automatic imposition of sanctions against countries that breached the terms of the pact. A majority of governments, led by France, did not want the Commission to have the right to impose sanctions automatically, but wanted the Council to be able to approve sanctions by means of a qualified majority vote. A minority of governments argued that giving the Council the last word on sanctions risked undermining the effectiveness of a supposedly stronger pact. Ordinarily Germany would not have been in that camp, but this was a rare case of Merkel making a concession to Sarkozy. The Council's common position reflected the majority viewpoint.

The EP too was divided on this issue. The European People's Party, the "governing" group, supported the Council's position. It may not have been coincidental that Joseph Daul, leader of the group, belonged to the ruling French center-right party. As Daul knew only too well, Sarkozy took a keen interest in the issue and mentioned more than once the importance of getting the EP behind the Council's position.

On the other side of the aisle, the Socialist Group, then under Schulz's aggressive leadership, advocated a position that did not call for sanctions to be fully automatic, but that would allow governments to prevent their imposition only by means of a reverse qualified majority. In other words, instead of being able to prevent the imposition of sanctions by forming a blocking minority, as the Council proposed, a country wanting to reject the Commission's recommendation would face the much more daunting task of having to form a supermajority. With the backing of the Liberals and other groups, Schulz swung the EP behind the reverse majority rule.

Despite intense pressure from Sarkozy and other national leaders, the EP collectively stuck to this position. For the sake of enacting the legislation by the end of 2011, France, the final holdout on the Council side, eventually relented. It was a sweet victory for the EP as a whole, despite the opposition of the European People's Party. The reverse majority rule improved the effectiveness of the legislation by making it more difficult for governments to wiggle out of their Stability and Growth Pact commitments. What difference the revised Stability and Growth Pact would make in practice, however, remained to be seen.

The Fiscal Compact. Not content with reform of the Stability and Growth Pact, Germany pressed toward the end of the 2011 for an EU treaty change that would require member states to include in their national legislation, preferably at the constitutional level, a requirement for a balanced budget (strictly speaking, not to run a deficit exceeding 0.5 percent of GDP). In the event of an excessive deficit, governments would have to correct any deviation within a short time.

As usual, Merkel first brought Sarkozy on board and then built up sufficient political momentum to win support for the idea in the European Council. Cameron's solitary stance against the Fiscal Compact emphasized the growing distance between Britain and the rest of the EU. It also infuriated Sarkozy, who reportedly told Cameron at an EU summit in October 2011: "You have lost a good opportunity to shut up. . . . We are sick of you criticizing us and telling us what to do. You say you hate the euro and now you want to interfere in our meetings."[41] British recalcitrance obliged the other governments to negotiate the proposed agreement outside the formal EU framework. Twenty-five national leaders duly signed the Fiscal Compact—officially the Treaty on Stability, Coordination, and Governance in the Economic and Monetary Union—in March 2012, with the prime ministers of Britain and the Czech Republic being the odd ones out.

The intergovernmental nature of the Fiscal Compact bothered the Commission and especially the EP. The Parliament, having reluctantly agreed to approve an earlier EU treaty change, on establishing the European Stability Mechanism, by means of the simplified amendment procedure, thereby obviating the need for a convention, was reluctant to allow another, further-reaching treaty change to take place by means of the simplified procedure.

Governments were averse to holding a convention, fearing that it would empower the EP and open a Pandora's box. Who knew what other items would appear on the agenda? Nor did they want to risk possibly unwinnable ratification battles. The EP acquiesced, but many MEPs felt that they were being steamrolled by governments when it came to fighting the eurozone crisis. As it happened, the decision to conclude the Fiscal Compact as an international agreement, outside the EU framework, negated the question of whether to hold a convention or use the simplified procedure to change the EU treaty.

New French leadership. In late 2011, François Hollande, the Socialist candidate and frontrunner in the French presidential election campaign, came out against the proposed Fiscal Compact. Sarkozy's seemingly uncritical attachment to Merkel compounded the president's unpopularity in France. Conversely, Hollande's emphasis on investment and stimulus spending, as an antidote to excessive austerity, boosted the opposition candidate's electoral prospects. Merkel made no secret of her preference for Sarkozy. The idea of a German chancellor publicly supporting a French presidential candidate offended many French people. Yet in an entity such as the EU, electioneering by members of the same pan-European party (Merkel and Sarkozy belong to the European People's Party) was a sign of the EU's political maturity.

By that time, Germany's preponderant power and unyielding position on economic austerity and structural reform had deeply alienated other member states, not just those struggling to stay afloat financially. Merkel, though far from isolated within the European Council, must have felt slighted by the widespread euphoria with which many other leaders greeted Hollande's decisive victory in May 2012. For them, Sarkozy's defeat meant not only the departure of an unpopular member of the European Council, but also a stinging rebuke for the hegemonic duo known derisively as "Merkozy."

Hollande's victory, moreover, put a definite Social Democratic stamp on the growing dissatisfaction with Merkel. Danish prime minister Helle Thorning-Schmidt, a Social Democrat, was jubilant, especially as Denmark held the rotating Council presidency in the first half of 2012. She pointed out that job creation and growth, Hollande's main objectives, were also the Danish presidency's priorities.[42] Though now president of the EP, Schulz could not disguise his partisan preference for Hollande and expressed delight that a counterweight was forming against Merkel in the European Council.

Soon after the French election, Hollande and Merkel held a bilateral summit, at which it was clear that the tone and substance of Franco-German relations had changed appreciably. As if to emphasize the point, the next meeting of the European Council, in May 2012, did not begin with a joint Franco-German position or policy statement. Even more striking, in June 2012, largely at Hollande's insistence, the European Council adopted the Compact for Growth and Jobs, which aimed to tackle unemployment, address the social consequences of the crisis, and improve economic competitiveness.[43] Nobody disputed the desirability of growth, which was precisely what austerity and budget discipline aimed to foster. Yet the word "growth" became a catchall, especially on the political left, for measures to stimulate economic activity through government spending. Merkel, though willing to go along with the Compact for Growth and Jobs, which was mostly rhetorical, and to revise the conditions for the terms of bailouts offered through the European Stability Mechanism, was not about to renegotiate the Fiscal Compact. Nor was she willing to contemplate mutualizing the sovereign debts of eurozone members by agreeing to issue eurobonds.

The differences between Merkel and Hollande became more apparent later in the year. Merkel repeatedly called for "more Europe," meaning a major transfer of sovereignty from the national to the European level of governance. Deeper political integration, involving far-reaching institutional reforms, would complement the shift of responsibility for fiscal and economic policymaking to Brussels and Strasbourg. This could come about only through extensive treaty change, which would be time-consuming and difficult to ratify. Hollande was less ambitious. The notion of holding a convention and negotiating treaty change hardly appealed to someone whose political party had been torn apart during the disastrous 2005 French referendum campaign on the Constitutional Treaty. He preferred to focus on issues affecting growth and employment that might be tackled immediately.

The distance between Hollande and Merkel made it unlikely that the European Council would agree at its December meeting on a far-reaching plan for "completion" of EMU. Indeed, the "roadmap for the achievement of genuine economic and monetary union" that the European Council adopted was a far cry from what Van Rompuy had proposed in a series of reports presented to national leaders throughout the year.[44] Merkel successfully resisted the idea of establishing an EU-level mechanism to help counter country-specific economic shocks, fearing that it would cost Germany too much and possibly reward countries that were not serious about structural reform. She also managed to limit the scope of the Single Supervisory Mechanism, a key initiative for financial-sector reform, to large banks and those already receiving state support, thereby shielding most German institutions from it.[45]

The December 2012 European Council marked a disappointing but not entirely unexpected end to three years of hectic summitry. Merkel's commitment to far-reaching eurozone reform increasingly appeared more rhetorical than real. Hollande was bereft of ideas that might help tackle high unemployment and sluggish economic performance throughout the EU. The two leaders seemed uninterested in working closely together. As one observer remarked, the December 2012 European Council "demonstrated once again that the Franco-German tandem does not function . . . [and] that the process towards a more ambitious renewal of the EU/EMU . . . will not be possible without a rapprochement between Germany and France," a rapprochement unlikely to happen before the German federal elections of September 2013.[46]

The ECB to the rescue. The president of the European Central Bank faced fewer political constraints than national leaders and could act decisively. Neither Jean-Claude Trichet nor his successor, Mario Draghi, hesitated to tell politicians what they should be doing, while fiercely protecting the independence of their own institution. Nevertheless, the ECB did not exist in a political vacuum. The ECB's pursuit of unconventional operations, notably the purchase of government bonds on the secondary market through the Securities Markets Program, generated considerable controversy within the bank, and especially in Germany, the self-proclaimed enforcer of ECB orthodoxy. German politicians and Bundesbank officials saw the ECB's action as contrary to the spirit of the EU treaty—as the ECB was not allowed to purchase government bonds on primary markets—and a diversion from the all-important task of maintaining price stability in the eurozone, which, in 2011, exceeded the ECB's target of just below 2 percent.

Frustrated by the ECB's seemingly irresponsible behavior, Bundesbank president Axel Weber resigned in protest in February 2011. In doing so, he removed himself from contention for the presidency of the ECB when Trichet's second term came to an end, in November 2011. Without a strong candidate of its own, Germany acquiesced to the appointment of Draghi to the position. Though Draghi was an internationally trained economist, the fact that he came from Italy, a country openly mocked in Germany for its fiscal irresponsibility, sent mild shock waves through the chancellery in Berlin and the Bundesbank in Frankfurt.

German fears seemed to be realized when the ECB launched a new long-term refinancing operation in December 2011, offering low-cost, three-year loans to banks in an effort to stabilize the rickety European financial system.[47] But Draghi held off from further massive bond purchases—for a while. Feeling more secure in office and less sensitive to German criticism, in July 2012 he finally said what the financial markets and many Europeans—though perhaps few in Germany—had long wanted to hear: that the ECB would do "whatever it takes to preserve the euro."[48] Proving that it was now the lender of last resort, in August 2012 the ECB launched its "outright monetary transactions" program, the successor, on a potentially limitless scale, to the Securities Markets Program. Proving also that it would not simply write blank checks, the ECB made recourse to outright monetary transactions conditional on beneficiary countries seeking assistance from the EU and the IMF and therefore subjecting themselves to strict conditionality. Nevertheless, the effect on the bond prices of beleaguered countries was immediate. Reassured that sovereign default was no longer a possibility, the financial markets settled down without the bank even having to put the new mechanism to the test.

Whereas the financial effect of Draghi's action was immediately beneficial, German and other commentators fretted about its long-term economic consequences. The political price was also potentially high. German faith in the ECB was further shaken, especially as the bank cut interest rates to 0.25 percent in November 2013, even though by that time eurozone inflation had fallen well below 2 percent. The seemingly wayward direction of the ECB, an institution modeled on the Bundesbank, caused alarm in Germany, the eurozone's largest economy and the EU's most influential member state.

A chronic crisis. The ECB's assertiveness in 2012 reduced pressure on the heavily indebted eurozone members, but did not end the crisis. The eurozone's continuing vulnerability became apparent in March 2013, when the situation in Cyprus spun out of control. The problem was rooted in the country's banks, which were heavily exposed to risky foreign loans, especially to borrowers in Greece. As a result, banks could not repay their own creditors, many of whom were Russian investors. The cost of rescuing the banks and of borrowing internationally became prohibitive for the Cypriot government, which dithered in early 2013 over requesting an EU-IMF bailout. When it finally concluded a rescue package, Cyprus agreed that all bank customers would pay a onetime tax on their deposits, to help raise €5.8 billion toward the cost of the bailout. This caused a huge backlash among ordinary Cypriots, who had taken for granted that their savings were secure.

Under the terms of the renegotiated agreement, the government decided not to tax deposits under €100,000, thereby penalizing wealthier—mostly Russian—depositors. Cyprus also agreed to a major restructuring of its banking sector, along with the usual austerity measures. Apart from the long-term costs of the crisis, the immediate impact was shocking. In order to prevent a run on the banks, the government closed all financial institutions for two weeks. When the banks reopened, customers were allowed to withdraw only €300 a day and faced controls on moving money out of the country. The imposition of capital controls demonstrated the extent of the eurozone's disarray.

The New Normalcy

Notwithstanding the Cypriot situation, the EU settled in 2013 into what looked like a period of new normalcy. EU summits became less frequent and frantic, and were no longer dominated by the eurozone crisis. Merkel and Hollande developed an uneasy coexistence, especially after Merkel won reelection to an unprecedented third term as German chancellor, in September 2013. Merkel's victory was not so much a ringing endorsement of her handling of the crisis as an acknowledgment that she personified German caution. Merkel was in a paradoxical position: strengthened by her decisive election victory and by her long experience at the center of EU affairs, but weakened by the loss of confidence throughout the eurozone in Germany's ability to provide sound leadership. The extent of the dissatisfaction with Germany soon became apparent when other member states and the Commission vociferously denounced Germany's large trade surplus as a contributory factor to the eurozone's economic instability.

Though not shy about advancing German interests, Merkel continued to wrap her preferences in a Franco-German cloak. Despite the reality of German hegemony, she seemed determined to maintain the fiction of Franco-German equality. There were institutional and personal dynamics at play. Personally, Hollande was in tune with the unflappable Merkel. Institutionally, the Franco-German duopoly was hardwired into Germany's political elites. So was an aversion to assertiveness and unilateralism on the international stage.

The crisis raised questions about how united the EU really was. Speaking in late 2011, Schulz saw a threefold distinction among member states: the Franco-German decisionmakers, other eurozone countries, and the rest.[49] He might have added that the United Kingdom was in a category of its own, being increasingly at odds with other member states and dissatisfied with EU membership. At the end of 2011, when Cameron refused to go along with the proposed Fiscal Compact, the depth of the division between the United Kingdom and the others became fully apparent.

The most obvious distinction within the EU was between eurozone members and nonmembers, which corresponded approximately to that between older and newer, and Western and Eastern European, member states. Most Central and Eastern European eurozone nonmembers saw themselves as "pre-ins," as countries waiting to meet the criteria for membership despite the fading luster of adopting the single currency. Poland, the largest of the new member states and a country that weathered the global financial crisis and ensuing economic recession better than most, was especially eager to participate in eurozone deliberations before formally becoming a member of the group. Poland's exclusion from meetings of eurozone leaders was particularly galling during the country's Council presidency in the second half of 2011.

"As guardian of the unity of the 27," Van Rompuy remarked at the time of his reelection as European Council president in 2012, "I have insisted all along on involving all Member States—all 27 even when it was about the 17 of the Eurozone—and all institutions."[50] That may have been so, but the launch of the Euro Summit, which removed eurozone-specific issues from the European Council proper, inevitably reinforced the distinction within the EU between eurozone and non-eurozone members, a distinction that more and more resembled that between first- and second-class citizens.

The crisis had drawn unflattering attention to the nature and quality of economic governance in the EU. The meaning of economic governance was notoriously imprecise, ranging from fiscal federalism at one extreme, to intergovernmental coordination of various socioeconomic policies at the other. Regardless of political preferences, a consensus had emerged among eurozone members on the need to strengthen the economic aspect of EMU, so that "economic and monetary union [could] finally stand on both legs," as Barroso put it.[51] Though still nominally the preserve of national parliaments and governments, by the mid-2010s, as the crisis seemed to stabilize, fiscal policy—the final frontier of European integration—was subject to much closer scrutiny by the Commission and far greater coordination among national authorities. This did not mean that fiscal policy was subject to supranational decisionmaking. Rather, economic governance had developed into a set of binding rules, expectations, institutions, and obligations guiding fiscal policy and structural reform primarily among eurozone members. Nevertheless, the economic aspect of EMU was far from sturdy.

Notes

1. On the Lisbon Treaty, see Paul Craig, *The Lisbon Treaty: Law, Politics, and Treaty Reform* (Oxford: Oxford University Press, 2013); David Phinnemore, *The Treaty of Lisbon: Origins and Negotiation* (Basingstoke: Palgrave Macmillan, 2013).

2. Brussels European Council, "Presidency Conclusions," June 16–17, 2005.

3. *Financial Times,* May 29, 2006, p. 4.

4. Brussels European Council, "Presidency Conclusions," June 15–16, 2006.

5. Nicolas Sarkozy, "Je serai le président de tous les Français," Paris, May 6, 2007, http://www.u-m-p.org/site/index.php/ump/s_informer/discours/je_serai_le_president _de_tous_les_francais.

6. Brussels European Council, "Presidency Conclusions," June 21–22, 2007.

7. "EU Summit: Leaders Strike Treaty Deal," *EurActiv,* October 19, 2007.

8. See Institute of International and European Affairs, *Ireland's Future After Lisbon: Issues Options Implications* (Dublin, 2008), pp. 32–49.

9. Brussels European Council, "Presidency Conclusions," December 11–12, 2008.

10. Brussels European Council, "Presidency Conclusions," June 18–19, 2009.

11. Constitutional Court of Germany, press release (72/2009) and judgment, June 30, 2009, http://www.bundesverfassungsgericht.de/en/press/bvg09-.html.

12. Tony Barber, "The Appointments of Herman Van Rompuy and Catherine Ashton," *Journal of Common Market Studies* 48, supplement (September 2010), pp. 55–67.

13. See Desmond Dinan, "The Post-Lisbon European Council Presidency: An Interim Assessment," *West European Politics* 36, no. 6 (2013), pp. 1256–1272.

14. General Secretariat of the Council, *The European Council in 2011* (Luxembourg: Publications Office of the European Union, 2012), p. 16.

15. See Bart van Vooren, *A Legal-Institutional Perspective on the European External Action Service* (The Hague: T.M.C. Asser Institute, 2010), pp. 11–13; "The EU's New Diplomatic Service," *EurActiv,* March 8, 2011.

16. CEPS, Egmont, and EPC, *The Treaty of Lisbon: A Second Look at the Institutional Innovations* (Brussels, 2010), pp. 76, 78.

17. See John O'Brennan, *The Enlargement of the European Union* (Abingdon: Routledge, 2006); Victoria Curzon Price, Alice Landau, and Richard Whitman, eds., *Enlargement of the European Union* (Abingdon: Routledge, 2012).

18. See D. Papadimitriou, *Romania and The European Union: From Marginalization to Membership* (London: Routledge, 2008); Martin Kalachev, *Bulgaria's Accession to the EU* (Saarbrücken: Lambert Academic, 2009).

19. Chirac is quoted in *European Report,* February 19, 2003, p. 15.

20. See Aroida Elbasani, *European Integration and Transformation in the Western Balkans: Europeanization or Business As Usual?* (Abingdon: Routledge, 2013); Sinas Kusic and Claudia Grupe, *The Western Balkans on Their Way to the EU?* (Brussels: Peter Lang, 2007); John O'Brennan, *The EU and the Western Balkans: Stabilization and Europeanization Through Enlargement* (Abingdon: Routledge, 2014).

21. Milada Anna Vachudova, "Corruption and Compliance in the EU's Post-Communist Members and Candidates," *Journal of Common Market Studies* 47, supplement (2009), p. 44.

22. Commission, "Enlargement: Kosovo," http://ec.europa.eu/enlargement/countries /detailed-country-information/kosovo.

23. On the Turkish case, see Ali Carkoglu and Barry Rubin, eds., *Turkey and the European Union: Domestic Politics, Economic Integration, and International Dynamics* (London: Cass, 2003); Esra LaGro and Knud Erik Jorgensen, eds., *Turkey and the European Union: Prospects for a Difficult Encounter* (Basingstoke: Palgrave Macmillan, 2005); Meltem Müftüler-Baç and Yannis Stivachtis, eds., *Turkey–European Union Relations: Dilemmas, Opportunities, and Constraints* (Lanham: Lexington, 2008); Belgin Akcay and Bahri Yilmaz, eds., *Turkey's Accession to the European Union: Political and Economic Challenges* (Lanham: Lexington, 2012).

24. Council, "Negotiations Framework: Principles Governing Negotiations," Brussels, October 3, 2005.

25. See George Christou, "The Cyprus Presidency of the EU," *Journal of Common Market Studies* 51, supplement (2013), pp. 80–88.

26. On the causes, conduct, and consequences of the eurozone crisis, see David Marsh, *The Euro: The Battle for the New Global Currency,* revised and updated ed. (New Haven: Yale University Press, 2011); David Marsh, *Europe's Deadlock: How the Euro Crisis Could Be Solved—And Why It Won't Happen* (New Haven: Yale University Press, 2011); Johan van Overtveldt, *The End of the Euro: The Uneasy Future of the European Union* (Farnham: Ashgate, 2011); Carlo Bastasin, *Saving Europe: How National Politics Nearly Destroyed the Euro* (Washington, DC: Brookings Institution, 2012); Costas Lapavitsas, *Crisis in the Eurozone* (London: Verso, 2012).

27. Brussels European Council, "Presidency Conclusions," December 14, 2007.

28. Quoted in *Europolitics,* October 22, 2008.

29. See "Czechs Blast 'Protectionist' Comments by Sarkozy," *EUobserver,* February 9, 2009, http://euobserver.com/institutional/27568.

30. "European Summit: Meeting Reaffirms Principles but Short on Actions," *Europolitics,* March 3, 2009.

31. Quoted in *Financial Times,* June 3, 2009, p. 1.

32. Valéry Giscard d'Estaing and Helmut Schmidt, "L'appel de Giscard et Schmidt," *Le Point,* May 27, 2010.

33. General Secretariat of the Council, *The European Council in 2011,* p. 6.

34. *Agence Europe,* 28 October 2011.

35. Quoted in "Jean Claude Juncker on Saving the Euro," *Spiegel Online International,* 24 January 2011, http://www.spiegel.de/international/europe/jean-claude -juncker-on-saving-the-euro-it-would-be-wrong-to-create-taboos-a-741183.html.

36. See, for instance, Martin Schulz, "A Return to Long-Term Thinking," speech, Berlin, November 6, 2012.

37. See *Le Monde,* 9 December 2011.

38. Council press conference, October 23, 2012.

39. W. Paterson, "The Reluctant Hegemon? Germany Moves Centre Stage in the European Union," *Journal of Common Market Studies* 49, supplement (2011), pp. 57–75.

40. Council, *Strengthening Economic Governance in the EU: Report of the Task Force to the European Council,* Brussels, 21 October 2010.

41. Quoted in *The Guardian,* October 23, 2011, p. 2.

42. "Hannes Swoboda Interview," *Agence Europe,* May 4, 2012.

43. General Secretariat of the Council, "Conclusions," June 28–29, 2012, Brussels.

44. Council, *Towards a Genuine Economic and Monetary Union* (Van Rompuy report), December 5, 2012.

45. See Janis A. Emmanouilidis, "Steps but No Roadmap Towards GEMU: The Results of a Disappointing Summit," European Policy Center Post-Summit Analysis, Brussels, 2012.

46. Ibid., pp. 10–11.

47. Dermot Hodson, "The Eurozone in 2011," *Journal of Common Market Studies* 50, supplement (2012), p. 184.

48. Speech by Mario Draghi, president of the European Central Bank, at the Global Investment Conference in London, July 26, 2012.

49. See *Agence Europe*, 26 October 2011.

50. Council, "Acceptance Speech by President of the European Council Herman Van Rompuy," Brussels, March 1, 2012.

51. José Manuel Barroso, "Statement by President Barroso at the Press Conference Following the European Council," Brussels, 25 March 2011.

10
Conclusion

THE EUROPEAN UNION BEARS MORE THAN A PASSING RESEM-
blance to its long-forgotten precursor, the European Coal and Steel Community. The Coal and Steel Community had a narrow purview and only six
member states; the EU covers most areas of public policy and has steadily
enlarged to envelop almost the entire continent of Europe. Nevertheless,
they share common traits that recur throughout the history of European integration: the primacy of national interests; the centrality of France and
Germany; Britain's ambivalence; the unavoidable involvement of the
United States; and the importance of individuals, ideas, and institutions.
The political rationale for the Coal and Steel Community—strengthening
national and regional security—also underpins today's EU, despite the latter's far greater weight as an economic entity. Most important, practical solutions to concrete and complex challenges, rather than an overarching
philosophical framework, shaped both organizations. The result has been an
accretion of institutions, power structures, and policies that run the perpet-
ual risk of being incoherent and occasionally unmanageable.

National Interests and Supranational Solutions
The Coal and Steel Community epitomized the postwar Western European
peace settlement. Although it was established to resolve a specific economic problem, its prime purposes were political and symbolic. The principle of supranationalism embodied in the High Authority and Court of Justice (the Common Assembly was too weak to mention), balanced by the
intergovernmentalism of the Council of Ministers, satisfied French security
concerns and helped rehabilitate Germany. The process of European integration contributed to a rapprochement between both countries and, in time,
to reconciliation as well.

The launch of the European Economic Community later in the 1950s demonstrated the durability of supranationalism as a solution to practical problems, this time the perceived need for greater trade liberalization and closer economic integration in order to accelerate modernization and growth. Again, however, practical politics were paramount: the six founding members struck a deal in the Rome Treaty that included, at French insistence, arrangements for agricultural subsidies and trade with overseas territories. Without those provisions, French advocates of the EC could not have overcome the resistance of cautious colleagues and suspicious compatriots.

Similarly, a combination of political and economic interests accounts for the emergence of economic and monetary union at key junctures in the history of European integration. France responded to Germany's economic resurgence and diplomatic revival in the early 1970s by floating the idea of EMU, which reemerged on the agenda of European integration more than a decade later, thanks to the success of the single market program. The unexpected prospect of German unification, following the fall of the Berlin Wall, increased the political salience of EMU. A felicitous combination of economic and political interests, primarily in France and Germany, ensured the conclusion of the Maastricht Treaty and implementation of EMU by the end of the 1990s, but fell short of convincing member states to cede the necessary sovereignty to put the process on a long-term, solid footing, which became painfully clear during the eurozone crisis a decade later.

As in other policy areas, the quest for closer foreign, security, and defense cooperation in the EU represented a practical response to new challenges, not a doctrinaire effort to deepen European integration. The proposed European Defense Community failed in the 1950s because of political opposition in France. The end of the Cold War seemed an opportune time for the new European Union to deepen foreign and security policy cooperation, and the protracted Balkan wars in the 1990s provided an impetus for closer defense cooperation. Nevertheless, sensitivity to national sovereignty proved insurmountable. New challenges in the aftermath of the terrorist attacks on the United States in September 2001, and the divisiveness of the war in Iraq, prompted member states to take a harder look at defense policy cooperation, not for the sake of European integration but for pragmatic security reasons.

Driven by necessity rather than ideology, what began as a modest common market for coal and steel expanded over the years into an entity touching on almost every aspect of public policy. At the same time, the EU widened as it deepened, with more and more countries wanting to join. The existing member states responded to enlargement in a pragmatic way. Applicant countries, in turn, wanted to join the EU for tangible economic and political reasons, such as greater market access, eligibility for agricultural subsidies and structural funding, or the consolidation of democracy. For the countries of Central and Eastern Europe, recently dominated by larger neighbors, EU membership had a compelling strategic dimension. Even so, their interest in joining the EU was primarily economic—as long as they could also join NATO.

Institutions, Ideas, and Individuals

The seemingly impersonal entity that these countries wished to join was shaped more by individual initiative and involvement than by anonymous social and economic forces. The case of Jean Monnet is instructive. His method involved building institutions to bind the countries of Western Europe closer together, ultimately transforming the nature of the relationship between them. But institutions were only one side of Monnet's triangular technique: ideas and individuals were the others. Monnet's remarkable life showed how institutions, ideas, and individuals mattered. Monnet was an opportunist who cultivated individuals upon whom he could call to move ideas along. Early 1950 was the right time to launch a new initiative; supranationalism was an ideal solution to a specific problem; and Robert Schuman was the right person to make it happen: hence the famous Schuman Declaration that resulted in the Coal and Steel Community. Sometimes Monnet's timing was right, but his ideas were off the mark (his advocacy in the mid-1950s of cooperation on atomic energy rather than a common market is a case in point).

Monnet's successors adopted a similar approach. Walter Hallstein thought that he had the right idea (greater supranationalism) and the right time (the need for a new financial agreement), but miscalculated badly (he gave Charles de Gaulle an opening to reassert intergovernmentalism). Jacques Delors became Commission president at an ideal time (member states were eager to reinvigorate economic integration) but initially promoted the wrong idea (economic and monetary union) before championing the right one (completion of the single market). For Monnet and Delors, the EU's most successful supranational leaders, policy goals were instrumental rather than being ends in themselves. Lacking a clear vision of the EU's ultimate shape or form, they sought to advance European integration by degrees. Thus they contributed to a situation in which the EU resembled a geological formation, with many layers of initiatives and reforms, taken over the years, deposited on top of each other.

As heads of supranational bodies, Monnet, Hallstein, and Delors stood on weak foundations of political authority. Being from France or Germany, the largest and most influential member states, undoubtedly enhanced their positions. National governments were the most powerful players throughout the history of the EU; national leaders were the most influential individuals; and France and Germany were the dominant member states. As European integration intensified and intruded more into everyday political life, national leaders devoted more time to EU affairs. The launch of the European Council in the mid-1970s allowed them to meet regularly to resolve politically sensitive issues and give the EU overall direction. The centrality of the European Council to the survival, let alone the success, of the EU was glaringly obvious during the eurozone crisis.

Frequent contact in the European Council shaped the leaders' impressions of each other, a situation that, in turn, helped shape the outcome of the summits. Although summit communiqués were mostly drafted well in advance, interaction among the summiteers determined their final form and content. What seems in retrospect to have been preordained could have turned out otherwise if different interpersonal dynamics had been at play. The long-running saga of the British budgetary question is an obvious example.

De Gaulle's assault against supranationalism in the mid-1960s showed how a powerful individual could shape the direction of European integration. De Gaulle's relationship with Konrad Adenauer further illustrated the importance of individual initiative and action in the EU. Together, they fended off Britain's rival proposal of a free trade area and set the Community on course to implement the customs union and common agricultural policy. The Elysée Treaty, which de Gaulle and Adenauer signed in January 1963, institutionalized the rapprochement between France and Germany at the core of the European Community.

Despite occasional strains in bilateral relations and poor personal chemistry between specific leaders, French presidents and German chancellors met regularly under the terms of the Elysée Treaty to resolve disputes and hatch plans for the EU. Other national leaders also met bilaterally or multilaterally, but none with the same frequency or sense of purpose as their French and German counterparts. The combination of bilateral summitry under the auspices of the Elysée Treaty and multilateral summitry under the auspices of the European Council provided a powerful platform for Franco-German leadership in the EU, regardless of differences between particular French and German leaders. Only with the onset of the eurozone crisis has the fundamental bond between France and Germany really been put to the test.

Personal relationships and professional networks oiled the wheels of the EU at every level. As the EU deepened and widened, many more politicians and officials became involved in policymaking and implementation at the European level. Armies of officials in national and regional capitals augmented the corps of Brussels-based bureaucrats. Around them revolved an ever-expanding circle of lawyers, lobbyists, concerned citizens, academics, and students.

Yet ordinary Europeans seemed left out. Europeans were always unsure about their singular political experiment. The rapid expansion of the EU's policy reach in the early 1990s fueled public fears about legitimacy and democratic control. Europeans complained about the EU's remoteness, the incomprehensibility of decisionmaking, and the unaccountability of the unelected but seemingly all-powerful European Commission, while failing to turn out for European Parliament elections or to take national politicians to task for their votes in the Council of Ministers. These resentments, sometimes allied with anxieties about national identity, increasingly flared into open hostility.

The perception of weak legitimacy widened the gap between the governed and the governing in the EU. The Nice Treaty, an ineffectual attempt at institutional reform, made things worse. The ensuing Constitutional Treaty engendered a backlash against what many people perceived as the EU's overweening ambition. Though the Lisbon Treaty rescued most of the provisions of the Constitutional Treaty that were aimed at improving the EU's performance and appeal, ten years of contentious treaty reform robbed the EU of much of its luster. The eurozone crisis, coming on the heels of the protracted treaty reform process, further eroded public confidence in the EU.

As the crisis ground on, the EU seemed condemned by its nature and structure, and by the tendency of member states to blame Brussels for their own inadequacies, to remain misunderstood and underappreciated. The EU's inability to resolve the crisis quickly and definitively exacerbated the problem. With traditional security concerns fading as rallying cries for integration, people generally judged the EU by its ability to deliver greater economic advantage, which it seemed incapable of doing. Together with the challenge of legitimacy, the challenge of meeting economic expectations is proving formidable for the EU more than sixty years after Robert Schuman's call for a supranational solution to postwar Europe's problems.

Europe Recast

Regardless of the EU's manifest failings, the events of the last decades have shown that the proponents of European union—the EU way—have convincingly won the argument over the future of Europe. Though Britain is once again flirting with the idea of leaving the EU, its economic well-being seems inextricably linked to membership. Far from wanting to leave, countries have flocked to join. Thus, in the 1990s, the countries of Central and Eastern Europe lined up to share much of their own, recently acquired, fragile sovereignty with the EU and its institutions, just as the countries of the Western Balkans do today.

Despite persistent economic problems, Europe is immeasurably better off than it was at the end of World War II. Standards of living are higher throughout the EU than were imaginable at that time. Europe's welfare states, which developed independently of the EU, are still largely intact. Responsibility for welfare policies resides at the national level, although the pressure of globalization and constraints of integration are reducing governments' fiscal choices, particularly for countries in the eurozone. The evolution of the EU since the 1950s, and especially since the acceleration of integration in the late 1980s, introduced a new kind of politics in Europe.[1] The machinery of EU government is deeply entrenched in the member states' consciousness. Media coverage of the EU, often highly critical, is pervasive and intense.

The EU's existence also reflects a fundamental change in relations among European countries. Alan Taylor's classic book *The Struggle for Mastery in Europe* is a salutary reminder of the tenor of intra-European relations in the nineteenth century, when the great powers vied for hegemony, destroying lesser powers without scruple.[2] National leaders enthusiastically followed the dictum of Carl von Clausewitz in treating war as a continuation of politics by other means, a practice that proved ever more suicidal as technology multiplied death and destruction with each new conflict. Realpolitik in Europe reached its zenith (or nadir) between 1914 and 1945, framed by the outbreak of World War I and the end of World War II. Revolution in Russia and the emergence of the Soviet Union, economic collapse and the Great Depression, and the rise of fascism tore Europe apart.

Europe has largely overcome, if not forgotten, the effects of those traumatic events. Communism and fascism are discredited beyond repair. Apathy, not extremism, is the chief danger to democracy in Europe today, despite an apparent surge in populism fueled by the eurozone crisis. Small states fret about the intentions of large states, but no longer worry about being swallowed up by powerful neighbors. The prospect of EU member states using force against each other is so remote that it is risible. According to Francis Fukuyama, "the end of history" means "the growing 'Common Marketization' of international relations, and the diminution of the likelihood of large-scale conflict between states."[3] Although that may make life duller, historians should welcome it, especially considering the alternative. Intra-EU bargaining in Brussels is today's manifestation of "the continuation of politics by other means." It may be boring, even Byzantine, but it is safe. The battlefields of Jena, Waterloo, Verdun, or Normandy have given way to meeting rooms in Brussels, tidily furnished with bottled water. The EU has helped to recast Europe in fundamental and highly beneficial ways.

Notes

1. See Alberta Sbragia, ed., *Euro-Politics: Institutions and Policymaking in the "New" European Community* (Washington, DC: Brookings Institution, 1992).

2. A. J. P. Taylor, *The Struggle for Mastery in Europe* (Oxford: Clarendon, 1954).

3. Francis Fukuyama, "The End of History?" *The National Interest* no. 16 (Summer 1989), p. 16.

Appendix 1

Acronyms and Abbreviations

CAP	common agricultural policy
CFSP	common foreign and security policy
Coreper	Committee of Permanent Representatives
EC	European Community
ECB	European Central Bank
Ecofin	Economic and Financial Affairs Council
ECSC	European Coal and Steel Community
EDC	European Defense Community
EEC	European Economic Community
EFTA	European Free Trade Association/Area
EMS	European Monetary System
EMU	economic and monetary union
EP	European Parliament
ESPRIT	European Strategic Program for Research and Development in Information Technology
EU	European Union
EUI	European University Institute
Euratom	European Atomic Energy Community
G7	Group of Seven major industrialized countries
G8	Group of Eight major industrialized countries
G-20	Group of 20 major economies
GATT	General Agreement on Tariffs and Trade
GDP	gross domestic product
IMF	International Monetary Fund
MEP	member of the European Parliament
NATO	North Atlantic Treaty Organization
OECD	Organization for Economic Cooperation and Development
OEEC	Organization for European Economic Cooperation

SEA	Single European Act
UN	United Nations
VAT	value-added tax
WTO	World Trade Organization

Appendix 2

The Ever-Wider EU, 1957–2013

Original Member States, 1957
Belgium
France
Germany
Italy
Luxembourg
Netherlands

1st Enlargement, 1973
United Kingdom
Denmark
Ireland

2nd Enlargement, 1981
Greece

3rd Enlargement, 1986
Spain
Portugal

4th Enlargement, 1995
Austria
Finland
Sweden

5th Enlargement, 2004
Czech Republic
Poland
Hungary
Estonia
Slovenia
Latvia
Lithuania
Slovakia
Cyprus
Malta

6th Enlargement, 2007
Bulgaria
Romania

7th Enlargement, 2013
Croatia

Appendix 3

Major Treaty Changes

Rome (1957)

General: establish the European Community

Institutions: establish the Commission, Council, Parliament, Court, and Economic and Social Committee

Policies: Customs union (by 1968); common agricultural policy (subject to negotiation); common commercial policy; competition policy; development assistance policy; regional policy; social policy

Single European Act (1986)

General: revitalize the European Community

Institutions: legitimize the European Council (launched in 1975); extend the use of qualified majority voting; strengthen the legislative role of the European Parliament (through the cooperation procedure); establish the Court of First Instance

Policies: complete the single market (by 1992); strengthen cohesion policy; legitimize cooperation on foreign policy (European Political Cooperation); strengthen environmental policy; strengthen research and development policy

Maastricht (1992)

General: launch the European Union

Institutions: extend the use of qualified majority voting; strengthen the legislative role of the Parliament (through the co-decision procedure); establish the Committee of the Regions; introduce the principle of subsidiarity

Policies: Economic and monetary union (by 1999); transform European Political Cooperation into the common foreign and security policy; introduce cooperation on justice and home affairs; strengthen environmental policy

Amsterdam (1997)

General: limited institutional and policy reform

Institutions: extend the use of qualified majority voting; strengthen the legislative role of the Parliament (extend the applicability of the co-decision procedure); limit the Parliament to 700 members

Policies: reform the common foreign and security policy; establish an area of freedom, security, and justice (reform cooperation on justice and home affairs); proclaim the EU's commitment to the principles of liberty, democracy, respect for human rights, and fundamental freedoms

Nice (2001)

General: limited institutional reform

Institutions: change the voting weights of the member states and allocate votes to the candidate countries; extend the use of qualified majority voting; change the composition of the Commission to one commissioner per member state until 2007; allocate seats in the Parliament to the candidate countries and increase the Parliament to 732 members

Policies: Reform the common commercial policy

Lisbon Treaty (2009)

General: strengthen political foundations of the European Union

Institutions: change the modalities of qualified majority voting; extend the use of qualified majority voting; empower the European Council to elect its own president; empower the Parliament to elect the president of the Commission; limit the Parliament to 701 members; appoint a High Representative for Foreign Affairs and Security Policy to chair the Foreign Affairs Council and also serve as vice president of the Commission; strengthen the role of national parliaments in European Union affairs

Policies: reform the common foreign and security policy; reform cooperation on justice and home affairs

Appendix 4

Chronology

1945

February	Yalta conference on postwar settlement
May	End of World War II in Europe
July–Aug.	Potsdam conference on postwar settlement

1946

September	Churchill's "United States of Europe" speech

1947

March	Truman Doctrine announced
	Britain and France sign Dunkirk Treaty (defensive alliance)
May	UN Economic Commission for Europe established
June	Marshall Plan announced
July	Committee on European Economic Cooperation established
October	General Agreement on Tariffs and Trade (GATT) launched
December	International Committee of the Movements for European Unity established

1948

January	Benelux customs union launched
February	Communist coup in Czechoslovakia
March	Brussels Treaty (defensive alliance of France, Britain, and Benelux) signed
April	Marshall Plan (European Recovery Program) enacted
	Organization for European Economic Cooperation (OEEC) established

| May | Congress of Europe held in The Hague |
| June | Berlin Blockade begins |

1949

April	North Atlantic Treaty signed in Washington
	International Ruhr Authority established
May	Federal Republic of Germany (West Germany) established
	Council of Europe launched
	Berlin Blockade ends

1950

May	Schuman Declaration
June	Negotiations to establish European Coal and Steel Community (ECSC) begin
	Outbreak of Korean War
October	Pleven Plan for a European Defense Community (EDC)
November	European Convention for the Protection of Human Rights and Fundamental Freedoms signed

1951

| February | Negotiations begin to establish EDC |
| April | Treaty establishing ECSC signed in Paris |

1952

May	Treaty establishing EDC signed in Paris
August	ECSC launched in Luxembourg
September	ECSC Assembly holds first session in Strasbourg

1953

| March | Ad hoc assembly adopts draft treaty for European Political Cooperation |

1954

| August | French National Assembly rejects EDC treaty |
| October | Paris agreement to establish Western European Union |

1955

May	Germany joins NATO
June	Messina conference on reviving European integration
	Spaak committee holds first meeting
October	Saar referendum
	Monnet launches Action Committee for the United States of Europe

1956

April	Spaak committee recommends atomic energy community and customs union
May	Venice conference approves Spaak committee recommendations
June	Negotiations to establish European Economic Community (EEC) and European Atomic Energy Community (Euratom) begin
October	Soviet intervention in Hungary
Oct.–Nov.	Suez crisis

1957

January	Saar rejoins Germany
March	Treaties of Rome (establishing EEC and Euratom) signed

1958

January	Launch of EEC and Euratom
	Hallstein Commission takes office
March	First plenary session of European Parliament (EP)
May	Collapse of French Fourth Republic
July	Stresa conference on establishing the common agricultural policy (CAP)
September	French endorse Fifth Republic in a referendum
December	De Gaulle elected president of France

1959

January	First stage of transition to common market begins
September	Stockholm Convention establishes European Free Trade Association (EFTA)

1960

December	Organization for Economic Cooperation and Development (OECD) established

1961

July	Association agreement with Greece signed
August	Britain applies to join European Community (EC) (together with Denmark, Ireland, and Norway)
November	France launches Fouchet Plan for a European political community

1962

January	Second stage of transition to common market begins
April	Fouchet Plan collapses

July	US president Kennedy outlines "grand design" for transatlantic relations

1963

January	De Gaulle vetoes Britain's EC application
	De Gaulle and Adenauer sign Elysée Treaty
July	Yaoundé Convention between EC and seventeen African states and Madagascar signed
September	Association agreement with Turkey signed

1965

April	Merger Treaty, fusing the executives of the EC, ECSC, and Euratom, signed
	Hallstein introduces controversial budget proposals
July	Empty chair crisis begins

1966

| January | EC enters third and final stage of transition to common market |
| | Empty chair crisis ends with Luxembourg Compromise |

1967

May	Britain applies a second time to join EC (together with Denmark, Ireland, and Norway)
July	Merger Treaty enters into force
	Rey Commission takes office
November	De Gaulle vetoes Britain's application a second time

1968

| May | Student and worker riots in Paris |
| July | Customs union completed eighteen months ahead of schedule |

1969

February	Barre memorandum on economic and monetary union (EMU)
April	De Gaulle resigns
July	Britain, Denmark, Ireland, and Norway reactivate EC membership applications
December	At a summit in The Hague, European leaders decide to revive the EC

1970

| January | Malfatti Commission takes office |

April	Agreement to finance EC through "own resources"
June	Accession negotiations with Britain, Denmark, Ireland, and Norway resume
October	Pierre Werner presents plan for EMU
	Foreign ministers adopt Davignon Plan for foreign policy cooperation (European Political Cooperation)
November	Foreign ministers hold first European Political Cooperation meeting

1971
| January | Second Yaoundé Convention and Arusha agreement enter into force |
| August | United States announces the suspension of dollar convertibility, formally ending Bretton Woods system |

1972
January	Accession treaties signed in Brussels
March	Launch of the monetary "snake" to reduce fluctuations in exchange rates among member states' currencies
	Mansholt becomes interim Commission president
September	Norwegians reject EC membership in a referendum
October	At Paris summit, EC leaders agree "to transform the whole complex of . . . relations [between member states] into a European Union" by the end of the decade

1973
January	Britain, Denmark, and Ireland join EC
	Ortoli Commission takes office
July	Conference on Security and Cooperation in Europe (CSCE) opens in Helsinki
October	Arab oil producers quadruple the price of oil and embargo port of Rotterdam
December	EC leaders discuss oil crisis at Copenhagen summit

1974
April	New British government renegotiates EC membership terms
July	Euro-Arab dialogue opens in Paris
September	EC leaders decide to form European Council
December	EC leaders hold last informal summit in Paris

1975
| February | Lomé Convention between EC and forty-six developing countries signed |

March	Inaugural meeting of European Council in Dublin concludes renegotiation of Britain's membership terms
	European Regional Development Fund established
June	British referendum on continued EC membership
	Greece applies to join EC
July	Agreement to establish Court of Auditors and strengthen budgetary powers of the EP
August	Thirty-five participating states conclude CSCE
December	Tindemans report on European Union

1976
| July | EC accession negotiations with Greece begin |

1977
January	Jenkins Commission takes office
March	Portugal applies to join EC
July	Spain applies to join EC

1978
July	At a meeting in Bremen, European Council agrees to establish European Monetary System (EMS)
October	Accession negotiations with Portugal begin
December	Member states decide to launch EMS in January 1978; eight decide to participate in the system's exchange rate mechanism

1979
February	Accession negotiations with Spain begin
March	Launch of EMS
May	Accession treaty with Greece signed in Athens
June	First direct elections to the European Parliament
September	Spierenburg report on Commission reform
October	Second Lomé Convention signed
November	"Wise men" report on EC reform
	Beginning of British budgetary question

1981
January	Greece joins EC
	Thorn Commission takes office
November	Genscher-Colombo initiative

1982
| February | Greenlanders decide in a referendum to leave EC |

1983

June   Solemn Declaration on European Union

1984

February   EP adopts Draft Treaty Establishing the
                           European Union
June   Second direct elections to the European Parliament
                       At Fontainebleau summit, EC leaders resolve British
                           budgetary question
December   Third Lomé Convention signed

1985

January   Delors Commission takes office
February   Agreement on Integrated Mediterranean Programs
March   Dooge committee recommends intergovernmental
                           conference on treaty reform
June   Portugal and Spain sign accession treaties
                       Belgium, the Netherlands, Luxembourg, France, and
                           Germany decide at a meeting in Schengen,
                           Luxembourg, gradually to abolish border posts
                       Commission publishes white paper on single market
                       At Milan summit, EC leaders decide to hold
                           intergovernmental conference
September   Intergovernmental conference starts
December   Intergovernmental conference ends with agreement on the
                           Single European Act (SEA)

1986

January   Portugal and Spain join EC
February   Foreign ministers sign the SEA

1987

April   Turkey applies to join EC
July   SEA comes into effect
September   Finance ministers strengthen EMS

1988

January   Balladur memorandum on EMU
February   Genscher memorandum on EMU
                       At Brussels summit, EC leaders agree on Delors I budget
                           package
June   At Hanover summit, EC leaders decide to establish Delors
                           committee on EMU

1989

June	Delors report on EMU
	Third direct elections to the European Parliament
July	Austria applies to join EC
November	Fall of Berlin Wall
December	At Strasbourg summit, EC leaders decide to hold intergovernmental conference on EMU and adopt Charter of Fundamental Social Rights for Workers

1990

May	Charter for European Bank for Reconstruction and Development signed
June	At Dublin summit, EC leaders decide to hold intergovernmental conference on political union concurrently with intergovernmental conference on EMU, beginning in December 1990
July	Stage One of EMU begins
	Cyprus applies to join EC
	Malta applies to join EC
October	German unification
	Britain joins exchange rate mechanism of EMS
November	US-EC Transatlantic Declaration signed
December	Intergovernmental conferences begin in Rome

1991

June	Outbreak of war in Yugoslavia
July	Sweden applies to join EC
December	Intergovernmental conference ends at Maastricht summit
	Soviet Union collapses

1992

January	EC recognizes independence of Croatia and Slovenia
February	Foreign ministers sign Treaty on European Union in Maastricht
March	Finland applies to join EC
May	EC and EFTA countries sign agreement for European Economic Area
	Agreement on CAP reform
	Switzerland applies to join EU
June	Danes reject Maastricht Treaty in referendum
September	Britain suspends participation in exchange rate mechanism of EMS
	Currency crisis deepens
	French narrowly approve Maastricht Treaty in referendum

November	Norway again applies to join EC
December	Swiss reject European Economic Area membership in referendum, implicitly rejecting EC membership
	At Edinburgh summit, EC leaders agree on Danish opt-outs from Maastricht Treaty and Delors II budget package
	Completion of single market program

1993

February	Accession negotiations with Austria, Finland, and Sweden begin
April	Accession negotiations with Norway begin
May	Danes approve Maastricht Treaty in second referendum
June	Meeting in Copenhagen, the European Council agrees on EC accession criteria
August	Currency crisis ends
November	Maastricht Treaty comes into effect, and the European Union (EU) comes into being
December	Commission publishes white paper on growth, competitiveness, and employment

1994

March	Dispute over institutional implications of enlargement ends with Ioannina Compromise
	Hungary applies to join EU
April	Poland applies to join EU
June	Fourth direct elections to the European Parliament
	Accession treaties with Austria, Finland, Sweden, and Norway signed
July	Stage Two of EMU begins
	European Monetary Institute established
November	Norwegians reject EU membership in referendum
December	European Energy Charter signed

1995

January	Austria, Finland, and Sweden join EU
	Santer Commission takes office
June	First meeting of Reflection Group to prepare intergovernmental conference
	Romania applies to join EU
October	Latvia applies to join EU
November	Estonia applies to join EU
	EU and twelve Mediterranean countries sign Barcelona Declaration

December	United States and EU sign New Transatlantic Agenda
	Reflection Group report on intergovernmental conference
	Lithuania applies to join EU
	Dayton peace plan for former Yugoslavia signed in Paris
	Bulgaria applies to join EU

1996

January	Czech Republic applies to join EU
March	Intergovernmental conference begins in Turin
June	Slovenia applies to join EU
December	At Dublin summit, EU leaders agree on EMU Stability and Growth Pact

1997

June	At Amsterdam summit, EU leaders conclude intergovernmental conference
October	Amsterdam Treaty signed
November	European Council holds special jobs summit in Luxembourg

1998

March	Inaugural session of European Conference (London)
	Accession negotiations with Poland, Hungary, Czech Republic, Estonia, Slovenia, and Cyprus begin
May	At special Brussels summit, EU leaders agree that eleven member states will participate in Stage Three of EMU (all except Britain, Denmark, Greece, and Sweden), and choose first president of European Central Bank (ECB)
June	Launch of ECB in Frankfurt

1999

January	Stage Three of EMU (single monetary policy and irrevocably fixed exchange rates among participating currencies) begins
March	Santer Commission resigns
	At Berlin summit, EU leaders agree on Agenda 2000 budget package
May	Amsterdam Treaty enters into force
June	Fifth direct elections to the European Parliament
July	Manuel Marín becomes interim Commission president
September	Prodi Commission takes office
October	At Tampere summit, EU leaders strengthen cooperation on justice and home affairs
December	At Helsinki summit, EU leaders recognize Turkey as candidate for membership

2000

February	Accession negotiations with Latvia, Lithuania, Slovakia, Bulgaria, Romania, and Malta begin
	Intergovernmental conference begins
March	At Lisbon summit, EU leaders launch strategy for economic modernization
September	Danes decide in referendum not to adopt euro
November	At a summit in Zagreb, Croatia, the EU and the countries of the Western Balkans launch the Stabilization and Association Process
December	Intergovernmental conference ends at Nice summit
	European Council proclaims Charter of Fundamental Rights

2001

January	Greece adopts euro
June	Irish reject Nice Treaty in referendum

2002

January	Euro notes and coins introduced
February	Convention on the Future of Europe begins in Brussels
June	ECSC comes to an end
October	Irish approve Nice Treaty in second referendum

2003

February	Nice Treaty comes into effect
April	Accession treaties with Cyprus, Czech Republic, Estonia, Hungary, Latvia, Lithuania, Malta, Poland, Slovenia, and Slovakia signed in Athens
June	Convention on the Future of Europe ends
	At a summit in Thessaloniki, Greece, the EU declares that all of the Western Balkan countries are potential member states
September	Sweden decides in a referendum not to adopt the euro
October	Intergovernmental conference to negotiate Constitutional Treaty begins

2004

May	The eight Central and Eastern European countries, plus Cyprus and Malta, join the EU
June	Sixth direct elections to the European Parliament
	European Council reaches agreement on the Constitutional Treaty
October	EU leaders sign the Constitutional Treaty in Rome

| November | José Manuel Barroso becomes Commission president |

2005

May	French voters reject the Constitutional Treaty in a referendum
June	Dutch voters reject the Constitutional Treaty in a referendum
	European Council suspends ratification of the Constitutional Treaty pending a "period of reflection"
October	Accession negotiations with Turkey and Croatia begin
December	EU leaders agree on a new multiannual financial framework for the period 2007–2013

2006

| June | European Council agrees to resume intergovernmental negotiation to rescue as much as possible of the Constitutional Treaty in the guise of a new "Reform Treaty" |
| December | Council partially suspends accession negotiations with Turkey |

2007

January	Bulgaria and Romania join the EU
	Slovenia adopts the euro
March	EU leaders issue Berlin Declaration to commemorate fiftieth anniversary of the signature of the Rome Treaty
June	European Council decides to launch a new intergovernmental conference to conclude the Reform Treaty
July	Intergovernmental conference begins
December	EU leaders sign the treaty in Lisbon (henceforth the "Lisbon Treaty")
	Schengen area enlarged to include the Central and Eastern European countries that joined the EU in 2004

2008

January	Cyprus and Malta adopt the euro
June	Irish voters reject the Lisbon Treaty in a referendum
September	Collapse of Lehman Brothers in the United States signals the seriousness of the global financial crisis
November	European Council holds the first of many extraordinary summits over the next five years to address the financial crisis

2009

January	Slovakia adopts the euro
June	Seventh direct elections to the European Parliament
July	Iceland applies to join the EU
September	José Manuel Barroso reelected Commission president by an absolute majority in the European Parliament
October	Irish voters accept the Lisbon Treaty in a second referendum
December	Lisbon Treaty comes into effect
	Herman van Rompuy becomes the first elected president of the European Council and Catherine Ashton becomes the first High Representative for Foreign Affairs and Security Policy
	Serbia applies to join the EU

2010

March	Greek financial crisis escalates dramatically
May	EU and International Monetary Fund (IMF) agree on a bailout for Greece
June	Eurozone finance ministers establish European Financial Stability Facility to provide emergency assistance to eurozone members
	European Council adopts Europe 2020 strategy for economic growth and structural reform
July	Accession negotiations with Iceland begin
September	Commission president Barroso delivers inaugural State of the Union address in Strasbourg
November	EU and IMF agree on a bailout for Ireland
December	European External Action Service officially launched
	European Council agrees on a treaty amendment to allow establishment of European Stability Mechanism, a permanent bailout fund for eurozone members

2011

January	Estonia adopts the euro
	First European Semester, to coordinate economic and fiscal policy among member states, begins
March	Eurozone leaders agree on the Competitiveness Pact
May	EU and IMF agree on a bailout for Portugal
October	European Stability Mechanism comes into operation
December	British opposition to the Fiscal Compact, intended to strengthen economic and fiscal policy coordination, obliges the other member states to conclude the agreement outside the formal treaty framework
	Lichtenstein joins Schengen area

2012

March	EU leaders, except those of Britain and the Czech Republic, sign the Fiscal Compact (officially the "Treaty on Stability, Coordination, and Governance in the Economic and Monetary Union")
June	European Council agrees to establish a European banking supervisory mechanism
July	ECB president Mario Draghi pledges to do whatever is needed within the institution's mandate to save the euro
December	EU receives Nobel Peace Prize
	European Council agrees on a roadmap for completion of genuine EMU

2013

February	EU leaders agree on a new multiannual financial framework for the period 2014–2020
April	EU brokers an agreement between Kosovo and Serbia, possibly facilitating Serbia's accession
June	Iceland announces suspension of its EU application
July	EU and United States start negotiations for Transatlantic Trade and Partnership Agreement
	Croatia joins EU
November	Ukrainian president Viktor Yanukovich rejects trade agreement with EU, sparking crisis in Ukraine

2014

January	Latvia adopts the euro
May	Eight direct elections to the European Parliament

Bibliography

Acheson, Dean. *Present at the Creation*. New York: Norton, 1969.

Alphand, H. *L'étonnement d'être, journal 1939–1973*. Paris: Fayard, 1977.

Alting von Geusau, Frans A. M., ed. *The Lomé Convention and the New International Economic Order*. Leiden: Sijthoff, 1977.

Annan, Noel. *Changing Enemies: The Defeat and Regeneration of Germany*. Ithaca: Cornell University Press, 1997.

Applebaum, Anne. *Iron Curtain: The Crushing of Eastern Europe, 1944–1956*. New York: Anchor, 2013.

Avery, Graham, and Fraser Cameron. *The Enlargement of the European Union*. Sheffield: Sheffield University Press, 1998.

Ball, George. *The Past Has Another Pattern*. New York: Norton, 1982.

Bastasin, Carlo. *Saving Europe: How National Politics Nearly Destroyed the Euro*. Washington, DC: Brookings Institution, 2012.

Baun, Michael J. *An Imperfect Union: The Maastricht Treaty and the New Politics of European Integration*. Boulder: Westview, 1996.

———. *A Wider Europe: The Process and Politics of European Union Enlargement*. Lanham: Rowman and Littlefield, 2000.

Behrman, Greg. *The Most Noble Adventure: The Marshall Plan and the Reconstruction of Postwar Europe*. New York: Free Press, 2008.

Beloff, Max. *The United States and the Uniting of Europe*. Washington, DC: Brookings Institution, 1963.

Benoit, Emile. *Europe at Sixes and Sevens: The Common Market, the Free Trade Association, and the United States*. New York: Columbia University Press, 1961.

Beyer, Henri, ed. *Robert Schuman: L'Europe par la réconciliation franco-allemande*. Lausanne: Fondation Jean Monnet pour l'Europe, 1986.

Bieber, R., et al. *1992: One European Market*. Florence: European University Institute, 1988.

Binoche, Jacques. *De Gaulle et les Allemands*. Brussels: Éditions Complexe, 1990.

Binzer Hobolt, Sara. *Europe in Question: Referendums on European Integration*. Oxford: Oxford University Press, 2009.

Bischof, Günter, Anton Pelinka, and Michael Gehler, eds. *Austria in the European Union*. New York: Transaction, 2002.

Bitsch, Marie-Thérèse. *Histoire de la construction européenne de 1945 à nos jours.* Brussels: Éditions Complexe, 1996.

Bjøl, Erling. *La France devant l'Europe.* Copenhagen: Munksgaard, 1966.

Bloch-Laine, François, and Jean Bouvier. *La France restaurée, 1944–1954: Dialogue sur les choix d'une modernisation.* Paris: Fayard, 1986.

Bloes, Robert. *Le "Plan Fouchet" et le problème de l'Europe politique.* Bruges: College of Europe, 1970.

Boltho, Andrea, ed. *The European Economy: Growth and Crisis.* Oxford: Oxford University Press, 1982.

Bossuat, Gérard. *L'Europe occidentale à l'heure américaine: Le Plan Marshall et l'unité européenne, 1945–52.* Paris: Éditions Complexe, 1992.

———. *La France et la construction de l'unité européenne: De 1919 à nos jours.* Paris: Armand Colin, 2012.

———. *La France, l'aide américaine et la construction européenne, 1944–1954.* 2 vols. Paris: Comité pour l'Histoire Economique et Financière de la France, 1992.

———. *Histoire de l'Union européenne: Fondations, élargissements, avenir.* Paris: Belin, 2009.

Bozo, Frédéric. *Mitterrand, la fin de la guerre froide et l'unification allemande: De Yalta à Maastricht.* Paris: Odile Jacob, 2005.

———. *Two Strategies for Europe: De Gaulle, the United States, and the Atlantic Alliance.* Lanham: Rowman and Littlefield, 2001.

Brandt, Willy. *My Life in Politics.* New York: Viking, 1992.

———. *People and Politics: The Years 1960–1975.* London: Collins, 1978.

Brinkley, Douglas, and Richard T. Griffiths, eds. *John F. Kennedy and Europe.* Baton Rouge: Louisiana State University Press, 1999.

Brugmans, Hendrik. *L'idée européenne, 1918–1965.* 2nd ed. Bruges: De Temple, 1966.

Brusse, Wendy Asbeek. *Tariffs, Trade, and European Integration, 1947–1957: From Study Group to Common Market.* New York: St. Martin's, 1997.

Bührer, Werner. *Western Europe and Germany: The Beginnings of European Integration, 1945–1960.* Washington, DC: Berg, 1995.

Bullen, R., and M. E. Pelly. *Documents on British Policy Overseas.* Series 2, vol. 1, *The Schuman Plan, the Council of Europe, and Western European Integration, 1950–1952.* London: HMSO, 1986.

———. *Documents on British Policy Overseas.* Series 2, vol. 3, *German Rearmament, September 1950–December 1950.* London: HMSO, 1989.

Bullock, Alan. *Ernest Bevin: Foreign Secretary, 1945–1951.* London: Heinemann, 1983.

Bulmer, Simon, and William Paterson. *The Federal Republic of Germany in the European Community.* Oxford: Oxford University Press, 1992.

Burgess, Michael. *Federalism and European Union: The Building of Europe, 1950–2000.* London: Routledge, 2000.

Bussière, E., M. Dumoulin, and É. Willaert, eds. *The Bank of the European Union: The EIB, 1958–2008.* Luxembourg: Imprimerie Centrale, 2008.

Butler, David, and Uwe Kitzinger. *The 1975 Referendum.* London: Macmillan, 1976.

Butler, R. A. *The Art of the Possible: The Memoirs of Lord Butler.* London: Hamilton, 1971.

Caldwell, Peter C., and Robert R. Shandley, eds. *German Unification: Expectations and Outcomes.* Basingstoke: Palgrave Macmillan, 2011.

Camps, Miriam. *Britain and the European Community, 1955–1963.* Princeton: Princeton University Press, 1964.

———. *European Unification in the 1960s: From the Veto to the Crisis.* New York: McGraw-Hill, 1966.

————. *What Kind of Europe? The Community Since de Gaulle's Veto.* Oxford: Oxford University Press, 1965.

Chace, James. *Acheson: The Secretary of State Who Created the American World.* Cambridge: Harvard University Press, 1998.

Chisholm, Michael. *Britain on the Edge of Europe.* London: Routledge, 1995.

Clarke, Peter. *Hope and Glory: Britain, 1900–2000.* 2nd ed. New York: Penguin, 2004.

Cloos, J. *Le traité de Maastricht: Genèse, analyse, commentaires.* Brussels: Bruylant, 1993.

Cockfield, Arthur. *Creating the Internal Market.* London: Wiley Chancery Law, 1984.

Cole, Alistair. *Franco-German Relations.* Harlow: Longman, 2001.

————. *François Mitterrand: A Study in Political Leadership.* London: Routledge, 1994.

Commission. *Homage à EmileNoël, secrétaire général de la Commission européenne.* Luxembourg: European Communities, 1988.

Coombes, David. *Towards a European Civil Service.* London: Chatham, 1968.

Corbett, Richard. *The European Parliament's Role in Closer EU Integration.* Basingstoke: Palgrave, 2002.

Couve de Murville, Maurice. *Une politique étrangère, 1958–1969.* Paris: Plon, 1971.

Croft, Stuart, John Redmond, G. Wyn Rees, and Mark Webber. *The Enlargement of Europe.* Manchester: Manchester University Press, 1999.

Daddow, Oliver J. *Britain and Europe Since 1945: Historiographical Perspectives on Unification.* Manchester: Manchester University Press, 2003.

————, ed. *Harold Wilson and European Integration: Britain's Second Application to Join the EEC.* London: Cass, 2002.

Dahrendorf, Ralf. *From Europe to Europe: A Story of Hope, Trial, and Error.* Cambridge, MA: Center for International Affairs, 1996.

de Gaulle, Charles. *Mémoires d'espoir, suivi d'un choix d'allocutions et messages sur la IVe et la Ve républiques.* Paris: Plon, 1994.

————. *Memoirs of Hope, Renewal, and Endeavor.* New York: Simon and Schuster, 1971.

de Ruyt, Jean. *L'Acte unique européen: Commentaire.* 2nd ed. Brussels: Editions de l'Université de Bruxelles, 1987.

Dedman, Martin. *The Origins and Development of the European Union, 1945–1995: A History of European Integration.* London: Routledge, 1996.

Dehousse, Renaud, ed. *Europe After Maastricht: An Ever Closer Union?* Munich: Law Books in Europe, 1994.

Deighton, Anne, ed. *Building Postwar Europe: National Decision-Makers and European Institutions, 1948–1963.* London: St. Martin's, 1995.

Delanty, Gerard. *Inventing Europe: Idea, Identity, Reality.* New York: St. Martin's, 1995.

Dell, Edmund. *The Schuman Plan and the British Abdication of Leadership in Europe.* Oxford: Oxford University Press, 1995.

Delors, Jacques. *La France par l'Europe.* Paris: Grasset, 1988.

Diebold, William, Jr. *The Schuman Plan: A Study in Economic Cooperation, 1950–1959.* New York: Praeger, 1959.

Dinan, Desmond. *Ever Closer Union: An Introduction to European Integration.* 4th ed. Boulder: Lynne Rienner, 2010.

————, ed. *Origins and Evolution of the European Union.* 2nd ed. Oxford: Oxford University Press, 2014.

Dockrill, Saki. *Britain's Policy for West German Rearmament, 1950–55.* Cambridge: Cambridge University Press, 1991.

———. *Britain's Retreat from East of Suez: The Choice Between Europe and the World.* New York: Palgrave, 2002.

Drake, Helen. *Jacques Delors: Perspectives on a European Leader.* London: Routledge, 2000.

Duchêne, François. *Jean Monnet: The First Statesman of Interdependence.* New York: Norton, 1994.

Duff, Andrew, John Pinder, and Roy Pryce, eds. *Maastricht and Beyond: Building the European Union.* London: Routledge, 1994.

Dumoulin, Michel, ed. *The European Commission, 1958–72: History and Memories.* Luxembourg: Office of Official Publications of the European Communities, 2007.

Dyson, Kenneth. *Elusive Union: The Process of Economic and Monetary Union in Europe.* London: Longman, 1994.

Dyson, Kenneth, and Kevin Featherstone. *The Road to Maastricht: Negotiating Economic and Monetary Union.* Oxford: Oxford University Press, 1999.

Eden, Anthony. *Full Circle: The Memoirs of Sir Anthony Eden.* London: Cassell, 1960.

Edwards, Geoffrey, and Alfred Pijpers. *The Politics of European Treaty Reform: The 1996 Intergovernmental Conference and Beyond.* London: Pinter, 1997.

Edwards, Geoffrey, and Helen Wallace. *Council of Ministers of the European Community and the President in Office.* London: Federal Trust, 1977.

Egan, Michelle. *Constructing a European Market: Standards, Regulation, and Governance.* Oxford: Oxford University Press, 2001.

Eichengreen, Barry. *The European Economy Since 1945: Coordinated Capitalism and Beyond.* Princeton: Princeton University Press, 2007.

———. *Globalizing Capital: A History of the International Monetary System.* 2nd ed. Princeton: Princeton University Press, 2008.

Ellison, James. *Threatening Europe: Britain and the Creation of the European Community, 1955–1958.* London: Macmillan, 2000.

Ellwood, D. W. *Rebuilding Europe: Western Europe, America, and Postwar Reconstruction.* London: Longman, 1992.

Emerson, Michael, et al. *The Economics of 1992: The EC's Assessment of the Economic Effects of Completing the Internal Market.* Oxford: Oxford University Press, 1988.

Endo, Ken. *The Presidency of the European Commission Under Jacques Delors: The Politics of Shared Leadership.* New York: St. Martin's, 1999.

Fimister, A. P. *Robert Schuman: Neo-Scholastic Humanist and the Reunification of Europe.* Brussels: Peter Lang, 2008.

Fondation Jean Monnet pour l'Europe. *Jean Monnet–Robert Schuman correspondance, 1947–1953.* Lausanne: Fondation Jean Monnet pour l'Europe, 1986.

———. *Temoignages à la memoire de Jean Monnet.* Lausanne: Fondation Jean Monnet pour l'Europe, 1989.

Fontaine, Pascal. *Le Comité d'Action pour les États Unis d'Europe de Jean Monnet.* Lausanne: Centre de Recherches Européennes, 1974.

Forster, Anthony. *Britain and the Maastricht Negotiations.* Basingstoke: Palgrave, 1999.

Friend, Julius W. *The Linchpin: French-German Relations, 1950–1990.* New York: Praeger, 1991.

———. *Mitterrand.* Boulder: Westview, 1999.

Fursdon, Edward. *The European Defense Community: A History.* New York: St. Martin's, 1980.

Gaddis, John Lewis. *The Cold War.* London: Allan Lane, 2005.

Gäiner, Maria. *Aux origines de la diplomatie européenne.* Brussels: Peter Lang, 2012.

Garton Ash, Timothy. *In Europe's Name: Germany and the Divided Continent.* New York: Random, 1993.

Geary, Michael J. *Enlarging the European Union: The Commission Seeking Influence, 1961–1973.* Basingstoke: Palgrave Macmillan, 2013.

Geddes, Andrew. *Immigration and European Integration: Towards Fortress Europe?* Manchester: Manchester University Press, 2000.

Genscher, Hans-Dietrich. *Rebuilding a House Divided: A Memoir.* New York: Broadway Books, 1998.

George, Stephen. *An Awkward Partner: Britain in the European Community.* Oxford: Oxford University Press, 1998.

Gerbet, Pierre. *La construction de l'Europe.* 4th ed. Paris: Armand Colin, 2007.

Giauque, Jeffrey Glen. *Grand Designs and Visions of Unity: The Atlantic Powers and the Reorganization of Western Europe, 1955–1963.* Chapel Hill: University of North Carolina Press, 2002.

Gilbert, Mark. *European Integration: A Concise History.* Lanham: Rowman and Littlefield, 2011.

Gill, Christopher. *In Their Own Words: The Advocates of European Integration.* East Haddon: S.E.K., 1996.

Gillingham, John. *Coal, Steel, and the Rebirth of Europe, 1945–1955.* Cambridge: Cambridge University Press, 2005.

———. *European Integration, 1950–2003: Superstate or New Market Economy?* Cambridge: Cambridge University Press, 2003.

Girão, José A. *Southern Europe and the Enlargement of the EEC.* Lisbon: Economia, 1982.

Girault, René. *Pierre Mendès-France et le rôle de la France dans le monde.* Grenoble: Presses Universitaires de Grenoble, 1991.

Gorman, Lyn, and Marja-Liisa Kiljunen. *The Enlargement of the European Community: Case Studies of Greece, Portugal, and Spain.* London: Macmillan, 1977.

Grant, Charles. *Delors: Inside the House That Jacques Built.* London: Brealey, 1994.

Greenwood, Seán. *Britain and the Cold War, 1945–1951.* New York: St. Martin's, 2000.

Griffiths, Richard T., ed. *Economic Development of the EEC.* Cheltenham: Elgar, 1997.

———. *The Netherlands and the Integration of Europe, 1945–1957.* Amsterdam: NEHA, 1990.

———. *Socialist Parties and the Question of Europe in the 1950s.* Leiden: Brill, 1993.

Gros, Daniel, and Niels Thygesen. *European Monetary Integration: From the European Monetary System Towards Monetary Union.* 2nd ed. London: Longman, 1999.

Gstöhl, Sieglinde. *Reluctant Europeans: Norway, Sweden, and Switzerland in the Process of Integration.* Boulder: Lynne Rienner, 2002.

Guirao, F., F. M. B. Lynch, and S. M. Ramírez Pérez, eds. *Alan S. Milward and a Century of European Change.* London: Routledge, 2012.

Haas, Ernst. *The Uniting of Europe: Political, Social, and Economic Forces.* Stanford: Stanford University Press, 1958.

Haines, C. Grove, ed. *European Integration.* Baltimore: Johns Hopkins University Press, 1957.

Hallstein, Walter. *United Europe: Challenge and Opportunity.* Cambridge: Harvard University Press, 1962.

Hanrieder, Wolfram. *Germany, America, and Europe.* New Haven: Yale University Press, 1989.

———. *West German Foreign Policy, 1945–63: International Pressure and Domestic Response.* Stanford: Stanford University Press, 1967.

Hansen, Lene, and Ole Waever. *European Integration and National Identity: The Challenge of the Nordic States.* London: Routledge, 2002.

Harper, John Lamberton. *America and the Reconstruction of Italy, 1945–1948.* Cambridge: Cambridge University Press, 2002.

Healey, Denis. *The Time of My Life.* London: Penguin, 1990.

Heath, E. *The Course of My Life: My Autobiography.* London: Hodder and Stoughton, 1998.

Heisenberg, Dorothee. *The Mark of the Bundesbank: Germany's Role in European Monetary Cooperation.* Boulder: Lynne Rienner, 1999.

Heller, Francis H., and John R. Gillingham. *The United States and the Integration of Europe: Legacies of the Postwar Era.* New York: St. Martin's, 1996.

Hendricks, Gisela. *The Franco-German Axis in European Integration.* London: Elgar, 2001.

Hitchcock, William. *France Restored: Cold War Diplomacy and the Quest for Leadership in Europe, 1944–1954.* Chapel Hill: University of North Carolina Press, 1998.

Hogan, Michael. *The Marshall Plan: America, Britain, and the Reconstruction of Western Europe, 1947–1952.* Cambridge: Cambridge University Press, 1987.

Holmes, Martin. *European Integration: Scope and Limits.* Basingstoke: Palgrave, 2001.

Horne, A. *Macmillan.* Vol. 1, *1894–1957.* London: Macmillan, 1988.

———. *Macmillan.* Vol. 2, *1957–1986.* London: Macmillan, 1989.

Howarth, David J. *The French Road to European Union.* Basingstoke: Palgrave, 2001.

Howe, Geoffrey. *Conflict of Loyalty.* New York: St. Martin's, 1994.

Howorth, Jolyon. *Security and Defense Policy in the European Union.* Basingstoke: Palgrave Macmillan, 2007.

Hug, Simon. *Voices of Europe: Citizens, Referendums, and European Integration.* Boulder: Rowman and Littlefield, 2003.

Institut Charles de Gaulle. *De Gaulle en son siècle.* 6 vols. Paris: Plon, 1991–1992.

Jacobson, Max. *Finland in the New Europe.* Westport: Praeger, 1998.

James, Harold. *Making the European Monetary Union.* Cambridge: Harvard University Press, 2012.

Jenkins, Roy. *European Diary, 1977–1981.* London: Collins, 1989.

———. *Life at the Center: Memoirs of a Radical Reformer.* New York: Random, 1991.

Jobert, Michel. *L'autre regard.* Paris: Grasset, 1976.

Jones, Seth G. *The Rise of European Security Cooperation.* Cambridge: Cambridge University Press, 2007.

Jouve, Edmond. *Le Général de Gaulle et la construction de l'Europe.* Paris: Librairie Générale de Droit et de Jurisprudence, 1967.

Judt, Tony. *Postwar: A History of Europe Since 1945.* New York: Penguin, 2005.

Kaiser, Wolfram. *Using Europe, Abusing the Europeans: Britain and European Integration, 1945–1963.* London: Macmillan, 1996.

Kaiser, Wolfram, Brigitte Leucht, and Morton Rasmussen, eds. *History of the European Union: Origins of a Trans- and Supranational Polity, 1950–72.* Abingdon: Routledge, 2009.

Kaiser, Wolfram, and J.-H. Meyer, eds. *Societal Actors in European Integration: Polity-Building and Policy-Making, 1958–1992.* Basingstoke: Palgrave Macmillan, 2013.

Kaiser, Wolfram, and Antonio Varsori, eds. *European Union History: Themes and Debates.* Basingstoke: Palgrave Macmillan, 2010.

Kaplan, Jacob J., and Günther Schleiminger. *The European Payments Union: Financial Diplomacy in the 1950s.* Oxford: Clarendon, 1989.

Kay, John, ed. *1992: Myths and Realities.* London: London Business School, 1989.

Kenen, Peter B. *Economic and Monetary Union in Europe: Moving Beyond Maastricht.* Cambridge: Cambridge University Press, 1995.

Killick, John. *The United States and European Reconstruction, 1945–1960.* Edinburgh: Keele University Press, 1997.

Kindleberger, Charles P. *Marshall Plan Days.* Boston: Allen and Unwin, 1987.

Kipping, Matthias. *Zwischen Kartellen und Konkurrenz: Der Schuman-Plan und die Ursprünge der europäischen Einigung, 1944–1952.* Berlin: Duncker and Humblot, 1996.

Kissinger, Henry. *The White House Years.* Boston: Little, Brown, 1979.

Kitzinger, Uwe. *Diplomacy and Persuasion.* London: Thames and Hudson, 1973.

Knudsen, Ann-Christina L. *Farmers on Welfare: The Making of Europe's Common Agricultural Policy.* Ithaca: Cornell University Press, 2009.

Kolodziej, Edward. *French International Policy Under de Gaulle and Pompidou: The Politics of Grandeur.* Ithaca: Cornell University Press, 1974.

Kotlowski, Dean J., ed. *The European Union: From Jean Monnet to the Euro.* Athens: Ohio University Press, 2000.

Koutrakos, Panos. *The EU Common Security and Defense Policy.* New York: Oxford University Press, 2013.

Kramer, Alan. *The West German Economy, 1945–1955.* New York: Berg, 1991.

Krause, L. B., and W. S. Salant, eds. *European Monetary Unification and Its Meaning for the United States.* Washington, DC: Brookings Institution, 1973.

Kreppel, Amie. *The European Parliament and Supranational Party System: A Study in Institutional Development.* Cambridge: Cambridge University Press, 2002.

Krotz, U., and J. Schild. *Shaping Europe: France, Germany, and Embedded Bilateralism from the Elysée Treaty to Twenty-First Century Politics.* Oxford: Oxford University Press, 2013.

Kuisel, Richard. *Capitalism and the State in Modern France: Renovation and Economic Management in the Twentieth Century.* Cambridge: Cambridge University Press, 1981.

Kusterer, Hermann. *Der Kanzler und der General.* Stuttgart: Neske, 1995.

Küsters, H. J. *Die Gründung der europäischen Wirtschaftsgemeinschaft.* Baden-Baden: Nomos, 1982.

Lacouture, Jean. *Pierre Mendès-France.* New York: Holmes and Meier, 1984.

Lapavitsas, Costas. *Crisis in the Eurozone.* London: Verso, 2012.

Large, David Clay. *Germans to the Front: West German Rearmament in the Adenauer Era.* Chapel Hill: University of North Carolina Press, 1996.

Laursen, Finn, ed. *The Amsterdam Treaty: National Preference Formation, Interstate Bargaining, and Outcome.* Odense: Odense University Press, 2002.

———, ed. *Designing the European Union: From Paris to Lisbon.* Basingstoke: Palgrave Macmillan, 2012.

———. *The Ratification of the Maastricht Treaty: Issues, Debates, and Future Implications.* Maastricht: EIPA, 1994.

———, ed. *The Rise and Fall of the EU's Constitutional Treaty.* Leiden: Brill, 2008.

Laursen, Finn, and Sophie Vanhoonacker, eds. *The Intergovernmental Conference and Political Union: Institutional Reform, New Policies, and International Identity of the European Community.* Maastricht: EIPA, 1992.

Laursen, Jean-Marie, ed. *Designing the European Union: From Paris to Lisbon.* Basingstoke: Palgrave Macmillan, 2012.

Lawson, Nigel. *The View from No. 11: Britain's Longest-Serving Cabinet Member Recalls the Triumphs and Disappointments of the Thatcher Era.* New York: Doubleday, 1993.

Lefèvre, Sylvie. *Les relations économiques franco-allemandes de 1945 à 1955: De l'occupation à la coopération.* Paris: Comité pour l'Histoire Économique er Financière de la France, 1998.

Leffler, Melvyn. *For the Soul of Mankind: The United States, the Soviet Union, and the Cold War.* New York: Hill and Wang, 2007.

Leffler, Melvyn, and Ode Arne Westad. *The Cambridge History of the Cold War.* 3 vols. Cambridge: Cambridge University Press, 2012.

Lerner, Daniel, and Raymond Aron, eds. *France Defeats the EDC.* New York: Praeger, 1957.

Lipgens, Walter. *Die Anfänge der europäischen Einigungspolitik.* Stuttgart: Klett, 1977.

——, ed. *Documents on the History of European Integration.* Vol. 1. Baden-Baden: Nomos Verlag, 1985.

——, ed. *Documents on the History of European Integration.* Vol. 2. Baden-Baden: Nomos Verlag, 1986.

——. *A History of European Integration.* Vol. 1, *1945–1947: The Formation of the European Unity Movement.* Oxford: Clarendon, 1982.

Lipgens, Walter, and W. Loth, eds. *Documents on the History of European Integration.* Vol. 3. Berlin: De Gruytes, 1988.

Lodge, Juliet, ed. *The 1999 Elections to the European Parliament.* Basingstoke: Palgrave, 2001.

Lord, Christopher. *Absent at the Creation: Britain and the Formation of the European Community, 1950–1952.* Aldershot: Dartmouth, 1996.

Loth, Wilfried. *Der Weg nach Europa, Geschichte der europäischen Integration, 1939– 1957.* Rev. ed. Göttingen: Vandenhoeck and Ruprecht, 1996.

Loth, Wilfried, and Robert Picht. *De Gaulle, Deutschland und Europa.* Opladen: Leske and Budrich, 1991.

Loth, Wilfried, William Wallace, and Wolfgang Wessels. *Walter Hallstein: The Forgotten European?* New York: St. Martin's, 1998.

Lowe, Keith. *Savage Continent: Europe in the Aftermath of World War II.* New York: St. Martin's, 2012.

Lucarelli, Bill. *The Origin and Evolution of the Single Market in Europe.* Aldershot: Ashgate, 1999.

Ludlow, N. Piers. *Dealing with Britain: The Six and the First UK Membership Application.* Cambridge: Cambridge University Press, 1997.

——. *The European Community and the Crises of the 1960s: Negotiating the Gaullist Challenge.* London: Routledge, 2006.

——, ed. *European Integration and the Cold War: Ostpolitik-Westpolitik, 1965– 1973.* Abingdon: Routledge, 2007.

Ludlow, N. Piers, Frédéric Bozo, Marie-Pierre Rey, and Leopoldo Nuti, eds. *Europe and the End of the Cold War: A Reappraisal.* Abingdon: Routledge, 2008.

Ludlow, Peter. *The Making of the European Monetary System.* London: Butterworths, 1982.

Luif, P. *On the Road to Brussels: The Political Dimension of Austria's, Finland's, and Sweden's Road to Accession to the European Union.* Vienna: Austrian Institute for International Affairs, 1995.

Lynch, Frances M. B. *France and the International Economy: From Vichy to the Treaty of Rome.* London: Routledge, 1997.

MacDonogh, Giles. *After the Reich: The Brutal History of the Allied Occupation.* New York: Basic, 2007.

Macmillan, H. *At the End of the Day, 1961–1963.* London: Macmillan, 1973.

————. *Pointing the Way, 1959–1961*. London: Macmillan, 1972.

Mahant, E. *Birthmarks of Europe: The Origins of the European Community Reconsidered*. Farnham: Ashgate, 2004.

Maier, Charles S., ed. *The Cold War in Europe: Era of a Divided Continent*. 3rd updated and expanded ed. Princeton: Markus Wiener, 1996.

Maillard, Pierre. *De Gaulle et l'Allemagne: Le rêve inachevé*. Paris: Plon, 1990.

Mangenot, Michel, and Sylvain Schirmann (eds.). *Les institutions européennes font leur histoire*. Brussels: Peter Lang, 2012.

Maravall, José. *The Transition to Democracy in Spain*. New York: St. Martin's, 1982.

Marjolin, Robert. *Memoirs, 1911–1986: Architect of European Unity*. London: Weidenfeld and Nicolson, 1986.

Marsh, David. *The Euro: The Battle for the New Global Currency*. Revised and updated ed. New Haven: Yale University Press, 2011.

————. *Europe's Deadlock: How the Euro Crisis Could Be Solved—And Why It Won't Happen*. New Haven: Yale University Press, 2011.

Martin, Stephen, ed. *The Construction of Europe: Essays in Honor of Emile Noël*. Dordrecht: Kluwer, 1994.

Massigli, René. *Une comédie des erreurs, 1943–1956: Souvenirs et refléxions sur une étape de la construction européene*. Paris: Plon, 1978.

Mayhew, Alan. *Recreating Europe: The European Union's Policy Towards Central and Eastern Europe*. 2nd ed. Cambridge: Cambridge University Press, 2014.

Mazzucelli, Colette. *France and Germany at Maastricht: Politics and Negotiations to Create the European Union*. New York: Garland, 1997.

McAllister, Richard. *From EC to EU: A Historical and Political Survey*. New York, 1997.

McNamara, Kathleen. *The Currency of Ideas: Monetary Politics in the European Union*. Ithaca: Cornell University Press, 1997.

Mélandri, Pierre. *Les États-Unis et le défi européen, 1955–1958*. Paris: PUF, 1975.

————. *Les États-Unis face à l'unification européene, 1945–1954*. Paris: Pedone, 1980.

Menon, Anand, and Vincent Wright, eds. *From the Nation State to Europe: Essays in Honour of Jack Hayward*. Oxford: Oxford University Press, 2001.

Middlemas, Keith, ed. *Orchestrating Europe: The Informal Politics of European Union, 1973–1995*. New York: Fontana, 1995.

Miles, Lee. *The European Union and the Nordic Countries*. London: Routledge, 1996.

Miles, Lee, and Anders Wivel. *Denmark and the European Union*. Abingdon: Routledge, 2014.

Miller, James Edward. *The United States and Italy, 1940–1950: The Politics and Diplomacy of Stabilization*. Chapel Hill: University of North Carolina Press, 1986.

Milward, Alan. *The European Rescue of the Nation State*. 2nd ed. London: Routledge, 2000.

————. *The Reconstruction of Western Europe, 1945–1951*. Berkeley: University of California Press, 1984.

————. *The UK and the European Community*. Vol. 1, *The Rise and Fall of a National Strategy, 1945–1963*. London: Cass, 2002.

Milward, A., F. M. B. Lynch, F. Romero, R. Ranieri, and V. Sørensen. *The Frontier of National Sovereignty: History and Theory, 1945–1992*. London: Routledge, 1993.

Monnet, Jean. *Memoirs*. Garden City: Doubleday, 1978.

Moon, Jeremy. *European Integration in British Politics, 1950–1963: A Study of Issue Change*. Aldershot: Gower, 1985.

Moravcsik, Andrew. *The Choice for Europe: Social Purpose and State Power from Messina to Maastricht.* Ithaca: Cornell University Press, 1998.

Morgan, Annette. *From Summit to Council: Evolution of the EEC.* London: Chatham, 1976.

Mourlon-Droul, Emmanuel. *A Europe Made of Money: The Emergence of the European Monetary System.* Ithaca: Cornell University Press, 2012.

Mowat, R. C. *Creating the European Community.* Tonbridge: Blandford, 1973.

Norman, Peter. *Accidental Constitution: The Making of Europe's Constitutional Treaty.* 2nd ed. Brussels: EuroComment, 2005.

Nugent, Neill. *The European Commission.* Basingstoke: Palgrave, 2001.

Occhipinti, John D. *The Politics of EU Police Cooperation: Toward a European FBI?* Boulder: Lynne Rienner, 2003.

Ovendale, R., ed. *The Foreign Policy of the Labour Governments, 1945–1951.* Leicester: Leicester University Press, 1984.

Owen, Geoffrey. *From Empire to Europe: The Decline and Revival of British Industry Since the Second World War.* London: HarperCollins, 1999.

Padoa-Schioppa, Tommaso, et al. *Efficiency, Stability, and Equity: A Strategy for the Evolution of the Economic System of the European Community.* Oxford: Oxford University Press, 1987.

Palayret, Jean-Marie, Helen Wallace, and Pascaline Winand, eds. *Visions, Votes, and Vetoes: The Empty Chair Crisis and the Luxembourg Compromise Forty Years On.* Brussels: Peter Lang, 2006.

Parsons, Craig. *A Certain Idea of Europe.* Ithaca: Cornell University Press, 2003.

Patel, Kiran Klaus, and Heike Schweitzer, eds. *The Historical Foundations of EU Competition Law.* Oxford: Oxford University Press, 2013.

Patel, Kiran Klaus, and Kenneth Weisbrode, eds. *European Integration and the Atlantic Community in the 1980s.* Cambridge: Cambridge University Press, 2013.

Pattison de Ménil, Lois. *Who Speaks for Europe? The Vision of Charles de Gaulle.* London: Nicolson and Weidenfeld, 1977.

Pelkmans, Jacques, and Alan Winters. *Europe's Domestic Market.* London: Routledge, 1988.

Peyrefitte, Alain. *C'était de Gaulle.* Vol. 1, *La France redevient la France.* Paris: De Fallois/Fayard, 1994.

———. *C'était de Gaulle.* Vol. 2, *La France reprend sa place dans le monde.* Paris: De Fallois/Fayard, 1997.

Phinnemore, David. *The Treaty of Lisbon: Origins and Negotiation.* Basingstoke: Palgrave Macmillan, 2013.

Pine, Melissa. *Harold Wilson and Europe: Pursuing Britain's Membership of the European Community.* London: Tauris, 2007.

Poidevin, Raymond. *Histoire des débuts de la construction européenne, mars 1948– mai 1950: Actes du Colloque de Strasbourg, 28–30 novembre 1984.* Brussels: Bruylant, 1986.

———. *Robert Schuman, homme d'état, 1886–1963.* Paris: Imprimerie Nationale, 1986.

Pompidou, Georges. *Pour rétablir une vérité.* Paris: Flammarion, 1982.

Pond, Elizabeth. *The Rebirth of Europe.* Washington, DC: Brookings Institution, 2002.

Priestley, Julian. *Six Battles That Shaped Europe's Parliament.* London: John Harper, 2008.

Pryce, Roy, ed. *The Dynamics of European Union.* London: Croom Helm, 1987.

Redmond, John. *The 1995 Enlargement of the European Union.* Aldershot: Ashgate, 1997.

Redmond, John, and Glenda G. Rosenthal. *The Expanding European Union: Past, Present, Future.* Boulder: Lynne Rienner, 1998.

Riddell, Peter. *The Thatcher Government.* London: Martin Robertson, 1983.

Rittberger, Berthold. *Building Europe's Parliament: Democratic Representation Beyond the Nation State.* Oxford: Oxford University Press, 2005.

Rosato, Sebastian. *Europe United: Power Politics and the Making of the European Community.* Ithaca: Cornell University Press, 2011.

Ross, George. *Jacques Delors and European Integration.* Oxford: Oxford University Press, 1995.

Roussel, Eric. *Charles de Gaulle.* Paris: Broché, 2002.

Ruane, Kevin. *The Rise and Fall of the European Defense Community: Anglo-American Relations and the Crisis of European Defense, 1950–1955.* Basingstoke: Macmillan, 2000.

Rueff, Jacques. *Combats pour l'ordre financier.* Paris: Plon, 1972.

———. *The Monetary Sin of the West.* London: Macmillan, 1972.

Sandholtz, Wayne. *High-Tech Europe: The Politics of International Cooperation.* Berkeley: University of California Press, 1992.

Sarotte, M. E. *1989: The Struggle to Create Post–Cold War Europe.* Princeton: Princeton University Press, 2009.

Schaad, Martin P. C. *Bullying Bonn: Anglo-German Diplomacy on European Integration, 1955–61.* New York: St. Martin's, 2000.

Schaetzel, Robert. *The Unhinged Alliance: America and the European Community.* New York: Harper and Row, 1975.

Schain, Martin, ed. *The Marshall Plan: Fifty Years After.* Basingstoke: Palgrave, 2001.

Scheinman, Lawrence. *Atomic Energy Policy in France Under the Fourth Republic.* Princeton: Princeton University Press, 1965.

Schirmann, Sylvain, and Sarah Mohamed-Gaillard. *Georges Pompidou et l'Allemagne.* Brussels: Peter Lang, 2012.

Schmid, Carlo. *Erinnerungen.* Berne: Scherz Verlag, 1979.

Schmidt, Hans A. *The Path to European Union: From the Marshall Plan to the Common Market.* Baton Rouge: Louisiana State University Press, 1962.

Schulz, Matthias, and Thomas A. Schwartz, eds. *The Strained Alliance: US-European Relations from Nixon to Carter.* Cambridge: Cambridge University Press, 2009.

Schulze, Max-Stephan, ed. *Western Europe: Economic and Social Change Since 1945.* London: Longman, 1999.

Schuman, Robert. *Pour l'Europe.* Paris: Nagel, 1963.

Schwabe, Klaus, ed. *Die Anfänge des Schuman-Plans, 1950–1951.* Baden-Baden: Nomos, 1988.

Schwartz, Thomas Alan. *America's Germany: John J. McCloy and the Federal Republic of Germany.* Cambridge: Cambridge University Press, 1991.

———. *Lyndon Johnson and Europe: In the Shadow of Vietnam.* Cambridge: Harvard University Press, 2003.

Schwarz, Hans-Peter. *Helmut Kohl: Eine politische Biographie.* Munich: Deutsche Verlags-Anstalt, 2012.

———. *Konrad Adenauer: A German Politician and Statesman in a Period of War, Revolution, and Reconstruction.* Vol. 1, *From the German Empire to the Federal Republic, 1876–1952.* Oxford: Berghahn, 1997.

———. *Konrad Adenauer: A German Politician and Statesman in a Period of War, Revolution, and Reconstruction.* Vol. 2, *The Statesman, 1952–1967.* Oxford: Berghahn, 1997.

Seidel, Katja. *The Process of Politics in Europe: The Rise of European Elites and Supranational Institutions.* London: Tauris Academic, 2010.

Serfaty, Simon, ed. *The Finality Debate and Its National Dimensions.* Washington, DC: Center for Strategic and International Studies, 2002.

Serra, Enrico, ed. *Il Rilancio dell' Europa e i Trattati di Roma.* Brussels: Bruylant, 1989.

Shore, Cris. *Building Europe: The Cultural Politics of European Integration.* London: Routledge, 2000.

Simonian, Haig. *Privileged Partnership: Franco-German Relations in the European Community, 1969–1984.* Oxford: Clarendon, 1985.

Smets, P. F., ed. *La penseé européenne et atlantique de Paul-Henri Spaak.* Brussels: J. Goemmaere, 1980.

Smith, Brendan P. G. *Constitution Building in the European Union: The Process of Treaty Reform.* The Hague: Kluwer Law International, 2002.

Smith, M. L., and Peter M. R. Stirk. *Making the New Europe: European Unity and the Second World War.* London: Pinter, 1990.

Soutou, Georges-Henri. *L'alliance incertaine: Les rapports politico-stratégiques franco-allemands, 1954–1996.* Paris: Fayard, 1996.

Spicka, Mark E. *Selling the Economic Miracle: Economic Reconstruction and Politics in West Germany, 1949–1957.* New York: Berghahn, 2007.

Spierenburg, Dirk, and Raymond Poidevin. *The History of the High Authority of the European Coal and Steel Community: Supranationality in Operation.* London: Weidenfeld and Nicolson, 1994.

Spinelli, Altiero. *The Eurocrats: Conflict and Crisis in the European Community.* Baltimore: Johns Hopkins University Press, 1966.

Steiner, Zara. *The Lights That Failed: European International History, 1919–1933.* Oxford: Oxford University Press, 2007.

Steinherr, Alfred. *Thirty Years of European Monetary Integration, from the Werner Plan to EMU.* London: Longman, 1994.

Stikker, Dirk U. *Men of Responsibility: A Memoir.* New York: Harper and Row, 1965.

Stirk, Peter M. R. *A History of European Integration Since 1914.* New York: Pinter, 1996.

Stirk, Peter M. R., and David Weigall, eds. *The Origins and Development of European Integration: A Reader and Commentary.* London: Pinter, 1999.

Szabo, Stephen F. *The Diplomacy of German Unification.* New York: St. Martin's, 1992.

Taylor, A. J. P. *From the Boer War to the Cold War: Essays on Twentieth-Century Europe.* London: Penguin, 1995.

Taylor, Paul. *The European Union in the 1990s.* Oxford: Oxford University Press, 1996.

Thatcher, Margaret. *Downing Street Years.* New York: HarperCollins, 1993.

Thody, Philip Malcolm Waller. *Europe Since 1945.* London: Routledge, 2000.

———. *The Fifth French Republic: Presidents, Politics, and Personalities.* London: Routledge, 1998.

Trachtenberg, Marc. *A Constructed Peace: The Making of the European Settlement, 1945–1963.* Princeton: Princeton University Press, 1999.

Tratt, J. *The Macmillan Government and Europe: A Study in the Process of Policy Development.* London: Macmillan, 1996.

Triffin, Robert, ed. *EMS: The Emerging European Monetary System.* Brussels: National Bank of Belgium, 1979.

Tsoukalis, Loukas, ed. *Greece and the European Community.* Farnborough: Saxon, 1979.

———. *The Politics and Economics of European Monetary Integration.* London: Allen and Unwin, 1977.

———. *What Kind of Europe?* Oxford: Oxford University Press, 2005.

Tugendhat, Christopher. *Making Sense of Europe.* New York: Columbia University Press, 1988.

Ungerer, Horst. *From EPU to EMU: A Concise History of European Monetary Integration.* Westport: Quorum, 1997.

Uri, Pierre. *Partnership for Progress: A Program for Transatlantic Action.* New York: Harper and Row, 1963.

Vaïsse, Maurice. *La grandeur: Politique étrangère du général de Gaulle, 1958–1969.* Paris: Fayard, 1997.

van Overtveldt, Johan. *The End of the Euro: The Uneasy Future of the European Union.* Farnham: Ashgate, 2011.

van Middelaar, Luuk. *The Passage to Europe.* New Haven: Yale University Press, 2013.

Varsori, Antonio, and Elena Calandri, eds. *The Failure of Peace in Europe, 1943–1948.* Basingstoke: Palgrave, 2002.

von der Groeben, Hans. *The European Community: The Formative Years.* Luxembourg: Office for Official Publications of the European Communities, 1987.

Wall, Irwin M. *France, the United States, and the Algerian War.* Berkeley: University of California Press, 2001.

———. *The United States and the Making of Post-War France, 1945–1954.* Cambridge: Cambridge University Press, 1991.

Wall, Stephen. *The Official History of Britain and the European Community.* Vol. 2, *From Rejection to Referendum, 1963–1975.* Abingdon: Routledge, 2012.

Weaver, Frederick S. *The United States and the Global Economy: From Bretton Woods to the Current Crisis.* Lanham: Rowman and Littlefield, 2011.

Werts, Jan. *The European Council.* London: HarperCollins, 2008.

Wexler, Imanuel. *The Marshall Plan Revisited.* Westport: Greenwood, 1983.

Wilkes, George, ed. *Britain's Failure to Enter the European Community, 1961–1963: The Enlargement Negotiations and Crises in European, Atlantic, and Commonwealth Relations.* London: Cass, 1997.

Williams, Charles. *Adenauer: The Father of the New Germany.* New York: Wiley, 2000.

Willis, F. Roy, ed. *European Integration.* New York: New Viewpoints, 1975.

———. *France, Germany, and the New Europe, 1945–1967.* Revised and expanded ed. Stanford: Stanford University Press, 1968.

Wilson, Harold. *Memoirs: The Making of a Prime Minister, 1916–1986.* London: Weidenfeld and Nicolson, 1986.

Winand, Pascaline. *Eisenhower, Kennedy, and the United States of Europe.* New York: St. Martin's, 1993.

Wood, Stephen. *Germany, Europe, and the Persistence of Nations: Transformation, Interests, and Identity, 1989–1996.* Aldershot: Ashgate, 1998.

Wright, Jonathan. *Gustav Stresemann: Weimar's Greatest Statesman.* Oxford: Oxford University Press, 2002.

Wurm, Clemens, ed. *Western Europe and Germany: The Beginnings of European Integration.* Oxford: Berg, 1995.

Young, Hugo. *This Blessed Plot: Britain and Europe from Churchill to Blair.* Woodstock: Overlook, 1999.

Young, John W. *Britain, France, and the Unity of Europe, 1945–1951.* Leicester: Leicester University Press, 1984.

———. *France, the Cold War, and the Western Alliance, 1944–1949.* New York: St. Martin's, 1990.

Zelikow, Philip, and Condoleezza Rice. *Germany Unified and Europe Transformed: A Study in Statecraft.* Cambridge: Harvard University Press, 1995.

Index

393

340; onset of, 330–331; overview of, 328–349, 335*fig*; Six-Pack in, 342–343; summits during, 340–342; threat, 336–347

Farmers, 97–99, 107
Fascism, 358
Faure, Maurice, 199
Featherstone, Kevin, 232
Federal goal, 235–236
Federal Republic of Germany. *See* West Germany
Federal Union, 4
Federalism: British, 4; dark ages, 12; Italian, 4–5, 69; as panacea, 32; spiritual dimension of, 11; war reviving interest in, 4
Federalist interpretation, 10–13
Fifth Republic, 96, 104
Finland, 254–255, 288
Finnish markka, 275
Fiscal Compact, 343
Fischer, Joschka, 270–271
Fisheries, 132, 181
FitzGerald, Garret, 148, 152, 154, 178
Five power Brussels group: at Council of Ministers meeting, 107–108; de Gaulle succumbed to by, 106
Foreign Assistance Act, 35
Foreign policy, of France, 38
Fouchet, Christian, 101–102
Fouchet Plan, 101–102
Four Power talks, 66
Fourth Republic, 87, 93–94
Franc, 220, 275–276
France, 146–147, 307–308; Adenauer maintaining relations with, 71; agricultural common market wanted by, 80; Britain reducing in rank, 67; Britain's EDC membership and, 65–66; CAP and, 97–99; civil war of, 24; common market as key for, 54; Constitutional Treaty rejected by, 318; Council of Ministers walkout of, 88, 105–107; crisis, 87; on customs union, 79; customs union interest of, 36; decolonization of, 53–54; deconcentration wanted by, 60; diplomatic revolution

launched by, 56; EC accepted by, 6; EC influenced by, 96–97; ECSC opposed by, 61–62; EDC rejected by, 67; Egyptian intervention of, 53, 54; empty chair crisis walkout of, 105–107; EMU preferences of, 233; enlargement adapted to by, 319; Euratom championed by, 73–74; European Assembly cause taken up by, 33; European integration and, 5–6; in Eurozone crisis, 344–345; farmers, 97, 107; foreign policy of, 38; franc, 220, 275–276; free trade area opposed by, 93–94; Germany controlled by, 65; Germany's rapprochement with, 37–48, 57, 64, 70–71; Germany's rift with, 9; intergovernmental conference and, 74–75, 78–79, 203–204; on Italy, 38; leadership, 344–345; Maastricht Treaty referendum, 245; in 1950s, 53–54; parliamentary victories in, 78; Parsons on, 17; under pressure, 40–43; qualified majority voting harming, 106; on Rome Treaty, 81–82; on Saar, 60; Saar returned by, 71; Schuman Plan protected by, 65; at Schuman talks, 58, 60, 61; social model, 79–80; steel production, 40–41; Suez crisis influencing, 77; Thoiry summit in, 3; transport policy resisted by, 111; treaty ratified by, 67; treaty timetable honored by, 92–93; US influencing, 41, 42; US reducing in rank, 67; after World War II, 38–42
France Telecom, 278
Franco-German friendship, 150–151
Franco-German union, 48
Free trade area: Britain launching idea of, 93; fending off, 92–97, 95*fig*; France opposing, 93–94
Freedom area, 288–290
Freedom Party, 298–299
Freeman, Orville, 99
French, 61
French Fourth Republic, 53
"From Summit to Swamp" (Gillingham), 15–16

About the Book

THOROUGHLY REVISED TO REFLECT A DECADE OF RECENT HISTORY —and incorporating newly available archival material and the latest scholarship—*Europe Recast* tells the story of European integration from its modern origins in the 1940s to the challenges of today. The book is an essential guide to unraveling the complexity of the EU system in the context of modern European history.

Desmond Dinan is professor of public policy at George Mason University and holds an *ad personam* Jean Monnet Chair there. His numerous publications include *Ever Closer Union: An Introduction to European Integration*, and he is editor of *Encyclopedia of the European Union*.